C. G. Jung has been and continues to be a pervasive yet often unacknowledged presence in twentieth-century art and intellectual life. This timely volume is the first comprehensive attempt to assess this presence and to demonstrate Jung's far-reaching cultural impact. The distinguished contributors represent a number of views, from traditional Jungian to the most contemporary post-Jungian stances, including feminist, non-Jungian, and anti-Jungian positions. Jung, as seen in this volume, addresses a wide range of contemporary issues related to religion, anthropology, popular culture, creativity, gender, and postmodernism. The essays reveal dimensions of his work that extend far beyond psychoanalytical theory and that show his hermeneutics to be a much more subtle and sophisticated methodology than previously allowed by his critics. The methodology appears, in fact, to have anticipated significant aspects of contemporary critical principles and practice.

The contributors to the volume were among the participants in a major international conference sponsored by Hofstra University and the C. G. Jung Foundation of New York, held in 1986 at Hofstra University.

Karin Barnaby is pursuing doctoral studies in comparative literature at New York University, and is Associate Editor of *Quadrant*. Pellegrino D'Acierno is Associate Professor of Comparative Literature and Director of Italian Studies at Hofstra University.

C. G. Jung
and the
Humanities

Written under the auspices of Hofstra University
and the C. G. Jung Foundation, New York

# C. G. Jung and the Humanities

## Toward a Hermeneutics of Culture

Edited by
KARIN BARNABY and
PELLEGRINO D'ACIERNO

Princeton University Press
Princeton, New Jersey

Library of Congress Cataloging-in-Publication Data
C. G. Jung and the humanities : toward a
hermeneutics of culture / edited by Karin Barnaby,
Pellegrino D'Acierno ; written under the auspices of
Hofstra University and the C. G. Jung Foundation,
New York.
p.   cm.
Selected essays and discussions from a
1986 conference sponsored by Hofstra University
and the C. G. Jung Foundation, New York.
Includes bibliographies and index.
ISBN 0-691-08616-8
1. Jung, C. G. (Carl Gustav), 1875-1961—
Influence—Congresses. 2. Psychoanalysis and culture—
Congresses.   3. Hermeneutics—Congresses.
1. Barnaby, Karin, 1944-   .
II. D'Acierno, Pellegrino, 1943-   .
III. Hofstra University.
IV. C. G. Jung Foundation for Analytical Psychology.
BF173.J85C15   1989
001.3—dc19
88-34257

This book has been composed
in Linotron Bembo

Clothbound editions of
Princeton University Press Books
are printed on acid-free paper,
and binding materials are chosen
for strength and durability.
Paperbacks, although satisfactory
for personal collections,
are not usually suitable for library rebinding

Printed in the United States of America
by Princeton University Press
Princeton, New Jersey

*In memory of Joseph Campbell*    mythologist, teacher,
hermeneut par excellence

# Contents

*Contents*

## Part II.    Creativity

# Illustrations

# A Note
## on Sources

---

Citations to the Princeton University Press edition of the *Collected Works of C. G. Jung* appear in abbreviated form (*CW* vol.: par., pg.) within the text. For a complete outline of the title and contents of each volume in the *Collected Works*, please see the listing at the back of this book.

Pellegrino D'Acierno

Karin Barnaby

# Preface

Because Jung's work encompasses so many varied fields of interest, his influence is still only in its beginnings. Today, interest in Jung is growing year by year, especially among the younger generation. Accordingly, the growth of his influence is still in its early stages; thirty years from now we will, in all probability, be able to discuss his work in very different terms than we do today. In other words, Jung was so far ahead of his time that people are only gradually beginning to catch up with his discoveries.[1]

In 1986, fourteen years after Marie-Louise von Franz's prognostication, Hofstra University and the C. G. Jung Foundation of New York jointly sponsored an international, interdisciplinary conference titled "C. G. Jung and the Humanities." The conference was convened as a means of reassessing the preeminent—albeit problematic—role that Jung has played in the history of modern thought and culture and, in particular, of determining Jung's specific contribution to the interpretative methodologies of the humanities and social sciences. As a corollary to this historiographic and retrospective task, the conference also actively sought to place Jung within the movement of contemporary thought and to generate a "post-Jungian" reading of Jung. Such a reading would be conducted from the perspective of our postmodern (and perhaps postpsychoanalytical) culture and would stage a confrontation between Jung's thought and recent critical developments in such areas as gender, creativity, popular culture, and above all, poststructuralist theory. Insofar as poststructuralism has to a significant degree privileged Freud over Jung, its introduction of the problematic of language and textuality challenges us to read Jung in a radically new way.

This volume presents selected essays and discussions from the conference and is intended as an updating of the Jungian project, conducted from within traditional Jungian parameters as well as from non-Jungian, post-Jungian, anti-Jungian, and even, as Leslie Fiedler puts it, "anti-Jungian Jungian" positions. As such, the volume can be read either as a series of compelling applications of Jung's theory of interpretation to a wide range of "local" problems belonging to the domains of the humanistic sciences, or as a historical index—an "archive in the making," as it were—that registers, however, partially and symptomatically, Jung's place in the culture of the eighties. Further-more, it records some of the possible disciplinary and methodological uses to which Jungian discourse can be put as the twentieth century— the century of Freud and Jung and of the culture of psychoanalysis— moves to its close.

It should be stressed, however, that the volume is conceived from the extra-analytical and cross-disciplinary perspective of the humani-ties. Consequently, it considers Jung's writings and the analytic disci-pline of which they are the foundation as part of the cultural sciences, that is, as part of a comprehensive interpretative project in which Jung's interpretation of the self and its "textual" productions (dream, myth, vision, art) are inseparable from his hermeneutics of culture. Indeed, the archetype is the culture of the self.

Jung was generally suspicious and at times highly critical of fixed theories and "law-and-order" methodologies. Psychic phenomena, as he observed them, had a "distressingly irrational character which proves refractory to any kind of philosophical systematization" (*CW* 18: par. 1731, p. 770). Furthermore, the psyche is not something un-alterably given that would yield itself to a fixed or definitive interpre-tative system. The psyche is a process, the "product of its own contin-uous development" (*CW* 5: p. xxvii), that is, an event *in* and *of* transformation, a structure profoundly plural and "dialogic" in nature. Jung reminds us: "Because I am an empiricist first and foremost, and my views are grounded in experience, I had to deny myself the plea-sure of reducing them to a well-ordered system and of placing them in their historical and ideological contexts" (*CW* 18: par. 1731, p. 770). This often-repeated claim to empiricism, to "natural interpretation,"[2] ought to be understood by and large as a historical defense of the sci-entific status of analytical psychology in its emergence from the re-futed views of positivism and the other late-nineteenth-century sci-ences. As an authorization of Jung's "anti-method," however, it can be seen to account for the vital and productive way the distinction be-tween theory and practice breaks down in his work. Furthermore, as Paul Feyerabend has so clearly demonstrated in his account of how science is much closer to myth than a scientific philosophy would grant, science, because of its "uneven development," must recognize the historical necessity and productivity of a "theoretical anarchism"[3] such as Jung's. From this point of view, the whole psychoanalytic en-terprise in its quality as a scientific avant-garde can be regarded histor-ically—and without any loss of its scientific validity—as the most mythological part of twentieth-century science.

Despite these preliminary cautions regarding system and method, Jung—as one of the twentieth century's greatest "readers" of the psyche and its productions relating to culture, from dream, through myth and art, to religion—did develop an interpretative methodology in his analytical practice, a "hermeneutics," which has in turn established itself in the so-called sciences of man (unfortunately, often in the form of emphatically un-Jungian applications of fixed interpretative codes). Jung's hermeneutics was above all a hermeneutics of the symbol and, as such, unfolded as a constructive and accumulative operation. The best metaphor for it is perhaps that of the child's "building game" proposed by Jung in *Memories, Dreams, Reflections*.[4] Its task was not so much the restoration of meaning to the symbol or dream text, but rather the opening of a process producing a plurality of meanings, without ever coming to a hard and fast decision about the ultimate meaning.

Consequently, a properly Jungian hermeneutics involves the deployment of a flexible (pluralistic), comparative, and interdisciplinary "exegesis" that seeks out interpretative possibilities—not conclusions—and whose canonic procedures *amplify* the symbol-text by adding to it a wealth of personal and collective, historical and cultural analogies, correspondences, and parallels. In other words, the Jungian interpretation unfolds as a production—a positing of meanings *in relation to* and not the uncovering of *the meaning*, as in the Freudian operation—thereby advancing the genesis of meaning, collaborating in the genesis of the hermeneutic secret. In this respect, Jung's "will to interpretation" is much closer to Nietzsche's "progressive" than to Freud's "regressive" hermeneutics. This constructive process is clearly set out by Jung in one of his infrequent methodological formulations of his hermeneutic approach:

> The essential character of hermeneutics . . . consists in making successive additions of other analogies to the analogy given in the symbol. . . . This procedure widens and enriches the initial symbol, and the final outcome is an infinitely complex and varied picture, in which certain "lines" of psychological development stand out as possibilities that are at once individual and collective. There is no science on earth by which these lines could be proved "right": on the contrary, rationalism could very easily prove that they are not right.[5]

Of course, Jung is characteristically cautious with respect to the epistemological—scientific and "semantic"—aspects of such an operation. As he points out in an immediately preceding passage: "If one takes them [the manifestations of the imagination] concretely they are of no value: if, like Freud, one attributes *semantic* significance to them, they are interesting from the scientific point of view; but if we regard them, according to *hermeneutic* conception, as authentic symbols, then they provide the directive signs we need in order to carry on our lives in harmony with ourselves."⁶

Here we move to the existential dimension of Jung's hermeneutics, especially with the almost Heideggerian projection of the "lifeline" constructed by the hermeneutic method, in which the analysand ultimately appropriates the analyst's "hermeneutic" position so as to undertake his or her own interminable analysis. In short, the forwarding of interpretation is the forwarding of individuation, and vice versa. It is important to stress that the "hermeneutic conception" elaborated in "The Relations Between the Ego and the Unconscious" (*CW* 7) rests on a crucial distinction between the analytic-reductive method (whether of Freud or Adler) and the synthetic-hermeneutic method. Jung, at least with respect to the choice of treatments for the patient, has inscribed within his own analytic practice what Paul Ricoeur has called the "conflict of interpretations."⁷ He incorporates the conflict into his own method by setting out the strategic uses of a negative or critical hermeneutics (Freud's) alongside those of a positive or constructive hermeneutics, determining the efficacy of each approach in terms of the typology and life-stage of the analysand. As we shall attempt to demonstrate below, Jung's awareness of the conflict of interpretations and his recognition of the possibilities of a "suspicious" hermeneutics forces us to posit a much more complex Jung—a Jung wise enough to account for the productivity of the "negative." As Jung, the good doctor who had a "finger for nuance," put it, the theories of Freud and Adler are "critical methods, having, like all criticism, the power to do good when there is something that must be destroyed, dissolved, or rendered, but capable only of harm when there is something to be built" (*CW* 7: par. 65, p. 45).

The reader in search of Jung's "synthetic or constructive method," especially the reader in search of a Jungian method for reading texts, would do well to scrutinize the extensive analysis of the "crab-dream" that Jung sets out in "On the Psychology of the Unconscious" (*CW* 7: pars. 121-165, pp. 80-102). There the reader will find the method of amplification at work in its most plenary fashion, as well as the delineation of the analytic and synthetic procedures. The distinction between interpretation on the objective level and that on the subjective level is extremely useful as a canon both for dream interpretation and for interpretation of cultural texts in general. It sets limits to the first or semanticizing operation while demonstrating the limitless quality of the second, recognizing that the undecidability of the crab can at best be articulated, but by no means resolved, by resorting to the archetypes. Moreover, the reader, especially if primed by contemporary literary theory, will find that Jung reads the crab-dream as what Paul de Man calls an "allegory of reading,"[8] that is, the dream is about the process of its own reading. Because the dreamer cannot read the crab-dream, because the dreamer cannot "cross over" the ford, the unreadability of the dream becomes the dream's message.

The question of Jungian dream interpretation immediately leads us to the question of his interpretative theory of culture. Jung did not formulate a theory of culture in a strict sense; he did not produce a series of major texts on culture comparable, say, to Freud's *The Future of an Illusion, Civilization and its Discontents*, and *Moses and Monotheism*, which establish a comprehensive economy of culture. Nor can his notion of the collective unconscious be properly called a "political unconscious" that accounts for the manner in which political and institutional structures govern the practices and performances of the self. This is not to say that a work like Jung's *Modern Man in Search of a Soul*, for instance, does not provide an interpretation of culture, by which psychical productions are linked to a larger public and historical economy of symbols and archetypes. Nor does such a claim intend to ignore the critique—quite political in its way—of post-Reformation civilization as a destructive series of "chronic iconoclasms," culminating in the "alarming impoverishment of symbolism that is the condition of our life" (*CW* 9i: par. 23, p. 13). It is, however, to say that Jung's hermeneutics of culture is intrinsically a hermeneutics of the self and of the way in which culture is in the self. His analogical approach to the imaginary relates individual consciousness to its own unconscious aspects, via personal associations, but more important to the larger cultural context, via amplifications drawn from history, mythology, folklore, anthropology, the arts, and comparative religion, among others. Jung's conviction that "If we want to understand the psyche, we have to understand the whole world" (*CW* 9i: par. 114, p. 56) gave his psychological investigations an extraordinary universality. According to Jung, comparative and transdisciplinary study of the human sciences was imperative for psychological understanding, and psychology, conversely, was indispensable to understanding the human sciences: "every science is a function of the psyche, and all knowledge is rooted in it. The psyche is the greatest of all cosmic wonders and the *sine qua non* of the world as an object" (*CW* 8: par. 357, p. 169).

By expanding the basis of psychological inquiry in this way, Jung extended the question of meaning to include the totality of human experience, unconscious as well as conscious, individual as well as collective. With such a global project in which psychological *explanation* and hermeneutic *understanding* were made to converge, the epistemological problem of the limits of the conscious understanding of unconscious meaning cropped up again and again. As Jung repeatedly points out: "the psychic phenomenon cannot be grasped in its totality by the intellect" (*CW* 9ii: par. 52, p. 27). Reason—"directed thinking" or what Jung also calls "thinking in words" (*CW* 5: par. 11, p. 11)—comprehends and functions within the reality of space and time and according to laws of logic and casuality. How can reason, then, comprehend an unconscious that defies logic and that operates according to an equivocal and "prelinguistic" language that resists "semanticization" in the Freudian sense?

As we have already pointed out in our discussions of the way in which Jung's approach internalizes the conflict of interpretations, his quarrel with Freud was ultimately a hermeneutic dispute about the question of the meaning of the unconscious. It is untenably simplistic to maintain, however, that the conflict of interpretation as waged by Freud and Jung was merely a polarization of the *critical* and *Romantic* positions that Ricoeur has found operating in the hermeneutic tradition: a *critical hermeneutics* intends "to elaborate the universally valid rules of understanding"; a *Romantic hermeneutics* appeals to a "living relation with the process of creation."⁹

Certainly, it is more valid, especially with respect to Jung's approach, to see the "double mark"¹⁰—the critical and the Romantic operations—that informs the interpretative positions of both thinkers. This doubleness of Jung's approach is, as we have already pointed out, at work in his distinction between the analytic-reductive approach and the hermeneutic-synthetic approach. Jung's distinction, it is clear, rests on a "misreading" of Freud by which the "double mark" is erased and Freud seen only in terms of his critical and reductive approach.

In some sense, it can be claimed that the present volume of essays seeks to interrogate the "double mark" of Jung's hermeneutics, thereby going beyond the traditional "myth-of-meaning" readings of Jung. Certainly, if we are to situate Jung properly within the context of those "suspicious" hermeneutics against which Jungian hermeneutics must compete (here we are thinking not only of those of Marx, Nietzsche, and Freud, the masters of what Ricoeur has called the "school of suspicion,"¹¹ but also the deconstructivist and anti-interpretative stances of poststructuralism), it is crucial to point out that Jung's hermeneutics is far more "suspicious" and "critical" than traditionally allowed. It is not enough, however, to indicate the interminable and indefinite, the polysemous and pluralistic dimensions of Jung's interpretative operation. Jung's pluralism rests on a profound suspicion of language or, at least, that language of directed thinking, which Derrida would call "logocentric." This negative aspect of Jung's overwhelmingly positive hermeneutics, his "suspicion of language vis-à-vis im-

ages," has been pointed out by Edward Casey in his essay included here
and is clearly at work in the following representative comments by
Jung: "I quite deliberately bring everything that purports to be metaphysical into the daylight of psychological understanding, and do my
best to prevent people from believing in nebulous power words (*CW*
13: par. 73, p. 49).

The implication of Jung's demystification of language (see, in particular, *CW* 5: pars. 4-46, pp. 7-33) must be understood as an essential
feature of his canon of interpretation; that is, his constructive-synthetic
method is permanently infiltrated by a margin of silence, by that which
absolutely resists interpretation. This sets it apart, to a certain degree,
from those hermeneutic theories of interpretation that J. Hillis Miller
criticizes for bypassing "the interference of the rhetorical dimension of
language in its grammatical and logical functioning."[12] Jung's bypassing of language then is a deliberate strategy for confronting the prelinguistic language of the unconscious archetypes that are rendered "dialogic" to the degree that they are personified and inserted into a
dramaturgy of sorts.

The attempt to see Jung's theory and practice of interpretation as a
more complex and more nuanced approach, to go beyond what might
be called "vulgar Jungianism" (the mechanical and reductivist allegorical rewriting of a "text" according to the master code of the archetypes), is the shared methodological task of the authors and discussants
featured in this volume. Not only does it emerge as a conscious project
in the section on "Post-Jungian Contributions" (essays and comments
by James Hillman, Edward Casey, Paul Kugler, David Miller, Andrew
Samuels, Carol Schreier Rupprecht, Beverley Zabriskie), but it is the
thread that runs throughout the volume, from the mythological analysis of Eileen Preston to the intricate discussions of the Trickster by
Stanley Diamond and Thomas Belmonte.

Sociologist R. Kevin Hennelly has suggested that Jung's model of
the psyche ought to be regarded in terms of a Kuhnian paradigm
shift.[13] Another approach, partially at the expense of the "scientific
side" of his theory, might be to regard Jung as an initiator of a discursive practice along the lines proposed by Foucault in his seminal essay,
"What is an Author?"[14] Whether Jung's model is regarded as a paradigm shift in the "harder" sciences or in the interpretative or cultural
sciences, it is certain that, as it comes to be internalized by various
disciplines, its full complexity will continue to emerge. Furthermore,
the ideological ways in which Jung has heretofore come to be institutionalized and canonized will be replaced by historiographic and textual analyses that grasp the true dimension of his work. For example,
an interpretative operation, if it is to escape its perfunctory status as an

allegorical act, must not merely call into question the materials it examines; rather, it must relentlessly turn back on itself and its procedures. One would be hard pressed to find a more exquisite methodological check on the interpreter's proclivity for projection than Jung's caution regarding the "prejudice" of the conscious (the interpreting) mind: "Between the conscious and the unconscious there is a kind of 'uncertainty relationship' because the observer is inseparable from the observed and always disturbs it by the act of observation. In other words, exact observation of the unconscious prejudices observation of the conscious and vice versa" (*CW* 9ii: par. 355, p. 226).

The complexity of this kind of self-reflective interpretative operation, involving conscious and unconscious factors simultaneously, both as interpretative subject and object, is complicated further by such arbitrary factors as "value," "feeling," and "attitude." Jung reminds us that "The psychic phenomenon . . . consists not only of meaning but also of value, and this depends on the intensity of the accompanying feeling-tones" (*CW* 9ii: par. 52, p. 27). By relating meaning to irrational functions of value and feeling, Jung introduces an experiential component that, in part, shifts meaning into the irrational domain, relocating it somewhere between consciousness and the unconscious in a mediating position, as it were. The final arbiter, however, between what is meaningful and what is meaningless, is the conscious attitude, which "regards a given fact not merely as such but also as an expression for something unknown" (*CW* 6: par. 818, p. 475). The inherent difficulty here is that, from its perspective, consciousness frequently equates the unknown with the meaningless, "projecting [its] own lack of understanding upon the object" (*CW* 8: par. 238, p. 238). It appears then that the decisive moment in the interpretation of meaning is the act of choosing between meaningfulness and meaninglessness: "Which element we think outweighs the other, whether meaninglessness or meaning, is a matter of temperament. . . . I cherish the anxious hope that meaning will preponderate and win the battle."[15]

Jung's contributions, the identification of unconscious aspects of meaning and the recognition of the reality of the collective unconscious, are as significant as they are radical: on the one hand, they liberate meaning from the confines of consciousness (i.e., from its logocentric identification and orientation), and on the other hand, they accord value and reality, however different and/or chaotic, to unconscious meaning. It is precisely in relation to the question of meaning that we discover the "postmodern" Jung: "Interpretations are for those who don't understand; it is only the things we don't understand that have any meaning" (*CW* 9i: par. 65, p. 31). Furthermore, this paradoxical finding, namely that meaning is not to be found in what we know but in what we do not know, is as ancient as it is contemporary: one need only remind oneself of the hard-won wisdom of Oedipus.

To relate this reassessment of Jung's work to the current critical preoccupation with the question of meaning would seem to open up a rich and mutually beneficial field of inquiry. Poststructuralist thought, particularly deconstruction, appears to offer an exceptionally useful critical perspective from which to formulate a contemporary understanding of Jung. For example, if we allow ourselves the liberty of a simplistic analysis of Jung from a deconstructive perspective, would we not locate his psychology of the unconscious, of the nonrational, on the periphery of Western rationalistic, logocentric culture? Indeed, was it not from a marginal position that Jung set out to call into question, to "deconstruct" (if we permit ourselves such an anachronistic use of the term) the "most cherished securities" of his time, foremost among them "the unequivocal superiority of rational conciousness"? "Since everybody believes or, at least, tries to believe in the unequivocal superiority of rational consciousness, I have to emphasize the importance of the unconscious irrational forces, to establish a sort of balance" (*CW* 18: par. 1585, p. 704).

Jung's systematic probing of psychic phenomena that have been historically marginalized and excluded appears, in some ways, to parallel deconstructive strategies. His bold pursuit of unconscious manifestations—the irrational, the illogical, the nonscientific, the fantastic, the esoteric and occult, alchemy, astrology, gnosticism, mysticism, parapsychology, Eastern religions, and primitive rituals—may have earned him the censure of the intellectual establishment while it rewarded him with his most crucial insights, namely the recognition of the symbolic and transpersonal nature of psychic phenomena. Could not Jung's "fundamental axiom," that "psychic phenomena should never be looked at from one side only, but from the other side as well" (*CW* 10: par. 292, p 141), and the maxim, borrowed from Disraeli, that "not too much importance should be attached to important things, and that unimportant things are not so unimportant as they seem" (*CW* 10: par. 292, p. 141), be understood as analogic Jungian formulations of deconstructive principles?

To the extent that familiarization with deconstructive theory could illuminate the overall phenomenon of Jung within the Western cultural context, could not Jungian theory also elucidate the psychological dynamics that underlie some of the deconstructivist discoveries? If we overlook, for the sake of the hypothesis, the discrepancy between the Jungian imagistic and deconstruction's linguistic models, we might cite as examples the hierarchical structuring of oppositional terms and the dislocation of those hierarchies via deconstructive reversals. These deconstructive operations show a striking similarity to basic archetypal dynamics, a similarity that can be attributed, as Jung would explain, to the common psychic origin of language and image: "Interpretations make use of certain linguistic matrices that are themselves derived from primordial images. From whatever side we approach this question, everywhere we find ourselves confronted with the history of language, with images and motifs that lead straight back to the primitive wonder-world" (*CW* 9i: par. 67, p. 33).

With regard to the oppositional dynamics found to be at work in discursive texts. Jung might have argued that they merely mirror the oppositional thinking that is, after all, a constitutive component of consciousness. Experience of the world, of existence itself, is possible solely in terms of the discrimination of opposites and is inseparable from, and in fact identical with, consciousness: "There is no consciousness without discrimination of opposites. . . . Nothing can exist without its opposite" (*CW* 9i: par. 178, p. 96). "It would be extremely illogical to assume that one can state a quality without its opposite." (*CW* 18: par. 1592, p. 708).

The privileging of consciousness over unconsciousness is to be expected, given that a consciousness establishes its identity in terms of what it is not, that is, in terms of the nonconscious or unconscious, which thereby becomes other or opposite. Jung offers the analogy of the birth and separation of logos: "The paternal principle, the Logos, eternally struggles to extricate itself from the primal warmth and primal darkness of the maternal womb; in a word, from unconsciousness. . . . Unconsciousness is the primal sin, evil itself, for the Logos" (*CW* 9i: par. 178, p. 96).

Jonathan Culler, in his work *On Deconstruction*, identifies logos as the "superior term" in strikingly similar fashion:

> In oppositions such as meaning/form, soul/body, intuition/expression, literal/metaphorical, nature/culture, intelligible/sensible, positive/negative, transcendental/empirical, serious/nonserious, the superior term belongs to the logos and is a higher presence; the inferior term marks a fall. Logocentrism thus assumes the priority of the first term and conceives the second in relation to it, as a complication, a negation, a manifestation, or a disruption of the first.[16]

This tendency of consciousness to privilege aspects identified with itself and to exclude opposite aspects is informed by the "polaristic structure of the psyche," described by Jung as an "energic system . . . dependent on the tension of opposites" (*CW* 9i: par. 483, p. 269), wherein the degree of polarization is always determined by the degree of one-sided concentration of energy. "The more one-sidedly, rigidly, and absolutely the one position is held, the more aggressive, hostile, and incompatible will the other become, so that at first sight there would seem to be little prospect of reconciling the two" (*CW* 7: par. 118, p. 78).

Jung's description is almost identical to a statement by Jacques Derrida: "In a traditional philosophical opposition we have not a peaceful coexistence of the vis-à-vis, but rather a violent hierarchy. One of the two terms governs the other (axiologically, logically, etc.), or has the upper hand."[17] To deconstruct these hierarchical oppositions, according to Derrida, "first of all, is to overturn the hierarchy at a given moment."[18] We could readily force a comparison to an analogic archetypal operation, which Jung has observed to be an inherent and essential mechanism of oppositional dynamics: "there are no general psychological propositions which could not just as well be reversed; indeed, their reversibility proves their validity" (*CW* 9i: par. 483, p. 269).

Reversibility or *enantiodromia*, a term borrowed from Heraclitus, is "the most marvelous of all psychological laws: the regulative function of opposites" in which "sooner or later everything runs into its opposite. Thus the rational attitude of culture necessarily runs into its opposite, namely the irrational devastation of culture" (*CW* 7: par. 111, p. 72). Classical Chinese philosophy represents this compensatory mechanism in the compelling symbol of the two contrary principles, "the bright *yang* and the dark *yin* . . . always when one principle reaches the height of its power, the counter-principle is stirring within it like a germ. This is another particularly graphic formulation of the psychological law of compensation by an inner opposite" (*CW* 10: par. 295, p. 142). The orientation of many of the essays in this volume is informed, explicitly or implicitly, by such oppositional dynamics, which can be observed not only in the relation between the unconscious and consciousness, but also in the relation between instinct and spirit (Preston), gnosis (Quispel) and the interiorization of deity (Dourley) and doctrine, Trickster and the sacred (Diamond, Belmonte), popular culture and high culture (Fiedler, Schechter, Carlin, Pladott), art and the historical-social context (Martin, Grabenhorst-Randall, Lassaw, Richenburg, Hasselriis), imagination and reality (Bly, Campbell, Pozzi, Hillman, Singer), woman and man (Rupprecht, Zabriskie, Samuels), and postmodern and traditional critical theory (Casey, Hillman, Kugler, Miller).

Our hypothetical delineations of some possibly fertile lines of inquiry do not pretend to be interpretative operations. Our observations of some of the more striking similarities—for the most part intuited—between Jung's archetypal psychology and deconstructive operations are intended, rather, to stimulate a rigorous comparative interpretative reading of Jung and postmodern critical theory, an enterprise that would perhaps realize the kind of post-Jungian reading of Jung that was projected by von Franz and that this volume hopes to generate.

This volume, then, has been organized under the sign of "hermeneutics"—and in the shadow of poststructuralism—to situate Jung within the so-called war between the various interpretative methodologies that has come to dominate today's intellectual marketplace; we also intend to effect a linkage of our interrogation of Jung to the current crisis in the humanities. Furthermore, the volume has been subdivided into three sections: an opening section comprising essays that operate more or less within the boundaries of traditional archetypal analysis, some of which extend the Jungian approach to relatively new areas of research, such as architecture and popular culture; a central section on creativity that, among other things, features discussions by prominent artists who have been influenced by Jung or who work with Jungian problematics; and a concluding polemical section that attempts to forge a "post-Jungian" understanding of Jung, what David Miller has called an "other Jung." Whether, of course, an "other Jung" does in fact emerge remains to be seen. What is of primary importance, however, is that an attempt—albeit provisional—has been made to contest the way in which the figure of Jung has come to be institutionalized and installed within late-twentieth-century culture. Now that poststructuralism, postphilosophy, and all the various postmarked disciplines have proclaimed and institutionalized the "disappearance of man" and have undermined the privileged status of the human subject, Jung more than ever—and unlike Freud—appears as the last humanist. His strong concepts of the self and of the process of individuation stand out as last-ditch—albeit abiding—efforts to understand the contingency of individual experience in all its depths.

This honorific function as "the last humanist" in the epoch of the "death of man" is of little consolation unless it is linked with Jung's relentless historical diagnosis of the modern human condition, a severe diagnosis whose historical specificity must not be attenuated by an illegitimate (read: non-Jungian) archetypal reading of history as the return of the same. Jung is just as strong a historian of modern humanity as he is a mythologist of modern humanity. He has "all-too-humanly" come to be regarded as the last hermeneut, that is, the last practitioner of the "myth of meaning," the last exegete of the symbol and its profundity, and as a corollary, the last and most secular exponent of numinosity, the last archaeologist of the self who captures the self's aura just as it dissolves officially into the archaeologies of language and institution.

Such mystification of Jung needed to be called into question, especially in the light of von Franz's comments regarding Jung's vanguardism and what David Elkind has called his "almost prophetic explanation for many contemporary phenomena from the Women's Liberation movement to youth's discovery of Eastern religions and drugs."[19]

It is also instructive to compare Freud's canonization with Jung's, their respective instaurations taking on the aspects of a horse race, with Freud having the head start of twenty years. Freud's work has been subjected to at least two strong "misreadings" or oppositional readings: the first undertaken by Jung himself, who rewrote Freud's account of the Oedipus complex in terms of archetypal symbolism; the second by Jacques Lacan, who rewrote Freud's account of the Oedipus complex in terms of language. Lacan's rewriting of Freud is extremely crucial to Freud's ascendancy in postmodern culture, for through it Freud was inserted within the problematics of language that dominate current concerns. All this serves to indicate that, despite his cultural pervasiveness, Jung has not yet found either his "Jung" or his Lacan. And perhaps the process of Jung's canonization/decanonization/recanonization will advance by different means. Regardless of how the language paradigm has come to dominate the human sciences, postmodern culture is overridingly a "society of the spectacle or the image,"[20] and no thinker provides more useful instruments for understanding the economy of the image than does Jung. It is hoped that the essays in this volume will contribute to our understanding, to the ongoing reassessment and problematization of Jung that is underway, both within the culture of psychoanalysis and in the culture at large. The usefulness of this volume lies in the fact that it regards Jung as a writer and a cultural figure. Recently Harold Bloom, in making a claim for "Freud as the greatest modern writer," has written: "It may be that Freud's importance to our culture continues to increase almost in direct proportion to the waning of psychoanalysis as a theory. His conceptions are so magnificent in their indefiniteness that they have begun to merge with our culture and indeed now form the only Western mythology that contemporary intellectuals have in common."[21]

A similar claim might be made for Jung, although Jung's writing has not yet been confronted as "writing." Unlike Freud's, Jung's is a language of the unconscious, a discourse infiltrated by the "other voice," as Jung puts it: "Everything I have written has a double bottom."[22] Here we move to the notion of Jung as a "trickster of writing," who locates in the oracular slippage of his writing the movement by which the epochal (post-Christian) question "But then what is your myth—the myth in which you do live?"[23] becomes the postmodern question "What myth are you lived by? What language are you spoken by?"

# Notes

1. Marie-Louise von Franz, *C. G. Jung: His Myth in Our Time*, trans. William H. Kennedy (New York: G. P. Putnam's Sons, 1972), p. 3.

2. See Paul Feyerabend, *Against Method* (London: Verso, 1979), pp. 69-80.

3. Ibid., p. 295. A study, grounded in close textual analysis, of the ways in which theory comes to be thematized—and thematized even when resisted—in Jung's written work needs to be undertaken. Such a study would focus on the language game by which Jung transposes the (self-) analytical experience onto the level of theory and would discuss the way in which theory is endorsed, resisted, pragmatized, personalized or "privatized," rendered scientific or philosophical, rendered mythological or metaphoric, and ultimately inscribed, whether as a method of interpretation or as interpretation itself, within a hermeneutics of meaning. For a preliminary discussion of the place of theory in Jung's work, see Andrew Samuels, *Jung and the Post-Jungians* (London: Routledge and Kegan Paul, 1985), pp. 4-6.

4. C. G. Jung, *Memories, Dreams, Reflections*, ed. Aniela Jaffé, trans. Richard and Clara Winston (New York: Vintage Books, 1965), p. 173.

5. C. G. Jung, *Two Essays on Analytical Psychology*, vol. 7 of *The Collected Works of C. G. Jung*, trans. R.F.C. Hull, Bollingen Series (New York: Pantheon Books, 1953), p. 287.

6. Ibid., p. 286.

7. See Paul Ricoeur, *The Conflict of Interpretations: Essays in Hermeneutics*, ed. Dan Ihde (Evanston: Northwestern University Press, 1974).

8. Paul de Man, *Allegories of Reading: Figural Language in Rousseau, Nietzsche, Rilke, and Proust* (New Haven: Yale University Press, 1979), p. 221.

9. Paul Ricoeur, *Hermeneutics and the Human Sciences*, ed. and trans. John B. Thompson (Cambridge: Cambridge University Press, 1981), p. 46.

10. Ibid.

11. Paul Ricoeur, *Freud and Philosophy: An Essay on Interpretation*, trans. Denis Savage (New Haven: Yale University Press, 1970), pp. 32-36.

12. J. Hillis Miller, review of Paul Ricoeur's *Time and Narrative* in *Times Literary Supplement*, October 9-15, 1987, p. 1104.

13. R. Kevin Hennelly, "Jung and the Social Sciences" (Paper presented at the C. G. Jung and the Humanities Conference, Hofstra University, 1986).

14. Michel Foucault, *Language, Counter-Memory, Practice: Selected Essays and Interviews*, trans. Donald F. Bouchard and Sherry Simon (Ithaca: Cornell University Press, 1977), pp. 113-138.

15. Jung, *Memories*, p. 359.

16. Jonathan Culler, *On Deconstruction* (Ithaca: Cornell University Press, 1982), p. 93.

17. Jacques Derrida, *Positions* (Paris: Minuit, 1972), pp. 56-57; trans. Alan Bass (Chicago: University of Chicago Press, 1981), p. 41.

18. Ibid., p. 41.

19. David Elkind, "Freud, Jung and the Collective Unconscious," *The New York Times Magazine*, October 4, 1970, p. 24.

20. Guy Debord, *Society of the Spectacle* (Detroit: Black and Red, 1983).

21. Harold Bloom, "Freud, The Greatest Modern Writer," in *New York Times Book Review*, March 23, 1986, p. 1.

22. Quoted in von Franz, *C. G. Jung: His Myth in Our Time*, p. 4.

23. Jung, *Memories*, p. 171.

# Acknowledgments

To speak of mere collaboration in connection with the production of the present volume does not do justice to the extraordinary process that generated it and saw it to completion. This volume represents the cooperative effort of three institutions—Hofstra University, the C. G. Jung Foundation of New York, and Princeton University Press—and several dozen individuals, a cooperation characterized by enthusiasm, support, and above all genuine friendship and mutual trust. The editors would like to thank these institutions and those individuals who served to "co-author" the volume. The greatest debt we have incurred as editors, however, is to Cathie Brettschneider, religion editor at Princeton University Press. We thank her for her superb judgment, advice, and patience, all of which were instrumental to the completion of this volume. We also express our deep appreciation for their friendship and faith to the late Dr. Joseph Astman, former director of the Hofstra Cultural Center, and to Dr. Aryeh Maidenbaum, executive director of the C. G. Jung Foundation of New York, in supporting the "C. G. Jung and the Humanities" conference. Finally, Joseph Campbell brought to this project a singular warmth and exuberance that will continue to radiate from this volume in the form of his deeply felt and unabashedly extemporaneous statement on creativity. We dedicate this volume to his memory.

C. G. Jung
and the
Humanities

# Introduction:
# C. G. Jung and
# the Humanities    Philip T. Zabriskie

The work and ideas of C. G. Jung have set moving several waves of influence. One area of influence is a school of psychological theory and therapy, that is, of clinical psychoanalytic practice. Another—that with which we are concerned here—has to do with the impact of his work on the study of the arts and humanities and in some measure with the impact of his work on the arts themselves. Although many people in these fields acknowledge no such influence, or know little of Jung, or actively resist his ideas (though they occasionally may be heard to speak of complexes, of introversion and extraversion, even of archetypes), the fact remains that Jung's contributions have the power to affect how we look at the history, labors, and creations of men and women in our own time as well as in his.

Jung has affected our vision in three main ways. The first has to do with his understanding of the unconscious. About this I shall make five assertions, paraphrases of what I believe were the central ideas that shaped Jung's views on life, art, and history—the subject matter of humanistic inquiry:

1. The unconscious is real, and its activity, its energy, in and amongst all of us, is continuous. The reality of the psyche and of its unconscious dimensions has to be recognized and emphasized over and over again. Our conscious minds are *not* the sole captains of our ships or even of our thoughts. Individually and collectively, we are continually being influenced, for better and worse, in our thinking, our feelings, our behavior, and our perceptions, by energies of which we are much of the time unconscious.

2. Because the unconscious is unconscious, we cannot know it directly; we know it by its fruits, by its manifestations. These manifestations may be discerned in dreams, in works of art, thought, and imagination, in patterns of behavior, and in the symbols that move people and nations.

3. In every manifestation of psyche there is a mixture of influences, a combination of factors. First, there is the work of the conscious ego. Second, there is the influence of the personal and largely unconscious complexes of the individual or the group to which he or she belongs.

3

And third, there is the influence of whatever combination of archetypal dynamisms may emerge from the collective psyche in that person's or that group's unconscious at that time.

It is from the interaction of these three levels of psychic activity that ideas (benign and malevolent), works of art, and collective movements arise. To observe or study this ever-varying interaction makes endlessly fascinating the lives of individuals, the relationships of men and women, and the output of the human spirit, from the sand paintings of a Navajo healer to Melville's *Moby Dick*; from the initiation dances of primitive peoples to the "ritual dance" at a summit conference; or such massive collective experiences as the civil wars in the United States or Ireland. Inherent in all of them is a mixture of conscious intent, personal complexes, and deep mythic powers.

4. The unconscious produces, in and through the works of the mind and the imagination, symbols; and these symbols of the psyche *always refer to psyche*. This is a difficult point to make. Robert Graves said in *The White Goddess* that every true poet writes to the Muse (or to the goddess) about herself and about the poet's experience of her.[1] The psyche reaches into matter and into the realms of the spirit, but its symbols do not stand for concrete objects or events, or for explicit metaphysical entities. The psyche's symbols, like psyche itself, may be grounded in empirical reality, but the symbols are not signs representing that reality. The mysteries of Eleusis were grounded in the life and experience of people who knew well the movements and cycles of death and growth in agriculture, but they were not about those cycles of the seasons. Rather the mysteries were about mystery, about the mysterious psychic process of purification, death, and new birth. If one dreams of a great bull, it is almost certainly not about an actual bull (unless perchance life puts one in close association with these animals). It is also not a sign, a disguised representation, of masculine aggression or sexuality. In the dreamer's experience the bull-energy of the psyche may be grounded in the dreamer's sexuality, but the image does not stand for that. Jung's attitude toward symbols (in dream, myth, art, religion) is difficult because it eschews a "this-means-that" correspondence. The bull is a symbol of psychic energy that has the force of—and may be expressed as—aggressive masculine sexuality; but it may also be expressed (or experienced) as phallic generative creativity that is as potent and as awesome as that of a god. This way of thinking about symbols opens up vast ranges of meaning; it also stands against all literalisms, all fundamentalisms, whether theological, political, critical, or psychological. Fundamentalist or literal attitudes restrict and kill psyche.

5. Lastly on this point about the unconscious, Jung believed that the

meaning of psychic symbols presses beyond the realm of the personal. Archetypal symbols in particular are transpersonal in meaning. As I have heard Joseph Campbell say in lectures, "The symbol is transparent to transcendence."[2]

In this regard Jung was inescapably religious—not doctrinal, but religious. Even in his youth, according to Henri Ellenberger, he would argue with fellow students who were secular materialists (whether in science or philosophy) and would sound like a theologian; when with theological students he would argue about the symbolic meaning of their creeds and sound like a skeptic or atheist.[3] Jung believed that life's story must be told on two levels, as in the old epics such as the *Odyssey* or in the narrative books of the Bible. Homer characteristically described what was taking place among the mortals: Odysseus, for example, stuck on Calypso's island weeping and helpless. Then, he described what happened among the immortals: the gods gathered on Olympus where Athena persuaded Zeus that it was time for Odysseus to move toward home, and Hermes was sent to carry the message. The poet talked about what happened on two levels. The story of Odysseus, the story of Achilles, Agamemnon, and Hector, the story of Moses, had to be told on both levels or it would not be a complete story, not yet a true story. So, said Jung, one must tell an individual's tale (or a people's tale) on two levels: tell the work of the conscious mind—the ego—and of what the writer or politician or citizen intended, and then tell what was happening among the archetypes, among the gods. Tell both levels or it is not a complete story, not yet a true story.

The second way in which Jung has affected our vision has to do with his somber sense of evil and tragedy. How can those involved in art and the humanities not deal with these great problems? Jung's was a dark view of the human psyche and history—born of his era, born of his own experience, born of his observation and study. He repeatedly spoke of the fearsome darkness experienced in the consulting room or among families, as well as on the battlefields of two world wars and in the societies of the warring nations. Every mythological system testifies to the reality and depth of horror and suffering. Individuals deal with it in different ways and with different resources. Richard Ellman, in his biography of James Joyce, tells of Jung's efforts to treat Joyce's psychotic daughter, and of how Jung concluded he could not help her. She was, he said, very like her father, having a remarkable imagination, but they "were like two people going to the bottom of a river, one falling and the other diving."[4]

The psyche is not a pastoral, sunlit glade, in Jung's view, or at least it is seldom so. He remarked once, when writing about Freud in 1939, on the occasion of Freud's death: "All that gush about man's innate goodness, which has addled so many brains after the dogma of original sin was no longer understood, was blown to the winds by Freud, and the little that remains will, let us hope, be driven out for good and all by the barbarism of the twentieth century" (*CW* 15: par. 69, p. 46). Though coming from a very different background, he sounds not unlike his Swiss contemporary, Karl Barth. But, unlike Barth, Jung went further. So deeply indeed do evil and wretchedness go into the nature of things that Jung was forced to brood about the dark Satanic nature even of God.

Third, humanists have been drawn to Jung because of his sense of the unending, wondrous creativity of the psyche. Again and again from talented hearts and minds or from unlettered people thoughts, intuitions, or symbols arise that carry the force of life and beauty, that can heal or rudely awaken, that can bring together the forces of work and love, of logos and eros. And such creativity is of the self, and it seems to exert its energies among people everywhere. I do not know if Jung had much feeling for music, but he loved (though not uncritically) philosophers and poets, shrewd peasants and medicine men. Moreover as a therapist he was forever in search of the creative ingredient in a sufferer's illness or complex. The products of creative imagination and feeling nurture our souls. They can correct our one-sided conscious view of things, for they arise from the objective psyche, so Jung thought, and almost always carry compensatory value for the partialness of what we are thinking and valuing consciously. Hence the importance, the revolutionary energy, and the loneliness of the artist.

With these thoughts in mind, I think that the phrase "C. G. Jung and the Humanities" implies a reciprocal undertaking. On the one hand, we here endeavor, as do others similarly engaged, to investigate how Jung's ideas, his work, his hypotheses, may shed light on other areas of humanistic work, for example in the study of literature or the arts; in philosophy, criticism, and theology; in education and in history. How may we in our day learn to tell history on two levels, as Homer did, or as Jung's ideas imply? On the other hand, how may those working in the arts or humanities bring to consciousness the complex workings of the psyche in the present day and generation? How may those who study the works of men, women, and society help us to see and understand the creative and destructive archetypal patterns that are shaping our lives and our future?

As in individual life, so in collective life, becoming conscious of what is moving and influencing the psyche presents the best hope of dealing creatively with those powers rather than being overwhelmed by them. As with Dionysus at Thebes in *The Bacchae*, there is no hope in repression or possession. The only way is to develop, with efforts of intellect, imagination, and heart, a conscious, respectful relation to the gods who are in our midst. In that endeavor there is both excitement and hope.

# Notes

1. Robert Graves, *The White Goddess*, rev. and enlarged ed. (New York: Farrar, Straus and Giroux, 1966), pp. 14, 444 and passim.

2. Joseph Campbell, *The Inner Reaches of Outer Space* (New York: Alfred van der Marck Editions, 1985). Campbell writes that the features of an environment, when seen with the vision of myth, become sacred, "become transparent to transcendence" (p. 20). Later he says that a culturally conditioned image or idea, when it becomes "a metaphor," is "thus to be recognized as transparent to transcendence" (p. 67).

3. Henri Ellenberger, *The Discovery of the Unconscious* (London: Allen Lane, The Penguin Press, 1970), pp. 687-688.

4. Richard Ellman, *James Joyce* rev. ed. (New York: Oxford University Press, 1982), p. 697.

# Part I

## The Archetypal Tradition

# Mind and Matter in Myth   Eileen Preston

Often myth is described as "archetypal." But what exactly do we mean when we say that myth is archetypal? My exploration of this question began with a study of the archetypal processes described by C. G. Jung in his work "On the Nature of the Psyche" (*CW* 8). Jung explained his theory by means of an analogy according to which consciousness was represented in terms of the scale of light or sound, with an upper and lower threshold delimiting it from the unconscious (*CW* 8: par. 367, p. 175; par. 417, p. 213). The illustrations included here are intended to demonstrate Jung's analogy. I then combine them into a symbolic model that will serve as the point of reference for an examination of imagery and figures in Egyptian mythology. My purpose is to show the nature of mythical images as psychological phenomena that reveal traces of the transformative process of human consciousness, and thereby to establish a more precise understanding of the archetypal quality of myth.

According to Jung's exposition, psychic processes are energized by instincts, which have both a physiological and a psychological aspect. In the organic substrate below the lower threshold of consciousness, the "drives" of instinct operate compulsively in a purely automatic, physiological way. Above the lower threshold, that is, within the field of consciousness, the processes resulting from instincts are not automatic or compulsive insofar as instinctual energy is subject to the control of conscious ego. They might thus be described as psychological. Toward the upper threshold, where instinct loses its influence over ego, the processes break free from instinct.

Extending his analogy of the scale of consciousness, Jung continued, "Just as in the lower reaches, the psyche loses itself in the organic-material substrate, so in its upper reaches it resolves itself into a 'spiritual' form" (*CW* 8: par. 380, p. 183). Spirit and instinct, then, are the opposite poles of the psychic sphere, and both being by nature autonomous, they constitute the boundaries of the field of consciousness.

Every instinct has its corresponding instinctual pattern or archetype, without which the instinct cannot function. The archetypes might be said to give the instincts both their form and their meaning. They regulate instinctual energy and are at the same time the instincts' inevitable fulfillment. Archetypes take their shape in consciousness as images with a very powerful mystical quality. This spiritual quality of the archetypal image would appear to be at variance with the nature of the corresponding instinct. "Archetype and instinct are the most polar opposites imaginable," affirmed Jung. Thus their opposition reflects the essential paradox of man, who "finds himself simultaneously driven to act and free to reflect." Nevertheless, these opposites show what he described as "a constant propensity to union" (*CW* 8: par. 406, pp. 206-207).

This spirit–instinct antithesis Jung saw as being one of the many processes of opposition in the psyche whose tension is the source of psychic energy. He likened the flow of energy between spirit and instinct to consciousness "sliding" along a scale: "At one moment it finds itself in the vicinity of instinct, and falls under its influence; at another, it slides along to the other end where spirit predominates and even assimilates the instinctual processes most opposed to it" (*CW* 8: par. 408, p. 207).

Using his analogy, Jung located the dynamism of instinct at the red end of the visible spectrum (see Figure 1). He insisted, however, that the instinctual image or archetype should be at the violet end of the spectrum. Violet, being a compound of blue and red, reflects the paradoxical nature of the archetype and its dual aspect, for the archetype must be regarded as a physiological dynamism, instinctual and unconscious (the red in violet), and at the same time as a psychological phenomenon; that is, it presents itself to the conscious psyche in the mediated form of a numinous, spiritual image (the blue in violet). Matter and spirit thus come together in the realm of psyche as conscious contents and in the form of an image. Like physiological instinct, however, the archetypes themselves are essentially unconscious. In terms of the analogy of the spectrum, therefore, Jung suggested that instincts and archetypes should be thought of as lying in the invisible realms of the infrared and ultraviolet, respectively, since the ultimate nature of both matter and spirit is transcendental.

At this point in the text, Jung reminds us that the alchemists expressed the mystery of the union of opposites in the symbol of the ouroboros—the circular tail-eating serpent (*CW* 8: par. 416, p. 213). Since the alchemical ouroboros naturally conveys the idea of an ongoing transformative process, and Jung's analogy of the spectrum illustrates the nature of the opposites transformed in conscious psyche, I have combined the two in order to represent the ongoing transformative process of human personality (see Figure 2).

If we reduce Figure 2 to its basic elements of color and shape, a symbolic model can be derived. It demonstrates the transformative process that is experienced when transcendental matter and spirit are inte-

**UNCONSCIOUS**

**SPIRIT**

**IMAGES**

visible spectrum

consciousness

**INSTINCT**

**UNCONSCIOUS**

Figure 1.   Spectrum.

Figure 2.    Ouroboros.

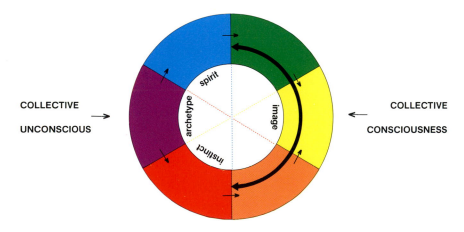

COLLECTIVE

UNCONSCIOUS

COLLECTIVE

CONSCIOUSNESS

spirit

archetype

image

instinct

Figure 3.    Model of the psyche.

grated in the conscious psyche through the manifestation of the arche-typal image (see Figure 3). The visual illustration, of course, has no representational value. It is no more than a conjured form on which to project interior experiences, which are difficult to prove empirically or even to approach directly. What I have attempted, therefore, is a sym-bolic approach. As a symbolic model, Figure 3 might be used to pro-vide terms of reference for the interior experiences involved in Jung's theory of archetypes.

The dark colors (red and blue and their compound violet) signify the more unconscious zones of the personal psychic sphere. The light colors (yellow and compounds orange and green) signify the more conscious zones. The original connection of instinct and spirit is sug-gested by their common source in the archetypal collective uncon-scious (violet), their propensity for union by their contrary circular direction. Instinct (red) moves as "drives" through its purely physio-logical operation toward its conscious psychological function under the influence of ego. Archetype (violet), clearly charged with the dy-namism of instinct (the red in violet), moves contrarily in spiritual forms toward its union with instinct and its manifestation in psyche as image. Yellow signifies the constellation of conscious psyche, the realm of human will, energized by the spirit–instinct tension. Itself a transformation of the first instinctual image, it is in turn a process whereby instinct is transformed and archetype mediated, so as to ap-pear in conscious form as image. The realm of image reaches into the influence of spirit at the upper limit (green combines the blue and yel-low). At the lower end it is permeated by instinct (orange combines the red and yellow). These realms (the green and orange) may be thought to constitute two of the different levels of consciousness on which archetypes operate, as the scale of consciousness "slides."

Whereas inwardly, individual consciousness is bounded by arche-types of the collective unconscious, outwardly, it faces the realm of the collective consciousness of the essential social human being. Ego, therefore, is affected not only by the flow of energy between the spirit–instinct poles within but also by the pressure of the social conscious-ness without. Jung describes the dynamics of the delicate balance that ego must maintain between the inner and outer collective spheres. In Figure 3, the sphere of influence of the collective, social consciousness forms the central area (yellow) of the realm of image, through which one may imagine consciousness sliding. Along with the spiritual and instinctual levels, it may be thought to constitute a third level of con-sciousness, the social level. We should expect, therefore, to find arche-types appearing in consciousness on these three levels.

With this symbolic model of psyche in mind, let us now turn to mythology. Myths and mythical images are treated here primarily as spontaneous psychic phenomena—as symbolic expressions of inner psychic events. The question is, if myth is accepted as such, what signs does it show of its archetypal origins? And specifically, to what extent is the spirit–instinct opposition expressed in the images, artistic or literary, that constitute the body of myth? Do they suggest a "sliding" of consciousness between the poles? Are they manifest under the influence of the outer as well as the inner collective spheres? Further, is the transformative process, the essence of which is integrating unconscious contents into consciousness, evident in the mythological image, which is itself a culmination of that process? What I am suggesting is that when we say that myth is archetypal, the presence of the themes of duality and transformation is implied. If these are shown to be inherent features of myth, since they are the forms fundamental to the archetypal processes of human consciousness, they might be said to constitute myth's primary archetypal quality. Let us, then, examine ancient Egyptian myth for traces of these two themes.

An investigation of the theme of opposition must start with the creation myth. The motif of most cosmogonic myths is the idea of separation, the breaking of the original unity that marks the beginning. Erich Neumann sees the cosmogonic myth as the archetypal image for the birth of consciousness.[1] If we examine the opposites that are differentiated in cosmogonic myths, therefore, might we not arrive at some idea of the nature of the duality that is basic to consciousness?

From the time of the Old Kingdom, the ancient Egyptian cosmogonic myths, according to the priests at Heliopolis, told how in the beginning was the primeval ocean, Nun, a dark, formless mass of water everywhere. Out of the primeval waters, on the occasion of the First Dawn, came Atum, the sun, the first light from out of the dark of Nun. Depictions of the First Dawn in the New Kingdom showed Nun personified lifting up Atum in a boat, with the scarabaeus beetle pushing up the sun's disk like a ball of eggs out of the sand. The beetle, therefore, symbolized the sun rising. Atum, the Complete One, He as well as She, created the first pair of gods, Shu and Tefnut. Thus the process of procreation was begun with the differentiation of elements. Shu, the male, was by nature air, and Tefnut, the female, was associated with moisture. These in turn gave birth to the pair of Earth and Sky, Geb and Nut. This pair lay together in eternal embrace until their father, Shu, the air, placed himself between Earth and Sky, and by holding up his daughter, kept the two apart (see Figure 4, second panel from the top). Then in the life-giving airy space, Sky was able to give birth to the stars and gods.

Figure 4.    Interior of an Egyptian coffin of the Twenty-first Dynasty.

This series of acts of differentiation, which runs through the Heliopolitan accounts of creation, indicates a fundamental duality in the Egyptian view of the cosmic order. Moreover, the nature of the duality can be surmised from an examination of the complexes of imagery through which it is expressed: the elements of sun and stars (fire), sky, light, air, form, and order are associated with an upper complex; the elements of ocean (water), earth, darkness, moisture, formlessness, and chaos are associated with a lower complex. Does not the ethereal, rarefied nature of the upper image complex appropriately convey the quality of spirit, whereas the material density of the lower one associates it with instinct, which is based in matter?[2] Neumann's idea of the cosmogonic myth as metaphor for the birth of consciousness can thus be traced in three stages according to the model in Figure 3. The primordial, undifferentiated unity out of which creation emerged might be thought of in terms of the violet part of the model, which illustrates the paradoxical nature of unconscious archetypes as spiritual forms charged with instinctual dynamism; creation myths project the archetypes' differentiation in consciousness as the spirit–instinct tension (blue and red); the physical life of the universe, which emerges from this polarization of the natural elements, reflects the psychic energy generated in consciousness by the spirit–instinct tension (yellow).

The flow of psychic energy between the poles of spirit and instinctual matter has its most apt expression in the myth that became popular in the New Kingdom of the sun's daily battle with Apophis, the snake of the underworld. The Egyptians imagined Re, a later, more general name for the sun, as journeying in a boat through the sky by day (see Figure 4, second panel from the top) and through the underworld passage of the earth by night in an eternal round. The passage was represented as a lion or sphinx-like creature with a head at each end of the body, the mouths of which marked the place where the sun entered the underworld in the west at evening and from where it rose in the east in the morning (see Figure 4, center panel). The solar journey through the earth was filled with dangers by the hour from the powers of darkness. Most formidable of these was the indestructible snake, spirit of chaos and nonexistence, which the sun continually had to defeat before emerging each day to begin his ascent of the sky as on the occasion of the First Dawn. The victorious encounter with the disintegrating powers of nonexistence in the dark, damp, lower world was an integral part of the regenerative process that ensured the continued existence of the sun.

The sun's perpetual rebirth in the circuit of the sky and earth naturally provided a powerful symbol of resurrection, which influenced religious ideas of immortality. The souls of the dead lying buried in the underworld, warmed to life by the rays of the sun as he passed through (see Figure 4, second panel from the bottom), were thought to be taken up by the sky along with the sun and to join him on his eternal round. Thus, an idea of immortality was formed in terms of the absorption by spirit (the sun and air) of the dynamism of instinctual matter (the soul of the mummified dead) and expressed through the image of a cosmic circuit that transcended the division between earth and sky.

The cyclical patterns of natural phenomena were familiar to the Egyptians not only from the daily rebirth of the sun god but also from the annual rebirth of the vegetation after the Nile flood. The personification of that annual process of nature was the god Osiris. It is not surprising, therefore, to find Osiris, like the sun, associated with immortality. Osiris, god of the ongoing fertility of the earth, was also Osiris, god of the eternal life of the souls of the dead. Pictorial art indicated his dual role. He was shown wrapped in white in mummified form, but with the visible parts of his body green. Through his own uprising as the vegetation, he promised resurrection after death. Belief in resurrection through Osiris spread toward the end of the Old Kingdom to such an extent that the Osirian cult was eventually assimilated with the solar cult. The gift of eternal life, originally the exclusive privilege of the king, was gradually extended, and by the beginning of the Middle Kingdom every dead Egyptian was given the name "Osiris" in addition to his own.[3] Figures of Osiris, made from wood or pottery, were hollowed out, planted with corn, and wrapped in linen like mummies. From the eighteenth dynasty, these figures were placed in burial chambers, the idea being that the dead one's soul would rise again like Osiris and the grain.[4]

The myth of Osiris's resurrection was the subject of funerary art. It told how Seth, the wicked brother of Osiris, killed and dismembered him, but his two sisters, Isis and Nephthys, restored the parts of Osiris's body, kept watch over the reconstituted corpse, and revived him so that Isis was able to conceive by him a son, Horus, who avenged his father and succeeded him as king of the living. Osiris became king of the dead. The dramatization of Osiris's resurrection became part of Egyptian burial ritual in which two priestesses playing the roles of the two sisters kept watch at the head and the foot of the mummified corpse.

The painted interior of a coffin from the Fitzwilliam Museum in Cambridge (Figure 4) shows the belief that the mummified deceased would rise again as Osiris in the hereafter. It also shows the extent to which the Osirian cult was eventually merged with the solar cult. By interpreting the panels from the bottom upwards, R. T. Rundle Clark has shown how they illustrate the transformation of the soul.[5] In the bottom panel of the coffin the headless mummy of the deceased, watched over by two spirits, lies inert in the underworld, but the beetle over it indicates the potential to arise. The second panel shows the soul in the form of the body of Osiris, which stirs to life as vegetation when the night sun illuminates the lower world. In the center panel the soul emerges with the sun from the mouth of the underworld passage on the east horizon, heralded by the morning stars. In the panel above is the representation of dawn as the Air God lifts up his daughter Nut, and Re in his boat carries the soul across the sky. In the top panel, the sun is shown as the beetle, but with a ram's head. Just as the beetle signified the rising sun, the ram indicated the setting sun on its nightly underworld descent. The beetle together with the ram, therefore, signified the complete cycle of the sun's eternal round. The ram-headed beetle as the culminating symbol on the mummy is not only the symbol of the sun in its absolute form but is at the same time an expression of the transcendental mystery of the everlasting life of the soul.

Combined with the myth of Re, the Osirian resurrection myth is a very powerful symbol of transformation. The soul can rise both with Osiris as vegetation that the *water* from the Nile pushes up through the *earth*, and with the sun god Re as solar *fire* through the *air* of the sky. Thus, the imagery reflects a process whereby disembodied spirit is incorporated in the elements of cosmic matter, and mortal matter is transcended and transformed into indestructible, spiritual form.

The myths can equally well be taken, therefore, as symbolic expressions of the transformative, psychological process of creative consciousness. Out of the psychic poles of unconscious spiritual form and unconscious instinctual energy is generated in consciousness an image. It is this experience of imagination that constitutes the re-creation of consciousness. And just as the birth of Re on the First Dawn, reenacted in each daybreak, constitutes the perpetuation of cosmic order, just as the resurrection of the dead Osiris, reenacted in every burial, constitutes the everlasting life of human beings, so the re-creation of consciousness, experienced in the transformation of archetype into image, constitutes the ongoing life of psyche.

Consciousness has been considered here as a process whereby instinct is transformed and archetype mediated, the process being reflected in the form of an image. Consciousness has also been considered in terms of a field of energy created by the tension between opposite poles, "sliding" according to influence from the opposed collective spheres. Would it not be logical to expect to find, therefore, that an archetype that is transformed into image at the upper level of consciousness (the green in Figure 3) under the influence of spirit has a more spiritual application, and that ideas associated with it are more conceptual in expression? And, by the same token, to find that an archetype transformed into image at the lower level of consciousness (the orange in Figure 3) under the influence of instinct has a more natural, material application, and the imagery associated with it is more perceptual or sensory in expression? In the case of Osiris, the meaning would be expressed on the spiritual level by his role as king of the souls of the dead and giver of eternal life. On the material or natural level, the meaning would be expressed through his connection with the fertility of the crops. The meaning lies in the experience of continuity—the ongoing life of the vegetation of the earth and of the human soul.

But what about the remaining level of consciousness, the outward sphere of influence of the collective conscious psyche (the yellow in Figure 3)? For, as consciousness "slides," ego must also maintain the balance between the inner and outer collective spheres. In the tradition of myth about Osiris, is the experience of continuity expressed on the social level under the influence of collective consciousness? To answer this question we must turn to the figure of Horus, Osiris's son.

Horus and his father's enemy, Seth, fought for rulership of Egypt in a long, fierce feud. Geb, the Earth god, intervened, at first dividing the land between the two, but finally revoking his decision and declaring Horus ruler of both parts. The myth is believed by some to reflect political events in predynastic times, before the unification of Egypt.[6] Whether the myth had historical reference or not, in Egyptian art and thought Horus and Seth represented the Two Lands, Lower and Upper Egypt, which were united under the first pharaoh's rule. Interpreted mythologically, then, the political union of Lower and Upper Egypt under one king's rule is the end of the discord between Horus and Seth and the establishment of Horus as Osiris's rightful heir. The religious ideas associated with the myth became inseparable from the question of kingship because of the identification of the pharaoh with the god Horus himself. The pharaoh was for the Egyptians the living Horus. And just as the ruling monarch was identified with Horus, so, by allusion to the myth, the dead king became "Osiris." His son succeeded him as "Horus" until he in turn died and became "Osiris," and his son in turn ruled.[7] The order and prosperity of the kingdom depended on the reciprocal benefits and ritual relations between the two: the safe transfer of the late king through the ordeal of death depended on the ritual duly performed through the devotion of his son; the new king's rule was only propitious if the land was blessed by the inundation and fruitful crops, manifestations of his father's supernatural power. In this way, the myth was the religious authority for the succession to the throne. It must be remembered, moreover, that it was the verdict of Geb that recognized Osiris's son Horus as successor to his father's throne. And Osiris himself, according to the genealogy of the priests of Heliolopolis, was the son of Geb. On the social level, therefore, the myth was intrinsically connected with the institution of the inherited rule of kings. Consequently, the mythical tradition of Osiris not only expressed the idea of spiritual and material continuity but was also a fundamental expression of the continuity of the social order.

The final, inevitable question remains. From the mythical images that appear in consciousness, do we have any indication of the nature of the original unconscious archetypal forms? What Jung says of the forms is that "there is not a single important idea or view that does not possess historical antecedents. Ultimately they are all founded on primordial archetypal forms whose concreteness dates from a time when consciousness did not *think* but only *perceived*" (*CW* 9i: par. 69, p. 33). While admitting the difficulty of proving the existence of the archetypes empirically, given that consciousness, by which we apprehend them, has no terms of reference outside of itself, Jung nevertheless explored an "indirect" means of approach through dream images. The unconscious fantasies of his patients as expressed in dream images led him to observe repeated themes: duality (light and dark, upper and lower, right and left, chaos and order), union of opposites in a third, rotation, centering, and quaternity (*CW* 8: par. 401, p. 203). If myth is to be taken as archetypal, we must look for the vestiges of these dream themes in myth also.

Two of the themes that Jung observed immediately associate themselves with the two basic features of creative consciousness examined here: the theme of duality in its various manifestations connects with the spirit–instinct tension; the theme of union of opposites in a third reflects the transformative process, which is the natural culmination of that tension. Insofar as these two features of creative consciousness are inherent features of myth, we can describe myth as archetypal. Jung, however, claims that human consciousness "is . . . itself a transformation of the original instinctual image" (*CW* 8: par. 399, p. 201). If so, it follows that union of opposites, the fundamental form of human consciousness, must be considered as the primary instinctual image or archetypal form. The presence of the theme of union of opposites in myth, moreover, must be said to constitute myth's primary archetypal quality.

# Notes

1. Erich Neumann, *The Origins and History of Consciousness*, Bollingen Series (Princeton: Princeton University Press, 1971), Part I, pp. 102-127.

2. A different version of creation is recorded in a text known as the "Memphite Theology," according to which the first gods were created not by Atum but by Ptah, conceived in his "heart" and materialized into existence by the creative utterances of his "tongue." By associating "heart" and "tongue" with mind and matter, Henri Frankfort shows how this version of creation also reveals a dualistic view. See Henri Frankfort, *Kingship and the Gods* (Chicago: University of Chicago Press, 1978), pp. 28 and 29.

3. See Erik Hornung, *Conceptions of God in Ancient Egypt* (Ithaca: Cornell University Press, 1982), p. 96; A. Rosalie David, *The Ancient Egyptians* (London: Routledge and Kegan Paul, 1982), p. 111; Barbara Watterson, *The Gods of Ancient Egypt* (Bicester, England: Facts on File Publications, 1984), p. 82.

4. Watterson, *The Gods of Ancient Egypt*, p. 75; Frankfort, *Kingship and the Gods*, pp. 185 and 186.

5. R. T. Rundle Clark, *Myth and Symbol in Ancient Egypt* (London: Thames and Hudson, 1978), pp. 254-256.

6. For a summary of the evidence, see David, *The Ancient Egyptians*, pp. 28-31.

7. Ibid., p. 107; Watterson, *The Gods of Ancient Egypt*, p. 103.

# Gnosis
## and Culture   Gilles Quispel

Gnosis is a Greek word that means "knowledge." It comes from the Indo-European root *gno* from which the English word "knowledge" is derived. In late antiquity gnosis was used to designate an intuitive awareness of hidden mysteries as opposed to discursive, analytical knowledge.

Gnostic comes from the Greek *gnostikos*, knowledgeable. It was used in classical times as an adjective, never as a substantive noun. At the beginning of the Christian era, in Alexandria, there was a school of rebellious Jews who called themselves "gnostics," knowers. Later they superficially christianized their views and brought forth such writings as the *Apocryphon of John*, ca. A.D. 100. They venerated the Unknown God beyond god and held that the human self was related to this Ground of Being. Until this day there lives in Iran and Iraq a sect that adheres to the same views. They are called Mandaeans, which means nothing more than "gnostics." In the second century there were other Christian movements, in Alexandria and elsewhere, whose views resembled those of the gnostics, but who did not call themselves gnostics. About A.D. 200 there was a catholic thinker in Alexandria, Clement Alexandrinus, who called himself a "true gnostic." This led to a generalization and to the practice of designating all leaders of movements later expelled from the Catholic church as gnostics.

Gnosticism or gnosis is a modern invention. It is used by present-day scholars to indicate all currents of pluriform antiquity that are not Catholic, such as Jewish Christianity, Encratism (rejection of marriage), and related currents. This has led to an enormous confusion. The designation should be limited to those schools and religions that are ostensibly dependent upon the myth of the *Apocryphon of John*, to Valentinians, to adherents of Basilides, and to Marcionites.

Gnosticism is not exclusively a Christian phenomenon. Jewish kabbalism has its origins in the heterodox Jewry of Alexandria, which produced the *Apocryphon of John*. The appellation "Adam Qadmon," well known from the kabbala, has been found in pre-Christian gnostic documents found at Nag Hammadi in 1945, in the form of "Geradamas," that is, "old, archetypal Adam." In the ninth century, these same Jewish revolutionaries gave rise, in southern Iraq, to the Islamic gnosis of the Ismailis, the religion of the Aga Khan.

All these gnostics proclaimed a new God, after the old one had failed. It is not correct, however, as Hans Jonas holds, that they disparaged the world excessively. A certain depreciation of matter and sex is characteristic of many philosophical schools of the Greeks, of Plato and the Platonists, and of the Stoic philosopher Posidonius and his followers. Christian Catholics had very strong reservations about the world and eros. The gnostics were no exception to the rule. The large majority of them, however, believed that the world was created to serve as a catharsis for the spirit, to make men and women conscious of their unconscious selves, a belief that, in effect, redeems the phenomenal world.

Gnosticism found its achievement and fulfillment in Manichaeism, as the *Cologne Mani Codex* shows. Mani, a Jewish boy who lived from 216 to 277, was brought up in a Jewish Christian community in Southern Mesopotamia. These people believed that God was the origin of both good and evil. Mani, who was a cripple, abhorred these views. At the age of twelve, and again at twenty-four, he was confronted with a vision of his self, his guardian angel or twin or Holy Spirit, who revealed to him that light and darkness, soul and matter, good and evil are radically opposed to each other. After that he wandered through Asia to proclaim the new doctrine and to found a gnostic Christian church, which has existed for more than a thousand years in Asia.

The Middle Ages, too, had their gnostics. They were sectarians called Albigensians or Cathars, members of a gnostic antichurch that was founded in 1167 at Saint Felix de Caraman, near Toulouse, and who lived in southern France and northern Italy. The Cathars were bloodily persecuted by the Roman Catholic Inquisition. They owed most of their ideas to the Bogomils of Bulgaria and eastern Europe, who, in turn, went back to the Paulicians, Barbeliots and Messalians of Armenia, where ancient gnosticism had survived.

According to medieval sources, the Bogomils and the Cathars were a mixture of Messalianism and Paulicianism. This seems to be true. Messalianism (a name based on a word that means "prayers") was a charismatic movement in Mesopotamia and Armenia. Messalians were divided into two classes, perfects and believers. The perfects were unmarried, wandered around in poverty, and were familiar with the *Gospel of Thomas*. In these aspects they resembled the Bogomils and Cathars. But the Messalians were not gnostics. They had been transplanted by the Byzantine emperors from Mesopotamia to Armenia, where they significantly influenced the rise of the Bogomils and Cathars.

The Paulicians were gnostics. They were a warlike tribe in Armenia, who had inherited the ideas of the Barbeliots and Marcionites and rejected the Old Testament. They had fled to the outskirts of the empire when persecuted by the Catholic authorities.

There is a direct link between ancient gnosticism and Catharism. The Cathars held that the creator of the world, Satanael, had usurped the name of God, but that he had subsequently been unmasked and told that he was not really God. In the same way, innumerable passages in the Nag Hammadi writings argue that the demiurge of this world pretended to be the only God, only to be informed that the Unknown God above him was the authentic deity. As Joseph Campbell has said, "The problem with Jehovah is that he thinks he is God."[1] This concept is so rebellious and strange that there must be a historical connection.

Gnosis is, in fact, the third component of European culture. There has always been faith, which goes back to Sinai and Golgotha. There has always been rationalism, which can be traced back to Athens and Ionia. There have always been people who had inner experiences and expressed themselves in imaginative thinking: Valentinus had a vision of a newborn child, the Logos or Christ, and started to compose his "tragic myth." Mani encountered his twin, the Holy spirit, and said, "I recognized him that he was my Self from which I had been separated."[2] Jacob Boehme saw a ray of light in a vessel and wrote his fantastic books. Gnosis originated in Egyptian Alexandria at the beginning of our era. Three cities, therefore, Alexandria, together with Jerusalem and Athens, determined the history of the West.

In modern times, gnosis was generated spontaneously in the heart of the German shoemaker Boehme, who influenced William Blake, Isaac Newton, and the New England transcendentalists, especially Emerson. In 1600, Boehme had a vision of a lovely vessel of joyous splendor, which initiated him into the innermost ground and core of nature's mysteries. Not knowing whether or not this vision was an illusion, he left his house in Görlitz and crossed over a bridge to the green countryside across the river. The visionary experience became more intense and clear. Boehme could intuit the heart of nature, so that he was overwhelmed with great joy, praised God, and kept silent about the illumination he had received. Much later, he wrote his imaginative books about his experience in which he used alchemistic terms and showed some familiarity with Jewish kabbalism. But his real discovery was the union of opposites, of darkness and light, hate and love, evil and good.

Gottfrid Arnold, a pious, radical, and extremely learned professor of church history, was a follower of Boehme. In 1699, disgruntled by orthodoxy, he wrote a book about the history of the church and the heresies, which he called *The Impartial History of the Church and the Her-*

*etics*, probably the most partisan writing ever published. The book exploded like a time bomb and caused a universal sensation. It was no wonder, since Arnold depicted the history of the church as a continuous story of decadence and perversity, and described all orthodox teachers, even Lutherans, as hypocrites. The heretics, on the other hand, he described as innocent lambs and true Christians. The heresies, in his view, were part of the history of the church and should be studied with the same empathy as orthodox teachings. Among Arnold's favorites were the ancient gnostics, which he knew exclusively through the works of Catholic heresy hunters, but whose importance and depth he sensed nevertheless.

This had important consequences for Western culture, because among Arnold's many readers, there was one who was perhaps the greatest poet of all time. In September 1768, Johann Wolfgang von Goethe, who had been studying in Leipzig, fell ill and returned home. There he met, through his mother, a group of devout people who came together regularly for prayer meetings. These were pietists, some of whom read kabbalistic texts, devoted themselves to alchemy, and read the gnostic books of Jacob Boehme. Occultism made up a goodly part of their pious beliefs. It was through these pietists that Goethe was introduced to Arnold's book, which was to influence his thought profoundly. He discovered that the heretics, considered mad and godless, were actually not so strange. Gnostic ideas, in particular, made a deep and lasting impression on him. All gnostic systems start in heaven, run their course on earth, and then return to heaven. Furthermore, gnostics believe that salvation is a necessity and that a spiritual person cannot be lost. Goethe liked all this immensely. In his youthful fervor he devised a gnostic system for himself, a cosmology, based upon the alternation of systole, concentration, and diastole, expansion. Later, when he created his *Faust*, he began the poem with a prologue in heaven, in accordance with the gnostic system, and then described the development of Faust on earth. Only toward the end of his life was Goethe able to complete the gnostic cycle of his great work by rewarding Faust with his elevation into heaven.

Goethe's friend, Wilhelm von Humboldt, had visited the monastery of Monserrat, situated on towering grey peaks, in Catalonia, Spain. It was a numinous landscape, in which monks venerated a mysterious Black Madonna, a tiny figure in an enormous church. Von Humboldt, deeply impressed, wrote an enthusiastic report to his old friend Goethe. His description so inspired Goethe that he wrote down the final scene of his Faust poem: the monks adoring the glorious Mother on their mountaintop; she, manifesting herself and saving Faust. This is not simply the Virgin Mary pitying a poor sinner; Faust is saved because he is—and only for as long as he remains—a noble member of the spiritual world. His salvation is not an act of God but a process that, of its own necessity, moves toward completion: "Saved from evil is the noble member of the spiritual world."[3] The Mother is not simply the Black Madonna of Monserrat; she is the eternally feminine or, rather, the womanly eternal. The poem ends: "The eternally feminine elevates us to herself."[4] This is Goethe's last word: the Mother is a mask of God; God is a woman.

This revolutionary vision had incubated and matured over a long time. Before Goethe, Boehme had written a good deal about Sophia, the bride of the Lord and of the wise man—the goddess who manifested the Ground of Being. Arnold had collected passages from the Bible about Sophia in order to provide a biblical foundation for such an unorthodox idea. In his *Impartial History*, he mentioned the gnostic concept of a goddess of wisdom, Sophia, who was a mysterious representation of a divine secret, the *prima materia*, the primeval foundation of all creation.

Goethe had absorbed all this and, as an old man, returned to the images of his youth. By making his hero return to the divine Sophia above, he made his *Faust* a gnostic myth. Goethe coined and immortalized the words—everyone knows them: "the eternally feminine"— that sum up the gnostic experience, a tradition that runs from the ancient gnostics and medieval Cathars to modern sages like Boehme, Blake, and Goethe, and later to Steiner, Jung, and Hesse.

Gnosis, I repeat, was the third component of the Western cultural tradition, alongside the rationalism of philosophy and the faith of the churches. Several critics of our age have discerned this importance of gnosis for our Western culture, but, in accordance with the ancient ecclesiastical heresy hunters, they considered it to be a negative factor. Foremost among them were Denis de Rougemont and Erik Vögelin.

Denis de Rougemont, a Swiss essayist who spent the war years in the United States, published his influential book *L'amour et l'Occident* in 1939. It is difficult to understand now why it made such a deep impression upon my generation. His thesis, based on the following facts, was that the Cathars of southern France were responsible for the celebration and veneration of adultery in literature, both in the Middle Ages and in modern times: (1) the perfects of Catharism did not marry and sometimes preferred to die, the so-called *endura*; (2) the poetry of the troubadours, which later originated in southern France, celebrated courtly love, that is, the devotion of a knight for his lady, who was not his wife; and (3) adultery is treated as an ideal in romances such as *Tristan and Isolde*. From these facts, de Rougemont draws a direct line to modern poetry and art, not only to Wagner but to almost everybody. The Cathars were to blame, in his opinion, because they were said to be the heirs of the Manichees who rejected marriage. In contrast to this, de Rougemont posits the marital fidelity of Christian orthodoxy as the true alternative and ideal solution.

What are we to think of these generalizations? It is true that adultery is a source of artistic inspiration, but should we be so severe on the weakness and frailty of human nature? Even de Rougemont must have changed his mind later, because he divorced his wife after the war. What is important here is that there is not a shred of evidence to prove that the troubadours were Cathars, or that the medieval romance was of Cathar inspiration, or that the Cathars were, in essence, medieval Manichees. Manichaeism had been completely annihilated both in the western and eastern Roman Empire before the end of the sixth century.

Eric Vögelin, a refugee from Austria, who taught at St. Louis, Stanford, and Munich, knew gnosticism well, though mainly through secondary literature. According to him, the essence of gnosis is that gnostics want to destroy the world and humanity and murder God. This tendency could also be observed in the millenarian, revolutionary groups of the Middle Ages, and in such figures as Karl Marx and Friedrich Nietzsche. Vögelin applied his insights to political science. Marxists, National Socialists, and liberals, he declared, all want to destroy or at least change the world. Greek thinkers like Plato and Aristotle, on the other hand, argue that order should be maintained in the state, because it reflects the immutable laws of cosmic order. Moreover, the people of Israel had been delivered from Egypt and its pagan idols and had learned to accept history as a source of divine revelation. Conservatism, Vögelin concludes, with its stress on order and history, is therefore the legitimate heir of Greece and Israel.

These ideas had a tremendous impact because they were well researched and profound. Nevertheless they contain a serious flaw. Vögelin is much indebted to Hans Jonas, who thought that the rejection of the world was typical and characteristic of ancient gnosticism. This is not correct. As already mentioned, all movements of late antiquity, including Neoplatonism and Catholicism, had their reservations about the material world. Gnostics, too, were suspicious of its creator, whom they held to be a lower demiurge. But as the *Tripartite Tractate*, one of the writings of the *Jung Codex*, demonstrates, this was not an exclusionary tenet of their belief. This treatise is incredibly optimistic: the world exists, matter exists, evil exists, the soul exists to train the spirit and make it conscious. The logos has to go through the inferno of matter and through the purgatorio of religion and ethics in order to acquire, through Christ, the liberation of the spirit. It is not the rejection of the world but the discovery of the unconscious self and the dynamic concept of God as Being-in-movement that is characteristic of gnosticism.

Vögelin's views should be corrected in the light of the new discoveries. And as far as murder is concerned, the gnostics have a good record. No ancient gnostic or Manichee, no Bogomil or Cather, no follower of Boehme or Blake, ever killed a Catholic. The Manichees and the Cathars were the only Christians ever to have lived according to the Sermon on the Mount. It is preposterous to put them on the same level with murderous Marx and bloody Nietzsche. Gnosticism, as distinguished from millenarianism and anabaptism, was nonviolent and apolitical. Is there any other faith or creed of which the same can be said?

The position of Emmanuel Le Roy Ladurie, in his book *Montaillou*, is somewhat different from that of de Rougemont and Vögelin; he does not attack gnosis, he ignores it. Le Roy Ladurie offers a very readable and attractive description, gleaned from detailed Inquisition records, of life in a French village near the Spanish border in the Pyrenees, between 1294 and 1324, where Cathars and Catholics lived together. His book represents sociology or social geography rather than historiography. In fact, what he has to say about the history of the Cathars is rather shallow. According to Le Roy Ladurie, Catharism is one of the chief heresies of the Middle Ages. It first appeared in the twelfth or thirteenth century in Languedoc and northern Italy, and in slightly different forms in the Balkans as well. It may have been affected by distant Oriental or Manichaean influences, but this, in his view, is only a hypothesis. Le Roy Ladurie is absolutely certain, on the other hand, that Catharism foreshadowed the great Protestant revolt of the Reformation three centuries later. His statements are full of errors and prejudices. First, Le Roy Ladurie ignores the fact that gnosis is a perennial philosophy, the "antibody," so to speak, in the Catholic "bloodstream." Second, the Reformation had nothing to do with gnosis; it was and is a reformed, transformed continuation of the Roman Catholic church, as its name *reformata ecclesia catholica* indicates. Catharism was not a heresy but a powerful counterchurch, founded in 1167 at the synod of Saint Felix de Caraman near Toulouse by Nikita, a Bogomil bishop from eastern Europe. Both the Bogomils and the Cathars were gnostics. They believed that an evil demiurge called Satanael had created this world. Beyond this shared belief, it is quite clear that the Cathars had, in fact, a certain originality. They believed in reincarnation, for example, whereas there is no evidence to suggest that the Bogomils had this belief. It is true that Manichaeism, on the other hand, believed in reincarnation. But Catharism does not owe anything to Manichaeism, since, as already mentioned, Manichaeism had been wiped out completely in the western and eastern Roman Empire long before the rise of Catharism and its avatars in eastern Europe.

## Jung and Gnosis

It was a well-kept secret twenty years ago, but today is common knowledge, that Hermann Hesse, when writing his influential book *Demian*, was leaning heavily on the *Septem Sermones ad Mortuos*, which Jung had written in 1915. One need only quote a few passages from Jung and then from Hesse to demonstrate this fact: "Hard to know is the deity of Abraxas. Its power is the greatest because man perceiveth it not. From the sun he draweth the *summum bonum* (the highest good); from the devil the *infimum malum* (the greatest evil); but from Abraxas LIFE, altogether indefinite, the mother of good and evil."[5]

Even more relevant is Jung's description of the first mandala that he ever drew (in 1916): "At the bottom of this universe, there is the dark Abraxas, the source and origin of everything. . . . From him springs the tree of life, its left branches symbolize the warmth of natural libido; its right, the love of God. Alongside the tree are the dove of the Holy Spirit, a female being, and celestial mother, Sophia, who pours from a chalice. The tree brings forth a child, the Self, called Erikapaios or Phanes, which are Orphic names for Eros, who breaks the world egg and creates the world."[6]

The following passage from Hesse's *Demian* contains almost identical images: "The bird fights its way out of the egg. The egg is the world. Who would be born must first destroy a world. The bird flies to God. That God's name is Abraxas. . . . Abraxas is a godhead whose symbolic task is the uniting of godly and devilish elements. . . . Abraxas was the god who was born god and devil."[7]

We know the source of these images. Jung's unknown and unknowable Godhead was inspired by Basilides, a profound gnostic from Alexandria, A.D. 150: "There was a time when there was nothing; not even the nothing was there, but simply, clearly, and without any sophistry, there was nothing at all."[8] Abraxas is a well-known figure on magic gems of antiquity that symbolizes the Godhead Iao, who combines heaven and earth, light and dark. Jung was also familiar with a relief of Phanes as a naked youth whose feet, hoofed like the goatlegs of the Greek god Pan, are standing on an upturned hemisphere, the world egg. Above his curly head, adorned with five shining rays, is the other half of the world egg.

Hesse had picked up on this. The bird that breaks forth from the egg became, for him, a symbol of his own individuation. From this ancient symbol, Hesse created a universal symbol, a fitting expression for his and our generation's most profound aspiration for wholeness, for the new being, for the healing of the split.

That was before the Nag Hammadi discoveries. In 1945, an Egyptian called Mohammed Ali—a blood avenger who proudly told me that he had eaten the heart of the victim he had killed—found a jar containing Coptic manuscripts with unknown gnostic texts. While he was in prison his mother had used some of them as kindling in her stove; the rest, some thirteen codices (books) containing fifty-two mostly unknown writings, he sold for about sixty dollars. Today, they would be worth about forty million dollars.

On May 10, 1952, I acquired one of the codices with Jung's help, the so-called *Jung Codex*, which contains five unknown scriptures from the school of Valentinus, from the second century A.D. The *Gospel of Truth* is the best known of the five. It is a gnostic meditation on the gospel written by Valentinus himself. It contains passages that are so beautiful that nothing in ancient literature, pagan or Christian, between the parables of Jesus and the *Confessions* of Augustine, can rival them. In one passage, the state of unconsciousness is compared to a nightmare: "One flees, one knows not where, or one remains at the same spot when endeavouring to go forward, in the pursuit of one knows not whom. One is in battle, one gives blows, one receives blows. Or one falls from a great height or one flies through the air without having wings. At other times it is as if one met death at the hands of an invisible murderer, without being pursued by anyone. Or it seems as if one were murdering one's neighbours: one's hands are full of blood."[9] Life in this world is compared to the journey of a mountaineer who has lost his way and his companions in the fog, until he hears his name called: "Therefore a gnostic has something transcendental. When he is called, he hears, he answers, he directs himself to Him who calls him and returns to Him. . . . He who thus possesses gnosis knows whence he comes and whither he goes. . . ."[10] The *Gospel of Truth* also contains an ecstatic confession. Valentinus explains quite candidly that he has sojourned in the Pleroma, the spiritual world of the eons, situated high above the seven heavens of the planets and the firmament of the fixed stars; the Pleroma where one encounters one's image and heavenly counterpart, the guardian angel or self, with whom one celebrates even here and now during one's lifetime the *mysterium coniunctionis* (a Valentinian expression), the sacred marriage of male and female, self and ego, the sacred marriage of wholeness and completion. Valentinus states that he has experienced this mystery: "This is the place of the blessed; this is their place. For the rest, then, may they who dwell in lower places know that it is not fitting for me, after having been in this place of rest, to say nothing more. But it is there that I shall dwell to devote myself at all times to God the Father of the All, and to the true brethren and sisters, those upon whom the love of the Father is poured out and in whose midst there is no eclipse of God."[11]

It was this passage that inspired a famous contemporary critic, Harold Bloom, professor of literature at Yale University, to write a novel—I call it a "gnovel"—titled *The Flight to Lucifer*, in which he translated the ecstatic gnostic experience into a space-travel experience. It is gratifying of course, to see ancient scriptures one has discovered enter modern culture and be assimilated to contemporary tastes, but when one compares the original with the adaptation, one notices a remarkable difference. In Valentinus's account, Christ is the focus of his heart and thought. It is Christ who reveals the gnosis of the Unknown God and the unknown self to an unconscious humanity. Christ is the Horos, whose illumination restores, confirms, and heals the bewildered mind of Sophia, worldly wisdom. In Bloom's account, Christ is never even mentioned. Is his translation treason? Or does it mean that modern men and women are too empty and shallow to understand Valentinus?

Jung's reaction seems more scholarly and dignified. When the discovery and acquisition of the *Jung Codex* was to be announced in 1953, a number of women in his entourage tried to persuade him not to attend the meeting where the presentation was to take place. They feared Jung would be branded a gnostic, whereas they wanted to present their hero as a meticulous scholar and scientist. Fortunately, Jung had the wisdom to understand the great value of the gnostic texts, which he had generously helped to acquire. It was in such an atmosphere of suspicion, discord, and insinuation, that Jung gave a reserved and scholarly speech on the psychological significance of the gnostic texts, of the *Gospel of Truth* in particular (*CW* 18: Addenda), which I paraphrase here:

Jung observed that this was not a gospel in the usual sense of the word, but rather a commentary on the gospel, which attempted to assimilate the strange and difficult content of the Christian message at the level of the Hellenistic–Egyptian spiritual world of that period. For the gospel's author, Christ was a metaphysical figure, a bringer of light, who had come from the Father to illuminate human unconsciousness, and to lead the individual back to his or her origin through self-knowledge. The symbols generated by the reception of the gospel reveal the reaction of the psyche, namely the unconscious, which responds with archetypal images, indicating how deeply the message has penetrated into the depths of the psyche and how the unconscious interprets the figure of Christ. These symbolic reactions, says Jung, began with gnosticism and continued, despite suppression and neglect, through the Middle Ages to the present. Even today such archetypal images can emerge spontaneously in healthy people as well as in patients. As a rule, however, modern men and women must be made conscious of their dark side with the help of artificial means, because they have forgotten the fundamental problem of Christianity, the moral and spiritual agnosia of the purely natural being. Christianity has brought considerable progress to the development of consciousness, and everywhere that this progress has not come to a standstill new receptions can be observed. Even Judaism has produced a process parallel to these Christian receptions, namely the kabbala.

The closest parallel to Christian gnosticism, however, is to be found in alchemy. And today, it is psychological analysis that continues the millennial process of coming-to-consciousness, producing the same symbols as did gnosticism, kabbalism, and hermetic philosophy. All these traditions show the same tendency to integrate the figure of the Son of Man into the innermost core of the personality while expanding it to a dimension comparable to the *purusha atman* of Hinduism.

Jung's interpretation of the *Gospel of Truth* and of gnosticism in general was accurate. The gnostic is in search of God and of self. The symbol for this search was the Son of Man who revealed the Unknown God and at the same time represented the archetype and the idea of the human. Jung, a genius, was able to interpret what was expressed in the gnostic writings, whose meaning was not understood at that time. He was familiar with the prophet Ezekiel's vision of the man on the chariot-throne, and he was familiar with Adam Qadmon of the kabbala, and so he was able to divine the meaning of the newly discovered gnostic manuscripts. The gnostic Son of Man, the god-man, is at the same time the self of the individual as well as the world-spirit, the Indian *purusha*. It was Jung's conviction that the Christian myth of the Son of Man would be the religious symbol that will dominate the future. And so the central symbol of the *Gospel of Truth* and of Christianity, the Son of Man, the god-man, continues to be relevant for modern believers because it reveals and expresses the core of their personality.

# Notes

1. Joseph Campbell, in private conversation at the "C. G. Jung and the Humanities" Conference, Hofstra University, November 1986.
2. R. Cameron and A. J. Dewey, *The Cologne Mani Codex* (Missoula: Scholars Press, 1979), p. 15.

3. Johann Wolfgang von Goethe, *Faust II* (Frankfurt: Insel Verlag, 1976), p. 396.

4. Ibid., p. 383.

5. C. G. Jung, *Septem Sermones ad Mortuos*, in *Memories, Dreams, Reflections*, ed. Aniela Jaffé, trans. Richard and Clara Winston (New York: Vintage Books, 1965), p. 383.

6. C. G. Jung, *Bild und Wort* (Olten: Walter Verlag, 1977), p. 76; my translation.

7. Herman Hesse, *Demian*, trans. Michael Roloff and Michael Lebeck (New York: Bantam Books, 1970), p. 78.

8. Basilides, in Hippolytus, *Refutatio VII*, 20 (Berlin: Wendland, 1916), p. 195.

9. James Robinson, *The Nag Hammadi Library* (Leiden: Brill, 1984), p. 43.

10. Ibid., p. 40.

11. Ibid., p. 48.

# Jung's Impact on Religious Studies   John Patrick Dourley

Jung's impact on religious studies is already immense. But only currently are the more radical implications of his thought for this discipline coming into fuller consciousness both in psychology[1] and in religious studies.[2] At the heart of the radical impact made by Jung's psychology on religious studies is its claim that it has discovered the dynamics of the psychogenesis of religious experience itself. In so doing his psychology has laid bare the origin of all the religions that have both graced and bloodied human history (*CW* 11: pars. 1-55, pp. 5-33). Nevertheless, Jung's identification of those archetypal energies universally endemic to the psyche, which inevitably breed religious consciousness in historical humanity, remains for many an ambiguous discovery. For it constitutes both a support and a threat to widespread factions in the communities of religious studies and theology, as well as to the believing constituencies they might serve beyond academe.

His discovery is profoundly supportive of religious studies because it shows that humanity, as long as it is endowed with its current psychic constitution, must give expression to its religious impulse. With the discrediting and political dispossession of institutional religion in the Enlightenment and its wake, Jung feared that collective religious expression in the twentieth century had taken on political rather than identifiably religious forms. Thus the energies previously channeled into religious commitment had been transformed into the various political "isms" with which the twentieth century has been so abundantly blessed and cursed.[3] Thus Jung had deep reservations about the transformation that moved the religious energies of the psyche from specifically religious to political expression. For this reason he argues consistently that humanity cannot rid itself of its religiosity, however disguised, as expressed in the *participation mystique* and in the *représentations collectives*, those archetypal powers that paradoxically provide the cohesive myths making societies possible even as they lower the consciousness of their national or tribal constituencies in doing so.

On this basis the religionist and the theologian are given profound assurance that the study of religion is the study of the deepest level of the human reality, namely, of the depths of the psyche from whence

36

deity addresses humanity in a conversation that can never end. But precisely because the conversation can never end and so continues into the present, Jung's psychology becomes the basis for a possible radical reinterpretation of the task of the religionist and the theologian. In the face of the full challenge of Jung's psychology their task might well assume the stature of a reflection on the ongoing conversation between deity and humanity under the rubric of how better to conduct this dialogue in the birthing of a safer God, in a myth with a wider empathy and, as such, possessed of a greater survival value than those divisive myths currently extant and ruling. As will be seen, this task would be greatly facilitated should the practitioner of these disciplines have individual, immediate, and experiential access to those energies in his or her psyche from which religion universally arises.

Many of those who are beginning to realize the wider implications of Jung's understanding of the psychogenesis of religion, however, rightly see it to be a mixed blessing. They are not wrong in looking upon it as a serious threat to claims of any faith position to have a so-called final revelation that might lay claim to an exclusive or even privileged grasp of an absolute saving truth. For such a mindset Jung's understanding of the psychogenesis of religion remains a threat because, while it can appreciate all mythical-religious expression, it cannot attribute an unqualified finality to any. On the contrary, the spirit of Jung's thought would suggest that humanity's dialogue with deity remains in a preliminary stage. It would view suggestions that this dialogue had reached full maturation in one or other of its discrete historical expressions as somehow juvenile. As such, Jung's psychology works an appreciative undermining of all current historical concretions of the religion-making propensities of the psyche, at least in their claim to an exhaustive finality. Indeed, his psychology, read organically, implies that all such expressions, valuable in themselves, seek now their own transcendence and so transformation—if not negation—toward a consciousness of wider embrace and greater empathy both prompted and demanded by the natural movement or *telos* of the psyche itself.

Three foundational elements in Jung's understanding of the psyche's religion and God-making propensities are at the basis of the fear of those who distrust his insight in these matters and at the basis of the hope of those attracted by it. These foundational elements can best be described as processes of interiorization, relativization, and universalization. Let us consider each one separately, though they admittedly intersect in the organic nature of his psychology.

Interiorization implies that for Jung the making of religion with its attendant myths, rites, dogmas and moralities is a psychic process that cannot accommodate any agency working on the psyche from beyond it. Thus for Jung efforts to "get God out of the psyche"[4] in the interests of preserving some kind of divine transcendence in principle unrelated to the human are doomed to failure. On this issue Jung is quite clear in the epistemological consequences of his psychology. Only that can be known that is known through the psyche.[5] If the experience of deity is not mediated through the native functioning of the psyche as both the possibility and the necessity of humanity's experience of divinity, it could not be mediated at all and God would remain, in principle, beyond human experience and so be of no significance to humanity.

Moreover, Jung might well look askance at the motives of those interested in "getting God out of the psyche." For Jung, success in this dubious enterprise would result in variations of depression or rage. For these are the inevitable consequences of being deprived or depriving oneself of those libidinal energies that fund life's efforts and that, in certain configurations of intensity, Jung identifies with the experience of God and of grace.[6]

Thus the elucidation of Jung's understanding of the wholly intrapsychic genesis of the creation of religion and deity reveals the hostility of his psychology to the enterprise, largely theologically motivated, of "getting God out of the psyche." For Jung's psychology establishes so intimate a link between human consciousness and those archetypal energies that convince it of deity's reality that a conception of God as "wholly other" than humanity is, for Jung, wholly inconceivable.[7] In Jung's mind such a conception of God remains one of the major pathologizing features of the Western religious tradition. For it removes from the fabric of life itself the psychic energies that fund life, or it projects the source of these energies beyond life into transcendent deities whose ability to lend energy to life is greatly impaired by the projection itself. This removal of the victim of belief from life's energies is further worsened when the believer is then asked in the name of faith to relate to such deity through myth, dogma, and creeds that for modern consciousness are all too often the vehicles of a "sacrosanct unintelligibility."[8]

But Jung's concept of interiorization does more than convict orthodox conceptions of divine transcendence of pathologizing their victims by removing God as the source of life from life itself. His own conception of interiorization, especially as expressed in his work on Job (*CW* 11) and on the symbol of the Trinity (*CW* 11: par. 169ff., p. 107ff.), moves from a trinitarian to a quaternitarian understanding of deity as present to humanity. In this move Jung introduces major features of the myth that invigorates his own psychology. It is a myth that bears an appreciative transcendence of the Jewish-Christian myth as well as other myths founded on a deity conceived to exist in potential discontinuity from humanity and human consciousness. For in the move to a quaternitarian model, Jung implies that deity in itself is no doubt intensely creative but is driven to create out of its need to become aware in created human consciousness of its own antinomy or self-contradiction. This clearly implies that human consciousness, infinitely weaker than its divine matrix, is yet gifted with that power of discretion that can perceive in the Godhead the contradiction the Godhead could neither perceive nor resolve in itself.⁹ Only then, through the cooperation of the human, can deity move to resolve the split in the ground of its being, not in the transcendent remove of a self-sufficient Trinity but in the processes of human historical consciousness.

Thus the radical immanence of Jung's conception of deity implies that human consciousness and creation as a whole are no arbitrary superadditions to deity's preexistent and splendid isolation. Rather, Jung would have it that human consciousness proceeds from the Godhead much as do those processions in the more traditional understanding of the Trinity—but with the added dignity and burden that in human consciousness alone can deity seek the resolution of the contradiction it could not find in itself. With this shift in perspective Jung lays to rest all theological pretensions to a Trinitarian God eternally perfectly differentiated in its own life process and moving to create beyond itself in a moment somehow consequent to and independent of its own differentiation. To get at the radical shift in paradigm this move implies, it could be said that Jung would understand human consciousness itself as the second principle in the processions of the Godhead. Thus understood, human consciousness would be the logos, but a logos that painfully reflects the split in its origin and, paradoxically, with the help of that origin, seeks to unify its opposites in the fourth. In this paradigm the age of the spirit would point to that stage of human consciousness that had first perceived and then resolved the primordial contradiction in its source at the insistence and with the help of that source itself.

Thus in Jung's myth it becomes equally true to say that humanity is involved in the redemption of God as to say that God is engaged in the redemption of humanity. The new and horrifying moral imperative attached to this position is humanity's charge, first to discern the unresolved contradiction in deity, and then to embrace the suffering burden of becoming the vehicle or container in which this contradiction can be resolved. Its resolution then becomes at once the challenge at the heart of the suffering in each individual life, the substance of history, and the basis of the philosophy of history latent in Jung's psychology. Such are some of the implications for the phenomenon of religion and its study of what I have called interiorization as it works in Jung's psychology. Let us pass to the second foundational element under discussion, that of relativization.

Jung understands the psyche to be enlivened by a dialectic in which an infinite pole, the unconscious, seeks its expression in the finitude of consciousness.[10] In another aspect of his thought related to his dialectic, he suggests that the archetypes may be of an inexhaustible fecundity as they express themselves in human consciousness. This aspect of his thought, too, would imply that they need many variant concretions even to approximate what they want to express in consciousness. Both points work toward a relativization of all expressions of the unconscious. This relativization is particularly true of its major expressions, which are inevitably mythical-religious and which provide humanity with the needed belief systems on which to found its personal convictions and social organization. In the context of a short paper, one must leave open the greater challenge of Jung's thought in this area. It would center on the question of whether the unconscious can ever exhaustively express itself in consciousness. The eschatological imagery of many religious traditions would seem to imply that it can and that this is the direction in which world history moves. Such, for instance, would be the import of the image of the New Jerusalem in which God will be all in all. Given the historical performances of the religions that bear such imagery when they try to realize it in or, more tragically, impose it upon historical society, it may be safer to hold the consciousness to which eschatological imagery points as a distant possibility. In holding eschatological hope at bay and thus bargaining for time in the face of its too often apocalyptic urgencies, especially as the human enterprise enters a new millennium, humanity both collectively and individually could work more responsibly toward the birthing of a safer myth through conscious dialogue with the unconscious.

For from the individual's immediate experience of those energies that give rise to religion universally, a growing and freeing appreciation of religious experience might well arise. This appreciation of religion, through the experience of its basis in the self, would both convict consciousness of religion's positive energies even as it relativized specific religious expressions and commitments. Such experience appears foundational to Jung's psychology and is the basis of the methodology and hermeneutic his thought contains. Practitioners of such a hermeneutic would be well aware that any religious revelation is made more intelligible through comparison with its historical variants. Where there were no variants one could assume one was dealing with the freakish, and so with that which held little value for the human condition. For example, one would best understand the Christian myth by looking for its extra-Christian variants, in such candidates as the myths and rites of Osiris or Dionysus, in the host of counterclaims to be in possession of the logos incarnate in whatever form, or in the modern variants of the *anthropos* myth in such secular religions as Marxism.

Thus the encompassing perspective that emerges from a Jungian conception of relativization is the bias that the effort of the unconscious to give itself full expression in human historical consciousness is still in progress and that any of its major expressions to date must be understood through a reflection on their variants. This reflection would at once illuminate what it is that seeks expression in these variants while persuading the mind that no variant to date exhausts the wealth of what seeks expression in it. Again claims to exhaustive possession of a saving truth are negated toward collective safety even as an openness to going beyond our current religious consciousness is made possible and necessary. This brings me to my last point, the Jungian conception of universalization.

If interiorization means that all religions originate from an intrapsychic dynamic, and if relativization means that no myth exhausts the archetypal energies that seek expression in it, universalization refers to the fact that all enduring myths have universal significance as expressions of the psyche's deepest movements. Needless to say, this is true not only of the so-called living religions but also of those called dead. For many an analyst has witnessed the truth of so-called dead religions with modern variants of their gods and goddesses alive and well in the contemporary psyche. Indeed one wonders what refusal of wealth prompted the psyche so widely to reduce the many gods to one.

The best example of the implications of universalization in Jung's writings are in those passages in which he effectively refutes the efforts of orthodox Christianity to turn the truth of Christ, understood as the unity of the human and divine in an isolated individual, into a unique event. Jung states explicitly that the unconscious could never buy the reduction of the unity of the divine and the human to one historical individual.[11] By this he means that the unity of the divine and the human is a universal human possibility whose realization in each life is demanded by the dynamics of the psyche in the natural process of human maturation. As such, incarnation becomes for Jung a major paradigm for processes of individuation understood as the progressive unification of the conscious and the unconscious.[12]

Thus there is a sense in Jung's thought in which the truth of Christ, for example, is a universal truth, but not in a sense that is of any consolation to that religious sensitivity that would claim uniqueness or finality for it and hold it to have a universal validity for all times and cultures. For when the universal truth of Christ is related to the implications of Jung's conception of relativization, this truth becomes but one concretion of the power of the self. This is not to deny its current importance, since, argues Jung with considerable justification, it continues to provide our society with its culture hero (*CW* 9ii: par. 69, p. 36). Jung makes this point explictly when he states that Christ is an image of the self, not the self an image of Christ (*CW* 9ii: pars. 122, 123, p. 68).

In this example taken from the Christian myth, one sees clearly how the processes of interiorization, relativization, and universalization conspire to work an appreciative undermining of any religious claims to uniqueness and finality while appreciating the power of the archetypal motifs these religions embody. One sees also how these processes, intrinsic to the dynamic of the unconscious as it generates religious experience, when engaged with consciously by individual and ultimately by society, could contribute to a more user-friendly myth and church as the basis of a more tolerant social consciousness. This would be the case because immediate experience of the unconscious would acquaint the individual with his or her personal myth as the basis of relating to collective myths. This would free the individual from the tyranny of a myth not one's own and in so doing, Jung would contend, make a most valuable contribution to a safer social climate by modifying collective absolutes toward individual spiritual needs.

The import of these remarks leads to the following conclusions about Jung's impact on the discipline of religious studies. There is a discernible norm in a Jungian hermeneutic that can be brought to bear on the field of religious studies. It would divide approaches to the field into those aware of the origin of religious consciousness and its expressions in the unconscious and those that are unaware of the origin of the content of their discipline. The latter approach could then justly be designated as unconscious in a negative sense because such an approach remains unconscious of the origin and so of the nature of religion itself.[13] In the neighboring field of theology this normative aspect of Jung's hermeneutic could lead to a new understanding of fundamentalism and of fundamentalist theology. Fundamentalism would be seen as that form of unconsciousness that is induced in the mind of the believer grasped and imprisoned by the archetypal power of the cherished myth. That theology could then be identified as fundamentalist in which the believing mind reflecting on its myth in the doing of theology remained unaware of the origin in the unconscious of both the myth itself and of the faith in the myth that prompts theological reflection upon it.

Thus, possibly the most significant implication of Jung's thought for the discipline of religious studies is his challenge and invitation to the practitioner to experience individually and immediately the energies that birth the material with which he or she deals. In doing so, Jung's approach could cultivate a newer empathy in the discipline itself through the transformation of the consciousness of its practitioners, which in turn could enable religious studies to become a significant contributor to the currently developing family of sciences of human survival.

# Notes

1. See Murray Stein, *Jung's Treatment of Christianity: The Psychotherapy of a Religious Tradition* (Wilmette, Ill.: Chiron Publications, 1985). See in particular chap. 1 where Stein presents an overview of Jung's interpreters to date and points to their inadequacy and chap. 4 where Stein states that Jung's psychology works to transcend Christianity.

2. See my *Illness That We Are: A Jungian Critique of Christianity* (Toronto: Inner City Books, 1984).

3. See, for instance, "Concerning the Archetypes, with Special Reference to the Anima Concept" (*CW* 9i: par. 125, pp. 61-62); see also "Archetypes of the Collective Unconscious" (*CW* 9i: par. 49, p. 23), where Jung refers to the "isms" as "the present politico-social delusional systems."

4. Such an effort is perceived and rejected by Jung in his denial that God could be "wholly other" in the manner conceived of in classical Barthian theology (*CW* 12: par. 11, p. 11, n. 6). The issue was central to his discussion and correspondence with Rev. Victor White O.P. from 1945 to 1960. See the White–Jung correspondence in *C. G. Jung Letters*, ed. Gerhard Adler, 2 vols., Bollingen Series (Princeton: Princeton University Press, 1975). It is also a central issue in Buber's attack on Jung. See *The Eclipse of God*, chap. 5: "Religion and Modern Thinking" (New York: Harper and Row, 1952).

5. Jung writes, "As a matter of fact, the only form of existence of which we have immediate knowledge is psychic." And again, "Not only does the psyche exist, it is existence itself" (*CW* 11: par. 16, p. 12, and par. 18, p. 12).

6. On the unity of conscious and unconscious in the birth of the self Jung writes, "The self then functions as a union of opposites and thus constitutes the most immediate experience of the Divine which it is psychologically possible to imagine" (*CW* 11: par. 396, p. 261). Again referring to the power and gratuity of the unconscious in its commerce with consciousness, he writes,

"The method cannot, however, produce the actual process of unconscious compensation; for that we depend upon the unconscious psyche or the 'grace of God'—names make no difference" (*CW* 11: par. 779, p. 488).

7. On this point Jung is explicit: "It is therefore psychologically quite unthinkable for God to be simply the 'wholly other,' for a 'wholly other' could never be one of the soul's deepest and closest intimacies—which is precisely what God is" (*CW* 12: par. 11, p. 11, n. 6).

8. The entire citation reads, "I have to ask myself also, in all seriousness, whether it might not be far more dangerous if Christian symbols were made inaccessible to thoughtful understanding by being banished to a sphere of sacrosanct unintelligibility. They can easily become so remote from us that their irrationality turns into preposterous nonsense" (*CW* 11: par. 170, p. 109).

9. For Jung the myth of Job captures this dialectic. "All this pointed to a *complexio oppositorum* and thus recalled again the story of Job to my mind: Job who expected help from God against God" (*CW* 11: Introduction, p. 358).

10. The dialectic between conscious expression and its unconscious matrix is implied throughout Jung's thought and made explicit in the paragraph in which he writes, "The conscious mind does not embrace the totality of man, for this totality consists only partly of his conscious contents, and for the other and far greater part of his unconscious, which is of indefinite extent with no assignable limits" (*CW* 11: par. 390, p. 258).

11. Arguing that the unconscious extends the unity of divine and human natures—the *homoousia* attributed only to Christ in orthodox dogma—to the human condition itself, Jung writes, "The Church, it seems to me, probably has to repudiate any attempt to take such conclusions seriously . . . since she cannot admit that nature unites what she herself has divided" (*CW* 11: par. 105, p. 61. Cf. also *CW* 11: par. 146, p. 89). Jung writes, "That is to say, what happens in the life of Christ happens always and everywhere."

12. The use of the paradigm of incarnation for individuation is particularly evident in his work "Transformation Symbolism in the Mass" (*CW* 11).

13. I do not deal here with the role of compensation in the production of religion by the unconscious. Let is simply be noted that Jung holds that the unconscious produces religion as collective compensation to collective one-sidedness and so always in relation to the social disorder it addresses. This social dimension does not mitigate my location of the genesis of religion in the unconscious. Rather for Jung the social dimension serves only to determine what form religion will take in its social historical concretion.

# The Trickster
# and the
# Sacred Clown
## Revealing the Logic
## of the Unspeakable    Thomas Belmonte

Lift up your hearts, my brothers, high, higher! And do not forget your legs either. Lift up your legs too, you good dancers; and better yet, stand on your heads!    —*Friedrich Nietzsche*

See, see! What shall I see?
A horse's head where his tail should be.    —*Mother Goose*

The Hopi clown or *Tsutskut* tears a living pup to pieces and smears his face with its blood. He drinks urine, eats excrement, is a phallic exhibitionist and a giver of wisdom to his people. The Navaho Black Dancer wallows in mud and carries the bloody exudate of body sores and polluting menstruation on his own person to heal his sick brethren. The Dakota *Heyoka* or contrary plunges his hand in a pot of boiling water and splashes it on his back, complaining cheerfully of the cold spray. He says "yes" when he means "no" and walks backward, naked in winter's cold, heavily robed in summer's heat. His Cheyenne counterpart, the *Hohnuhke'e*, was the bearer of the thunder lance, acting and speaking by opposites, fearless of lightning, a hermit sitting on his head, leading his people in battle—rushing the enemy head-on in suicidal charges. Masked Iroquois False Faces and Kwakiutl Fools (like English Mummers) go about begging and demanding. They violate all rules of hospitality. They abuse and torment their neighbors. They scatter cinders and hot coals on visiting guests, and they are esteemed and feared for the power that the spirits have conferred upon them.[1]

Trickster is a scatophagus and a satyr, a torturer and a Christ figure whose descent into corporeal humanity redeems through self-sacrifice. He is a selfish embodiment of unbridled "id" and an enforcer of commensal and redistributive imperatives. He is the menacing boy-child, tricking for treats, wreaking cruel mischief, surprising the elders with his teachings in the temple and becoming the prophet who guides to deeper truths.

Ethnology is a sober science. To visualize the performances of False Faces and English Mummers as obedient to the notations of the same choreographer, to hear the "avid" ravings of Flathead Indian "Bluejay" figures and birdlike Irish "madmen of the glen" as alternate voices of the same oracle, and to see the obscene abuse of a Hopi "mudhead" clown and a South Indian Raniga buffoon as the pornographic gestures of the same demon-tempting exorcist, strikes the positivist ethnographer as absurd. Contexts of time and place give both scientific and interpretive ethnography the empirical density that makes its descriptions run "thick."[2]

But the sparse information that ethnology provides on tricksters and clowns arranges itself as driftwood on the shore of a dream. Exposed to the bleaching, dessicating light of analysis, these fragments from near and far reveal the fluid dynamics of the lunar tides that washed them onto the bank. The key question posed by this backwash of primordial forms is whether or not a theory of culture based on the premise of plasticity can be reconciled with a theory of universal symbolic forms based on a deterministic unity of mind.

## Trickster and the Anthropological Study of Symbolic Universals

The existence of universal symbolic structures in the domains of myth and religion is not generally questioned by the social sciences. But neither is the universality per se of such structures the proper subject of normal social scientific discourse. To venture onto such inviting but hazardous territory is to leave behind the familiar complexity of the local sociocultural context, with its moorings in the particularities of knowable history. The theorist of the forms of universal as opposed to local knowledge is rarely possessed of a disciplined ethnographic or historical imagination. Freud, Jung, and Lévi-Strauss are alike vulnerable to charges of mentalism on the one hand and biologism on the other. All deny the absolute autonomy of the cultural level and all reduce its multitudinous and emergent properties to a theory of neural residues. Such theories, it must be admitted, have yet to attain the epistemological rigor of medieval alchemy.

It is not my intention here to correct this state of affairs. Presumably, we know more now about the causal connections that link brains to minds, selves to societies, and social interactions to shared (cultural) understandings than Jung did. My aim is not so much to revive or to rescue Jung but rather to rephrase and rethink some of his key concerns and questions in terms of the economics of both individual consciousness and cultural knowledge. Jung had neither a theory of information and feedback nor a theory of communications. In a sense, his predicament paralleled that of cellular biology up until recently. Before the discovery of the replicating codes that control the processes of organic life, biologists described their subject in terms of the intrinsic properties of protoplasm. Now they are all cryptographers of DNA. The study of symbols is undergoing a similar revolution. It is my contention that what Jung termed "archetype" is actually a *biosocial* manifestation of a widespread natural phenomenon, originally identified by Claude Shannon as a self-healing code. Had Jung formulated his theory of the archetypal synapse connecting mind, myth, and culture now, he would have undoubtedly adopted a perspective based on cybernetic as opposed to linear notions of causality and that positioned any symbolic process within its total semiotic context and dominant media environment. Once this step is taken, a great deal of the crass reductionism that mars Jung's psychology melts away and his most valuable intuitions become available for reconsideration by humanists and scientists alike.

Here I apply such a perspective to the most recalcitrant of archetypal forms, the figure of the trickster-clown. For this purpose I take some admittedly tricksterish liberties with the ethnographic material and assume a close psychosocial relation between the shape-shifting mythological figure and the ritual humorist, the sacred clown. Moreover, in my compressed treatment of the latter, I make no attempt to classify and analyze systematically the scenarios of masquerade, inversion, possession, and *sparagmos* (dismemberment of the sacrifice) that variably structure the clown's performance in cultures widely separated in time and space. Finally, whereas most discussions of the trickster refer the entire complex to an existential principle of heroic resistance to the constraints of social order, I do not so much reject as set aside this notion at the outset. If the essential elements of the trickster's seemingly nonsensical code can be deciphered successfully, they can suggest how the considerable expenditures of psychic energy attending the complex might be compatible with social and historical needs for both flexibility and order. Archetypal symbols are metacommentaries that both display and resolve a nested hierarchy of relationships. My core thesis is that the clowns and contraries described earlier are solving complex equations of unity and differentiation. They are, however, communicating their results on a sensory and cognitive channel for which there are few receptors remaining in the information economies of high-literate, urban civilizations.

## The Archetype as a Deep Structure

Perhaps because of its formation as a vanguard discipline in singular and combative opposition to the claims of scientific racism, cultural anthropology—especially its American variant—continues to display an evangelical hostility toward any theory of mind that asserts the priority (or even the parity) of essence in relation to experience. The exile of Jung to a place far beyond the borders of admissible argument in academic anthropology must be seen in light of the discipline's Boasian foundations as well as Jung's own failure to invent and refine a terminology that would do justice to the novelty of his ideas.[3]

Nor did Jung ever clarify with any rigor the evolutionary premises of his psychology. He was uneasy with the hydraulic and Newtonian machinery of Freud's *Project for a Scientific Psychology*, and he knew that Darwin's survivalist materialism could not easily account for the creative and transcendent character of human mentality. But he was no special creationist. He uncritically accepted an instinctual and Lamarckian ground for the evolution of mind and embraced Haeckel's notion of ontogeny recapitulating phylogeny in the embryo as a fair description of the growth of the individual psyche. Like Konrad Lorenz and Edward Wilson, Jung was a sociobiological structuralist for whom the terms of mental life were at once transpersonal and preformed.[4] But he was not by implication a genetic determinist. For Jung, archetypes were always "forms without content," the structures of which were comparable to "the axial system of a crystal." Just as particular crystals of water or carbon might vary endlessly, as snowflakes or diamonds, so might the objects, events, and personages of an archetype be transformed and rearranged without ever violating the rules of archetypal assembly: "The only thing that remains constant is the axial system, or rather, the invariable geometric propositions underlying it. The same is true of the archetype. In principle, it can be named and has an invariable nucleus of meaning—but always only in principle, never as regards its concrete manifestation." (*CW*9i: par. 155, pp. 79-80).

Here Jung's archetype resembles nothing less than Chomsky's colorless green idea, sleeping furiously in the recesses of the soul. Thus re-visioned in linguistic terms, the archetype is a message inscribed on a neural cartridge, composed of arbitrary signs that appear in rule-governed or formal configurations. Universal myths are syntactic structures, ultimately constrained by neural schemata, but capable of creative transformation in that they are never locked into a particular metaphoric content.

## Myth as a Therapy of the Word

The Jungian archetype is more than the transform of unfulfilled wishes and much more than a mere social mortar. It affirms and represents. It is an epistemology, a way of setting forth premises and first principles. It is a psychic tool for making explicit information about the spacing and sequencing of generations and sexes, givers and takers, leaders and followers, and for reconciling the anxieties of the living with their memories of the dead. Archetypal tales make sense; that is, they communicate information about order and how to create more of it under certain conditions of social and cultural organization. They are not merely prescriptive or cautionary so much as corrective of distortions that arise in the course of the composing and enacting of primordial social scenes. Myth, in this view, is an instruction for doing that heals. It is the earliest of logotherapies. As Aristotle so well understood (and as Hippocrates did not), mythical language is curative. Through catharsis its tragic poetry yields inner harmony to the soul (*sophrosyne*).[5]

The archetype is a metaphor nesting within a metaphor, an "as if" proposition bridging the gap between matter and mind, action and ideation, object and percept, self and other. But the archetypal myth is more to Jung than a collection of "as if" propositions. These are assembled at another level into an "if only" form. All myth has a lamentative, grieving, as well as a laughing aspect and, like grief and laughter, is restorative. The archetype is a link or rebinding (*religio*) of the present with the past. It exists outside of history precisely because human beings are historical, because they are creatures capable of alienation.

For Jung, as for Freud, culture is an unstable and precarious attainment, always in danger of lapsing into the regression of unrestrained appetite or setting into the rigid, if porcelain, molds of renunciation and sublimation. But whereas for Freud the claims of religion and myth are fundamentally irrational, representing the triumph of either desire or terror, for Jung the religious imagination resolves the dialectic of impulse and renunciation, rendering human life not only possible but possessed of a potential for joy. In the Jungian view, myth is not so much the return of the repressed as it is the return of the human being, of Unamuno's "man of flesh and bone, walking solidly upon the earth."[6]

No archetypal figure represents to consciousness the agon of culture and nature more parsimoniously than the trickster figures that recur in various animal-human guises in the vast majority of recorded mythologies. Freudians describe such figures as providing drastic relief from the intolerable pressure of instinctual cravings, and Jung would seem to echo this notion when he describes the Winnebago trickster as "a faithful copy of an absolutely undifferentiated human consciousness."[7] But in his famous essay on the theme, Jung enjoins his readers "to never forget that in any psychological discussion we are not saying anything *about* the psyche, but that the psyche is always speaking about itself."[8] Jung goes on to describe the trickster figure as a "reflection" and an "epitome" as well as a "component" of personality. For Jung, as for Socrates, the reflectant properties of the mind are the beacons of its dynamic, unfolding inner life. If the original "psychologems" are neglected—if the process of self-constitution in the language of myth is blocked—the equilibrium of the person-in-society is disrupted and the contents of desire are experienced as threatening and alien. Put in another way, when the mind's ordering eye is blinded and its mythic voice muffled, pathology will result as fascist or racist hatred and the projection of one's own animality onto others. Apparently for Jung, archetypal imagery allows the mind to view itself as a balanced totality, as a republic of contending but mutually interdependent processes. The archetype is above all an oracular message, a governor or a steersman in Norbert Wiener's cybernetic sense—a package of information as well as a burst of energy. It is, at the intrapsychic level, a system-stabilizer (recalling Ray Birdwhistell's kinesics)—an answer to the question "Who is speaking?"[9]

## Trickster and the Paradoxes of Play

Superficially considered, the archetype of the trickster and the cognate performances of the sacred clown present a challenge to any notion of myth as a grammar that determines the relations of agents, actions, and objects in the genesis of self and society. The clown is after all a "Lord of Misrule" who makes of things a mess. The trickster rabbit-man or spider-man, the bug-bunny, dissolves back into the world even as he defecates, urinates, and ejaculates its distinctive features. The performances of sacred clowns are likewise founded on scatological flows where the envelope of what Niebuhr called "the particularity of the body" is punctured (like the bladder on the scepter of a fool),[10] to channel the jets of self back to the odorous ground of creation, as bare-handed predation, as phallic-aggressive copulation, and as grinning, self-satisfied coprophagy. Stevenson describes a ritual of the Zuni clown society, the *Koyemci*:

the acme of depravity is reached after the chief takes his final departure from the plaza. The performances are now intended solely for amusement. The one who swallows the largest amount of filth with greatest gusto is the most commended by the fraternity and onlookers. A large bowl of urine is handed to a man of the fraternity, who, after drinking a portion, pours the remainder over his head. Each man endeavors to exceed his fellows in buffoonery and in eating repulsive things, such as bits of old blankets or splinters of wood. They bite off the heads of living mice and chew them, tear live dogs apart, eat the intestines and fight over the liver like hungry wolves.[11]

Such performances have been variously interpreted as providing comic relief at the long and tedious maize ceremonies of which they form a part, as Freudian representations of male anxieties concerning female blood-knowledge or life-knowledge, and as creators of a ritual anti-structure that can correct for hierarchical trends in unstable egalitarian clan systems.[12] Jung will have none of this. The clown is not simply a reflection of local color, not even a rectifier of local wrongs. Rather he expresses what Bateson once referred to (recalling Pascal) as "the algorithms of the heart."[13] His savage pantomime displays at the deepest level possible—the level alluded to by Blake in his poem of the strangled babe—the courage of conviction.

But the clown's act of courage is also an act of play. As such, it may be viewed as a primordial form of scientific inquiry, based on the logic of reversals and the exploration of Russelian types of paradox of the "I am lying" sort.[14] Primitive societies, as oral knowledge economies, have high levels of tolerance for inclusive levels of paradox. Oral cultures may be more playful than high literate cultures where play, in effect, becomes the reserve of children and philosophers.

The masked Mayo-Mexican clown who mocks the stations of the cross in the most lurid of terms clenches a crucifix tight between his teeth. His acts that amuse and shock teeter on a conceptual ledge, as he converts the message "This is play" to the derivative "Is this play?" to generate an oscillating experience of humor and horror in his spectators.[15] Ritual inversion has traditionally been viewed as a form of reaffirmation and release from traditional moral imperatives. That the clown himself might be a metaphysician in Whitehead's terms, who lays the foundation of his culture's forward movement into an uncertain future, is only rarely conceded. Arden King has suggested that Native American peoples with vital and ongoing clown performance did not initiate revitalization movements, since their ritual humorists were able to build conceptual bridges between the past and the future.

Thus the clown's performance clarifies the epistemological possibilities of his people's cosmology. He factors out the fundamental signs of social health and disease, and he poses entropy and order as human alternatives open to realization in a concrete flow of events.[16]

## Trickster, *Thanatos*, and the Language of Negation

The Greek trickster, Hermes, was the patron of herdsmen, thieves, graves, and heralds. He was the god of boundaries and of all those engaged in the risky business of crossing them.[17] Like Charlie Chaplin's tramp, perpetually hopping from the wrong to the right side of the tracks (until claimed by infinity), the trickster-clown gives us a fleeting glimpse of the process of creation as order and chaos in alternation.[18] In the clown's laboratory of far-from-equilibrium states, structure is renewable only if it is able to make contact with its negation. The clown breaks the bottle that imprisons Faust's homunculus, and the psyche is revealed for what it is—a whirlwind, a flame that feeds on dissipation.[19]

The word "folly" and its cognate "fool" derive from the Latin *follis*, referring to a pair of bellows or a windbag. The word "buffoon" likewise derives from the Italian *buffare*, "to puff."[20] What then is the relationship between the blowhard and the fool and the proverbial sadness of clowns? The aging Jung cited *Corinthians* to illustrate the blind ambition of the ego: "Are you not puffed up, and have not rather mourned?" (*CW* 9ii: n. 3, p. 23). The girthful, mirthful fat man of the sideshow, weeping for the phallus that has been reabsorbed into his flesh, is the trickster's saddest sacrifice at what is both a satyricon and funeral of the self. Taken to such gross extremes, folly does its cruel work and the ego's flatulent hot air fizzles out of the exhausted balloon. Pathetically human at last, now it can share and mourn. The labor of the clown-turned-shrink has not been in vain.

The trickster creates form through dissolution, that is, scato/logically. He is in fact a "scatterbrain" (in colloquial American terms, a "shithead") who unites in the notation of the body the forces of chaos and logos. Note that here unification is attained not through Platonic contemplation and argument but via the induction of that absolutely human biopsychic convulsion known as laughter. The laughter of the trickster-clown is, as Bakhtin describes it, "laughter directed at those who laugh . . . laughter that degrades and materializes as it digs a bodily grave for a new birth."[21]

Jung was convinced that archetypes do not fade away. They are as irrepressible as the psychic schedules and tensions they polarize and encode. But Jung is notably weak in accounting for the metamorphoses of archetypal contents in the flux of history, from the celebrations of communal ritual and shared folktale to neurotic compulsion and private dream or "night/mare." If archetypes are conceived as attaining a social identity only under certain organizations or modes of production and communication, the problem of their efflorescence, eclipse, and resurgence becomes accessible to analysis. Archetypes solve problems in a particular medium or code. The switch or translation from one code to another always involves a trade-off of information gained and lost. "Any particular representation," writes David Marr, the late mathematician of vision, "makes certain information explicit at the expense of information that is pushed into the background and may be quite hard to recover"[22] Thus do cultures of the voice and the book respectively bear a very different relationship to the realm of the invisible and the unseen. They take notice of different worlds and generate opposed notions of what is "obvious."

Feathers and wings, Marr points out, are incomprehensible to biologists who lack a knowledge of aerodynamics.[23] Myths likewise can take flight only in a domain of specific atmospheric pressures and conditions. They can thrive only where interaction, work, and communication are arranged in more or less closed circuits of commensal, erotic, and political flows that return upon themselves in the form of the gift, the dance, and the feast. The archetype of the trickster and the child could be a living idea in the world of Bruegel's *Kermesse* and might thrive even at the civilizational level, in genuinely theocratic places, like Llasa, Cuzco, and Beauvais.

In his critical analysis of the Platonic utopia, Stanley Diamond makes the point that the ideological burden of all complex stratified societies is to redefine and thus to remake human nature in such a way as to establish a permanent isomorphism between the slave and his labor. If work has been oversimplified, standardized, and degraded, then in that measure must human nature be subjected to a process of shrinkage and contraction. Images of human wholeness are anathema to the new common sense of the rational bureaucratic state, and so the philosopher and the scribe become the pallbearers of the trickster god.[24]

But as Eric Havelock has emphasized, the final privatization of the mythic imagination was the work of writing. Literacy, when internalized, creates detachment from language as it locks the word in visual space. The book creates a new cartography of the spirit, in that it splits the fields of force connecting words to things, and humans to other beings, mapping the universe in chapter and verse and creating the Cartesian intellect.[25]

"My sons must never work," intones the Nez Perce chieftain, Smohalla, "men who labor cannot dream, and wisdom comes through dreaming."[26] Echoing him, Jung declared, "the primitive mentality does not invent myths, it experiences them"(*CW* 9i: par. 261, p. 154). In societies where all knowledge must be coded orally, where the word is an event (the Hebrew *dabar*), the name of the god is sufficient as a summons, and the dream image is an order to revise, a form of second sight. In such societies, tricksters, clowns, and rites of reversal are sensible and sacramental. They set forth critical insights about security and danger and set them apart as well in a sanctum, a place holy and accursed, bounded and ochre-lined. "Wise men see outlines," quipped Blake, "and therefore they draw them."[27] The clown draws them upside down.

"Bare negation," Bakhtin tells us, "is completely alien to folk culture."[28] The language of icon and dream works without simple negatives. In this deficiency, it is homologous to most zoosemiotic systems, a point stressed by Bateson in a classic paper on primitive art.[29] Thus, in order to communicate an absence of aggressive intent, the animal bares its teeth and raises its paw in the pose of the greeting-strike. Dream language and mythical language can only negate through reversal and positive assertion, through (again invoking Bakhtin) "the peculiar logic of the inside out and the turnabout."[30] Thus Jung recognizes the cruelties of the trickster as the blessings of a savior. "The wounded wounder is the agent of healing . . . the sufferer takes away suffering."[31] So also does the clown mediate his people's encounter with death. Mischa Titiev reflected on their meaning in his Hopi field journal as follows:

> With the passage of the years, I have more and more come to hold the belief that clowns are often equated with the dead and that much of the mockery arousing laughter stems from the notion that since death is the opposite of life, those who represent the dead, as do clowns, should also do and say the *opposite* of what is normally expected. This is a surefire way of arousing laughter; but in such cases the factor of amusement is entirely secondary, whereas the primary purpose is to behave like the dead—that is, to do things opposite to the way they are done by the living.[32]

Titiev's equation of the Hopi clowns with the deceased is especially intriguing in light of Freud's observation that severe depression, generically so similar to intense grief, is often accompanied by a sadistic, exhibitionistic component. If the clown is indeed, at one level, a cadaver, his sadomasochistic behavior dramatizes the ambivalent rage of the kin-based community toward the release-as-abandonment of the dead as they transform into ancestors.[33] But to brand the clown's performance as neurotic is to place a visitor bearing gifts under the house-arrest of reason. Like Lenny Bruce remanded for psychiatric observation, he is likely to shoot up with morphine and make his way back home.

The wonderland of the dead, as James Hillman has emphasized, can never be safely navigated with the compass of the dayworld. In the Egyptian underworld, the dead walk upside down and defecate through their mouths. "What is merely shit from the daytime perspective," Hillman writes, ". . . becomes soul food when turned upside down."[34] The scatological feasts and urine dances of the otherwise sober Zuni become comprehensible at last, as eucharistic celebrations of unity with the people on the other side.

The use of reversal and the use of analogic coding are fundamental to the mythic mentality and to the sensorium for which it is the axis. The clown can only personify death by "hanging upside down" and by, in effect, turning up the volume of his performance so that the song becomes a scream, converting information back into noise. As such, he is a figure of great, even ultimate, power—a Superman, or better, an upended "Batman," who can swirl all the roiling energies of the psyche into a single bolt of existential lightning.

Myth talk is double-talk to the literate mind. The image of the skull, as Weston LaBarre has shown, was for the paleolithic mind a potent image of health. (Recall "skoal," the Scandianavian toast!)[35] The myth symbol always partakes of this duality, a point elaborated by Freud in his classic paper, "The Antithetical Sense of Primal Words." The semantic life of the primal word was achieved in the systole and diastole of contrast. The ancient Egyptian word for "strong (*ken*) was an alternator meaning "strongweak." By the same process, the English "tub" reverses to "boat," "reck" to "care," and over time the Anglo-Saxon word for "good" (*bat*) becomes "bad." (The Bat or Badman is, of course, a "better" or good man.)[36]

In bisections such as these, we see two lines converging from the thought of Jung and Lévi-Strauss. But whereas for Lévi-Strauss, myth is "inauthentic" and the trickster a mere mediator between culture and nature on the one hand, hunting and agriculture on the other—a binary operator in a Pythagorean triangle—Jung's archetype is embedded in a drama of ecstasy and awareness.[37] The trickster is no referee at a structuralist quiz show but a poor slob—a contestant—a tragic hero on another channel, the matricide Orestes questing for atonement as a joker.[38]

For Freud, a character like Orestes was an Aeschylean symptom, a poet's daydream of life as it might be in a world where all juries can be bribed for the sake of His Majesty, the Ego.[39] For Jung, the mythic utterance was an "outering" of the soul's contents that clarified the happening as a doing. One trivialized such dream wisdom at one's own risk. One scoffed at the trickster only to find oneself the aching victim of a banana peel, or worse—far, far worse.

"No psychic value," Jung wrote, "can disappear without being replaced by another of equivalent intensity."[40] If we banish Hermes the *psychopompos*, the escort of souls to Charon, he returns as a hound of Hell. Terrified of death, we become murderous and cowardly, sentimental as a Nazi. But if we can achieve recognition of the trickster as a personification of the shadow side of our being, of what Blake called "the Devouring," our frightful shuddering transforms to carnival laughter and our stalled pilgrimage toward self-possession can proceed. Bakhtin recounts how, among the "grottessche" unearthed during the Renaissance, were terra cotta figurines of senile pregnant old women, their heads thrown back in uproarious laughter.[41] Death cleanses the world and prepares it for renewal, and renewal is the special province of that which is female in both sexes. Not for nothing do children who lose a tooth receive a gift from the fairy. They have experienced the body's downward movement toward decay and deserve a token-glimpse of the anima.

The human mind speaks a finite number of languages. The language of hammers and nails (i.e., the language of instrumental reason) has served the species well in its quest for power and technological mastery. The language of myth, however, is rarely focused on such goals. As Gregory Bateson reminds us, the recurrent concern of myth is with those "universal minima" that are necessary to the health of many overlapping systemic fields—individual, social, and natural. Myth sets forth an "epistemology of the sacred" and reminds us that God, understood as the totality of these open and overlapping, mutually sustaining systems, will not be mocked.[42]

Moreover, if we attempt to achieve mastery of this god by resorting to the language of hammers and nails, we succeed only in bringing about his death. For most of us, however, a perspective that takes in the total field of relations is disorienting, if not unbearable. When, in the *Bhagavad-Gita*, the Lord Krishna, disguised as a wise and gentle charioteer, reveals his many-sided being to his pupil, Arjuna, the result is terrible and blinding. The trembling young warrior begs the god to reassume his familiar human form.[43] Unless the image of the god-asself is properly modeled, it can be neither recognized nor understood by that part of the mind that we identify as consciousness. But effective work with models implies a capacity for play and a readiness to forget. "To know God as He is," says Meister Eckhart, "we must be absolutely free from knowledge."[44] Thus can we better understand why the Winnebago trickster cycle does not begin in some primordial landscape but at a solemn ceremonial banquet, a war-party, at which the chief-who-will-be-trickster breaks the most sacred of taboos and sheds the raiments of his worldly station before his metamorphosis into an infantile wanderer.

At the entrance to the Egyptian underworld, the heart of the deceased was weighed against a feather. To enter paradise one had to be lighthearted. Christ and Buddha alike are light enough to walk on the surface of the water.[45] But levitation is not only the special province of mystics. In trickster's cathedral, under the great conical circus tent, levitation transforms to the levity of a happy dream. Jumbo the elephant steals the show on a red rubber ball. The novice clowns, like flying monks (or nuns) are shot from the cannon through the cosmic spaces of the Big Top, while far above the center ring, the Flying Wallendas defy death, erecting human pyramids on the high wire. For all its hostility to the official church, Moscow built a great hall for its circus, acknowledging that without its liturgy of renewal and transcendence, the morale of the people might suffer. Thus do we obtain insight into the medieval meaning of "carnival," from *carnem levare*, to lay aside the flesh.[46]

Whether we choose to think of the cluster of symbols surrounding the trickster in terms of archetypes, binary operators, or safety valves, we are compelled to recognize the psychocultural coherence of the assemblage in the cross-cultural and trans-historical recurrence of such themes as the boundary-crossing, the ego's inflationary greed, and the denial and acceptance of death. Here I have tried to show how the logic of play, paradox, and reversal operates at a number of levels to unite sacred and profane aspects of the trickster myth and the clown's performance. I have proposed a powerful system-stabilizing or therapeutic function for the dialogue between clown, self, and society, not, following Freud, because of the instinctual effluent that is presumably discharged, but because of the knowledge that is created when the biologically grounded mind achieves a means of coding the unspeakable. If we have parted company with Jung in this discussion, it is in our understanding of the archetype as an advanced and, by implication, recently acquired function of the human mind and not as a throwback to the murky realms of instinct.

In summation, the trickster reveals himself to us as a composite symbolic figure of high density and energy, a psychosocial battery of sorts, that fuels the life of the mind by coding out its elementary polarities. These polarities are inclusive and paradoxical, expressive of identity and difference between the animal and the human being, between the ego and the self, and between the self and the body, with its messy cravings and necessities. The trickster is both a troublemaker and a sorcerer whose gestures can either sicken or heal. The outcome will depend on the individual's ability to receive and decode the meaning of the magician's "hocus pocus" in terms that make cultural sense. If the scope of self-knowledge is restricted by the paucity and thinness of available symbolic and ritual codes, the individual will experience the promptings of the archetype as fear and hatred of the stranger. The sorcerer will have triumphed in a monstrous irony.

Jung was perhaps too optimistic when he declared that the spiritual impoverishment of modern (Protestant) men and women would lead to a more genuine experience of individuation. If we agree with him that "the symbolic process is an experience *in images of images*," we are forced to ask by what hermeneutic means can a person deprived of access to the lexicon and grammar of mythic images decipher and re-integrate his or her private meanings in terms that can enrich the social experience of love and work? (*CW* 9i: par. 82, p. 38).[47] The problem is analogous to that encountered by primitive peoples who attempt to reclaim a lost heritage in the language of the conqueror. As Jung's lesser known contemporary and peer Coomaraswamy wrote: "To have lost the art of thinking in images is precisely to have lost the proper linguistic of metaphysics and to have descended to the verbal logic of 'philosophy.' "[48] If the trickster can never be fully repressed, he can be made to suffer the fate of Cassandra, ignored and unheeded until the fateful night of fire and rout.

## Trickster Denied: Last Laughter at Armageddon

"Repressed contents," Jung wrote, "are the very ones that have the best chance of survival."[49] Jung's essay on the trickster can, in fact, be read as a trenchant critique of positivism and its well-established successor, "rational"—as opposed to hermeneutic—Freudo-Marxism, with its confident definition of "health" as a balance in the supply and demand of sex and bread. For capitalist and socialist alike, it is sufficient to follow the "standard operating procedures" (fiscal and psychiatric) for the deployment and control of both wealth and libido. As long as these prove effective in regulating an economy of appetites, rationality will present itself as the governor rather than the by-product of the system. When such a system breaks apart, however, business as usual becomes a contradiction in terms and the ancient figure of the monkey-clown suddenly reappears to leap on the back of reason. In systems organized around the premises of Freudo-Marxism, however, this "monkey-business" is nothing less than the work of a familiar, even lovable if rough beast, a tropical captive breaking its bonds—King Kong clutching his shrunken Fay and mounting the Empire State.

The Jungian definition of "health" is not predicated on a system of rational price supports for the microeconomies of pleasure and necessity, but neither does it prescribe the abdication of reason. Jung's jeremiad is not directed against reason but rather against its hypertrophied impersonator—technocratic rationality. The real and present danger facing the postmodern mind was, for Jung, the breakdown in communications between the diverse regions of the psyche. Deprived of the oral-mythic system of maps and messengers, the self would, at best, come to experience itself (recalling Camus) as a disembodied, potentially homicidal, stranger. At worst, entire populations might suddenly find themselves in the grip of a terrifying psychedelia, dominated by an addictive and compulsive wish to kill an insurgent enemy—the "jew-nigger-commie-gook or flaming fairy"—within. Whatever his own problematic relationship to the racist alternative was, the older Jung finally knew that the trickster would have the last laugh at Armageddon.[50]

On May 9, 1939, on the occasion of Freud's eightieth birthday celebration, Thomas Mann delivered an encomium to the founder of psychoanalysis that was actually a poem of gratitude to Jung. "Nobody has ever focused as sharply as he," declared Mann, "the Schopenhauer-Freud perception that 'the giver of all conditions resides in ourselves'. . . . A great and costly change he [Jung] thinks is needed before we understand how the world is 'given' by the nature of the soul."[51] For Jung, as for Mann, myth was the soul's mode of confession and admission, of itself to itself, its way to accountability and an image of truth.

Thomas Mann himself sought this image in Hans Castorp's hallucinated dream-poem at the storm-tossed peak of the magic mountain. In his vision of sensuous youths watering horses by a golden sea and simian hags dismembering, to devour, a living babe, Mann granted his "guileless fool" of a hero an initiate's glimpse into the mystery of the dying god. He led him to the doors of that chamber whose reasons reason cannot know. He invited him to ponder the *coincidentia oppositorum*, to plead with Nicholas of Cusa for an understanding of liberty's sphere in a determined universe. He groped before the perplexities of the quantum as theorized by Niels Bohr, with its leaping circus acrobats of velocity and position. But could he himself have foreseen the terrible voyage of the so-called Little Boy, from Los Alamos to Hiroshima, become the Fat Man engulfing Nagasaki, fulfilling Oppenheimer's prophecy at Trinity: "I have become Death, shatterer of worlds."[52]

# Notes

1. For an excellent summary of the ethnographic literature on both trickster figures and sacred clowns, see Mahadev K. Apte, *Humor and Laughter: An Anthropological Approach* (Ithaca: Cornell University Press, 1985), esp. chaps. 5 and 7. Robert Pelton reviews and rethinks the West African material in *The Trickster in West Africa: A Study of Mythic Irony and Sacred Delight* (Berkeley: University of California Press, 1980), and Enid Welsford places the European fool in panoramic historical and literary perspective in her classic study, *The Fool: His Social and Literary History* (London: Faber and Faber, 1935; reprint ed., Gloucester, Mass.: Peter Smith, 1966). Excellent, if theoretically diverse, discussions of the Native American material can be found in Laura Makarius, "Ritual Clowns and Symbolical Behavior," *Diogenes* 69 (Spring 1970): 44-73; Edward Norbeck, "Rites of Reversal of North American Indians as Forms of Play," in *Forms of Play of Native North Americans: 1977 Proceedings of the American Ethnological Society*, ed. Edward Norbeck and Claire R. Ferrer (St. Paul, Minn.: West Publishing Co., 1979); Verne F. Ray, "The Contrary Behavior Pattern in American Indian Ceremonialism," *Southwestern Journal of Anthropology* 1 (1945): 75-113; and Julian Steward, "The Ceremonial Buffoon of the American Indian," in *Evolution and Ecology: Essays on Social Transformation*, ed. Jane C. Steward and Robert F. Murphy (Urbana: University of Illinois Press, 1977). Insightful poetic and aesthetic commentaries of Native American clowning can be found in Jamake Highwater, *Ritual of the Wind* (New York: Viking, 1977) and *The Primal Mind* (New York: Harper and Row, 1981). A detailed description of the Cheyenne contrary can be found in George Bird Grinnell, *The Cheyenne Indians: Their History and Ways of Life*, 2 vols. (New York: Cooper Square, 1962), 2: 79-86 and 204-210. The Navaho Black Dancer is described by Gladys Reichard in *Navaho Religion: A Study of Symbolism*, 2d ed. in one vol., Bollingen Series (Princeton: Princeton University Press, 1974), pp. 183-184. Vivid descriptions of Hopi clowning are provided by Alexander M. Stephen in his *Hopi Journal*, 2 vols. (New York: Columbia University Press, 1936), esp. pp. 328-331 and p. 554.

2. Clifford Geertz, "Thick Description: Toward an Interpretive Theory of Culture," in his *The Interpretation of Cultures* (New York: Basic Books, 1972), pp. 3-32.

3. For an excellent discussion of Jung's relation to the social thought of his time, and of the confining nature of his terminological apparatus, see Ira Progoff, *Jung's Psychology and its Social Meaning* (New York: Dialogue House Library, 1985), esp. p. 225.

4. Jolande Jacobi elucidates the points of similarity and difference in the work of Jung and Lorenz in *Complex/Archetype/Symbol in the Psychology of C. G. Jung*, trans. Ralph Manheim, Bollingen Series (New York: Pantheon, 1959), pp. 92-93.

5. On the therapeutic forms and uses of speech in classical antiquity, and their exclusion from the praxis of scientific medicine, defined by Virgil as "the silent art" (*muta ars*), see Pedro Lain Entrelago, *The Therapy of the Word in Classical Antiquity*, trans. L. J. Rather and John M. Sharp (New Haven: Yale University Press, 1970), esp. pp. 240-247.

6. Miguel de Unamuno, *The Tragic Sense of Life in Men and Peoples*, trans. J. E. Crawford Flitch (London: Macmillan, 1921), chap. 1. When one compares their positions concerning the potential healing functions of the mythic voice and image, the abyss separating Jung and Freud becomes unbridgeable. Freud did not deny that an active mythic imagination could serve as a safeguard against pathology, but he hardly considered religious minds to be healthy. Rather, "their acceptance of the universal neurosis spares them the task of constructing a personal one" [Sigmund Freud, *The Future of an Illusion* (Garden City, N.Y.: Anchor Books, 1964), p. 72]. For Jung, it was not so much religion as Freud's millennium of the therapeutic that was the illusion. The inflated and disembodied ego of the secular intellectual, epitomized by the Freudian analysand, was a symptom of severe and chronic psychic distortion. In a letter to Arnold Künzli, Jung disparaged Kierkegaard in terms he might well have applied to Freud, as a man who "could settle everything in the study and need not do it in life." In the same letter, he described Kierkegaard's personality as "a jangling hither and thither of displeasing fragmentary souls" and contemptuously dismissed the pivotal Freudian problem of anxiety as a "poltroonery of the ego, shitting its pants" [Jung to Arnold Künzli, March 16, 1943, *Letters, Vol. 1: 1906-1950*, ed. Gerhard Adler and Aniela Jaffé, trans. R.F.C. Hull, Bollingen Series (Princeton: Princeton University Press, 1973), pp. 332-333].

7. C. G. Jung, "On the Psychology of the Trickster Figure," in Paul Radin, *The Trickster: A Study in American Indian Mythology, with Commentaries by Karl Kerényi and C. G. Jung* (New York: Schocken, 1972), p. 200.

8. Ibid., p. 209.

9. Birdwhistell's work reveals how, in the context of small-group interaction, people "give themselves away," in unconscious gestures that clarify questions of identity with respect to status, power, and gender. If we conceive of the psyche as both polyvocal and polytheistic (recalling the work of James Hillman), the archetype likewise functions as a "giveaway," marking its acces-

sion to the podium of the self by its distinctive mode of signing. See Ray Bird-whistell, *Kinesics and Context: Essays on Body Motion Communication* (Phila-delphia: University of Pennsylvania Press, 1970). The work of Claude Shannon on "self-healing" codes and Norbert Wiener on the applications of cybernetics to an improved understanding of sociocultural phenomena is rel-evant to the rethinking of Jung's concepts in linguistic terms. In the early ter-minology of information theory, a monitor was known as a "tell-tale" that clicked into operation in response to actual performance, to guide the heat-seeking missile to its target, or to indicate the arrival of the elevator at the door and thus prevent the passenger from stepping to his doom down an empty shaft. Jung clearly perceived the archetype as such a "tell-tale," a story told by the mind to itself in the interests of guidance. See Norbert Wiener, *The Human Use of Human Beings* (New York: Avon, 1967), p. 36. For an explication of Shannon's theorem and its general relevance to Jung, see Jeremy Campbell, *Grammatical Man: Information, Entropy, Language and Life* (New York: Simon and Schuster, 1982), esp. chaps. 5 and 19.

10. Reinhold Niebuhr, *The Nature and Destiny of Man: A Christian Interpre-tation* (New York: Scribners, 1941), p. 54. See also William Willeford, *The Fool and His Scepter: A Study of Clowns and Jesters and Their Audience* (Evanston: Northwestern University Press, 1969).

11. Matilda Coxe Stevenson, *The Zuni Indians: Their Mythology, Esoteric Fraternities, and Ceremonies*, 23d Annual Report of the Bureau of American Ethnology, 1901-1902 (Washington, D.C.: U.S. Government Printing Office, 1904), pp. 437-438.

12. Steward, "The Ceremonial Buffoon of the American Indian"; Makar-ius, "Ritual Clowns and Symbolical Behavior"; Jacob Levine, "Regression and Primitive Clowning," *Psychoanalytical Quarterly* 30 (1961): 72-83; Louis Hieb, "Meaning and Mismeaning: Toward an Understanding of the Ritual Clown," in *New Perspectives on the Pueblos*, ed. Alfonso Ortiz (Albuquerque: University of New Mexico Press, 1972).

13. Gregory Bateson, "Style, Grace and Information in Primitive Art," in his *Steps to an Ecology of Mind* (New York: Ballantine Books, 1972), p. 139.

14. Bateson, "A Theory of Play and Fantasy," in *Steps to an Ecology of Mind*, p. 180.

15. Ibid., p. 182.

16. See Ross N. Crumrine, "Čapakoba, The Mayo Easter Ceremonial Im-personator: Explanations of Ritual Clowning," *Journal for the Scientific Study of Religion* 8 (Spring 1969): 1-22; Arden King, "North American Indian Clowns and Creativity," in *Forms of Play of Native North Americans*, ed. Norbeck and Ferrer; Alfred North Whitehead, *Modes of Thought* (New York: Macmillan, 1983), p. 67. In an essay that has just come to my attention, Barbara Babcock offers an interpretation of the trickster that converges in many intriguing ways with the viewpoints being expressed here. Babcock rethinks the literature on the trickster in terms of Victor Turner's concepts of "liminality," "structure," and "anti-structure." She rejects a functionalist model and enlists Arthur Koestler's notion of "the bisociation of two matrices" as the foundation of

creativity. Tricksters and clowns are "double-minded" in order to break the constraining molds of the apparent and the real. Through negation and symbolic inversion, the trickster "introduces death and with it all possibilities to the world." See Barbara Babcock, "A Tolerated Margin of Mess": The Trickster and His Tales Reconsidered," in *Critical Essays on Native American Literature*, ed. Andrew Wiget (Boston: G. K. Hall, 1985), pp. 179-182; Victor Turner, *The Ritual Process: Structure and Anti-Structure* (Chicago: Aldine, 1969); Arthur Koester, *The Act of Creation* (New York: Dell Publishing Co., 1964), pp. 35-36.

17. For a discussion of the many offices of Hermes, see Walter Burkert, *Greek Religion: Archaic and Classical*, trans. John Raffan (London: Basil Blackwell, 1985), pp. 156-158.

18. For a provocative discussion of the clown's transgression of boundaries as exemplified in the films of Charlie Chaplin, see Willeford, *The Fool and His Scepter*, chap. 8.

19. For a discussion of the new systems theory, which accounts for the genesis of chemical order through fluctuations under far-from-equilibrium conditions, see Ilya Prigogine and Isabelle Stengers, *Order Out of Chaos: Man's New Dialogue with Nature* (New York: Bantam, 1984). Prigogine refers to the "canning" of Faust's homunculus on p. 128.

20. Willeford, *The Fool and His Scepter*, p. 10.

21. Mikhail Bakhtin, *Rabelais and His World*, trans. Helene Iswolsky (Bloomington: Indiana University Press, 1984), pp. 20-21.

22. David Marr, *Vision: A Computational Investigation into the Human Representation of Visual Information* (San Francisco: W. H. Freeman, 1982), p. 21.

23. Ibid., p. 27.

24. Stanley Diamond, "Plato and the Definition of the Primitive," in *Primitive Views of the World*, ed. Stanley Diamond (New York: Columbia University Press, 1964).

25. Eric A. Havelock, *Preface to Plato* (Cambridge, Mass.: Harvard University Press, 1963); see also Walter Ong, *Orality and Literacy: The Technologizing of the Word* (London: Methuen, 1982), and Claude Lévi-Strauss, *Myth and Meaning* (New York: Schocken, 1979), p. 17.

26. Thomas E. Sanders and Walter W. Peck, eds., *Literature of the American Indian* (New York: Glencoe Press, 1973), p. 334.

27. Gregory Bateson attributes this line to Blake in *Mind and Nature* and in *Steps to an Ecology of Mind*. In his *Note-Book, 1808-11*, Blake wrote, "Madmen see outlines and therefore they draw them," but a careful search of his writings (via concordance) failed to uncover the line attributed to him here. Though putative, the citation is nevertheless in harmony with Blake's philosophy. In Blake's view, wisdom and madness merge in the mind of the myth-making artist whose task it is to give definitive form to those visions of unity and boundary that escape the censorship of instrumental reason. As Bateson points out repeatedly, Blake's epistemology prefigures the discoveries of modern information theory, with its emphasis on instruction as prior to substance, and its demonstration that information (perception of difference) must be concen-

trated at outlines. See Bateson, "Metalogue: Why Do Things Have Outlines?" in *Steps to an Ecology of Mind*, pp. 27-37, and *Mind and Nature: A Necessary Unity* (New York: E. P. Dutton, 1979), p. 97n. See also William Blake, *Complete Writings*, ed. Geoffrey Keynes (London: Oxford University Press, 1969), p. 549; and David V. Erdman, ed., *A Concordance to the Writings of William Blake*, 4 vols. (Ithaca: Cornell University Press, 1967).

28. Bakhtin, *Rabelais and His World*, p. 11.

29. Bateson, "Style, Grace and Information in Primitive Art," in *Steps to an Ecology of Mind*. Bateson credits Otto Fenichel with the insight that "primary process" is without negatives and markers of time, but Freud was explicit on these points. In his paper "Negation" he wrote, "in analysis, we never discover 'No' in the unconscious." As early as 1915, Freud had remarked on the capacity of the unconscious to tolerate contradiction. For Freud, as for Jung, the logic of desire is timeless and affirmative. The relicts of pure desire that float to the surface of consciousness are the mind's natural objects of humor and terror. Sigmund Freud, "The Unconscious," in *Collected Papers*, vol. 4, ed. Joan Riviere (New York: Basic Books, 1959), p. 119, and "Negation" in *Collected Papers*, vol. 5, ed. James Strachey (New York: Basic Books, 1959), pp. 181-186. Fenichel's work is still relevant to students of myth in that it clearly amplified the metaphoric foundations of the dreamwork in a way that often reveals the structuralist debt to psychoanalysis. In Fenichel's refinement of Freudian technique, neither the dream nor the myth can be reduced to a wish-impulse without a linguistic understanding of the semiotic processes that intervene. In his paper, "Examples of Dream Analysis," the word "bees" in a patient's dream is shown to be an apt metaphor for "dangerous pleasure." "After all," he writes, "what does a child know about bees? They make honey and they sting." According to Fenichel, the association of the clown, the dwarf, and the prodigy is not fortuitous, since all are united in their declaration of "the greatness of the little one" (i.e., the pregenital "female" phallus of the emotionally injured child). Thus the prevalence of transvestite or female "trick-shooters" in vaudeville. (Annie, get your gun!) Of course, the crucial difference between such Freudian interpretations and the neo-Jungian viewpoint of the author hinges on the identification of clowning behavior as so much symptomatic flotsam or as a primal form of "lay analysis." See "Examples of Dream Analysis" in *The Collected Papers of Otto Fenichel*, 1st ser., ed. Hanna Fenichel and David Rapaport (New York: W. W. Norton, 1953), p. 126, and "The Symbolic Equation: Girl = Phallus," in *The Collected Papers of Otto Fenichel*, 2d ser., ed. Hanna Fenichel and David Rapaport (New York: W. W. Norton, 1954), p. 13.

30. Bakhtin, *Rabelais and His World*, p. 11.

31. Jung, "On the Psychology of the Trickster Figure," p. 196.

32. Mischa Titiev, *The Hopi Indians of Old Oraibi: Change and Continuity* (Ann Arbor: The University of Michigan Press, 1972), p. 256.

33. Sigmund Freud, "Mourning and Melancholia," in *Collected Papers*, vol. 41, pp. 152-170.

34. James Hillman, *The Dream and the Underworld* (New York: Harper and

Row, 1979), p. 39. In an intriguing parallel observation, Edmund Carpenter points out that the female ivory figurines of the Greenland Thule culture (so similar to the Upper Paleolithic Venus effigies) were perforated at the feet for inverted suspension and as such represented deceased ancestors. See Edmund Carpenter, *Eskimo Realities* (New York: Holt, Rinehart and Winston, 1973), pp. 146-147.

35. Weston LaBarre, *Muelos: A Stone Age Superstition about Sexuality* (New York: Columbia University Press, 1984).

36. Sigmund Freud, "The Antithetical Sense of Primal Words," in *Collected Papers*, vol. 4, pp. 184-191.

37. Claude Lévi-Strauss, "The Structural Study of Myth," in his *Structural Anthropology* (Garden City, N.Y.: Doubleday, 1967), pp. 202-228. In his interview with George Charbonnier, Lévi-Strauss defines myth as "the most fundamental form of inauthenticity," that is, as an extreme form of abstract, and therefore detached (as opposed to concrete and involved), knowledge of the other. George Charbonnier, *Conversations with Claude Lévi-Strauss* (London: Jonathan Cape, 1969), pp. 53-56.

38. According to David Miller, Orestes is unique in possessing the flaws of both *hubris* (as masculine aggression) and *erinus* (as maternal passion and fury). He requires a double catharsis, of separation and unification. Miller seems to agree with Aeschylus, that pious Athena is up to the job of curing this fellow, but dialectical "splitting" of this severity requires the more drastic catharsis of laughter. See David Miller, "Orestes: Myth and Dream as Catharsis," in *Myths, Dreams and Religion*, ed. Joseph Campbell (New York: E. P. Dutton, 1970), pp. 26-47.

39. Sigmund Freud, "The Relation of the Poet to Daydreaming," in *Collected Papers*, vol. 4, p. 180.

40. C. G. Jung, "The Spiritual Problem of Modern Man," in *The Portable Jung*, ed. Joseph Campbell (New York: Penguin Books, 1971), p. 470.

41. Bakhtin, *Rabelais and His World*, p. 25.

42. Gregory Bateson and Mary Catherine Bateson, *Angels Fear: Towards an Epistemology of the Sacred* (New York: Macmillan, 1987), pp. 9-15, 135-144.

43. *The Bhagavad-Gita: Krishna's Counsel in Time of War*, trans. Barbara Stoler Miller (New York: Bantam, 1986), pp. 97-107.

44. Cited by A. K. Coomaraswamy in "Bhakta Aspects of the Atman Doctrine," in *Coomaraswamy: 2. Selected Papers: Metaphysics*, ed. Roger Lipsey, Bollingen Series (Princeton: Princeton University Press, 1977), p. 392.

45. Coomaraswamy discusses metaphors of obesity and weight and strategies for "reducing" in Eastern mysticism, in "On the Indian and Traditional Psychology, or Rather Pneumatology" in *Coomaraswamy: 2. Selected Papers*, p. 123. For a discussion of levitation in both Buddhism and Christianity, see his *Hinduism and Buddhism* (Westport: Greenwood Press, 1971), p. 68 and p. 83n.

46. James Hillman sees the moment of "*carnem levare*" as one of "psychization that removes the naturalistic attitude." Far from representing a mere "exuberance of flesh," the circus, in Hillman's view, is an "*opus contra naturam that*

overcomes gravity and establishes a thoroughly pneumatic world." See *The Dream and the Underworld*, p. 178.

47. Mary Douglas presents a cogent critique of Jung's "eulogy of spiritual poverty as a source of strength and self-knowledge." "The fullest self-knowledge," she writes, "will take account of the social conditions which affect the development of the self." See Mary Douglas, *Natural Symbols* (New York: Vintage Books, 1973), p. 152.

48. Coomaraswamy, "Primitive Mentality," in *Coomaraswamy: 1. Selected Papers: Traditional Art and Symbolism*, ed. Roger Lipsey, Bollingen Series (Princeton: Princeton University Press, 1977), p. 289.

49. Jung, "On the Psychology of the Trickster Figure," p. 205.

50. For a troubling discussion of the projective psychodynamics of technocratic racism, as "actions taken toward an *Other*, a term we may define as the negation of the socially affirmed self," see Joel Kovel, *White Racism: A Psychohistory* (New York: Columbia University Press, 1984), pp. xxix-xxx.

51. Thomas Mann, "Freud and the Future," in his *Essays of Three Decades*, trans. H. T. Lowe-Porter (New York: Alfred A. Knopf, 1965), p. 149.

52. Reflecting on his experience on the mountaintop, Hans Castorp reveals his creator's debt to Jung. "Now I know that it is not out of our single souls we dream. We dream anonymously and communally, if each after his fashion. The great soul of which we are a part may dream through us, in our manner of dreaming, its own secret dreams, of its youth, its hope, its joy and peace— and its blood sacrifice." *The Magic Mountain*, trans. H. T. Lowe-Porter (New York: Vintage, 1969) p. 495. In his *Journal*, Mircea Eliade recalls Cusa's principle, similar to the *enantiodromia* of Heraclitus on the one hand and to Niels Bohr's explication of the quantum on the other. Eliade asks, "How is liberty possible in a conditioned universe? How can one live in history without betraying it, without denying it, and still partake of a transhistorical reality?" Neither Freud nor Jung successfully resolves the political and ethical dilemmas of a life dedicated to the attainment of a therapeutic gnosis, with its potential for regression into the serene death-in-life of stylitism. See Mircea Eliade, *No Souvenirs: Journal, 1957-1969*, trans. Fred H. Johnson, Jr. (San Francisco: Harper and Row, 1977), p. 31. Paul Chilton describes the mythic and phallic vocabulary of nuclear strategy including the successive use of the terms "Little Boy" and "Fat Man" to designate the first atomic devices in "Nukespeak: Nuclear Language, Culture and Propaganda," in *The Nuclear Predicament*, ed. Donna U. Gregory (New York: St. Martin's Press, 1986), pp. 127-142. Oppenheimer's ominous recollection was from the eleventh book of the *Bhagavad-Gita*. In most translations, the word "death" (*Kala*) is translated as "Time," but the meaning in Sanskrit is the same.

# Jung
# Contra
# Freud

## What It Means
## To Be Funny    Stanley Diamond

The trickster cannot be exiled from the human species, although representatives of this or that establishment have tried, time and again, in the history of Western civilization to banish him/her/it for good. But always Trickster returns, in fact never leaves, a heterogeneous and androgynous beauty of a figure. The more totalitarian a state, the more society operates by reductive signals, driving symbols underground, the harsher the efforts to cast out Trickster. The trickster is no aberration, which we call upon to vent our frustrations; nor is it conceptual. It is rather integral to the definition of the human existence, one half of the tragicomic whole of the human experience.

There is a striking episode in the film based on the *The Seventh Cross*, Anna Seagher's largely forgotten novel about the early anti-Nazi resistance in the Germany that was to become Hitler's. A trapeze artist, a veteran circus performer, who was a courier for the underground, is after a long chase—punctuated by his many brilliant leaps and cunning escapes—finally trapped on a high roof by a Nazi death squad. The circus performer realizes the hopelessness of his position, spots a tower above the roof, and climbs to the top at breakneck speed, hesitates for a moment, and then in full view of his frustrated pursuers, launches himself into a magnificent swan dive, vital and defiant, until the instant of his death.

I have no idea what Freud would say about such a man, but I am sure—I think I am sure—that Jung would recognize him as a descendant of the trickster, as a being of ultimate humor, a comic performer, as are all the traditional partners in a circus—the clowns, the high-wire artists—all bound together by a defiance of death inevitably linked to a comic sense of life. Typically, as one might have anticipated, circus performers, like gypsies, are just about impossible to regiment. (Even the commercialized three-ring affairs that pass for circuses in American society still resonate to some degree with the tragicomedy, the daring, and the parodistic acts that explain the circus's continued hold on the

67

urban imagination.) Can one imagine an honest clown as a Nazi? So as it turned out, I was not surprised to hear from friends of mine in Germany whose families had been in the anti-Nazi underground that circus performers were among the avant-garde in the spontaneous resistance to fascism. Like gypsies, they have no love for the state, a primitive horror of being counted and classified, and a life of their own that somehow survived the overburden of modern society.

Of course, such people had comrades in the anti-Nazi enterprise. Among them were artisans, shoemakers in particular, who refused to knuckle under to *der Staat über Alles*. And I was reminded that it was the anarchist artisans who were at the heart of the Paris Commune.

But perhaps the most remarkable element in the anti-Nazi underground through the entire period of fascist domination were the children, the youth, ranging in age from ten to eleven to eighteen, nineteen, twenty, and older. These young people who named themselves the Edelweiss Pirates (Edelweiss sometimes varying with the locality), also known as Navajos (particularly in Cologne), demystified the fascist denouement of high German civilization in a recapitulation of primitive opposition to the state. They snapped their fingers under the noses of the Nazis. And, in a calculated opposition to the *Hitlerjugend*, whom they ambushed and challenged, dressed as "sloppily" as possible, spoke as dangerously as possible, stole from Nazi depots, danced and sang to the beat of American jazz, and in response to "Heil Hitler" typically said, "Heil Benny Goodman." The courage and insight of these children is well documented in German archives, wherein they are considered to be criminals, traitors, inferior elements, and so on. Wherever the fascists imposed order, they proclaimed disorder. And in their local territoriality they exposed for our distanced observation the impossibility of any absolute state tyranny, even in a technocratic society; the closer one came to the localities, the more holes appeared in the self-advertised, seamless Nazi structure, and the more corruptible the neighborhood Gauleiters are revealed to be. These underground children seemed to understand that terrorism was a sign of impotence and could not be equated with omniscience. And, moreover, they knew that their anti-Nazism, their band-organized primitivism, must eventually be opposed to the order of the state itself. In fact, they were sophisticated enough to despise without completely particularizing the Nazis; that is, if their comic rage were stimulated by the *Hitlerjugend*, it carried past that and penetrated the very structure and meaning of state hegemony. They knew in their skins, and parodied, the morbid themes in German culture that smoothed the way for fascism. One is reminded of Goethe's assertion that he would rather live under injustice than in disorder.[1] Or Weber's frigid notion of the bureaucratic future and his consequent definition of social responsibility, which included the helplessness of the person, now and forever a functionary. Or Hegel's projection of the divine order of the universe, the ultimate hierarchy that rationalizes and reflects quotidian hegemony. It is this notion of order/disorder that contextualizes the duplicity and comic reversals of the trickster and that motivated the Edelweiss Pirates, the young Navajos. A typical song in opposition is worth relating:

> We all sat in the tavern
> with a pipe and a glass of wine,
> a goodly drop of malt and hop,
> and the devil calls the tune.
>
> Hark the hearty fellows sing!
> Strum that banjo, pluck that string!
> and the lasses all join in.
> We're going to get rid of Hitler,
> and he can't do a thing.
>
> The Hamburg sirens sound,
> time for Navajos to go.
> A tavern's just the place
> to kiss a girl goodbye.
> Rio de Janeiro, *caballero*, ahoy!
> An Edelweiss Pirate is faithful and true.
>
> Hitler's power may lay us low,
> and keep us locked in chains,
> but we will smash the chains one day,
> we'll be free again.
> We've got fists and we can fight,
> We've got knives and we'll get them out.
> We want freedom, don't we, boys?
> We're the fighting Navajos.
>
> Out on the high road, down in the ditch.
> There's some Hitler Youth
> Patrolmen, and they're getting black as pitch.
> Sorry if it hurts, mates, sorry we can't stay.
> We're Edelweiss Pirates, and we're on our way.
>
> We march banks of Ruhr and Rhine
> and smash the Hitler Youth in twain.
> Our song is freedom, love and life,
> We're Pirates of the Edelweiss.

> Polar bear, listen, we're talking to you
> Our land isn't free, we're telling you true.
> Get our cudgels and come into town
> and smash in the skulls of the bosses in brown.[2]

Why and how and at what people laugh is perhaps the most revealing of human actions. According to Freud, humor is basically confined to wit, including punning and wordplay. But wit can hardly be disconnected from *schadenfreude*, that is, the enjoyment of another's discomfort, humor at the expense of the other, of which Freud was, of course, fully aware. Wit, he says, emerges from the unconscious—that reservoir of unresolved ambiguity and not-so-free association. Wit can be morbid, light, gentle, heavy, slow, but it is always *en passant*, and one is always laughing at the other, or at least admiring oneself. But more important, I think, for an understanding of the configuration of Freud's work, his notion of wit—wordplay—is the key to his insistent significations. Indeed, one could extend Freud's notion of wit to some of the most precious, and perhaps amusing, Freudian signs. Why should an umbrella stand for a penis? Does that include all umbrellas, open, closed, or functioning in a driving rainstorm? Not that Freud ignored contexts. But where did he draw the line? One can of course make a slight joke, a witticism about an umbrella standing for a penis, and then reversing it by saying: of course, there's no way a penis can stand for an umbrella. It may be of some interest that several years ago while working with a secluded people in North Central Nigeria, I was struck by the shape of certain pillars of stone that they defined as shrines: a narrow pillar, perhaps anywhere from six to nine feet high, with a circle of small stones around the base, and a loose round stone that crowned the top. This reminds me of a penis, I said to myself and later to them, and they laughed, agreeing, but added "Of course, it is not." That had the effect of chilling the Freudian interpretation I was about to undertake. In other words, there was no repression of the point, hence no Freudian signification. Their understanding of what they themselves had constructed was not reducible to psychoanalytic interpretations of any sort.

One could have a certain amount of fun at Freud's expense, putting into question the entire corpus of linguistic transmutations. One would wind up with a quite impressive gestalt of private figures. Stated more moderately, Freud had to put everything to use: nothing took off by itself. Humor was compressed into wit, and wit was pressed into the service of the unconscious, that is, as Freud defined the unconscious. But Freud had no visible sense of the comic, of the trickster, laughing everything out of existence, in the mode of that doubleness so evident in the mythology and rituals of primitive peoples. How often does a clown parody the most serious struggle for identity that an initiate might be undergoing? Perhaps one could say that the trickster is the personification of the unconscious—the creator and destroyer of the world—the vessel of every imaginable, and often grotesquely debased, human fantasy (cf. Jung's "shadow" that follows each of us). But that would be incomplete, a stab in the dark. How can one exhaust the meanings of the human spirit? How can one reduce, or split, the tragicomedies of existence? Given Freud's dependence on aspects of the Greek drama, one questions why he ignored pre-Socratic insights on the one hand, and transcendent moments—as in Sophocles' own resolution of the blind king's dilemma in *Oedipus at Colonus*—on the other.

It has been said that Freud was a great novelist, and Freud himself asserted that he had originally cast his final work as a novel. Perhaps an apt description of this master of nuanced language would be as a major and keen-witted, if monothematic, tautologically repetitive storyteller. But because Freud had no demonstrable sense of the trickster, of the *comic* duality, of transcendence, of the irreducibly sacred—that is, of humanity in its fullness—he had not much of a sense of culture either. Or putting it another way, the understanding of culture embraces the qualities that he scanted. In his slender and curiously unrevealing autobiography, he concludes by insisting that he began with the problem of culture, ends with the problem of culture, and that the notion of culture has always been his fundamental concern. But the declarations are insubstantial. For, in the Freudian account, symbols are reduced to significations, and significations fall most often beneath the level of consciousness. Art and religion are summarily dealt with, that is to say, they are each in its own way the result of certain deformations, or projections. In the Freudian world, there is a great determination: everything seems, indeed must be, explainable. And one senses that the absence of explanation, the denial of the omniscient language of science, or the acceptance of mystery are impermissible—and more than that, they are heresies. The Freudian world is a perfect mesh of projected and retrojected mythic events that fit and explain, once and for all, individual psychodynamic manifestations.

This leads directly to Freud's complex confrontation with Jung. Once Jung separated himself from Freud, his intoxication with the conundrums of human culture became increasingly evident. He refused to acknowledge the generality of Freud's theory of neurosis and the primacy of his related historical explanations, and in making his objections specific he referred to Freud's Jewish background (only one generation removed from the *shtetl*) as accounting for the web of Freudian significations and, more pertinently, for the cerebral intensity of the work, in the absence of a deeply developed cultural context. In a word, life was not a text, and culture was not reducible to Freud's notion of origins, acting out, and neurotic repression. Nonetheless, Jung's respect for the depth of Freud's insights within the therapeutic milieu that he carved out of the society in which he worked, and for his methods, never wavered.

One of the more interesting, and subtle, confrontations between Freud and Jung, as the latter became increasingly intrigued by and to some degree dependent on primitive cultural formulations (e.g., the trickster) was with reference to the book of Job. Here, Jung's *Answer to Job* is also an answer to Freud, an answer more generally to Old Testamentarian repressive ethical tabulations, as well as a presentation of an alternative theology. Freud of course could hardly see himself as an exclusionary builder of laws, or as a prophet, but Jung's insight is, I think, sound. Moreover, *Answer to Job* is Jung's novel in response qua novel to *Moses and Monotheism*, wherein Jung claims that Job's words have not only reached the ear of God but have elicited a sympathetic response. One notices at once the availability of the sacred in Jung's perspective, as opposed to Freud's stern distancing of God the Father. If there is so much suffering on earth, the God of Job concludes—rather as a divine female would—that it is then his responsibility to descend and live for a season as a human being—with the sanction that he must never, under any circumstance, use his divine power to extricate himself from the human predicament. This decision by God "to change his own nature" (*CW* 11: par. 625, p. 397) implies the presence of the feminine principle, namely Sophia, as Jung contends: "Yahweh has allowed himself to be extensively influenced by Sophia" (*CW* 11: par. 625, p. 398). Hence the appearance of Jesus Christ, who suffers as a man to the point of his crucifixion "as if Job and Yahweh were combined in a single personality. Yahweh's intention to become human, which resulted from his collision with Job, is fulfilled in Christ's life and suffering" (*CW* 11: par. 648, p. 409). Here Jung is deploying the notion of grace, which has never been an Old Testament virtue, but which in Western iconography is introduced into the world through the figure deified and adopted by those who were to call themselves Christians.

Now there is not much humor in *Answer to Job*; it is a grave work. But it is a metaphor for the necessity of grace. Clearly, grace and the capacity for the comic—that is, for trickster reversals—walk hand in hand. (See the trapeze artists with which this essay began.) There is more to consider. In the absence of the trickster figure—that sense of comic reversal that we witness as a kind of residue at the beginnings of

European civilization in the Dionysian satyr play—there can be no sense of tragedy. Tragedy and comedy, not wit but comedy, are twin sisters. The struggle for identity and the capacity to obliterate identity, to blow it away and hence exert the mastery of an unrepressed and unrepressive morality, is what defines grace. One should note that Jung's notion of the good in *Answer to Job* is simply the absence of evil "with its implication of great variety in acceptable human actions," as opposed to Freud's conception of the good, which is always associated with the deadly struggle against the forces of darkness by means of a single process, making for a uniformity of the human experience.

In line with such confrontations, of course, is Jung's notion of archetypes as the ground for culture. Culture thus becomes the basis of human being—the specificity of the archetypes aside. And with culture comes the self-constitution of reality, followed by individuation—the attainment of mature meanings through the career of the person in the world, developing through the very texture of kin relations, to the attainment of a self. And here Jung criticizes Western civilization by stating that these meanings are rarely attained, that most people are condemned to lives of social behaviorism, beyond which they cannot emerge, the collapse occurring after the attainment of sexual potency; a new, procreative family structure; and a vocation.

Jung's break with Freud was most fruitfully perceived as a confrontation of incompatible cultural visions. Jung abandoned Freud, as Freud would have it, even becoming anti-Semitic, as others would have it; but above all, he attempted to understand Freud's representation of the West and, correlatively, the problematic of the West itself, most clearly drawn in Jung's essays on art, loneliness, and religion. It is claimed by a number of Freud's biographers that after his defection, and the gathering force of his heretical work became obvious, Freud, at the very mention of Jung's name, would fall into a faint. One can see why. Jung was the Goy, the absolute other, whom one could nevertheless reach out and touch but never grasp: Jung was the subordinated female. He represented the possibility of a culture beyond Freud's experience, a refusal to fit into the profoundly brilliant but exclusive mode of Freud's own understandings and misunderstandings.

It is in the figure of the trickster that we best catch a glimpse of Jung's more encompassing vision of culture, a vision in which the desperate defiance of the trapeze artist, the comic daring of circus performers, the irreverence of children, the ambivalence of the human spirit and the transcendent striving toward unity, are but some of the different aspects of the trickster dynamic. It was, perhaps, Jung's insight into the essential union of opposites, into trickster reversals, and his recognition of the connection between comedy and tragedy, between grace and suffering, that was incompatible with Freud's more rigidly delineated view of civilization. Moreover, it is perhaps this Jungian vision of culture that offers greatest insight into Jung's problematical relationship with Nazi Germany, about which something remains to be said.

Was Jung's flirtation with the German psychoanalytic association at the beginning of the Nazi period solely the result of his desire to internationalize the group and thus prevent its fascisization? Is there any sound evidence that Jung was, even if for a short time, drawn to the false promise of social-cultural revival in which the Nazis dealt?[3] No, he was not drawn to the Nazis but to the possibilities of a cultured German nation. This mistake casts a shadow of a personal tragedy, not a tragedy but the brooding intimation of one, and lends support to Freud's pessimism and skepticism about the illusions of civilization, even when presumably opposed to the character of civilization itself. Was Jung then another illusionist, trading in cheap mysteries and odd beliefs? If so, Freud would have had the last laugh, at the expense of the other, of course. And he would have been right, if limited, because even in defeat, as Western civilization disintegrates, Jung's vision was more spacious.

# Notes

1. "I would rather put up with an injustice than tolerate a state of disorder"; Johann Wolfgang von Goethe, quoted in Thomas Wiseman, *Children of the Ruins* (Boston: Little, Brown, and Co., 1986), p. 73.

2. Detlev J. K. Peuckert, *Inside Nazi Germany: Conformity, Opposition, Racism in Everyday Life* (New Haven: Yale University Press, 1987), p. 157.

3. After examining the available information regarding Jung's anti-Semitism and pro-Nazi convictions, I see no reason to change my opinion that Jung was (1) not an anti-Semite and (2) not a Nazi in any recognizable sense of the term. Volume 10 of Jung's Collected Works, *Civilization in Transition*, particularly paragraphs 371-487, will be of interest to the reader in this connection. In addition, it would seem to deserve note that a senior colleague of mine, Paul

Radin, had known Jung for many years in Switzerland and had participated actively in several Ascona conferences. Radin was a Jew, having been born in East Prussia, and he was a scholar of international stature, perhaps the most cultivated anthropologist of his period. Politically he had strong radical sympathies, and his being Jewish was important to him in a number of dimensions. Yet, when I was preparing a list of contributors for his Festschrift, which I edited, he added Jung's name to it. I consequently wrote to Jung in Switzerland. He replied promptly, courteously, and full of praise for Radin, but he felt he was then too old to undertake another project.

# Popular   John Carlin
# Culture   Leslie Fiedler
# Symposium   Harold Schechter

*Schechter*: How useful is Jung in giving us insight into the nature of popular art and the way it works on the community at large? This is the central question that any critic who is interested in the relation between myth and popular culture must ask. Jung himself, as far as I know, was not much concerned with popular art, although he mentions Rider Haggard's *She* as an example of the anima archetype. In his essay on the trickster, however, he refers to an interesting article, called "Daily Paper Pantheon," by an English psychoanalyst named Alan McGlashan, in which McGlashan talks about the parallels between comic strip characters and the great figures of classical mythology. In my work, I looked (under the influence of Professor Fiedler) at the connections between "pop art" and Jungian archetypes. Popular art is full of archetypes and is a rich source of material for anyone interested in archetypal images; in fact, popular art consists almost entirely of these images, unelaborated by any kind of aesthetic development. Ultimately, however, the question arises: How valid is it to look at pop art in light of Jung's theories, given the apparent discrepancy between the concept of myth, in the exalted sense that Jung means that term—as an embodiment of the highest and most enduring truths—and the essentially *schlocky* nature of popular art, the vast bulk of which is utterly exploitative and ephemeral?

*Fiedler*: I am interested only in the kinds of popular literature that live long and please many, so that, as far as I am concerned, we should not spend much time talking today about more ephemeral works, however interesting. We should concentrate on works that, despite critics who say they are without literary merit and despite the fact that they often distort history and the ideas contained in them are truly vicious and antisocial, somehow manage to live on and on and on. Among these works is Rider Haggard's *She*, which has been mentioned, as is quite proper in light of the fact that it was a book that obsessed Jung, who refers to it over and over again. The cases of *Tarzan of the Apes* and *Sherlock Holmes* are similar, and I hope we manage to talk about them before we are through. I am determined, in any case, to deal with the

76

best-selling popular novel of all time, the "top of the pops," as it were, whose fiftieth anniverssary we are celebrating this year. I am referring to *Gone With the Wind*, of course, which is not only being resold in book form and replayed as a film but has been memorialized in an actual icon. Recently in the *TV Guide*, there appeared an ad for a porcelain bisque figure of Vivien Leigh as Scarlett O'Hara, which can presumably be bought and set up in a place of honor in any household, quite like the Blessed Virgin or sacred figures of other sects.

I am interested in the archetypal context of such works, which I consider to be what gives them, despite their aesthetic and ethical weakness, so long a life. I guess this makes me, in a sense, a Jungian. But I am, I should like to make clear, also an *anti*-Jungian insofar as I find Jung's definition of what an archetype is, especially his view of its ontological status, quite unacceptable. Archetypes seem to me to be not as Jung believed, eternal and immortal, but rather invented at particular points in history, changing as that history changes and sometimes eventually dying when their psycho-social uses are exhausted.

I should add in a kind of parenthesis that there is something else I object to in Jung, as I have been strongly reminded when I recently reread Jung's absolutely fascinating, immensely puzzling, and totally wrongheaded essay on the book of Job, called *An Answer to Job*. It is not merely that he seems quite incapable of understanding the Jewish psyche; but that as a Hebrew of the Hebrews and a Pharisee of the Pharisees, which is to say an unreconstructed monotheist, I have trouble coming to terms with Jung's strange brand of polytheistic Christianity or, better perhaps, Christianoid polytheism.

I believe, moreover, that archetypes are not universal in their appeal, since the psycho-social needs they serve belong to particular constituencies, defined by sex, race, class, and generation. An example of such a parochial archetype is the one in which I have been interested for a long time, the uniquely American myth of interethnic male bonding in the wilderness. It has not yet outlived its usefulness, having survived all the way from James Fenimore Cooper's *Leatherstocking Tales* through *Star Trek*, where it reappears in the relationship of Captain Kirk and Mr. Spock. At the present moment it exists in several popular television shows, most notably perhaps *Miami Vice*, at the center of which Tubbs and Crockett are united by a bond threatened whenever women come into their lives. This suggests that the myth they embody is profoundly misogynist and presumably will disappear when (if ever!) men's fear of women disappears. The archetype was invented for white Anglo-Saxon Protestant males in early nineteenth-century America, but it has lasted into the modern, postmodern, bourgeois, postbourgeois world. Though its end cannot be predicted, its moment of origin can be dated exactly. It was the year 1800, with the appearance in print of the adventures of the trapper Alexander Henry, from which Cooper may have derived it, though perhaps he caught it from the general ambience of his world, out of the air around him.

*Carlin*: I want to state for the record that I find most popular culture not worthy of serious attention, but that holds true for virtually all forms of cultural expression: novels, movies, theater, and so on. What is important about popular culture and makes it worth studying in an academic context is that it is a vast ocean of information through which we cannot help but swim. What I hope we will do here today is discriminate among levels of popular cultural expression. So let us say, in very basic terms, that there are three ways to apply theory constructively to popular culture. The first critical analysis of cultural, as opposed to aesthetic, expression was the Marxist approach. In general, this analysis looked to popular forms of expression as representations of certain stereotypes or ideologies about the societies in which they were created. This method allowed the analyst to reveal certain aspects of the social structure that were repressed on a conscious level.

The second way is a psychological analysis, which comes closest to Jung's concept of the archetype. This is another way of looking at popular culture, not in terms of its own intrinsic values, but how it illustrates or allows us to peek into the psyche of the civilization in which it is created and then, of course, to link that psyche to other civilizations and to other cultures, both historically and geographically.

But I think in a contemporary context there is a third way of looking at popular culture, which is more sensitive to its own values and appreciates it as an aesthetic rather than socio-economic or psychological structure. This third approach takes the aesthetics of popular culture on its own terms. The reason why this approach is the least employed is that it is perhaps the most difficult and truly challenging to the ideological assumptions upon which most academic analysis rests. In some ways, as critics, we want to like what is the worst about pop culture, what is the most *schlocky*, what is the most degraded, as opposed to pop culture that has academic or intellectual pretensions, because that often leads to a middlebrow result. What is interesting about intelligent pop culture is not so much its refinement but its ability to challenge our notion of what is "high" culture. I think this potential is obvious to anyone who grew up after World War II in an environment that is so heavily saturated with the semiotic information of American pop culture. It remains to be seen whether this potential will be actualized and what its final effect will be.

I cannot avoid being conscious of the irony of regarding pop culture in this context as something we can shape and control, because I think the reason we are actually here and why people are fascinated by pop culture is precisely because it is beyond our control. It is not really an individual means of expression in the same way that we tend to look at fine art. In some ways it is a collective form of expression and therefore more suited to the late twentieth century than the sort of nineteenth-century notions of individuality and autonomous expression that one typically finds admired in art.

*Schechter*: Regarding the myth of interethnic male bonding in the wilderness, you say that archetypes are invented with history. I wonder whether there are analogues to that myth in ancient cultures—in the story of Gilgamesh, for example. In other words, is the myth you identify actually just a cultural inflection of a more universal pattern? Perhaps the most useful thing that Jung provides the critic of pop culture is a way of putting the products of the entertainment industry into some kind of meaningful context, of allowing us to see that the fictions we consume so avidly on television and film are really updated versions of narratives that have entertained human beings since storytelling began. Exactly *why* we need to hear "the same old stories" over and over again—just what those myths mean to us—is hard, perhaps impossible, to say. But what I wonder about here is the issue of universality, since as Jung, Joseph Campbell, and others point out, myths have both a universal and cultural aspect, and any particular telling is simply a local variant of the archetypal pattern.

*Fiedler*: I know what you mean, and though your arguments are plausible, I am not convinced. I have no doubt that there are elements in other myths of male bonding analogous to some of the elements in the essentially misogynist and uniquely American myth of male bonding in the wilderness. What interests me, however, are not those analogies but the profound differences that separate their peculiar configurations in different cultures. Close to the time of the appearance of the American myth, for instance there is Defoe's account of the relationship between Robinson Crusoe and Friday on their desert island. But the difference of that basic mythic structure from the one I have been talking about is demonstrated by the fact that the first word that Crusoe teaches Friday, in English of course, is "master." Theirs is not a relationship of equals like the American myth that involves the disparate recognition of such equality, despite ethnic differences. That American myth, in fact, comes into existence only when Europeans encounter in

79

what they had thought of as *una terra senza gente* an uninhabited world, of people culturally quite different from themselves but undeniably human. At that moment the ex-European becomes a Euro-American, quite unlike Crusoe who remains an unreconstructed Englishman. When that confrontation occurred, a myth was invented that continues to haunt the common memory of all Americans. (I almost said "collective unconscious," a term that I find confusing and unsympathetic and have therefore vowed never again to use.)

One might have expected that that original myth would disappear with the urbanization of America, when it is more typically Afro-Americans than Native Americans that Euro-Americans meet in their daily lives. It has, however, proved adaptable to the new circumstances, though it must be understood that it has never been universal in its appeal, since it satisfies the psychic needs of only the white member of the union that white writers seem never to tire of relating. Let me tell you an illustrative anecdote. A recent movie that embodies perhaps better than any other the myth of interethnic male bonding in its black-and-white version is called *The Defiant Ones*. In it there is a moment when the black and the white comrades who have been fleeing from a chain gang are on the verge of escaping. The black comrade, who is already safely in the boxcar, reaches his hand out to help his companion who has fallen behind him. I saw this film twice when it first appeared: once before an audience of primarily white college students and for the second time in a downtown theater, where the audience was made up largely of black high-school kids. The first time the onlookers cheered wildly; but the second time, as those two hands clasped together, the audience—almost as one man, one black man—screamed out: "You'll be sorry!"

*Carlin*: Is it true that the meaning of these myths or archetypes is defined by their context?

*Fiedler*: In myths, true myths, the deep meaning is present always and necessarily in encrypted form. This makes it possible for the audience to accept its meanings without asking, "Do I believe this or don't I believe it?" It simply settles back and says, "Let's make believe." But sometimes, depending on the nature of the audience, those covert or encrypted meanings are different. The reading of a myth by any group is always in some sense self-serving.

*Question*: All three of you have used the term myth consistently, obviously with reference to Jung. Should you say something here about what you mean by myth?

*Fiedler*: I have been desperately trying to avoid defining myth because I always find it a better strategy to leave key terms undefined and let them define themselves in the course of the discussion; but I cannot resist your challenge. For me myth is primarily what its etymological origin suggests: *mythos*, fable, story. A myth is essentially a narrative, whether told in words on a page, images on a screen, stained-glass windows, or whatever. It is a particular kind of story, multivalent, plurisignificant, and polysemous containing multiple meanings; it is therefore capable of psychically satisfying many audiences. Another way of saying it is that myth is a kind of communal dream that, like our own personal dreams, tells a kind of truth that demands to be told for the sake of our health and well-being, but that cannot otherwise be expressed, certainly not in discursive, rational terms. In a sense it can be called "a lie that tells the truth," or rather a single lie that tells many truths, sometimes contradictory ones, since in dreams there is no either/or.

*Carlin*: I think one of the reasons we use the term "myth" here is to establish a connection between things that are happening in contemporary culture on television and in movies or advertising and things that have a historical significance. So there is a kind of transversal between the forms that one finds in history and in the present that links them together and makes them intelligible as a sequence. What we traditionally think of as myths are old stories passed down through this sequence to us; and what we think of as popular culture are the stories that are all around us, created by us and for us.

One important thing to be aware of in terms of the contemporary interface of myth and theory is that in many respects theory is the most acceptable contemporary form of myth. Claude Lévi-Strauss was right when he suggested that Freud's Oedipus complex was not so much an analysis of myth but a version of that myth set in the style most acceptable to our times—scientific analysis. We like our myths to be in this form because we live in an acutely self-conscious culture that does not like to think of its expressions as primitive or naive.

So I think in some respects what we should do here is not just celebrate a Marxist, Freudian, or Jungian analysis but try to understand how these analyses tell us something about ourselves and the culture in which we live. The positive result of this could make us more aware of the postmodern mythic structures that persist despite the forms they currently take. Through this we can understand how these timeless stories and structures can still function in our culture as myths have always done; yet we can also still feel that somehow we have evolved beyond the instinctive, preliterate relation to the ritual forms embodied in myth.

*Schechter*: I, too, would like to address the question of the meaning of myth. At the moment, my favorite definition of the term comes from the Roman historian Salust, who says, "Myths are things that never happened but always are." This suggests that myths are not strictly determined by historical circumstances. There is a certain repertoire of narrative patterns or stories that are available to the human unconscious or psyche.

*Fiedler*: Though there is a limited repertoire of narrative patterns, the meanings of them differ depending on the social context. This is especially true at the oral stage, but remains so even when the patterns are fixed in print. It is, of course, their covert or encrypted meanings that change, so it is even possible (this is something that much intrigues me) that they preserve on an unconscious level responses to the world around us that on a conscious level we have come to think of as archaic, outgrown, even antisocial. One of the functions of archetypal literature is to allow the expression of attitudes and beliefs that, on the level of high culture and ordinary social discourse, we disavow. In this sense the myths of popular culture are subversive myths, as the dead myths that are embodied in the scriptures and serve to reinforce our conscious values are not. Let me give you an example. In the late 1960s and early 1970s, there appeared a new constituency for a new archetypal popular literature, the so-called Youth Cult books. An examination of the most popular of these books, however, reveals the disconcerting fact that though this generation was profoundly pacifist, their favorite books celebrated war and combat heroism. After demonstrating in the streets against United States involvement in the war in Vietnam, they went back to their own rooms where they read such things as the *Dune* tetralogy by Frank Herbert, which celebrated the warrior as hero and the ideal of *Jihad*, combat aimed at total extinction of the enemy: genocide. To understand this, one must understand that one of the functions of popular culture is to pay homage to the dark forces that we presumably disavow, what is called in Hebrew the *yetzerhara*, the evil impulse or, in other words, Satan, the Devil.

Another instance that illustrates this is the popularity of Ken Kesey's *One Flew Over the Cuckoo's Nest*, first read by young members of the so-called counterculture in the early 1960s. It became an immensely popular film in the late 1970s appealing to everybody of all generations. I attended a showing of that film in San Francisco when it opened. Present in the audience were the aging hippies, not yet quite turned into yuppies, who had originally loved that book and assured its success in the marketplace. It was clear from their response that they still loved it despite the fact that it is not merely basically racist but deeply, fundamentally misogynist in the grand tradition. It is a book, that is to say, that celebrates interethnic male bonding in the relationship between Patrick McMurphy and Chief Bromden, and it portrays woman, more specifically white woman, in the form of Big Nurse, as the enemy. Despite this fact, an audience that consisted of feminists and fellow travelers of feminism cheered wildly, males and females alike, as McMurphy attempted the rape-murder of Big Nurse at the climax of that film. But why, I asked. Because the dark side of their ambivalence, their *yetzerhara*, was reacting against the beliefs to which they subscribed on a conscious level, betraying in them a deep hunger for what they consciously considered taboo. Misogyny, that is to say, moves the American audience still, as it has all the way back to the times of James Fenimore Cooper and Mark Twain.

*Schechter*: That points to another powerful myth that is also relevant to the counterculture, that of the trickster, which manifests itself in Kesey's Merry Pranksters, yuppie politics, and so forth. The emergence of that incarnation of anarchy and antiauthoritarianism in 1960s America seems to confirm Jung's theory of archetypal compensation on a culture-wide scale.

*Fiedler*: Yes, there is no doubt that Patrick is an embodiment of the trickster, but he is also an embodiment of *machismo*, which appeared at the moment when all right-minded people were supposed to be ashamed of yearning to be *macho*.

*Carlin*: To me, being more a student of the 1960s rather than someone who was moving around and doing things in that period, the hippie movement was one of the most profoundly misogynist movements in American culture. The self-representations of the hippies, as far as I have been able to see, typically have to do with women walking around with bare feet, with bandanas around their heads and babies in their arms. There were precious few female thinkers, or even cult figures, relative to earlier periods in American culture, such as the 1920s. One of the most interesting and influential visual aspects to come out of the hippie era were underground comic books like *Zap*, whose pages, largely drawn by R. Crumb and S. Clay Wilson, were among the most fiercely antifemale works of art I have ever seen. I mention this because the general reputation of the period was one of liberation and free-thinking. I do not think it was until the mid-1970s that there was any recognition of how the persistence of traditional female stereotypes in the underground media had a measurable social influence.

*Fiedler*: I think that what you say is basically true, but what I was talking about is the reaction in the late 1970s to the film version of Kesey's book. At that point in time, feminism, which had remained somehow dormant in the early 1960s, came to full life.

*Carlin*: From a psycho-social point of view, what you are saying about myth is exactly what Freud said about dreams: we express things in dreams that we cannot express in our conscious lives. This forms an outlet, a balance, that contributes to our mental health.

*Fiedler*: As a matter of fact, the words I use instead of myth or archetype, when they seem to me to have become clichés, are "communal dreams."

*Schechter*: To illustrate something similar to what Leslie is talking about: the notorious horror film called *The Texas Chainsaw Massacre*, which is arguably the most nightmarish movie ever made, was created by a group of counterculture types. In fact, its director, Tobe Hooper, had made only one earlier film, a gentle comedy about the peace movement called *Eggshells*. By the early 1970s, in fact, the fantasies coming out of the counterculture were increasingly dark and disturbing: Woodstock had turned into Altamont, the Beatles' "Let It Be" into the Stones' "Let It Bleed," Alice's Restaurant into the human barbeque stand operated by *Chainsaw*'s family of cannibal killers. The obsessive fascination with these nightmares of violence and horror among a generation committed to the values of peace, love, and flower power seems to confirm Leslie's point. But what is also interesting about Hooper's film is that it is a kind of fairy tale, a cinematic version of a widespread folk motif known as "The Bloody Chamber," the most famous example of which is *Bluebeard*. I wonder if the most valuable thing about Jungian theory is that, by allowing us to make that kind of connection, it gives us insight into the way the human psyche deals with certain basic fears and anxieties by assimilating them to ancient—and therefore reassuringly familiar—story patterns.

*Fiedler*: I see what you are saying. What dismays me is the tendency on the part of some Jungians to level everything out until finally the infinite variety of myth threatens to turn into the boring uniformity of monomyth, as a kind of entropy triumph. In any case, I am interested in specifics.

But let me return to a question raised earlier that I have been longing to explore: the question of aesthetics. Are aesthetic criteria relevant in discussing the popular arts? I think that anybody who believes that all literature is words on a page gets into trouble when dealing with popular literature, because in popular literature the medium is not the message; the myth is the message. A myth is in some ways independent of the medium in which it happens to appear. Consequently, a great popular work can be and often is, translated from book form into film without losing its archetypal resonance and power. So also can that film be chopped up with commercials, edited, and shown on television without losing such power. Its images can be made into bisque porcelain dolls, carved in soap, or scrawled on the wall without losing that power. One can understand what it means to say that the myth is independent of its medium by thinking, for instance, of the myth of Baldur. Asked if he knows that myth, someone might answer yes, at which point it would be proper to ask, "In what language and in what words do you know it?" And the answer would scarcely matter, since like all mythic literature, that myth is primarily not the words in which it is told but the images in the head that exist first. Such myths, I am trying to suggest, are in fact known to us primarily as a sequence, a primordial dream narrative, that only on waking demands language to express it.

*Carlin*: There is an important distinction that we have not made and should be making. One has to distinguish between popular culture itself and the utilization of popular culture by self-proclaimed artists. Take, for example, Andy Warhol, who, depending on one's point of view, can be seen as a brilliant conceptualist who uses pop culture to make us aware of its hidden power over us, or as a rather naive and limited mediumistic artist who simply translates gaudy popular imagery into extremely expensive, elite commodity forms.

One could also make a similar statement about a film like *The Texas Chainsaw Massacre*, which I think is a wonderful film. It can be understood as a version of a fairy tale, or as a self-conscious film that poses as a version of a fairy tale, and then it distorts and utilizes that structure in a deliberate way. Let me give you an example of this in the film, which will also bring back the misogynist theme we have been discussing. *Chainsaw* began a very important genre in recent American film, along with John Carpenter's *Halloween*, of the teenage female hero who triumphs over a monstrous male attacker. These films are distinguished not only by having a central female hero but also by having as their theme the triumph of the woman, the woman being the sole survivor of a traumatic physical ordeal, who destroys a male monster who pursued her throughout the film. These films seem to me to be deliberate feminist myths, although I am not sure that they work completely on this level. But I am convinced that the filmmakers were consciously trying to rework traditional male adolescent myths from a feminist perspective. Rather than the women being the passive victims of these nightmare situations, they become the active saviors.

*Schechter*: I do not see it that way at all. What is interesting about that movie is that it, as well as Hitchcock's *Psycho*, was based on an actual and extremely sensational case that occurred in Wisconsin in the late 1950s and that produced a wave of national revulsion as well as morbid fascination. The crimes in question, which were committed by a Wisconsin farmer named Edward Gein, included grave-robbing, necrophilia, and supposedly cannibalism. From my point of view *The Texas Chainsaw Massacre* illustrates one of the major functions of myth, which is to assimilate extremely threatening material to preexisting narrative patterns, which in effect give shape and therefore some kind of intelligible meaning to this otherwise incomprehensible stuff. Again, I think that for the myth critic the real danger of Jungian criticism, wherever it is applied, is that it reduces everything to a kind of intrapsychic allegory featuring a stock cast of archetypal characters, so that this work becomes a drama about the anima's relationship to the animus; that work becomes the story of the ego's confrontation with the shadow, and so on. This is interesting—but only up to a point. After that, as Leslie suggests, you have to focus on the cultural dimension of the myth. For example, another film that I have focused on recently is *The Incredible Shrinking Man*. On one level it, too, is an updated, science fiction version of an age-old folktale, the story of the Thumbling hero. But its nightmarish portrayal of a helpless, infantilized male, trapped in an increasingly oppressive 1950s household, is also a reflection of powerful male anxieties very prevalent in postwar suburban America.

*Fiedler*: I would like to pick up on something *The Texas Chainsaw Massacre* suggests to me. It is—you will not be surprised to hear—one of the favorite movies of Stephen King, and it illustrates aptly a quality of the particular kind of popular literature that he himself produces. He has several times observed that when he creates most successfully, he creates literature of terror. When he cannot quite make that level, he settles for horror; and when that fails, he "grosses them out." In a certain sense, grossness and vulgarity are essential to all popular culture, which satisfies in us, I suspect, a profound distaste for high culture, indeed for everything that Huckleberry Finn would call "Sivilization." Implicitly, popular literature is hostile to the whole tradition of Christian humanism, aimed at canceling out what Walt Whitman called "those long overdue accounts to Greece and Rome."

*Carlin*: One thing that is very important about what has been said, and this may be an unavoidable contradiction in trying to analyze popular culture, is that we like to be grossed out, but only in very controlled, deliberate forms. So when we talk about a movie like *The Texas Chainsaw Massacre*, we single it out because it is an incredibly horrible film, a purposefully gross experience. But at the same time, it is a very poetic and formally self-conscious film. I think the reason we use it as an example, or why we use someone like Walt Whitman, or even Stephen King to a certain degree, is because these are far from the lowest forms of popular culture. *Texas Chainsaw* is not *Friday the 13th*. *Chainsaw* is a formal, controlled film that stands up to repeated viewings and is not entirely dependent upon its initial shock value. It begins and ends with a similar shot and pays a great deal of attention to its camera work, its manipulation of stock characters, and its relation to the history of film and to literature.

*Fiedler*: I am sympathetic to what you say, but I feel obliged to issue a word of warning on this score, more to myself, perhaps, than to you. I keep reminding myself that I must distrust any attempt to pretend, after the fact, that certain vulgar popular works that I love for quite other reasons possess the formal beauty and coherence that I was taught in school to consider essential to great art. We all have a tendency as critics and as teachers to try to kidnap into high culture works that we respond to passionately for quite disreputable reasons. By doing so, we eventually turn them into required reading in schools. This, however, is the worst thing, I believe, that can be done with essentially popular writers like Mark Twain or James Fenimore Cooper or, for that matter, Dickens or Balzac or Dostoyevsky. It falsifies their work less, I believe, to ignore or even to ban it than to require it, to make it a part of official high culture, thus suggesting that it is, in terms of moralists, "good for us."

*Carlin*: I think that in trying to distinguish between levels of popular expression, one thing that is important is a lesson that can be learned from the two central American authors of the nineteenth century who developed our aesthetics of popular culture. I am thinking here not of Mark Twain or James Fenimore Cooper but of Walt Whitman and Edgar Allan Poe. It is important to note that they incorporated popular elements into their work in dramatically different ways, and that these two different approaches persist into the present. Poe was a writer who obviously tried to gross people out, or at least to horrify them, and he did so in the most controlled and formal manner possible. To create his famous "unity of effect," he went so far as to write his stories backward, so he knew where they were going from the time he began. Whitman's approach was the exact opposite. Whereas Poe used symbols in a rigorous, stable pattern, Whitman tried to place them in flux. This "drifting" approach to writing embodies the anarchistic spirit of popular culture, the freedom and looseness of everyday speech, rather than the archetypes of popular imagination. And this is a way of getting back to the idea of not just talking about the archetypical or ritual forms of popular culture—how they link up with each other, how they tell us something about the culture that our society has developed from, and what are the particular forms of the society in which we live. But there are aesthetic strategies that go along with this, and I think that despite the caveat that Professor Fiedler just made, we cannot help but be interested in aestheticizing certain forms of popular culture and forming new canons or hierarchies to help define what we are and how we will be seen by future readers. The questions then become, what cultural baggage do we want to carry along with us, and what can we afford to leave behind? The answers are far more complex, and difficult to judge objectively, than most people think.

*Question*: Is that the nature of popular art? How do you take those classic images of Poe's art and compare them to popular icons of horror and grossness, to movies of terror like *The Texas Chainsaw Massacre*?

*Carlin*: I think they are very similar. Poe's comment about German gods was simply to hide the fact that he ruthlessly plagiarized from those sources, and he wanted to throw people off, kind of like Washington Irving, who became famous, it turned out, simply by translating German myths and folk tales into an American idiom.

*Fiedler*: Poe has always interested me as an example of an inadvertently popular writer—or to put it as paradoxically as possible, one who became popular by creating for the mass audience a myth of the true artist as necessarily alienated, *un*popular. It is possible that Poe himself actually believed that he wanted to be, as his French critics were convinced he did, an aristocrat of the spirit, a cultural dandy; but he ended up by writing some of the most popular stories and poems in the English language. It is a well-known fact that children seven or eight years old respond to his poems and that his fiction is equally popular.

Whatever he may have desired, he was gifted with an undeniable mythic power, and it is not an accident that he has ended up being known to a larger audience than has ever read him—those viewers of Vincent Price horror films. His case is the opposite to that of Walt Whitman, who desired to be a great popular writer but lacked the power to find deeply archetypal themes available to the largest popular audience. Whitman was not in his own time a popular poet; he is not now a popular poet; and he will never be one. And this joke on him is compounded by the fact that his most untypical poem, "O, Captain, My Captain," is the one by which the mass audience remembers him. It is a poem that he came to pretend he despised but for which he seems to have had a sneaking sort of affection himself. There is a moral in all this that I have reflected on for a long time but cannot define exactly.

I promised at the beginning of this session that I would eventually talk about *Gone With the Wind* as the great archetypal book of our time. And I shall therefore attempt to say a word or two, before we are finished, about the myths at its heart. Clearly, the basic myth and controlling metaphor, the very leitmotiv of Margaret Mitchell's book, is rape. Sherman's march to the sea is portrayed as the rape of the South. Reconstruction is portrayed in the same fashion. But there is a literal as well as a metaphorical rape in the tale. Three people attempt to rape Scarlett before the book is over; the first is the Yankee soldier, whom she disposes of by shooting him in the face. The second is a black man, driven mad by the freedom that, according to Miss Mitchell, he neither desired nor could endure. Scarlett is rescued in the nick of time by an Uncle Tom character called Big Sam. The only accomplished rape is marital rape, the rape of Scarlett by Rhett. In describing the assault, Miss Mitchell makes clear that the ancient archetype that underlies it all is the myth of Persephone. Rhett turns into Dis, the god of the underworld, described in terms of darkness, blackness, death; and for a moment it seems, as in the ancient story, her violation will bring eternal winter on the world. But Scarlett, we are asked to believe, likes it; in fact, it is suggested—however coyly—that for the first time in her life, with Rhett, she has been brought to the point of orgasm, or as she puts it, she felt for the first time a thrill of passion equal to the thrill of hatred she experienced when she shot the Yankee soldier.

That this book remains popular in a time when on a politically conscious level most women, many of whom respond to *Gone With the Wind*, consider rape the supreme indignity, suggests that myth transcends morality even as it transcends form and medium. Most popular literature, that is to say, moves us at a level beyond good and evil, or what at any moment we call "good" and "evil," though we know at a deeper level that all such ethical distinctions are provisional or temporary, that they will—before long—change. Indeed there is something in us that yearns desperately for such a change, which will make possible the release of instincts and impulses that contemporary ethical standards force us to repress, except of course as they are expressed for us symbolically, vicariously, in the trashy taboo subliterature of our time and place. But this is precisely why would-be censors, who consider what they happen to believe at a given moment as true for all time, distrust such books, films, and television shows and, however vainly, call on the police and the courts to suppress them.

*Carlin*: I do not think we are trying to be moralists here and pass ethical judgment on these myths. I would like to change tack briefly and focus attention on a kind of myth that we see in our society that is quite positive. What myths really do is teach us things, and often what they do is teach stereotypes that may unfortunately reinforce existing bad stereotypes. That leads us to criticize them and focus our attention on the persistent effect of myths on the popular imagination and on mass consciousness. But there is another thing that myths do that I think is important and not quite so negative. They help us to live with the world into which we were born. One of the characteristics of our culture that may be different from previous cultures is that virtually all our information comes through representations rather than through sensory apprehension of reality. And what a lot of the self-consciousness of contemporary pop culture does is to help us adjust to this hyperrealistic aspect of our culture. Perhaps one final illustration I can suggest is the work of the science fiction writer Philip K. Dick. On one level his work is offensively sexist. But on another level his work is among the best I have found in representing and dealing with the changes in human consciousness wrought by the new media. Along with William Burroughs and J. G. Ballard, Dick has taken the somewhat degraded genre of science fiction and turned it from adolescent technological fantasies into modern myths about the relation between technology and psychology. I think this is an important lesson to be learned, and therefore their postmodern myths teach us how to cope with the rapid changes in our culture that have not been dealt with elsewhere on a conscious level.

*Schechter*: I do not think these pop myths are negative at all. Even the horror movies we have discussed are necessary for the psychic health of the community, since they offer us ways of releasing the repressed— of venting taboo fantasies.

# Folk Theater, Community, and Symbols of the Unconscious

Dinnah Pladott

Can psychological concepts aid us in the reading of literary texts without overlooking or leaving out "their literary specificity"?[1] Could psychology possibly even enlighten us about the functional relation between form and content in such texts? The question came to me as I was puzzling over the curious status of Jewish (Yiddish) drama and theater (1830s–1930s). Here lies the curiosity of the phenomenon. Internally, within the Jewish community (first in Europe, then in America), the Yiddish theater was heatedly criticized by Jewish thinkers for being vulgar, unliterary, popular (in the sense of being unsophisticated and aesthetically inferior), and completely lacking in integrity in its shameless pandering to the masses.[2] Aspiring playwrights, critics, and later historians denounced its deemphasis of the written play in favor of improvisatory scenes, the reenactment of ritual procedures, interpolated dance and song sequences, *shticks* and the *shund* mode.[3] But while the intellectual elite leveled this criticism, the masses of Jews from all social and economic strata, as well as people from outside the Jewish community, flocked to participate in the performances of the Jewish theater. In America, Henry James (*The American Scene*, 1907) and Hutchins Hapgood (*The Spirit of the Ghetto*, 1902) were the forerunners of the scores of artists and theater arts enthusiasts who were to comment in the next decades on the power of Yiddish and Hebrew performances as a theater of the people. Analogous interest in Jewish productions had been expressed much earlier all over Europe.

How could a mode of theater that attracted such interest and attention be simultaneously so vilified for its "lack of aesthetic refinement" and its intellectual mediocrity? As I have shown elsewhere,[4] the Jewish theater was first and foremost a folk theater: a theater drawing life and shape from the roots of Jewish folk tradition, culture, and lore, and attempting to satisfy its community's emotional cravings and spiritual needs.[5] I submit that as a folk theater it is empowered, rather than hindered, by its simple structures to respond to the community's crises and to represent them in the most concise and compressed manner that the community feels it needs.[6]

Once we shift our perspective and consider the Jewish drama as a form of communal and tribal cultural activity, its simple and even crude shape turns out to be an asset rather than a liability. If we cease to judge such a theater for its failure to present its audiences with the intricately wrought stories of individualized characters, we may begin to appreciate its representation of the typical tales of representative figures. The refusal of the Jewish theater to adhere to criteria of strict realism; its delineation of character and situation in broad and general strokes; its invocation of the surreal as well as the real, the legendary as well as the factual, the supernatural as well as the natural, may then be perceived as integral and well-motivated aspects of the theatrical undertaking. If we consider the possibility that as in the folk tale, the fairy tale, or even jokes, folk drama manifests various conscious and unconscious predicaments that have been displaced or condensed into the symbolic action, the disruptions of "logic" and the flights of imaginative fancy begin to make aesthetic sense. If we no longer search for the faithful depiction of the surface reality of actual mundane events, we are in the position to appreciate the symbolically rendered conflicts and unravelings of psychic complications and stages of spiritual development, which are relevant to Jews and non-Jews alike.[7] Such symbolic and condensed representation is constrained by the limits of intelligibility.[8] The simplicity of composition in all these types of popular culture is then functionally motivated, ensuring the communicability of the unconscious materials. The utilization of popular models (in the sense of the unrefined and the familiar) thus acquires a functional *raison d'être*.

## A Case Study: *The Dybbuk*

In a previous study,[9] I have undertaken to examine one of the most "popular"—in both senses of the term: pleasing to the greatest number of spectators and falling into the category of the so-called lowbrow art—and most critically vilified of Jewish plays in order to lay bare its covert enactment of the internal drama. Anski's *The Dybbuk* (1917) is a different specimen, beloved by both spectators and critics. Nevertheless, it exemplifies the intriguing fact that even the most "artistically successful" Jewish plays are simple, and even simplistic, in shape. The Hebrew production of *The Dybbuk* was a "cult of Red Moscow, one of the chief cults of the Russian intelligentsia."[10] This reception was matched by the enthusiasm the production evoked as it toured (in Yiddish) across the American continent and is symptomatic of the Jewish theater's appeal to non-Jewish audiences. The enigma of the Jewish drama lies, as usual, in the magnetic power exerted by a play that could be (and was sometimes) dismissed as "nothing more than a melodrama patterned upon thwarted love and the mystique of retribution because of a broken bond."[11] In the following discussion I outline the manner in which this mere melodrama makes it possible to create a most surprising combination between the general and the particular: between problems of what Jung calls "the individuation process" (*CW* 5: par. 459, p. 301; *CW* 6: pars. 757-762, pp. 448-449; *CW* 7: par. 266ff., p. 173ff.) and specifically Jewish or folk thematic materials, such as "Jewish pathos, Jewish religious ecstasy," and "an artistic Jewish *weltanschauung*, born in the Jewish synagogue . . . nurtured by true Jewish spirit rather than by ethnic accident."[12]

### The Enacted Story

The chronologically reconstructed plot, or *fabula*, of the play is simple. A young couple, Leah and Hannan (in the English transliteration of the Hebrew names), are betrothed by their fathers, Reb Sender and Reb Nissan, at birth. They grow up completely ignorant of this fact, but providence leads them to meet and fall in love, for their spirits are predestined to a loving union. When Sender, Leah's father, decides to break his promise to his dead friend Nissan and to marry Leah to the rich Menashe rather than to the poor Hannan, the latter—who is a devout and industrious Yeshiva student—plunges himself desperately into the study of mysticism and kabbala. These forces he invokes in his defense before he dies of grief. And indeed, as she stands under the traditional wedding canopy, after she has implored the intercession of a legendary pair of ever-faithful lovers, Leah is overcome by the dybbuk (or obsessive spirit of the dead). From her mouth speaks the voice of her dead beloved, claiming her as his rightful spouse. Sender takes Leah to the Chassidic rabbi, the *tsaddik* (holy man), to undertake a ritual procedure of exorcism. But a dream provokes the rabbi to convoke a *beth din*, a rabbinical trial court, to try to ferret out the original injustice that brought on the obsessive dybbuk. A significant dream, in which Hannan's grave appears to Leah, prompts Leah earlier to include him in her visit to the cemetery, where she goes according to the Jewish custom to invite her dead mother to the wedding.

When the past is revealed, Reb Sender is sentenced to give half his fortune to charity and to say *Kaddish*, the prayer for the dead, throughout his life for the dead Nissan and Hannan whom he had wronged. Only then does the rabbi proceed to carry out the exorcism ritual, replete with the lighting of black candles and dancing. Finally the holy man does drive the spirit away by a threat of excommunication. Although Leah's body is freed from the dybbuk, however, her heart is still commanded by her love for the dead Hannan. She dies at the very conclusion of the exorcism ritual to join her lover in heaven.

Anski himself outlined some of the dramatic and folk elements that make the play universally meaningful to theater audiences:

> From the Old Testament to the present, the central idea of all Jewish creativity is: physical force is not the force that wins. This is the basic idea of the prophets, of the *Aggada* [Jewish fables], of Jewish folklore. The physically stronger is defeated because he is spiritually weaker. There is no idealization of physical force in Jewish folk creation and in Jewish folk tales. . . . The Jewish hero does not struggle for power or women or wealth, and his weapons are spiritual rather than physical. The sole motif of the Jewish folk tale is spiritual struggle.[13]

In *The Dybbuk* the struggle between the physical and the metaphysical is represented by a host of folkloristic elements. The Chassidic Jewish culture is itself of great interest as an example of a type of life of the spirit that accepts sensory as well as extrasensory perceptions as significant data and is in total disagreement with the dominant, rational, and empirical emphasis of the mainstream Jewish religious tradition. In addition, the play clearly deals with a whole spectrum of contrasts: a contrast between the world of the living and "the other world," the world of the dead, which is nevertheless actively present and involved in the action; a contrast between the world of the haves, such as the rich Sender, and the world of the have-nots, the poor, represented by Nissan and Hannan, as well as by the *Batlonim* (unemployed individuals who devote their time to religious study), and by the beggars who dance at the wedding; a contrast between the commonsense pragmatism of daily life—highlighting the importance of the concrete and the mundane, which guides the actions of men like Sender—and the love that knows no bounds, experienced by Hannan and Leah; a contrast, finally, between the dry, contemplative rationalism of the Talmudist Hennoch and the intuitive, mystic soaring of the kabbalist Hannan. Thus the action of the play spans (in the manner typical of folk artifacts, such as the folk tale or the fairy tale) an empirical world that is rational and factual, and another world, an irrational or arational world, that must be taken "largely upon faith . . . a world where Hamlet's father may return as a ghost without being assailed upon scientific and rational grounds."[14]

Even this cursory summary supports the claim that Jewish plays tend to "function allegorically."[15] That is, their overt concern with specifically Jewish problems is dramatized by characters and situations that actually represent abstract concepts, social groups, or attitudes.

On one level, it is a reaffirmation that a viable and beautiful cultural Jewish heritage exists, manifesting a humanist and humane rejection of victimization in any form. On another level, it touches upon truths that transcend both ethnic and local orientations. This second level is rendered more intelligible with the aid of Jungian concepts.

### The "Exemplary Action"[16]

A variety of typical psychic and spiritual predicaments are involved here.[17] Most notable is the traditional journey of the hero and the heroine toward a discovery and integration of the various (and contradictory) aspects of their identity. We are presented with the typical conflicts that attend the quest for self-discovery. Sender represents the "child-eating father,"[18] who blocks the natural development of both Hannan and Leah. The struggle with the parental interfering figures reflects not a personal but a symbolic process whereby the libido is developed and transformed (*CW* 5: par. 204ff., p. 142ff.). By killing the "terrible" and destructive aspect of the parent, the protagonist "liberates the fruitful and bountiful aspect."[19] Male as well as female protagonists must overcome the parental obstruction in order to discover the unity of conscious and unconscious, intellect and feeling, sexual and nonsexual love, feminine and masculine aspects, self and soul.[20] But Jung cautions us, "interpretation in terms of parents is a *façon de parler*. In reality the whole drama takes place in the individual's own psyche, where the 'parents' are not the parents at all but only their imagos" (*CW* 5: par. 505, p. 328).

In *The Dybbuk* the struggle that normally culminates in the symbolic "slaying of the parent" is immensely complicated. Leah's mother and Hannan's parents are long dead, suggesting the difficulty for both Hannan and Leah of integrating the complementary parts of their identity. " 'Beyond the grave' or 'on the other side of death' means, psychologically, 'beyond consciousness' " (*CW* 7: par. 302, p. 191), comments Jung. Von Franz elaborates the symbolic significance of the exclusion by absence (wittingly or unwittingly engendered) as that of the suppression or repression of some aspects of consciousness: "It means that some aspects of collective consciousness are so much in the foreground that others are ignored to a great extent."[21] The absence of the mothers, and the fact that Leah is the only female protagonist, reveals that there is a real difficulty here with the representation of the feminine principle. It appears "that the whole feminine world was repressed."[22] The patriarchal world of *The Dybbuk* seems to have tipped the necessary balance between the masculine and the feminine principles.

The consequences go beyond the subordination of women. The female figures—the mother, the beloved, and later on the daughter—are

95

essential if the hero is to achieve the process of individuation and self-realization. One of the attributes of the mother, according to Jung, is her role as gateway to the unconscious: "the 'mother,' as the first incarnation of the anima archetype, personifies in fact the whole unconscious" (*CW* 5: par. 508, p. 330). The mother imago, Jung tells us, is "at first identical with the anima [and] represents the feminine aspect of the hero himself" (ibid.). The absence of mothers in *The Dybbuk* suggests therefore that there is difficulty in gaining access to the unconscious as well as to the feminine component of identity. The problem is acute for the male protagonist, in whom the anima operates as the soul. Jung defines the anima as "the inner personality [which] is the way one behaves in relation to one's inner psychic processes; it is the inner attitude, the characteristic face, that is turned toward the unconscious" (*CW* 6: par. 803, p. 467). This "inner personality," the soul, or anima, in the case of the male hero, is concerned with "the relation to the subject" and is opposed by its complementary "outer face, the persona," which "is exclusively concerned with the relation to objects" (*CW* 6: par. 801, p. 465; cf. *CW* 7: par. 305, p. 192). A weakening of the one strengthens the other.

The Dybbuk suggests that the results of the suppression of the female principle are far more pernicious than the merely social oppression of women, since they lead to a predominant reliance on the object-directed persona or mask, with a concomitant suppression of the whole instinctual and libidinal realm (*CW* 5: par. 223, p. 157). The domination of the persona explains Sender's opposition to the love match on the grounds of commercial and financial justification (the groom's poverty) rather than on emotional self-justification (e.g., a hatred or a feud, as in *Romeo and Juliet*).

In view of these submerged conflicts, the marriage with the rich Menashe, which Sender wants to impose on his daughter, has far-reaching implications. In a natural marriage, the woman "is going to make contact with her spiritual and mental side."[23] Nevertheless, comments von Franz, "in alchemical symbolism the feminine figure is often first married to the wrong kind of man, and it is the heroic deed to separate the couple. The hero has to win his partner and separate her from the wrong man."[24] Hannan's adamant struggle to prevent the wrong marriage, even from the realm of the repressed and buried, the unconscious world of the dead, underscores the importance of the deliverance for the creation of balance and harmony. Each of the two protagonists needs to discover and unite with the psychic qualities represented by the other.

Leah's action, when she goes to the cemetery to invite both her dead mother and the dead Hannan to her wedding, reveals a determination to reestablish contact with the repressed aspects. On her mother's grave she reclaims the feminine, instinctive, feeling aspect that has been so brutally censored by her father. On Hannan's grave she reclaims a type of "spiritual and mental side" which, as we shall see, imbues rational intellectualism with the humanizing intuitive and mystical inspiration. Hence this double invitation throws into relief the affinity between the entities represented, respectively, by the figure of the mother and the figure of the dead beloved, and the contrast to the parental and male logos values that Sender represents.

A further level of meaning is revealed where the Hannan–Leah love story intersects with the other stories in the play. As we consider the pairs Sender–Nissan and Hannan–Hennoch, whose "souls were bound together in loyal friendship,"[25] we recognize the pattern of the friends who are twin-like in their fraternal love. And yet they reaffirm Neumann's comment that "the twin-brother motif in mythology . . . expresses the mutual affinity of opposites."[26] Nevertheless, continues Neumann, "consciousness of the bond between the male opponents is the beginning of masculine consciousness."[27] The action of the play hinges on the fact that such "consciousness" does not take place. Sender's transgression of his vow to the dead Nissan reinforces his initial rejection of Nissan, who represents what Sender considers not merely an opposite but a veritable "inferior personality component" (*CW* 5: par. 269, p. 183), which he adamantly refuses to accept. Jung calls this entity the shadow.

The shadow "contains all those elements in the personality which the ego condemns as negative values."[28] Yet Neumann elaborates on its double significance: "the shadow only half belongs to the ego, since it is a part of the personal unconscious. On the other hand, it is also constellated by the figure of the antagonist in the collective unconscious, and the importance of the shadow as an authority rests precisely on its position mid-way between the personal conscious and the collective unconscious."[29] The shadow is therefore both "the dark brother" and a potential ally. "Only by incorporating this dark side does the personality put itself in a posture of defense," explains Neumann, and he adds "that is why in myths the shadow often appears as a twin, for he is not just the 'hostile brother,' but a companion and friend."[30] Sender's adamant repudiation of his shadow, first in the poor Nissan and later in his equally poor son Hannan, is another disruption of the necessary balance between the opposites. As Jung explains it, "seen from the one-sided point of view of the conscious attitude, the shadow is an inferior component of the personality and is consequently repressed through intensive resistance. But the repressed contents must be made conscious so as to produce a tension of opposites, without which no forward movement is possible" (*CW* 7: par. 78, p. 53). Sender's failure is further illuminated by Neumann's observation: "Only by making friends with the shadow do we make friends with the self."[31]

The centrality of the encounter with the "shadow brother" is underscored in *The Dybbuk* by the repetition of the twin motif. Hannan and Hennoch reenact the fraternal bond (expressed even in the similarity between their nearly homophonic names) and the ideological clash between brothers. In Act I, Hannan argues against the "cold and dry" rationalism of the traditional wisdom in the Gemara and Commentaries. He introduces instead the mystic teachings of the kabbala, which replace the dualistic separation of good and evil by an a priori acceptance of sin as potential good: "There is no need to wage war against sin. Elevate it! As a goldsmith purifies the gold from its dross . . . so must sin be purified of its uncleanliness until only holiness remains."[32] This kabbalistic stance mirrors the psychological insight that "evil incitements provide us with opportunities to increase consciousness."[33]

In Hebrew and Yiddish, evil is significantly denoted by the Aramaic epithet *Sitra Achra* ("the other side"), implicitly acknowledging its intimate relation to goodness. Hannan's arguments recognize that the shadow, the Satanic "other side,"[34] has a potential "positive value and a luciferian light-bringing quality."[35] They recall Neumann's assertion that "this shadowy link with the archetype of the antagonist, i.e., the devil, is in the deepest sense part of the creative abyss of every personality."[36] But Hennoch is staggered by this position: "Sanctity in Satan! I can't, I can't conceive it."[37] Hennoch retreats from befriending the shadow, peremptorily reminding Hannan that "such ecstatic soaring is most dangerous."[38] Instead, he clings to the circumscribing protective shield of the traditional and rational Gemara, which "embraces a man like a harness of steel and prevents him from turning off the proper road either to the right or to the left."[39] Hannan's death, which resolves this argument (a perennial Jewish tug of spiritual arms), implies that Hennoch, the representative of the rational and analytical moral attitude, buries his repressed and denied intuitive and integrative twin.[40]

## The Communal Lesson

*The Dybbuk* manifests a variety of repressive processes, whereby censored and negated (denied) contents are abolished and buried out of conscious sight.[41] The tragic denouement of the play, however, provides a persuasive illustration of the fact that the repressed materials do not remain submerged without inflicting psychic damage. Hannan has not been able to release his captive beloved from the hateful, wrong marital union. Hence, he has not been able to "redeem his own soul, his own feminine counterpart," which is the precondition to a fertile and creative life.[42] But the needs of the individual, both male and female, for the balancing of antinomian halves must be satisfied. The concluding moments of the play emphasize that the various dichotomies implicit in the diverse repressive procedures are untenable: the conflicting components of the conscious and unconscious self are fragments of the same whole. "I have departed from your body. I come to your soul," says the voice of Hannan to Leah after the dybbuk has been successfully exorcised.[43] Moreover, the symbolism of light and darkness, of "higher" good emanating from "lower" evil, which dominates the final moments of the play, is crucial. Hannan, the shadow brother associated in Act III with "the Powers of Blackness,"[44] is repeatedly linked by Leah at the conclusion of the play with the redemptive light of the heart and soul: "My heart was drawn to you as to a bright star. . . . But you went away, and my light was put out and my soul withered. . . . A great light flows about me. I am joined with you, my destined bridegroom. Together we will soar higher, higher, higher."[45]

As Jung put it, "an exciting narrative that is apparently quite devoid of psychological intentions is just what interests the psychologist most of all" (*CW* 15: par. 137, p. 88). *The Dybbuk* seems to be an excellent illustration of this point. It suggests that the folk drama may, like the fairy tale and the folk tale, manifest what Neumann describes as "a complete, self-contained action 'in archetypal place.' " And his conclusion applies equally forcefully to all types of folk literature: "precisely because it is an archetypal action, its meaning must be taken in a collective human sense and not personalistically, that is, not as something that takes place in a particular man or a particular woman, but as a universal 'exemplary action.' "[46] When we recognize the "exemplary action" enacted in the Jewish drama, we are better equipped to acknowledge its welding of shape and content and to comprehend its fascination for both its Jewish community and the non-Jewish spectators.

Some critics may debate the point whether such psychic truths are "universal and eternal," as Jung believed, or whether they are culturally transmitted and inherited. But whether the psychological and spiritual predicaments I have pointed to rest in the human collective unconscious or in the writer's cultural heritage, the point is that the play—and it is typical of other Jewish plays—contains serious and penetrating truths within its simple folk structure. Moreover, *The Dybbuk* demonstrates the conjunction of the psychological and the ethical that is characteristic of even the most "popular" of the Jewish folk dramas. This conjunction has been celebrated by Jung: "If people can be educated to see the shadow-site of their nature clearly, it may be hoped that they will also learn to understand and love their fellow men better" (*CW* 7: par. 28, p. 26). The Jewish folk play, exemplified by *The Dybbuk*, reaffirms the essential and necessary bonds among all people and illustrates the catastrophic results of any attempt to create absolute barriers, whether they are between components of the personality or between the sexes, or between social, economic, and ideological groups.

Gary Saul Morson has already made a persuasive case for the futility of trying to "prove" a theory by the readings that it produces.[47] My goal is neither to "prove" a theory nor to produce a better, or a definitive, reading of *The Dybbuk*. I merely outline an explanation or a functional motivation for both the Jewish drama's simplicity of form and its selection of popular contents. I also underscore the predominantly conative (influencing) role of folk theater within the Jewish community. Jung has recommended telling children fairy tales and legends "because these are instrumental symbols with whose help unconscious ideas can be canalized into consciousness, interpreted, and integrated" (*CW* 9 ii: par. 259, p. 169). If the Jewish folk theater fulfilled a similar function, its compelling power and its capacity to fascinate people both within and outside its immediate community become more comprehensible.

# Notes

1. Shoshana Felman, *Literature and Psychoanalysis: The Question of Reading* (Baltimore: Johns Hopkins University Press, 1982), p. 6.

2. See David S. Lifson, *The Yiddish Theater in America* (New York: Thomas Yosselof, 1965), pp. 17-66.

3. *Shund*, explains Nahama Sandrow, "means trash. . . . It is art for the masses." That is, it is "artistically primitive" and may "lean heavily on insulting repartee and on puns." Nahama Sandrow, *Vagabond Stars: A World History of Yiddish Theater* (New York: Harper and Row, 1977), pp. 110-111.

4. Dinnah Pladott, "The Jewish (Yiddish) Theater as a Species of Folk Art," *Identity and Ethos: A Festschrift for Sol Liptzin on the Occasion of his 85th Birthday*, ed. Mark Gelbert (Bern: Peter Lang, 1986).

5. Historians are unanimous in their agreement about the folk roots of the Jewish theater, (see Isaac Goldberg, *The Drama of Transition* (Cincinnati: Stew-

art Kidd, 1922); B. Gorin, *The History of Yiddish Theater*, 2d ed., 2 vols. (New York: Max Maisel [Library Publishers], 1923); Alexander Mukdoiny, *Teater* (in Yiddish) (New York: Mukdoiny Jubilee Committee, 1927); Jacob Mestel, *Unzer Teater* (in Yiddish) (New York: Yiddisher Kultur Farband, 1943); Sister Frances Jerome Woods, *Cultural Values of American Ethnic Groups* (New York: Harper and Brothers, 1956); Lifson, *The Yiddish Theater in America*, and Sandrow, *Vagabond Stars*. They are also unanimous in their agreement about the responsiveness of Jewish playwrights to the demands of their audiences. They condemn this tendency, however, as an unnecessary pandering to the masses (see Sandrow, *Vagabond Stars*, pp. 85-122), overlooking the link between the folk theater's function and its utilization of artistic forms. As Peter Bogatyrev and Roman Jakobson describe the creation and development of folk art, this is the process in which the folk theater, as a species of folk creation, is shaped by the constant interaction of the artist and the community. The created folk art, say Bogatyrev and Jakobson, cannot survive without the ready comprehension, acceptance, and repeated performance by the community. Peter Bogatyrev and Roman Jakobson, "Folklore as a Special Form of Creativity," in *The Prague School: Selected Writings 1926-1946*, ed. Peter Steiner (Austin: University of Texas Press, 1982. Cf. Jan Mukarovsky's description of the evolution of a folk song; Jan Mukarovsky, "Personality in Art," in *Structure, Sign and Function: Selected Essays by Jan Mukarovsky*, ed. John Burbank (New Haven: Yale University Press, 1977), p. 161.

The corollary of this observation is the fact that in the folk theater, the focus is on the addressee, rather than on the addresser, of the act of communication; cf. Roman Jakobson's famous model, "Linguistics and Poetics," in *The Structuralists from Marx to Lévi-Strauss*, ed. Richard and Fernande de Georges (New York: Doubleday Anchor, 1972), pp. 85-122. Folk playwrights do not express their own individual attitudes and dreams or yearnings but those of their community. This is essential for the act of communication between artist and audience to be successfully consummated and for the work to have any impetus or validity. These playwrights are prevented from foregrounding either the "poetic function" (which emphasizes the artistic "message" as such) or the "emotive function" (which emphasizes the expression of the addresser). Instead, they foreground the "conative" and "phatic" functions regarding their influence and effect upon the community of spectators. Intent on reaching and affecting the audience, and supremely concerned with eliciting a fruitful response from the viewers, folk playwrights are conscious of the need to maintain a continuous contact between addresser and addressee. They therefore go to great lengths in order to insure that their code and their context are clear and persuasive at all times, so as to communicate successfully their appeal to the spectators' sensibilities and perceptions. See Jakobson, "Linguistics and Poetics," p. 95.

6. Mukarovsky describes the process wherein a folk song of twenty-one quatrains has been reduced by the community, over the sixty years of its existence, to merely seven stanzas. He comments that the process of attenuation was far from being "simply mechanical" but was "also artistically intentional."

The aesthetic intention of the song writer was countered and modified by the creative response of the community, since the seemingly "mechanical" forgetting of the vanished stanzas has, in fact, reshaped the song into "a very economical and really firmly constructed ballad." Mukarovsky, "Personality in Art," p. 161.

7. For a slightly different slant, see Victor Turner, *From Ritual to Theater: The Human Seriousness of Play* (New York: Performing Arts Journal Publications, 1982), pp. 89-101. See also Mircea Eliade, *Myth and Reality*, trans. Williard R. Trask (New York: Harper Colophon Books, 1963), pp. 195-202; Joseph Campbell, "Bios and Mythos: Prolegomena to a Science of Mythology," in *Myth and Literature*, ed. John B. Vickery (Lincoln: University of Nebraska Press, 1966), pp. 15-23; Geza Roheim, "Myth and Folktale," in *Myth and Literature*, pp. 25-32. Analyses of folk tales and fairy tales by C. G. Jung, Erich Neumann, and Marie-Louise von Franz are notable illustrations of this point; Bruno Bettelheim, *The Uses of Enchantment: The Meaning and Importance of Fairy Tales*, (New York: Vintage, 1977), represents a Freudian addition.

8. Cf. Sigmund Freud, *Jokes and Their Relation to the Unconscious*, trans. James Strachey (London: Pelican Books, 1978), p. 238.

9. Pladott, "The Jewish (Yiddish) Theater as a Species of Folk Art."

10. Lifson, *The Yiddish Theater in America*, p. 105.

11. Ibid., p. 302.

12. Mukdoiny, *Teater*, p. 33, 38ff.

13. S. Anski, *The Dybbuk*, in *The Great Jewish Plays: Five Outstanding Plays by Leivick, Anski, Asch, Pinski, Hirshbein*, ed. and trans. Joseph C. Landis (New York: Avon, 1925), pp. 23-24.

14. Goldberg, *The Drama of Transition*, p. 425.

15. Sandrow, *Vagabond Stars*, p. 199.

16. Erich Neumann, *Amor and Psyche: The Psychic Development of the Feminine*, trans. Ralph Manheim, Bollingen Series (Princeton: Princeton University Press, 1956), p. 141.

17. For example, the story of the star-crossed lovers who are destroyed by parental obstruction immediately suggests the repression of eros by the parental representatives of authority, societal pressures, and civilization, cf. Herbert Marcuse, *Eros and Civilization* (New York: Vintage, 1978). The point is emphasized by the fact that, unlike the Montagues and Capulets of *Romeo and Juliet*, Sender's opposition to Leah's love for Hannan is motivated by greed rather than by a personal hatred. He views marriage as a social and commercial transaction rather than as an expression and a consummation of erotic love.

18. Erich Neumann, *The Origins and History of Consciousness*, trans. R.F.C. Hull, Bollingen Series (Princeton: Princeton University Press, 1973), p. 178.

19. Ibid., p. 163.

20. Ibid., pp. 195-209, 353-355; cf. Bettelheim, *The Uses of Enchantment*, pp. 91-95.

21. Marie-Louise von Franz, *Problems of the Feminine in Fairytales* (Zurich: Spring, 1972), p. 25.

22. Marie-Louise von Franz, *Interpretation of Fairytales: An Introduction to the Psychology of Fairytales* (Zurich: Spring, 1973), p. 79.

23. von Franz, *Problems of the Feminine in Fairytales*, p. 14.

24. Ibid.

25. Anski, *The Dybbuk*, p. 61.

26. Neumann, *The Origins and History of Consciousness*, p. 180.

27. Ibid.

28. Ibid., p. 351.

29. Ibid., p. 352.

30. Ibid., pp. 352-353.

31. Ibid., p. 353.

32. Anski, *The Dybbuk*, p. 31.

33. von Franz, *Interpretation of Fairytales*, p. 92.

34. Anski, *The Dybbuk*, p. 32.

35. von Franz, *Interpretation of Fairytales*, p. 92.

36. Neumann, *The Origins and History of Consciousness*, p. 353.

37. Anski, *The Dybbuk*, p. 32.

38. Ibid., p. 31.

39. Ibid.

40. Cf. Neumann, *The Origins and History of Consciousness*, p. 353.

41. See Francesco Orlando, *Toward a Freudian Theory of Literature*, trans. Charmaine Lee (Baltimore: Johns Hopkins University Press, 1978).

42. Neumann, *The Origins and History of Consciousness*, p. 212.

43. Anski, *The Dybbuk*, p. 68.

44. Ibid., p. 61.

45. Ibid., pp. 67-68.

46. Neumann, *Amor and Psyche*, p. 141.

47. Gary Saul Morson, "Literary Theory, Psychoanalysis, and The Creative Process," *Poetics Today* 3, no. 2 (1982): 157-172.

# Individuation and Entropy as a Creative Cycle in Architecture

Anne Griswold Tyng

Carl Jung's cycle of individuation has profound implications today as a framework for understanding a dramatic interaction between human creativity and the law of entropy. Jung's cycle, in four stages of transformation and renewal (*homo, serpens, lapis,* and *anthropos-rotundum, CW* 9ii: par. 391, p. 248), has an extraordinary correspondence with a cycle of individual creativity and with the much-larger-scale cycles of creative attitudes that underlie changing styles in the history of architecture.

Like Jung's cycle, each of the cycles I have traced in architecture from the Great Pyramids to the present[1] follows a recurring pattern of four phases. For example, it moves from the contained rectilinearity of the early Roman basilica to the spatial expansion of Hagia Sophia at Istanbul, to the vertical energy of Charlemagne's Palace Chapel at Aachen, toward a phase of greatest disssolution and entropy in the diminishing spiral form of the Ziggurat of Samarra, finally breaking through to a synthesis of fresh energy in the simple cubic forms of Cistercian churches and abbeys. This creative cycle has a rigorous basis in its connection to the law of entropy and Jung's cycle of individuation.

Entropy, the Second Law of Thermodynamics, predicts the loss of energy and order within a closed system. The prediction of probable disorder and loss of energy does not explain the occurrence of life or of human creativity. An explanation is suggested by the cycle of psychic death and rebirth in the process of individuation. In Jung's view, the psychic transformation occurs in four phases, three phases based on *causal* sequence, with the fourth phase of psychic rebirth characterized as a *synchronistic* phenomenon. Although entropy is predicted as probable, laws of probability predict both the probable and improbable (causal and synchronistic) and the ratios between them. Thus, within the predictable, there is always a proportion of the improbable. The improbable synchronistic event, as proportionately predictable, offers an explanation for the occurrence of life and the development of human creativity.

Over time in natural evolution, each of many recurring cycles toward probable entropy was improbably encompassed within a larger contained energy system to begin a new cycle. This occurs in the hemoglobin molecule where multiple fourfold carbon bonds, rounded disc-like hemes, helical and spiraling molecular complexity are all contained in a simple larger-scale fourfold order. Synchronistic events of counterentropy built up ever higher levels of improbable order in cycles contained within cycles. The energy of life and creativity has occurred as improbable order within probable disorder. This cycle offers a scientific basis for resolving the conflict between evolutionists and "creationists": the evolutionary flow toward entropy of a casual sequence culminates in the synchronistic or "catastrophic" event of counterentropy ("creation"). Thus the law of entropy combines with laws of probability that predict a proportion of the improbable.

We are not only improbably alive, counter to probable entropy; we also have energy and an extraordinary capacity for creativity. Human creativity is the extension of life energy. It is the repeated assertion of order over disorder, integration over disintegration, the assertion of new forms of contained energy over forms that dissipate energy. Within the cycle, the process toward entropy is marked by moments of equilibrium, offering new geometric principles of orientation for consciousness and creativity, while each level of creative equilibrium offers new possibilities in the next flow toward entropy.

Each of the four phases in the cycle of individuation constellates contents of the unconscious mind that have been split into four components. Jung diagramed this process in the archetypal geometry of the octahedron and called these diagrams "quaternios" (*CW* 9ii: par. 358ff., p. 226ff.). In the cycle, energy flows to the unconscious, back in time and to deeper and deeper levels of the unconscious. From "higher Adam" to "lower Adam" to "serpens" to the plant form of the Tree of Paradise and its four rivers, to the "lapis" or philosopher's stone, and finally to the four basic elements of fire, air, earth, and water. The breakthrough to the next stage of "anthropos-rotundum" marks a psychic rebirth, an improbable synthesis. It is both end and beginning. Opening up to contents of the unconscious mind brings about thresholds of momentary balance on the path toward apparent disintegration. At the same time it leads to conscious assimilation and a breakthrough to a profound reordering of consciousness—an intuitive leap to a higher level of consciousness and energy.

Jung described the archetype that characterizes each step in this process as consisting of both form potential and psychic energy: "Its form . . . might perhaps be compared to an axial system of a crystal, which, as it were, preforms the crystalline structure in the mother liquid, although it has no material existence of its own. . . . [It] may vary endlessly. . . . The only thing that remains constant is the axial system, or rather, the invariable geometric proportions underlying it. The same is true of the archetype. In principle, it can be named and has an invariable nucleus of meaning—but always only in principle, never as regards its concrete manifestation" (*CW* 9i: par. 155, pp. 79-80).

The invariable proportions of the only regular forms possible in three-dimensional space occur in the five Platonic solids. The Pythagoreans perceived the basic geometry of the five Platonic solids as archetypal dice—the source of all forms of the universe: the cube represented the earth, and the three solids with triangular faces were the tetrahedron-fire, the octahedron-air, and the icosahedron-water; the fifth solid, the dodecahedron with pentagonal faces closest to a circle, was a symbol of the cosmos. Comparing these Western symbols of the universe to those of the Far East reveals basic similarities. The calligraphy of the seventeenth-century Zen artist Sengai for the universe, a rectangular earth linked by a triangle to a circular sky, correlates with the Pythagoreans' cubic earth linked by triangulated fire, air, and water to a cosmos formed with more rounded pentagons. Since the five Platonic solids are the only possible regular forms in three-dimensional space, they represent an essence of the archetypal order of possible orientations in space. They are now known to define the bonding possibilities of atoms and molecules of organic and inorganic matter. The ordering principles of the five solids and their extensions into helix and spiral are proposed as archetypal energy/form diagrams. These archetypal energies underlie the changing creative attitudes that produced historic shifts in architectural styles.

Each historic cycle in architecture is marked by four phases of shifting form empathy. I have described the underlying geometry of these four phases as *bilateral, rotational, helical*, and *spiral*. Each geometric stage diminishes in degrees of order toward entropy, from contained energy and simplicity to greater complexity and less symmetry. The geometry of each stage is evolved from movements of the previous geometric order as effected by forces of polarity and rotation. The four phases articulate steps of geometric possibility in three-dimensional space from contained simplicity to expanding complexity. The human attitudes evoked by these geometric archetypes have accumulated profound meaning over time. In architecture the underlying geometric archetype of each phase expresses a tendency or potentiality of attitude and form empathy but has no material existence in itself.

In the history of architecture, one such cycle began with the Renaissance, named by historians as a period of rebirth. Four phases of this cycle are clearly distinguished in the Renaissance, High Renaissance,

Mannerism, and Baroque (pushed to its extreme in Rococo). In Florence the spirit of the Renaissance appeared a generation earlier than elsewhere. Contained and balanced *bilateral* energy/forms were expressed in the serene cubic symmetry of the palaces of the merchant princes: in Benedetto da Maiano's Strozzi Palace, Michelozzo's Medici Palace (begun 1444), Brunnelschi's (1446) or Alberti's (1458) Pitti Palace, and Alberti's Ruccelai Palace (1455). This phase saw a recurrence of empathy for the rectilinear basilica form in churches: Brunnelschi's S. Lorenzo (1421) Florence, based on a regular composition of squares, and Alberti's S. Andrea (begun 1470) Mantua, with its rectangular nave terminating in an apse (its original form had no transept, dome, or choir).

Brunnelschi's dome of the Florence cathedral (1420-1436) and his Sta. Maria degli Angeli (1434-1437) Florence mark a breakthrough to a new phase of empathy for *rotational* form in centralized rounded church plans that reached its height from 1500 to 1525. Nikolaus Pevsner characterizes the centralized plan of this extraverted phase of confidence in human creativity: "The building has its full effect only when it is looked at from the one focal point. There the spectator must stand and by standing there, he becomes himself 'the measure of all things'. Thus the religious meaning of the church is replaced by a human one. Man is in the church no longer pressing forward to reach a transcendental goal, but enjoying the beauty that surrounds him and the glorious sensation of being the center of this beauty."[2] Early centralized plans include the east end of Michelozzo's SS. Annunziata (1444) and Alberti's S. Sebastiano at Mantua (1460). Giuliano da Sangallo's Sta. Maria della Carceri (1485) Prato has its central dome on a Greek cross, although it still maintains a simple cubic exterior; whereas in the pilgrimage church of Sta. Maria della Consolazione (begun 1508) at Todi, the Greek cross has flowered into four subsidiary domes around a higher central dome. Bramante's Tempietta (1502) Rome is a classic example of this phase and was originally planned to be placed in a larger circular court. Rotational empathy is also the powerful underlying order of Renaissance plans of ideal cities.

While Bramante's 1506 plan for St. Peter's in Rome proposed a hemispherical dome, its underlying empathy for rotational form had given way to *helical* form empathy in Michelangelo's St. Peter's (built 1588-1590) with its main dome pulled vertically to a tapering sphere on a high drum. It has been described as a powerful thrust that draws energy upward.[3] This marks the shift toward introversion and the contained verticality that is also announced most powerfully in the energized helical stairs at Palazzo Contarini (1499) Venice; at the Francis I wing of the Chateau de Blois (1512), inspired by Leonardo da Vinci;

and at the double-helix stair that is the central feature in Francis I Palace at Chambord (1519). (Leonardo's brilliant intuition of the double-helix stair, two intertwined stairs that never meet, was matched only by scientists five hundred years later in the discovery of the DNA molecule's double-helix structure.) Chambord abounds with single-helix stairs as well as vertically extended towers and lanterns as a rich example of helical form empathy. Vertical tensions appear in Michelangelo's Laurentian library (begun 1524, which has been called Mannerist. Mannerism, particularly in its superficial connotation, does not do justice to the profound expressions of the more inclusive helical phase). The library's unusual stairway (1559), Michelangelo's earlier 1537 design of the Capitoline stairs that widen as they ascend, and Bernini's (1663-1666) Scala Regia demonstrate the fascination with verticality in the shift from the horizontal tensions of extraversion to the vertical tensions of introversion. The pull between earth and sky, tortured polarities of heaven and hell, of good and evil, of life and death, of light and dark, and the concern with vertical time all take over from horizontal spatial expansion and radiantly confident extroversion. Parmigianino's ascetic Madonna with the Long Neck is in tension with the physicality of Aretino's and Romano's pornography. It is a phase of personal and individual tensions between spirituality and sexuality.

The build-up from rotational tensions between the individual and the collective on the conscious plane to the helical tension stretching the individual between the conscious and the unconscious is further complicated in the *spiral* phase by the combined horizontal and vertical tensions between the individual striving for uniqueness and the pull of the collective unconscious. The increase of entropy reaches its extreme in spiral space/time complexity. Forms are energized in undulating concave/convex walls of Guarino's Palazzo Carignano (1679-1692) Turin and Borromini's San Carlo alle Quatro Fontane (plan 1638-1641 and façade 1665-1676) Rome. Tapered spiral lanterns penetrated with light occur in Borromini's St. Ivo (begun 1642) and Guarini's Sta. Sindone (1667-1694) Turin. The oval, in infinite variations and modifications, is the dominant and powerful underlying order in church plans: Borromini's San Carlo alle Quatro Fontane, Bernini's Sant' Andrea al Quirinale at Turin, his Sta. Maria dell' Assunzione at Arriccia, and Guarini's Church of the Immaculate Conception at Turin with its three interlocking ovals contained within a single larger oval. Further dematerialization occurs in lingering extremes of rococo entropy, as in Pöpplemann's Zwinger (1711-1722) Dresden, in the lavishly encrusted patterns on ceilings and walls that are dissolved with light.

This cycle has moved toward entropy from simple to complex, from the solid to the dematerialized, from serenely contained energy of building forms to their highly energized dissolution. The clear changes of style are not brought about by whimsical shifts of architectural vocabulary but are found in the directing energy of underlying archetypes—orienting principles of cube, sphere, helix, and spiral—acting as the bridge between creativity and the collective unconscious.

In the cycle, four dynamic shifts in human orientation direct energy first upward, next outward, then downward, and finally inward. Upward-directed energy correlates with orienting principles of the square, with bilateral symmetry, orthogonal or rectilinear form, and with the balanced spiritual joining of the so-called masculine and feminine principles. Outward-directed energy correlates with the circle, with expansion around in all directions from a center, and with extroversion and dominance of the "masculine" principle. Downward-directed energy correlates with the vertical pole or contained verticality of the cylinder, along with the literal joining of "masculine" and "feminine" principles. Inward-directed energy correlates with the triangle or its three-dimensional version as a cone or spiral and with the dominance of the "feminine" principle.

From square to circle to pole to triangle, or from cube to sphere to cylinder to cone, the cycle progresses from simple to more complex forming principles. The cycle also proceeds from contained energy to apparent loss of energy in greater and greater interaction with the environment outward, downward, and inward, a causal sequence that makes an acausal upward leap to a larger encompassing system of contained energy. The spontaneous return to upward-directed energy, an orientation defined by the cube or rectilinearity, appears in history as a rebirth or renaissance.

Great architecture was produced by architects who understood the archetypal power of geometry. Louis Sullivan was deeply involved in geometry and wrote that any one of a group of basic patterns and lines is a "container of energy" and a "directrix of power."[4] Frank Lloyd Wright wrote that "Geometry is the grammar so to speak of the form. It is its architectural principle, but there is a psychic correlation between the geometry of form and our associated ideas which constitutes its symbolic value. There resides always a certain 'spell power' in any geometric form which seems more or less a mystery, and is, as we say, the soul of the thing."[5]

Louis I. Kahn went further in his understanding of the place of geometry in the creative process. Probably Kahn's earliest written articulation of a three-stage process of creativity was in a letter to me in Rome in 1953. He described the first stage as "the Nature of a Space." Next came "Order," and finally "Design." At the time, he was giving a problem to students at Yale to design a theater and was discouraged that they were all simply modifying existing theater designs. He wrote that "Innumerable architects are still just modifying what has long lost its life. . . . External spaces must wait until the 'Nature of the Space' unfolds, and before 'Order' can be evolved or created. Now that is the reason why I had difficulty explaining Order before. The basis from which Order could be derived was absent."[6]

It recently occurred to me that Kahn's three stages are missing a link in order to form a cycle of creativity—a cycle with a much shorter timespan and one that would occur many times over within each phase of the historical cycle. The creative process would begin with the challenge to design a building. This event correlates with the extroverted attitude of the rotational phase. Next the architect looks at history or at precedents, a phase that correlates with the empathy for physicality and with time in the helical phase. Many do not go beyond this stage. They get stuck at that level, which may account for the abundance of superficiality in architecture. The introverted spiral phase would involve going beyond history and beyond tangible forms to the essence or meaning of the spaces to be created—as Kahn said, "the Nature of a Space" or "what a space wants to be." Going beyond history and beyond memory, one is freed from any one specific form and looks for intangible qualities open to all the orientations of space and time. At this stage in the cycle the architect is then open to the possibility of an intuitive leap to Order, the particular geometric archetype that fits the Nature of the Space. To be open to Order demands a struggle that is free of ego, free of limitations of space and time. The momentary balancing of all tensions of polarity and rotation allows a creative breakthrough that corresponds to a renaissance in the historical cycle. To discover Order is to be in touch with laws of form, universal natural principles that do not belong to anyone but also belong to everyone. When this stage is reached, the Design process can begin, the creation of tangible expression that answers to circumstantial needs, budget, site, program, structure, mechanical systems, and materials.

Today architecture appears to have reached a phase of greatest entropy. The dramatic breakthrough at the beginning of this century from eclecticism to the cubic horizontality of Frank Lloyd Wright's Prairie Houses, epitomized in the serene sweep of the Robie House (1906), was rationalized in the International Style, in Mies Van Der Rohe's Barcelona Pavilion, in Le Corbusier's Villa Savoie. Curvilinear forms with rotational empathy appeared in Mendelsohn's Schocken store, Chemnitz, and the curved base of the Philadelphia Savings Fund Society Tower in Philadelphia. Buckminster Fuller's Dymaxion House and tensegrity domes are monuments to this pragmatic, extroverted, inventive phase of form empathy.

The shift from extraversion to the introverted tensions of helical form empathy occurred in the work of the highly introverted architect Kahn in his Richards Medical Towers (1957-1961). Wright's Johnson Wax Tower (1949) expresses a similar form empathy but, ahead of its time, did not strike the same responsive chord, perhaps because it was a later addition to the Johnson Wax office building with its pronounced rotational empathy. London's Post Office Tower, the Tokyo Tower, and Goldberg's Marina Towers in Chicago expressed helical tensions of this phase, followed by a proliferation of towers by John Portman and others. Kahn's and my proposed City Tower (1952-1957), in its spatial undulation, literally defines helical energy/form tensions, with a suggestion of a tapered spiral in its expanded buttressed base.

The more deeply introverted spiral phase takes on an almost pure expression in Wright's Guggenheim Museum (1946-1959), again ahead of its time. Combined horizontal and vertical tensions appear in the buttressed walls of Kahn's Business Institute in Ahmedabad, India and in his convoluted exteriors at Dacca, where undulating clusters of cylinders sliced with circular and triangular openings have a baroque energy. Much of the highly publicized current architecture of this phase has lost its power in superficial and personal "historicism" split off from the archetypal energy of the collective unconscious. Perverse and too-clever witticisms of postmodernism are the limp froth of this spiral form empathy. Many mirrored and faceted towers are dematerialized images without meaningful inner order or clarity of space and structure. Yet Richard Roger's and Renzo Piano's Pompidou Center in Paris and Norman Foster's Hong Kong Bank have a level of integrity and vitality. If architects go to deeper levels of "what a space wants to be," the intuitive leap to Order could bring about a new renaissance in the history of architecture.

Kahn's Kimbell Museum (1966-1672) heralds such a breakthrough. It is not dissolved by light, but it reflects and contains the sun's fire numinously in low cycloid vaults. Unlike the static reflection from a semicircular vault toward a center-point, the dynamically reflecting cycloid, like the moving sun, is defined by a rotating circle. The length of the vaults sweeps horizontally between earth and sky, between the sun's fire reflected within as light in motion and without as more visibly moving light along the length of the vault of falling water. At Kimbell, Kahn synthesizes the four elements of earth, air, fire, and water of Jung's final quaternio to bring a fresh and profound spirit to architecture.

Jung's powerful concept of the cycle of individuation is the inspiration for proposing a cyclical dimension to the chronological view of history that describes collective human creativity. Correlation of collective creativity with psychic concepts of Jung's cycle also gives greater depth and meaning to a proposed cycle of individual creativity. Jung's cycle of psychic individuation, historic cycles in architectural history, and a cycle of individual creativity all illustrate a dynamic interaction between the probable loss of energy in the law of entropy and the proportionately predictable yet improbable synthesis of a more encompassing energy—the intuitive creative leap to higher consciousness and renewal.

# Notes

1. Anne G. Tyng, "Geometric Extensions of Consciousness," in *Zodiac 19* (Milan: Edizione di Communita, 1969), pp. 130-162.

2. Nikolaus Pevsner, *An Outline of European Architecture*, 7th ed. (Hammondsworth, Middlesex, England: Penguin Books, 1964), p. 182.

3. H. W. Janson, *History of Art* (Englewood Cliffs, N.J.: Prentice-Hall; New York: Harry N. Abrams, 1973), p. 369.

4. Louis Sullivan, *A System of Architectural Ornament According with a Philosophy of Man's Powers* (New York: Press of the American Institute of Architects, 1924), plate 3.

5. Frank Lloyd Wright, *The Japanese Print* (1912; New York: Horizon Press, 1967), no page numbers.

6. Louis I. Kahn, letter to author, in Rome, Italy, December 8, 1953.

# C. G. Jung
## and the Temple
### Symbols of Wholeness      John M. Lundquist

C. G. Jung's researches into the human psyche reach into the heart of one of the most profound and influential symbols of human history: the temple. Jung documented at the psychic level the entire range of experience that we know from temple practices worldwide. This includes the universal validity of the symbolism of the center, the mountain, the tree and the water of life, the sacrality of the circle and the power of circumambulation, initiation and secrecy. The combination of religious symbolism with ritual and sacral building practices well known among ancient peoples is extant among such modern groups as the Pueblo and Oglala Sioux. Jung's work provides a possible account of the origins of these instances, ancient and modern.

Writing of the "other" and more mature personality that he discovered as a youth, Jung found that "there existed another realm, like a temple in which anyone who entered was transformed and suddenly overpowered by a vision of the whole cosmos, so that he could only marvel and admire, forgetful of himself."[1] Much later in his life, in 1944, Jung had a serious heart attack and was hospitalized. He came very close to death, and during the time that he was unconscious he experienced "deliriums and visions." He had a sense of being high up in space, of seeing the earth below him, and a vision of much of the Asiatic portions of its geography. Suddenly, after having contemplated the Indian Ocean, he turned around and looked to the north. Then he turned to the south and saw in space "a tremendous dark block of stone . . . about the size of my house . . . floating in space." A temple had been hollowed out into the stone, similar to rock temples he had actually seen on the Gulf of Bengal. He wrote:

> As I approached the steps leading up to the entrance into the rock, a strange thing happened: I had the feeling that everything was being sloughed away; everything I had aimed at or wished for or thought, the whole phantasmagoria of earthly existence, fell away or was stripped away from me—an extremely painful process. Nevertheless something remained; it was as if I now carried along with me everything I had ever experienced or done, everything that had happened around me. I might also say: it was with me,

and I was it. I consisted of all that, so to speak. I consisted of my own history, and I felt with great certainty: this is what I am. . . . Something also engaged my attention: as I approached the temple I had the certainty that I was about to enter an illuminated room and would meet there all those people to whom I belong in reality. There I would at last understand—this too was a certainty—what historical nexus I or my life fitted into. I would know what had been before me, why I had come into being, and where my life was flowing. . . . I felt sure that I would receive an answer to all these questions as soon as I entered the rock temple.[2]

This extraordinary vision of a visit to a temple, described by Jung, encompasses the primary elements of temple visits as they have actually been experienced by people for centuries. As one enters the temple, ordinary time is stripped away and one experiences sacred time and space. One enters the most holy place ("an illuminated room") and experiences the ultimate revelation: the discovery of oneself, one's consciousness of history, and a knowledge of one's place in history. In ancient times, kings and priests would go into the holy of holies once a year to consult the tablets of destiny in order to discover the course of a peoples' fate for the coming year.[3] In India, as well as in the mystical traditions of western Christianity, the sacred mountain (the archetype of the temple) was viewed as the place to which one went to find self-revelation, wisdom, integration, and union with deity and with the cosmos.[4]

Jung's description of his experience is remarkably parallel to other descriptions of revelation in a temple setting in a number of cultures. In the Vision Quest of the Oglala Sioux the young man desiring purification and vision from the deity (*Wakan Tanka*) would "go to a high place," would there orient a spot of ground by creating a squared circle (a mandala configuration), and would sleep with his head at the center pole, where he would hope to receive in dreams and vision what would be of value to him and to his people.[5] Similarly, it was at the high place of Gibeon where Solomon received the wisdom from God that allowed him to carry out his royal mission in ancient Israel (see I Kings 3, 2 Chronicles I).

Jung's most important discovery as it relates to the temple is the role of the mandala (the squared circle) as the archetype of wholeness. Temple plans are often mandalas. The temple, as documented in many cultures, is the place where wholeness is realized. The critical role Jung found the mandala to play in his therapeutic practice contributed greatly to the formulation of his theory of archetypes. Jung recognized one patient's description of a circle as "a mandala, the psychological expression of the totality of the self" (*CW* 9i: par. 542, p. 304). Further, the motif of the mandala, Jung postulated, was based on the squaring of the circle. In this squaring, Jung saw a central point within the psyche that served not only as a reference point but also as a source of energy for the psyche itself. "Their basic motif is the premonition of a centre of personality, a kind of central point within the psyche, to which everything is related, by which everything is arranged, and which itself is a source of energy." He described the totality of the psyche as comprising three elements: consciousness, the personal unconscious, "and finally an indefinitely large segment of the collective unconscious whose archetypes are common to all mankind" (*CW* 9i: par. 643, p. 357).

The mandala appears again and again as a religious symbol, becoming established as an archetype that indicates an ultimate unity of the self. In the early years following the deaths of both the Buddha and Christ, both figures were represented in mandala configurations, the Buddha as a twelve-spoked wheel, and Christ as the center of a mandala with the four gospel writers. When he first described the mandala-shaped core of the psyche, Jung was unaware of its significance as an ancient symbol of the godhead and the cosmos. He discovered the historical implications of the mandala much later.[6]

For an understanding of temple architecture, as it represents the archetype of unity, the identification of the circle with the symbol of the mandala is essential. The circle forms the basic shape, or is otherwise a principal feature in the temple, as seen in many historical traditions.[7] For a circle to be realized architecturally, however, it must first be oriented in the form of a square. As has been observed before,[8] the square complements the circle, representing the conscious realization of organic psychic unity. Rudolf Arnheim writes of the two spatial systems on which our world view is built, the cosmic, where "matter organizes around centers," and the parochial, where "the curvature of the earth straightens into a plane surface."[9] It is the architectural combination of these two units of space that we see in temple buildings worldwide and throughout history.

Mandalas take several forms: painted on cloth, laid out on the ground, and expressed in three-dimensional architecture. The painted mandalas of the Buddhist tradition, which were themselves temple documents and were deposited in temples for safekeeping in Tibet and Japan, were vehicles of meditation that possessed "the essence and totality."[10] In the Tibetan tradition, where in the *Yoga tantra* meditation played a major role in achieving enlightenment, mandalas played a major role as condensed images of the universe.[11] Mandalas not only served as vehicles for meditation, they also found architectural expression as the basic form of temples in the Hindu and Buddhist traditions. In those traditions, mandalas are temples. In India, where architecture was the chief science and was based on a knowledge of sacred texts, the mandala was carefully laid out on the ground prior to the raising of the sacred structure.[12] The stupa is the most characteristic three-dimensional representation of the mandala. And indeed, within Buddhism, the erection of a stupa was prescribed as one of the chief means of attaining buddhahood.[13]

In his autobiography, Jung recorded a profound personal experience at the famous stupas of Sanchi:

> When I visited the stupas of Sanchi, where Buddha delivered his fire sermon, I was overcome by a strong emotion of the kind that frequently develops in me when I encounter a thing, person or idea of whose significance I am still unconscious. The stupas are situated on a rocky hill whose peak can be reached by a pleasant path of great stone slabs laid down through a green meadow. The stupas are tombs or containers of relics, hemispherical in shape, like two gigantic rice bowls placed one on top of the other (concavity upon concavity), according to the prescripts of Buddha himself in the *Maha-Parinibbana-Sutta*. . . . The largest of these buildings is surrounded by a wall which has four elaborate gates. You come in by one of these and the path turns to the left, then leads into a clockwise circumambulation around the stupa. At the four cardinal points stand statues of the Buddha. When you have completed the circumambulation, you enter a second, higher circuit which runs in the same direction. The distant prospect over the plain, the stupas themselves, the temple ruins, and the solitary stillness of the holy site held me in a spell. I took leave of my companion and submerged myself in the overpowering mood of the place.[14]

Here we see yet another important example of the profound way in which visits to temple sites influenced Jung personally and professionally. Along with his description of the manner in which stupas were built (the mandala structure: the combination of circle and square), Jung introduced two additional specific concepts that play a central role in the relationship between temple symbolism and his work on archetypes: circumambulation and orientation. As was the case with his experience at the stone temple in India, quoted at length above, this experience demonstrates several of the fundamental ritual characteristics of temple practice: He exits the realm of profane or ordinary time and enters the temple and the realm of sacred time; but two new elements are introduced: circumambulation and orientation. The combination of these two ritual processes, by which he experienced the squaring of the circle as he rose higher in the stupa at each circuit, took him beyond the experience of unity of the self with historical consciousness that he had experienced in the earlier visit to the stone temple.

Writing of an earlier period in his life Jung stated, "During those years, between 1918 and 1920, I began to understand that the goal of psychic development is the self. There is no linear evolution; there is only a circumambulation of the self. Uniform development exists, at most, only at the beginning; later, everything points toward the center. This insight gave me stability, and gradually my inner peace returned. I knew that in finding the mandala as an expression of the self I had attained what was for me the ultimate. Perhaps someone else knows more, but not I."[15] Immediately before this Jung had written, "It became increasingly plain to me that the mandala is the center. It is the exponent of all paths. It is the path to the center, to individuation."[16]

The mandala represented a microcosmic image of the universe in Tibetan Buddhism, and in Japanese Buddhism a source of essential wholeness. In both the Buddhist and the Hindu traditions, moreover, the mandala served simultaneously as the actual ground-plan and as the spiritual foundation for temples. In the ancient Near East, the temple served as both the geographical and the ideological center of society. Jung's discovery of the mandala as an archetype of wholeness and centrality leads to a larger experience of this archetype as actualized in temples built by many cultures of the world.

Circumambulation as a ritual component of temple practice is attested in many cultures of the world. It is attested in a remarkable way in ancient Israel in Psalms 48:12-14 (in the King James Version):

> Walk about Zion, go round about her, number her towers,
> consider well her ramparts, go through her citadels; that you
> may tell the next generation
> that this is God, our God for ever and ever. He will be our guide
> for ever.

In order to make the relation between temple practice and circumambulation more clear, I am going to make what is admittedly a vast cross-cultural jump to the Oglala Sioux. The Sioux preserve remarkably ancient patterns in their ritual structures, patterns that bear close comparison with other cultures of the world, particularly those of south Asia. According to the account of Black Elk, the great nineteenth-century prophet of the Sioux, the sacred pipe was brought to his people by a sacred woman called White Buffalo Cow Woman. When this woman arrived to reveal to the Sioux the knowledge of the rites by which they should govern their religious and social lives, she entered the lodge that had been prepared for her coming and immediately circumambulated in a sun-wise direction. Then, having finished her instruction to those assembled, she again circumambulated before leaving.[17] Black Elk himself interpreted this event in the light of the life cycle, which he related to the four cardinal directions, each standing for one of the ages of the human being.[18] We thus see the intimate interconnection between circumambulation—which gives us the circle, the symbol of perfection and totality—and orientation—the symbol of the square, thus the squared circle, the mandala, and its relation to the human life cycle, indicating that the individual achieves wholeness at the center in the Oglala tradition, a remarkable validation of Jung's researches.

Jung's experience at the stupas of Sanchi also introduces the critical role that orientation to the four cardinal directions played in recorded temple-building practices.[19] In the temple-building cultures, dire consequences were thought to follow from an incorrect orientation of the building to the cardinal directions.[20]

The main point here is that the temple is the physical, the ideological, and the psychic center of a society; its presence binds a society together, and the physical orientation of the building corresponds to the human need for psychic orientation. As the individual circumambulates the temple, pausing at the four corners, as Jung did in the stupa of Sanchi, or as White Buffalo Cow Woman did in the Oglala lodge, that person is depicting and symbolizing the human need for orientation. Aniela Jaffé wrote that "The spatial orientation performed by Brahma and Buddha may be regarded as symbolic of the human need for psychic orientation. The four functions of consciousness described by Dr. Jung . . . thought, feeling, intuition, and sensation [which I believe can be correlated with the four cardinal directions of the Sioux, with the stages of the life cycle that they assign to each one] equip man to deal with the impressions of the world he receives from within and without."[21] Circumambulation and orientation are related to wholeness, to the human life cycle, to integration. As Jung said, the mandala "is the exponent of all paths. It is the path to the center, to individuation."

Jung was particularly interested in the role that secrecy played among various peoples he observed. Secrecy is an integral part of temple-centered societies.[22] It was especially among the Pueblo that Jung documented this aspect of traditional society. He noted the exceptionally closemouthed attitude of the Pueblo regarding the rituals that men in the community carried out in their sacred mountains that gave the Pueblo "pride and the power to resist the dominant whites. It gives him cohesion and unity; and I feel sure that the Pueblos as an individual community will continue to exist as long as their mysteries are not desecrated."²³ He further wrote that "There is no better means of intensifying the treasured feeling of individuality than the possession of a secret which the individual is pledged to guard. The very beginnings of societal structures reveal the craving for secret organizations."²⁴

Secrecy not only plays a social role, in that it reinforces social cohesion; it also plays a major role in the life of the individual, since "the individual on his lonely path needs a secret which for various reasons he may not or cannot reveal. Such a secret reinforces him in the isolation of his individual aims."²⁵ Jung lamented the fact that there were no secrets left in the Western world: "their sacraments have long ago ceased to be secrets." What is more, the secrecy that he observed among the Pueblo gave him insight into the situation of ancient Eleusis, whose mysteries we do not know today because they were not betrayed anciently. "This was not, I felt, mystification, but a vital mystery whose betrayal might bring about the downfall of the community as well as of the individual."²⁶

In 1927, Jung had a dream, which in my interpretation is saturated with temple symbolism and which, he concluded, "brought with it a sense of finality. I saw here that the goal had been revealed. One could not go beyond the center. The center is the goal, and everything is directed toward that center. Through this dream I understood that the self is the principle and archetype of orientation and meaning."²⁷

The dream was set in Liverpool, which Jung interpreted to mean "pool of life." In the dream, Jung, accompanied by a number of Swiss who themselves did not share with him in the revelation, finds himself in Liverpool, which is represented as a mandala-shaped city, designed much on the order of an ancient Near Eastern city, with a crowded, dirty lower city where the masses live, and an acropolis or citadel, high above the lower city where the city's temples and public buildings are located. The "real city" was high above, on a plateau, which Jung and his companions reached after a climb. This aspect of his dream invokes the image of the labyrinth, of the arduous initiatory journey one must make before reaching the temple, the center.

Having reached the plateau, Jung and his companions found "a broad square dimly illuminated by street lights, into which many streets converged." The city's quarters were arranged radially around the square. A round pool stood in the center of the square, thus creating the squared circle, the mandala, indicating the location of the temple in the topography of the dream. A small island stood in the center of the pool. On the brightly illuminated island, which stood out amidst the darkness that surrounded it, a magnolia tree stood. The tree seemed to be the source of light on the island. Jung's companions were aware only of the inclement weather—rain and cold and darkness—

and did not see the tree. Jung was the initiate here and, although surrounded by companions, was alone proceeding through the initiatory process that led through the darkness, up the mountain, into the deeper recesses of the temple, until he reached the holy of holies, a place bathed in light, where a tree of life, nourished by the waters of life, grew. We see then that Jung experienced ritual-like initiation based on temple symbols both in the ruins of ancient temple buildings, as we saw above, and in dreams, which according to Ira Progoff is the characteristic modern format for initiation across life-cycle thresholds.[28]

The combination of temple symbols referred to above and that occurred in Jung's dream—mountain, tree of life, and waters of life—represents a "primordial landscape," the scene that is depicted in ancient Near Eastern creation texts as representing the state of the world in primeval times. This scene is depicted both architecturally and ritually in ancient Near Eastern temples, since we know that ancient and traditional temple rituals are centered around the creation, the state of the world in its primordial perfection, a state that should serve as a paradigm for human beings at each transitional period in their lives.[29] In terms of ancient Near Eastern temple symbolism and architectural and ritual practices, the combination of the island, the tree, the water, and the light places us in the holy of holies; it was there where revelation occurred, where the world was set aright again each year, where the will of deity was made known to the king during the New Year festival. How significant it thus is that one of the central messages of Jung's life became apparent in this dream: "One could not go beyond the center. The center is the goal, and everything is directed toward that center. Through this dream I understood that the self is the principle and archetype of orientation and meaning. . . . Out of it emerged a first inkling of my personal myth."[30]

A recent television show documenting the main formative elements in the history of American architecture spent a considerable segment of the telecast discussing Jefferson's Monticello. The commentators spoke of Jefferson's Arcadian classical dream of America. They discussed the architectural eccentricities of Monticello itself and noted the fact that on the very top of the building, which itself sits on top of a hill, Jefferson left an unfinished, empty room. As the camera gave the viewer a clear look at the architectural plan of the building through an aerial view, it became evident that Monticello is architectually a mandala structure. The central theme of the show was America's search for a usable past. Jefferson, it seems, was himself incorporating into his life's work the symbols of a distant past that obviously still had deep significance for him as he tried to forge out a destiny for the new country.[31]

The great achievement of Jung is that he discovered a "usable past" for all of us. He located the past of temple symbolism in the present of human psychic activity. "Wholeness," he wrote, "is nevertheless empirical in so far as it is anticipated by the psyche in the form of spontaneous or autonomous symbols. These are quaternity or mandala symbols, which occur not only in the dreams of modern people who have never heard of them, but are widely disseminated in the historical records of many peoples and many epochs. Their significance as *symbols of unity and totality* is amply confirmed by history as well as by empirical psychology" (*CW* 9ii: par. 59, p. 31).

To enter the temple and proceed to the holy of holies is to find the true self, which is co-eternal with the deity who sits enthroned over the primordial mound in the most holy place. The squared circle (the temple) is a natural archetype of wholeness. The circumambulation of the mandala represents perfection. Perfection thus obtained means the attainment of selfhood. "Everything points toward the center." The attainment of the center must be maintained as a secret. The knowledge and insight gained at the mountain, the source of the stream of water, whence comes all life ("Do you not think that all life comes from the mountain?" the old Pueblo man asked Jung[32]) must be kept from the uninitiated who, like Jung's Swiss companions in the dream, could not understand why a Swiss would settle in Liverpool.[33]

Circumambulation, as in the stupa, proceeds to ever deeper interiors and to ever higher levels. Having attained the "highest depth" of the temple, one enters the realm of timelessness,[34] where one's true self becomes more evident and more authentic, where one's life course—the meaning of one's life—becomes clear. The penetration of the mandala takes on the aspect of a journey through the unconscious into circular and quaternity symbols. These symbols are realized architecturally in the temple structure itself. This journey is a journey to and into light (the "illuminated room" of Jung's early experience, or the brightly illuminated island of the Liverpool dream). The temple, the squared circle, represents wholeness and renders the journey to wholeness in both architectural and ritual form. "The temple, a monolith, represents the *lapis*, the philosopher's stone, in which and on whose account the entire sacrificial operation takes place."[35]

*Acknowledgment*

I wish to thank Ms. Elizabeth Kopley for generous editorial assistance, which improved both the style and the content of the article.

# Notes

1. C. G. Jung, *Memories, Dreams, Reflections*, ed. Aniela Jaffé, trans. Richard and Clara Winston (New York: Vintage Books, 1965), p. 45.

2. Ibid., pp. 290-291.

3. John M. Lundquist, "What is a Temple? A Preliminary Typology," in *The Quest for the Kingdom of God: Studies in Honor of George E. Mendenhall*, ed. H. B. Huffmon, F. A. Spina, and A.R.W. Green (Winona Lake, Ind.: Eisenbrauns, 1983), p. 216.

4. R. C. Zaehner, "Standing on the Peak," in *Studies in Mysticism and Religion presented to Gershom G. Scholem* (Jerusalem: The Magnes Press, 1967), pp. 381-387.

5. Black Elk, *The Sacred Pipe*, ed. Joseph Epes Brown (Baltimore: Penguin Books, 1971), pp. 44-46.

6. Marie-Louise von Franz, *C. G. Jung, His Myth in Our Time*, trans. William H. Kennedy (New York: G. P. Putnam's Sons, 1975), pp. 139-141.

7. John M. Lundquist, "The Legitimizing Role of the Temple in the Origin of the State," in *Society of Biblical Literature 1982 Seminar Papers*, ed. Kent Harold Richards (Chicago: Scholars Press, 1982), pp. 284-285.

8. Stella Kramrisch, *The Hindu Temple*, vol. 1 (Delhi: Motilal Banarsidass, 1976), pp. 21-22; Marie-Louise von Franz, "The Process of Individuation," in *Man and His Symbols*, ed. C. G. Jung (New York: Dell Publishing Co., 1984), p. 234.

9. Rudolf Arnheim, *The Power of the Center: A Study of Composition in the Visual Arts* (Berkeley: University of California Press, 1982), pp. vii-x.

10. Miyeko Murase, *Tales of Japan: Scrolls and Prints from the New York Public Library* (New York: Oxford University Press, 1986), p. 20, for the etymology of the word *mandala*. Cf. Giuseppe Tucci, *The Theory and Practice of the Mandala*, trans. A. H. Broderick (New York: Samuel Weiser, 1970).

11. bSod nams rgya mtsho, *Tibetan Mandalas, The Ngor Collection. Explanation to Iconography* (Tokyo: Kodansha, 1983), p. 18.

12. Kramrisch, *The Hindu Temple*, pp. 21-39.

13. Murase, *Tales of Japan*, p. 14.

14. Jung, *Memories*, p. 278.

15. Ibid., pp. 196-197.

16. Ibid.

17. Black Elk, *The Sacred Pipe*, pp. 4-9.

18. Ibid., p. 5.

19. Lundquist, "What is a Temple?", p. 210.

20. Kramrisch, *The Hindu Temple*, pp. 38-39.

21. Aniela Jaffé, "Symbolism in the Visual Arts," *Man and His Symbols*, pp. 266-267.

22. Lundquist, "What is a Temple?", pp. 218-219.

23. Jung, *Memories*, pp. 249-250.

24. Ibid., p. 342.

25. Ibid., p. 343.

26. Ibid., pp. 249-250.

27. Ibid., pp. 198-199.

28. Ira Progoff, "Form, Time and Opus: The Dialectic of the Creative Psyche," in *Form als Aufgabe des Geistes*, ed. Adolf Portmann, Eranos Jahrbuch 1965 (Zurich: Rhein Verlag, 1966), pp. 287-291.

29. See Mircea Eliade, "The Prestige of the Cosmogonic Myth," in *Diogenes* 23 (1958): 1-13; Roy A. Rappaport, "The Obvious Aspects of Ritual," in his *Ecology, Meaning and Religion* (Richmond, Calif.: North Atlantic Books, 1979), pp. 200-201; John M. Lundquist, "The Common Temple Ideology of the Ancient Near East," in *The Temple in Antiquity*, ed. Truman G. Madsen (Provo: Brigham Young University Religious Studies Center Monograph Series, 1984), p. 66.

30. Jung, *Memories*, pp. 198-199.

31. The program "What Is American Architecture?" was Part 1 of an eight-part series called *Pride of Place: Building the American Dream*, aired on PBS on March 29, 1986.

32. Ibid., p. 251.

33. Ibid., p. 198.

34. Rappaport, "The Obvious Aspects of Ritual," pp. 186-187. See also Mircea Eliade, *The Sacred and the Profane: The Nature of Religion*, trans. Willard R. Trask (New York: Harcourt, Brace and Jovanovich, 1959).

35. von Franz, *C. G. Jung*, pp. 227-228.

# The Image
## of the Vessel in the
## Architecture of
## Frank Lloyd
## Wright   Neil Levine

More than any other modern architect—perhaps more than any other architect, period—Frank Lloyd Wright sought to integrate architecture with nature in such an organic and intimate way that one might not be able to tell, as he liked to say, where nature leaves off and the building begins.[1] Often, he literally enmeshed building and landscape. At other times, he closely imitated the particular shapes of natural forms, such as a snail's shell, or an aspect of natural phenomena, such as the swirling movement of water. But what is more interesting and important for us, in the context of Jungian thought, is the fact that Wright realized that, in order to represent nature within the conventions of art, he had to develop a model or archetype that could both contain his thought and yet allow it to expand freely, following a natural pattern of growth and change. The archetype of spatial containment and representation that ultimately came to dominate his work and to serve as his means for translating the world of nature into the terms and forms of architecture was the image of the vessel.[2] Of even further interest in this context is the extraordinary degree to which that choice of imagery was intimately related to the particular events of Wright's personal life, thus encoding in the forms he evolved an added layer of psychological significance.

Wright practiced architecture for over seventy years, dying at the age of 91, just before the Guggenheim Museum, in New York City, was completed in 1959. The image of the vessel, however, which is so explicit in that climactic building, emerged in Wright's work only midway through his career, when he was about 55. It contrasted in almost every way with the more traditional and conventional image of the hut that had previously dominated his architecture in an equally powerful and explicit way.

The first significant building that Wright designed was the house he built for himself and his young family in 1889, in Oak Park, Illinois, the suburb to the west of Chicago where he chose to live when he left

Wisconsin to work in that city (Figure 1). With its exaggerated triangular gable set above a supporting base of bay windows, the form of the house was clearly modeled on that of the hut, an image that the French Enlightenment theorist Marc-Antoine Laugier had convincingly explained to be the natural model of the classical Greek temple.[3] For Wright, as for so many architects before him, the archetypal model of the hut represented a mediating term between nature and architecture, an idealized image of *shelter*. And it was this model that thus served as the basis for Wright's development of the Prairie House, his most important contribution to the history of modern architecture during the early years of his practice.[4]

Throughout Wright's work of the next twenty years or so, this basic image of shelter-as-construct retained its authority despite all his attempts to open up the space of his Prairie Houses to the larger environment surrounding them. In the house he built in 1904, for Mamah and Edwin Cheney, also in Oak Park, the triangular shape of the hipped roof, though much suppressed, still provides an overriding image of self-containment, which is further reinforced by the central fire-

Figure 1.    Frank Lloyd Wright House, Oak Park, Illinois.

place that pins the house to its site and gives it its intrinsic meaning (Figure 2).

But things began to break apart, so to speak, and come back together in entirely new ways, when Wright ran off to Europe in 1909 with Mrs. Cheney. The following year he returned, not to his family in Oak Park, but to the hills of southern Wisconsin, to the land his Welsh forefathers had settled in the previous century, in order to build there a place where he and Mamah Cheney could live together. In that building, as in his private life, Wright broke all the rules of convention in order to try to establish a purely natural, totally unmediated relationship with the landscape.

In the house built in 1911, which he named after the legendary Welsh bard Taliesin, Wright completely inverted his earlier process of design and made the preexisting landscape the core of the building. The hill-crown became the central focus of the design, and the house itself was allowed to grow irregularly around it, in a casual and extremely naturalistic manner (Figure 3). The loosely grouped wings of house and studio created a roughly C-shaped court, following the contours of the hill, just below its crown, The hilltop was preserved in its natural state and thus rose up through that architectural embrace.

In order to make Taliesin appear to grow out of the hillside and "belong to that hill, as trees and the ledges of rock did," Wright instructed the stone masons to imitate the rough pattern of rock strata that they might see in the walls of the quarry located just over the next hill.[5] In this way, Wright believed, the house would come to represent the image of a rock outcrop and thus translate into three dimensions what the Welsh word Taliesin meant—the "shining brow" of the hill embraced by the house.[6]

Figure 2.    Edwin H. Cheney House, Oak Park, Illinois.

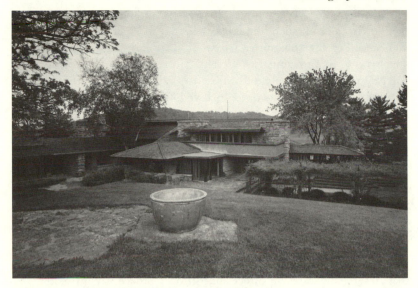

Figure 3.   Taliesin, Spring Green, Wisconsin.

Wright referred with almost religious reverence to that hill and
claimed that the house was designed to consort with it. Taliesin became his alter ego, and the hill its female companion.[7] He described
Taliesin as "a house that hill might marry and live happily with ever
after," in perfect natural union, just as he hoped he and Mamah Cheney
would.[8] House and hill were to complement one another, together creating a much larger whole.

That ideal union, however, was soon shattered by the arson and
multiple murders at Taliesin in the summer of 1914. Wright's cook
went mad, setting fire to the house when Wright was away, then hack-
ing to death Mamah Cheney, her two children, plus four of their em-
ployees. The utter horror of this tragic event destroyed, it would seem
forever, Wright's naive belief in the possibility of a completely natural
and direct identification of architecture and nature.

Wright spent most of the next seven or eight years far away from his
Wisconsin home, working on the Imperial Hotel in Tokyo, where,
instead of imagining an architecture at one with a benevolent landscape, he spoke of "building against doomsday"; he interpreted the
process as a confrontation with the violent and irrational forces of vol-
canos and earthquakes, embodied in the image of "the sacred Fujiyama
brooding in majesty and eternal calm over all."[9] Wright returned, almost with a vengeance, to historical forms and conventional compo-
sitions, even recalling, in Hollyhock House, the house he built in 1919–
1921 for the oil heiress Aline Barnsdall in Los Angeles, the pyramidal,

hieratic shapes of Maya temples. Regressive and defensive by comparison with Taliesin, such buildings, whether in Japan or not, were designed under the shadow cast by a mythic Fujiyama, that volcanic
shape now symbolizing for Wright nature's inexorable, intractable
force (Figure 4). Rarely returning to Taliesin during this period,
Wright now described its once "beloved" hill-crown as "the smoking
crater of a volcano."[10]

It is against this background of displacement and alienation that one
can see—in another house Wright designed for himself, though this
time for the desert—the new model that would revitalize and redirect
his thinking (Figures 5 and 6). This extraordinary house was never
built, nor did Wright ever publish the drawings or even mention the
project in print, a significant fact in its own right. It was apparently
designed, between 1921 and 1924, while he was living in Southern
California, most probably for a site in Death Valley, very near the volcanic Ubehebe Crater.[11] Conceived for the vast, scarred expanse of
that desert landscape, in direct apposition to the dormant crater, the
building seems to emerge from its site as a direct response on Wright's

Figure 4.   Hollyhock (Aline Barnsdall) House, Los Angeles, California.

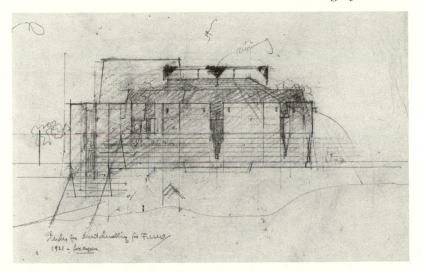

Figure 5.   F. L. Wright, project for his own "Desert Dwelling," Death Valley, California, c. 1921-1924.

part to his recent traumatic experience. It is, in effect, a transformation and sublimation of nature through the healing effects of time.

The house is clearly as symbolic and as imagistic in intention as was Wright's original Oak Park house. The actual living section of the small building is tucked onto the rear of an octagonal court, which is entered on axis and open to the sky. The plastic, reinforced-concrete walls of the octagon open out like the petals of a desert flower to hold in tension an overhead awning. A central oculus is situated directly above a circular pool of water, cut into the desert floor just in front of a monumental chimney that divides into two the stairways leading to balconies and the actual rooms behind. At first glance, the house has the appearance of a barbican, obviously defensive in nature. But soon that image dissolves into something more like a man-made crater—a cistern or vessel, protected from, yet receptive to, the elements. Seen in this way, the design appears to grow out of the ground in an entirely unpredictable yet natural way.

What underlies the form is indeed the image of a cistern or pot. During the years Wright was in Japan, he collected many works of Oriental art, which he then incorporated into his rebuilding of Taliesin. The most striking of these were the various vessels, and particularly the large tea jars, that he placed on the ledges and parapets of his house back in Wisconsin, as if to signify some new meaning he was trying to return to those walls embracing the hill-crown he had come to think of as the "smoking crater of a volcano." The idea of the fired vessel or

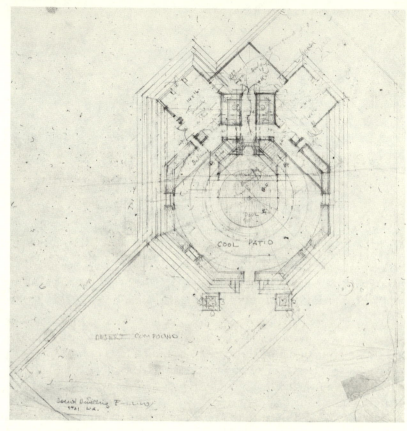

Figure 6.  F. L. Wright, project for his own "Desert Dwelling," plan.

pot thus became for Wright an image of regeneration, and its shape, totally continuous and protective yet wholly responsive to its contents, presented a new model for representation.[12]

Unlike the model of the hut, the vessel or pot was plastic rather than clastic, spatial rather than structural. Unlike other archetypal models, such as the cave or the tent, the pot provided a continuous image of inside and outside at once while remaining stable and permanent in shape. The earthenware vessel or pot was, by its very nature, *of* the earth and, according to Wright, the actual historic prototype for the kiva, the earliest sacred and monumental architecture of the Indians of the American Southwest.[13]

In his only essay devoted to the history of architectural development, a part of which was published in the following decade, Wright described how the earliest men and women, who "probably first lived in stone caves,"[14] soon learned a new method for shaping the structures around them subsequent to their change from basket-making to the production of pottery:

> While still dwelling in caves . . . man perhaps learned to make utensils out of wet clay. He burned them hard for use. These utensils he seems to have made with a higher faculty. His instinct became an aesthetic sense of environment. It taught him something of form. He learned from the animals, the serpents, the plants that he knew. Except for this faculty he was no more than another animal.
>
> Still clinging to the cliffs, he made whole caves out of wet clay and let the sun bake the cave hard. He made them just as he had made the vessels that he had previously put into the fire to bake and had used in the cave in the rocks. And so, once upon a time, man moved into his first earth-built house, of *earth*.
>
> This large clay cave or pot of the cliff-dwellers, with a lid on it, was among the first man-made houses. The lid was troublesome to him then and has always been so to subsequent builders.[15]

From the mid-1920s on, this new, more plastic and more integral model of the vessel was adapted by Wright to all kinds of architectural situations. It gave him the basis for expanding his notion of architecture-as-space to the extent that he now began talking of buildings as vessels of space and of "the reality of the building" as "the space within."[16] Iconicizing, as it were, the fluid medium of architecture, the fired-clay vessel came to embody, in its very being, the symbolic idea of regeneration Wright was always to ascribe to the creation and modeling of space.[17]

In Taliesin West—the desert camp he finally built in Scottsdale, Arizona, in the 1930s, to serve as the winter headquarters for the Taliesin Fellowship, the apprenticeship program he instituted in 1932—Wright made the basic image of the vessel of the earlier Death Valley project as explicit as it would ever be. With their wood and canvas lids clamped over rubble-stone bases, the separate top-lit structures look like a group of ancient pots lying upright on the mesa floor. Wright used unlidded portions of the buildings to contain plants and flowers, as in the section devoted to his private office that is just at the entrance to the complex. In the focal corner of the living room of his domestic quarters, he hollowed out a small, well-like garden court. And, within its glass enclosure, he framed and displayed, as if floating miraculously in space, two Han dynasty cinerary urns, like prehistoric relics unearthed and newly brought to light, which thus dramatize and, as it were, materialize the underlying image of the vessel as a symbol of regeneration (Figure 7).

At about the same time that he was planning Taliesin West, Wright produced a number of house designs—such as the one for the Hannas in Palo Alto, California, or the one for Ralph Jester in Palos Verdes, on the Pacific coast south of Los Angeles—that develop the imagery of the building-as-vessel into its most logical geometric shapes, the hexagon on the one hand and the circle on the other. Furthermore, these designs directly relate the expression of spatial containment and flow to the revitalizing quality of water. In the Spivey project for a canal-side dwelling in Fort Lauderdale, Florida, of the same years, Wright finally made the entire space of the building conform to the shape of a pot, reflecting in its "streamlines" the swirling movement of the water and providing views out through the screen of perforated concrete blocks as if through a glass-bottomed boat.

For the most significant commission he was to get to build in his

Figure 7.    Taliesin West, Scottsdale, Arizona.

later years, the Solomon R. Guggenheim Museum, in New York City, Wright turned a Babylonian ziggurat upside down and hollowed it out to create a great vessel of space that spirals around and down in rhythmic motion, to give the visitor the feeling of being suspended in space, and in time, in a fluid environment that Wright likened to the impression created by "a still wave, never breaking, never offering resistance or finality to vision" (Figure 8).[18] The museum was intended by its curator Hilla Rebay to be a "temple of spirit," wherein the nonobjective paintings Guggenheim had collected could organically exert their elevating and healing "cosmic power."[19] As in the earlier Death Valley project, a circular dome of light is connected to a pool of water below to form an axis mundi relating sky to earth. The double convex pool itself is here shaped like a seed-pod, so as to symbolize, according to Wright, the fluid source of life that in fact generates the spiral growth.[20] Indeed, taking the elevator to the top and descending the ramp as Wright expected one to do, the visitor would always come back to that point of origin and thus perceive the building as a cyclical pattern of eternal return, a direct spatial experience of the idea of regeneration and of the integrative power of modern art.

In this regard, it is perhaps interesting to note in conclusion how the archetypal image of the vessel can in fact be related back to the story

Figure 8.  Solomon R. Guggenheim Museum, New York.

of Taliesin itself. The Welsh bard Taliesin was a legendary folk hero who was unwittingly inspired to his poetic genius by the drops of magic liquid that spewed out from the boiling cauldron that the witch Ceridwen had brewed for her own son.[21] The vessel, before it burst apart from the heat of the fire, was thus the very source of Taliesin's artistic power. And it is therefore not surprising that one of the last things Wright did to complete his own architectural image of Taliesin was to set on the hill-crown he had so poignantly left untouched almost a half-century earlier an enormous aqua-blue, Ming ceramic pot, as if to acknowledge in plastic form the model that underlay his own regeneration and, at the same time, the return of all things to their source (see Figure 3).

*Acknowledgments*

I would like to thank the Frank Lloyd Wright Memorial Foundation and, in particular, Bruce Brooks Pfeiffer, its Director of Archives, for their generous help and advice over the past years. I am also grateful to the Graham Foundation for Advanced Studies in the Fine Arts for their support of my work on Frank Lloyd Wright.

This essay is a revision of part of an article titled "Frank Lloyd Wright's Own Houses and His Changing Concept of Representation," recently published in Carol R. Bolon, Robert S. Nelson, and Linda Seidel, eds., *The Nature of Frank Lloyd Wright* (Chicago and London: University of Chicago Press, 1988), pp. 20-69. The material will be incorporated in a more expanded form in my forthcoming book on Wright's entire career.

# Notes

1. See, e.g., Frank Lloyd Wright, *An Autobiography* (London, New York, and Toronto: Longmans, Green and Co., 1932), p. 173; and *Architectural Forum* 68 (January 1938): 83 (special issue devoted to Frank Lloyd Wright).

2. On the subject of the symbolism of the vessel, see, e.g., Erich Neumann, *The Great Mother: An Analysis of the Archetype*, trans. Ralph Manheim, Bollingen Series, 2d ed. (Princeton: Princeton University Press, 1963); Volume 5 of Jung's *Collected Works*; and Emma Jung and Marie-Louise von Franz, *The Grail Legend*, trans. Andrea Dykes, 2d ed. (Boston: Sigo Press; London: Coventure, 1986), esp. pp. 113-160.

3. Marc-Antoine Laugier, *Essai sur l'architecture*, 2d ed. (Paris: Duchesne, 1755).

4. For his discussion of the Prairie House as an expression of "the sense of 'shelter' in the look of the building," see *An Autobiography*, p. 138ff.

5. Ibid., pp. 171, 174.

6. Ibid., p. 173.

7. For a more extended treatment of the feminine character of such archetypal images of the earth and, by extension, the vessel itself, see Neumann, *The Great Mother*, esp. pp. 39-119.

8. Wright, *An Autobiography*, p. 171. It should be noted that following her divorce in August 1911, Mamah returned to her maiden name, Borthwick.

9. Ibid., p. 213. In the second edition of his *Autobiography*, published in 1943, Wright retitled the chapter dealing with the "great earthquake" of 1923 "Building Against Doomsday." For a more extended treatment of this whole problem in Wright's career, see my "Hollyhock House and the Romance of Southern California," *Art in America* 71 (September 1983): 150-165.

10. F. L. Wright, "Taliesin III," typescript letter of June 8, 1926, TS. XXI/4, John Lloyd Wright Collection, Avery Library, Columbia University, New York.

11. I am extremely grateful to Bruce Brooks Pfeiffer, Director of Archives of the Frank Lloyd Wright Memorial Foundation, for making this project known to me as well as for suggesting the Death Valley site.

12. Historically, the centrally planned building type, whether circular or octagonal, was usually associated with martyria or baptistries, the most significant, perhaps, in the Western Christian tradition being the fourth-century Church of the Holy Sepulchre in Jerusalem, the Church of the Nativity in Bethlehem, and the Baptistry of Constantine in Rome. Wright had earlier used the clerestoried octagonal form for the studio-library complex he added to his Oak Park house in the mid-1890s in what would appear to be a knowing reference to the sacred meaning that Medieval and Renaissance architects attached to the type. For a further discussion of the type, see André Grabar, *Martyrium: Recherches sur le culte des reliques et l'art chrétien antique* (Paris: Collège de France, 1943-1946); Rudolf Wittkower, *Architectural Principles in the Age of Humanism*, Columbia University Studies in Art History and Archaeology, No. 1 (New York: Random House, 1965), esp. pp. 1-32; Staale Sinding-Larsen, "Some Functional and Iconographical Aspects of the Centralized Church in the Italian Renaissance," *Acta ad archaeologiam et artium historiam pertinentia* 2 (1965): 203-252; and Wolfgang Lotz, *Studies in Italian Renaissance Architecture* (Cambridge, Mass., and London: MIT Press, 1977), pp. 66-73.

13. For a contemporaneous discussion of this issue, see Alfred Vincent Kid-

der, *An Introduction to the Study of Southwestern Archaeology, with a Preliminary Account of the Excavations at Pecos* (New Haven: Yale University Press, 1924), esp. pp. 78, 81, and 119-123.

14. F. L. Wright, "Some Aspects of the Past and Present of Architecture," in *Architecture and Modern Life*, by Baker Brownell and Wright (New York and London: Harper and Brothers, 1937), p. 23.

15. Ibid., p. 24.

16. See, e.g., F. L. Wright, *An Organic Architecture: The Architecture of Democracy*, The Sir George Watson Lectures of the Sulgrave Manor Board for 1939 (London: Lund Humphries and Co., 1939), p. 3.

17. Both Vincent Scully and William Jordy have previously remarked on the significance of the container or "vase" in the later work of Wright, though without giving it the representational meaning I am ascribing to it, or taking it back to its sources in his work and thought of the teens and twenties. See Vincent Scully, *Frank Lloyd Wright*, The Master of the World Architecture Series (New York: George Braziller, 1960), p. 30; and William H. Jordy, *American Buildings and Their Architects*, vol. 4: *The Impact of European Modernism in the Mid-Twentieth Century* (Garden City, N.Y.: Doubleday, 1972), pp. 353-359.

18. *Architectural Forum* 88 (January 1948): 137 (special issue devoted to Frank Lloyd Wright).

19. For a discussion of Solomon Guggenheim's curator Hilla Rebay's "spiritualist" conception of nonobjective painting, see Joan Lukach, *Hilla Rebay: In Search of the Spirit in Art* (New York: George Braziller, 1983), esp. pp. 134-210. For the interaction between client and architect, see *Frank Lloyd Wright: The Guggenheim Correspondence*, selected and with commentary by Bruce Brooks Pfeiffer (Fresno, Calif.: The Press at California State University; Carbondale and Edwardsville, Ill.: Southern Illinois University Press, 1986).

20. F. L. Wright, *The Solomon R. Guggenheim Museum. Architect: Frank Lloyd Wright* (New York: The Solomon R. Guggenheim Foundation and Horizon Press, [1960]), p. 21.

21. The translation that was most popular during Wright's own childhood was *The Mabinogion*, trans. Lady Charlotte Guest (1838-1849; reprint, London: Bernard Quaritch, 1877). For a much more elaborate discussion of the legend in terms of European culture in general, see Robert Graves, *The White Goddess*, amended and enlarged ed. (New York: Farrar, Straus and Giroux, 1983). For a somewhat different interpretation of Wright's use of Welsh myths, see Thomas Beeby, "The Song of Taliesin," *Modulus, The University of Virginia School of Architecture Review* (1980-1981): 2-11.

# Part II
# Creativity

# Creativity  Joseph Campbell

This business of creativity was greatly illuminated for me by a letter that Schiller wrote to a young poet who was having writer's block. Schiller said to him, "Your problem is that you bring the critical factor down, before you have allowed the lyric to make its statement." Now, every creative act is going to be unprepared for, and consequently it is going to break rules. Any person in any of the arts must learn how to deal with this problem of knowing how a thing ought to be, and how it turns out as you bring it forth. You spend years studying the rules of art, that is, how it ought to be, according to certain essential laws for the development of a cogent form, but what comes out is not in that form. When you are in the act of creating, there is an implicit form that is going to ask to be brought forth, and you have to know how to recognize it. So, they say, you are to learn all the rules—and then you must forget them. As the lyric factor is beginning to move you, the mind is supposed to watch for the emergent form, because anything that comes out of the proper ground of inspiration is formed already. There is an implicit form intrinsic in it, and your job is to recognize it.

This personal creative act is related to the realm of myth, the realm of the muses, because myth is the homeland of the inspiration of the arts. The muses are the children of the goddess of memory, which is not the memory from up there, from the head; it is the memory from down here, from the heart. It is the memory of the organic laws of human existence that sends forth your inspirations. One can help oneself to know something about these laws by studying myths, particularly comparative mythologies. Each mythological system develops in a way that is different from that of another. By comparing the ways, one can see what archetypal form is being applied to this, that, or another mode of what might be called "life-prejudices," that is, what one thinks life ought to be, as the prejudices begin to take over and shape things.

I have become increasingly aware of the fact that there are two entirely different types of mythologies in the world. There are mythologies that emphasize, with more or less force, the sociological situation to which the myth is to be applied. These are socially based mythologies, and they insist on the laws of that social order as being *the* laws. We find this kind of mythology in the Bible. I imagine two thirds of the Old Testament is the statement of rules. Moses goes into the tent of the meeting and Yahweh gives him a set of rules, and then he goes the next day and there is another set, and this goes on and on and on. If you are going to live according to the rules, not of nature but of society, you have to have them written out for you. And again, throughout the Book of Kings, the kings are always making sacrifices on the mountaintops, but the text says that Yahweh did not approve of one or the other king because he neglected some set of rules. What was the worship on the mountaintops? It was the worship of the goddess Nature, that is what it was! So then, when you are studying mythology to find what the rules of nature are, avoid the Bible.

The nature rules live in the human heart. The society rules and gods are always "out there." But the source of the lyric is in here, in the heart. And that is the sense of the inward-turned meditation. There is where the god is that is dictating to you. There is where the muses live, in your own heart, not out there in some book.

The classic example of this mythology is the Dionysian system. I was in San Francisco recently where I, John Perry (a Jungian analyst), and Mickey Hart (the drummer of the Grateful Dead), together with Jerry Garcia put on a program. Mickey Hart had composed a piece that he called "The African Queen Meets the Holy Ghost" especially for that conference, the name of which was "Ritual and Rapture from Dionysus to the Grateful Dead." It was my idea. I had had my first rock and roll experience at a performance of the Grateful Dead in Oakland six months earlier. Rock music had always seemed a bore to me, but I can tell you, at that concert, I found 8,000 people standing in mild rapture for five hours while these boys let loose everything on the stage. The place was just a mansion of dance. And I thought, "Holy God! Everyone has just lost themselves in everybody else here!" The principal theme of my talk was the wonderful innocence and the marvel of life when it recognizes itself in harmony with all the others. Everyone is somehow or other at one with everybody else. And my final theme was that this is the world's only answer to the atom bomb. The atom bomb is based on differentiation: I-and-not-that-guy-over-there. Divisiveness is socially based. It has nothing to do with nature at all. It is a contrivance and here, suddenly, it fell apart.

The socially oriented people, the church leaders, political leaders and so forth, always get nervous when Dionysus gets going. The descriptions of the Dionysian movement that we get from the Greeks and Romans are from the point of view of people who do not like Dionysus. You have the case of Pentheus, the Man of Sorrows, who is torn apart. Well, Pentheus is exactly Christ being torn apart. He is the one that comes out of love and says, "Yes, of course you are torn apart.

Your individual will and your individual enclosure in yourself is broken, and all the rules are gone."

Following rules is precisely the theme of T. S. Eliot's *The Waste Land*. Eliot got the title for the poem from the Waste Land theme in the twelfth- and thirteenth-century Grail romances. When Parzival, in the Grail castle, saw the wounded king before him, he was moved to ask, "What ails you, Uncle?" but there was a rule that a knight does not ask unnecessary questions. Here is an example where following rules inhibits spontaneity and the emotion of compassion, which is the only emotion that counts in the realm of religious experience. The awakening of compassion, "com-passion," "*Mit-leid*," "suffering-with," enveloping that person's pain in your skin, so that you are suffering with him or her equally, this is the awakening of the heart. That is what it is all about, and that is what the lyric moment is: the awakening of the heart.

Years ago, when computers were beginning to come into their own, it is said that Eisenhower went into a room full of computers, and he put a question to them: "Is there a god?" So the computers started twinkling and doing the things computers do, and after about ten or fifteen minutes of this mysterious performance, a voice was heard, and the voice said, "Now there is."

When I bought my computer—anyone who has tried to work a computer knows what my experience was—I thought, well, I wonder what god it is that is in there? Being somewhat an expert on gods, I lived with this computer for a couple of months, and then I recognized the god. It was Yahweh of the Old Testament: a lot of rules and no mercy! But then, when you get to know the rules and your fingers obey them, it is fabulous what that thing can do!

This is the way it is with the rules in art. You have to learn to know them, and if it is a proper, up-to-date local art, the rules will have something to do with the life of people here and now, not a big smoochy general thing about life, but how it is here and now, what our problems and our mysteries are, here and now. You have to know your own day. You have to know your own relation to your own day, and then forget it! Let the thing build into you, the way my knowledge of my computer is built into me now. And then each of you can sing.

One of the big problems for young artists today—and I think I know a lot about them, because I have been living with artists ever since I graduated from college, which is a long time ago—is that they are all terribly frustrated in the bringing forth of their art, primarily because they have studied sociology. They always think there is a moral to be pointed out, something to be communicated.

Artists are not very good at telling you how it is that they got to be good, but there is one artist that I know of who did, and that was James Joyce. In *A Portrait of the Artist as a Young Man* he gives the best clue that I know of on how to create a work of art. In the last chapter, Stephen Dedalus explains to his friend, Lynch, the essential points of the artist's work. He tells him that there are two kinds of art. There is proper and improper art. Improper art is kinetic. Improper art moves you either with desire to possess the object or with loathing and fear to resist it and avoid it. Art that excites desire for the object he calls "pornographic." All advertising is pornographic art. Art that excites loathing and criticism of the object he calls "didactic," and so much of our writing, particularly in the first half of this century, has been di-dactic writing, what I call the work of "didactic pornographers."

Proper art is static. It holds you in ecstatic arrest—arrest at what? Joyce brings up Aquinas at this point, who says that in the art moment, the first experience is *integritas*, the beholding of one object set apart from all objects in the world. This is a thing, and within that thing what is important is the relation of part to part, and part to the whole, the rhythm, the rhythm of beauty. And this is the key of all art. This is the key of form. The rhythm is implicit in your own body. It is implicit in your expression. And when the rhythm is properly, fortu-nately achieved, the result is radiance, rapture, beholding it. Why? Be-cause the rhythm before you is the rhythm of nature. It is the rhythm of *your* nature. Cezanne says somewhere, "Art is a harmony parallel to nature." Art is the rendition of the interface between your inner nature and the nature out there.

The natural mythologies are also art in that sense. They are modes, they are rhythms, in which everything is an expression of nature. When I was a student in Paris, back in the 1920s, I knew a sculptor, a very great sculptor, Antoine Bourdelle, who used to say, "L'art fait ressortir les grandes lignes de la nature" (Art brings out the great lines of nature). And that is all it does. And why is it that you are held in aesthetic arrest? It is because the nature you are looking at is *your* na-ture. There is an accord between you and the object, and that is why you say, "Aha!"

In one of the Upanishads it says, when the glow of a sunset holds you and you say "Aha," that is the recognition of divinity. And when you say "Aha," to an art object, that is the recognition of divinity. And what divinity is it? It is *your* divinity, which is the only divinity there is. We are all phenomenal manifestations of a divine will to live, and that will and the consciousness of life is one in all of us, and that is what the artwork expresses.

Now this is what is meant by an archetype of the unconscious. An archetype of the unconscious is a recognized form, but the problem with it, when you begin to talk about it, is that it is not recognized at all; it is talked about. The thing gets to be a cliché, and it is no good any more. This is another great difficulty in the creative life. If you know exactly what it is you are creating, it is not going to work. You have turned it into a sign or a concept instead of a thing in itself. It has to come out beyond speech, as life does.

My great friend, Heinrich Zimmer, had a saying: "The best things cannot be told; the second best are misunderstood." The second best are misunderstood because they talk about what cannot be told and one thinks one knows what they are saying. This is the way religion is. The idea of God is an idea that is metaphoric of something that cannot be told, and yet we say that God is good, God is merciful, God is just, and God loves these people and not those, etc., etc. We are not talking about God at all. We are talking about our *idea* of God. Meister Eckhart, in the thirteenth century, said, "The ultimate leave-taking is leaving god for God." The word that is missing is the other word. The European languages lack that very important word. Monotheism is idolatry in that it imagines its god to be the God for which you leave this one. The Hindus have the word Brahma or Atman. No Hindu, nobody east of Suez, would mistake god for God, mistake a god for Brahma. Gods are all metaphors of this ultimate mystery, the mystery of your own being. So God is not "out there"; God is in here. This is the source of the lyric, and what you are writing about is the word of God that is coming out. That is what is meant by inspiration. That is what is meant by the "Word of God." That life that is of your essence is talking through your inspiration. So let the mind up here relax and listen, not dictate, and recognize the implication of the word.

# The Road
## to Mecca     Robert Bly

It is amusing to talk about creativity here, because we are talking in the presence of two enemies: the university and the conference. James Hillman objects to our adopting for this discussion the magic word "creativity," and I sympathize with that objection. Creativity has become a cover word. Where could we put the emphasis? I would say that people who spend their lives creating art are *adventurers moving between two worlds*, travelers on the road to Mecca. How to do that? Rumi has a wonderful poem in which he says:

> The road to Mecca is hard: Thieves, blowing wind,
> and only camel's milk to drink![1]

My idea is to talk of five qualities or companions—inescapable partners—on the road the traveler has no choice but to take.

The first companion for the adventurer is *matter*. Daydreaming is utterly distinct from art, because in the daydream one flies through the air and is not tied down to matter. Being tied down produces the proper tension. Christ did not enter Jerusalem by himself but on a donkey; so the artist enters art. In poetry the sound is the donkey. In painting the canvas and the paints, colored by minerals, are the donkey. If a teacher in the workshop allows or encourages the young poet to use too many abstract words, the poet evades the struggle. The donkey vanishes. I insist on naming matter as the first true companion on the road. Computer poetry is not poetry at all because the donkey refuses, for reasons of its own, to enter the computer. I think most of us are willing to ride on the donkey. A few lines by Gerard Manley Hopkins (from "Pied Beauty") will give the mood of such art:

> Glory be to God for dappled things—
>    For skies of couple-colour as a brindled cow;
>       For rose-moles all in stipple upon trout that swim;
> Fresh-firecoal chestnut-falls; finches' wings;
>    Landscape plotted and pierced—fold, fallow, and
>    plough;
>       And all trades, their gear and tackle and trim.

> All things counter, original, spare, strange;
>> Whatever is fickle, freckled (who knows how?)
>> With swift, slow; sweet, sour; adazzle, dim;
> He fathers–forth whose beauty is past change;
>> Praise him.[2]

The second companion on the journey to Mecca I would name *spontaneity*. The child is full of that. Blake loved the child. Spontaneity helps the child to move effortlessly between worlds. The difficulty is for adults to preserve spontaneity. "Adult" and "dull" often seem interchangeable adjectives with us. "The roaring of lions, the howling of wolves, the raging of the stormy sea and the destructive sword are portions of eternity, too great for the eye of man."[3] That is what Blake said. Freud pointed out the distressing contrast between the radiant intelligence of the child and the feeble mentality of the average adult. What destroys spontaneity? Bureaucracy, the Ph.D. program, fundamentalism, the interior critic. The thin-nosed interior critic gets stronger each year in our culture, and such a critic has killed almost all spontaneity in our daily conversation and on talk shows. What is called "workshop poetry" is not in good shape, either. The Taoists in China advise owning little, refusing responsibility, ignoring degrees, and laughing at criticism as ways to keep the spontaneity and radiance of the child alive. A Taoist painting that I particularly love shows a man walking or dancing along, a frog seated firmly on his head. It is not elegant; it is likely that the frog will do God-knows-what to his hair. The old tradition suggests that if you cannot stand a frog peeing in your hair, do not become an artist.

In one of his poems Hölderlin describes the dance of spontaneity for an adult as "swaying":

> All the fruit is ripe, plunged in fire, cooked
> And they have passed their test on earth, and one law is this:
> That everything curls inward, like snakes,
> Prophetic, dreaming on
> The hills of heaven. And many things
> Have to stay on the shoulders like a load
> of failure. However the roads
> Are bad. For the chained elements,
> Like horses, are going off to the side,
> And the old
> Laws of the earth. And a longing
> For disintegration constantly comes. Many things however

145

> Have to stay on the shoulders. Steadiness is essential.
> Forwards, however, or backwards we will
> Not look. Let us learn to live swaying
> As in a rocking boat on the sea.[4]

The third companion on the journey I would call *nature* itself. Georgia O'Keefe painted a canvas with only a cow skull and a rose. By nature I do not mean human nature. We love human nature in this century. But nature in art means mountains, animals, leaves, ocean water, redwood trees, muskoxen, wind, the nonhuman. Wordsworth declared that the child does not become an adult by moving from childhood to adolescence to adulthood, but on the contrary by moving from childhood to *nature* to adulthood. Do we doubt that Dürer and Van Gogh followed that sequence? Ancient Chinese artists insisted on it. One Chinese artist of the Tang dynasty, before he dared to touch brush to paper, would go into the woods and sit silently with grass or water for several hours. Then he would return to his house, and his family would pull him by an ingenious pulley arrangement up to his painting room, where he would stay for ten or twelve hours until he had finished his painting. When he was an ordinary human being again, with human thoughts, his family would pull him back down.

A small clay figure of Dionysus has survived that shows him grieving, his face mysterious and calm. In one hand he holds an egg, and the mood is courage. Joseph Campbell reminds us that each egg contains in its yolk the sun itself. Since that is so, the human being is not alone and need not be anxious. An early poem of mine (called "Poem in Three Parts") ends with the anxiety gone or diminished:

> I
>
> Oh, on an early morning I think I shall live forever!
> I am wrapped in my joyful flesh,
> As the grass is wrapped in its clouds of green.
>
> II
>
> Rising from a bed, where I dreamt
> Of long rides past castles and hot coals,
> The sun lies happily on my knees;
> I have suffered and survived the night
> Bathed in dark water, like any blade of grass.
>
> III
>
> The strong leaves of the box-elder tree,
> Plunging in the wind, call us to disappear
> Into the wilds of the universe,

Where we shall sit at the foot of a plant,
And live forever, like the dust. [5]

The fourth companion on the journey I would name *destruction*. Destruction and creation go hand in hand. In Hindu mythology, Shiva, the god of creation, is also the god of destruction. How can anything be created unless something else is destroyed? We have to be careful in recommending "creativity" as a life aim, because inside it there is destruction. The *Book of Job* says that when one's life is perfectly even and ordinary, and all is going well, be careful, because something will come up from underneath to smash it. On the road to Mecca one cannot avoid this "something" that gathers, rises from underneath, and smashes the evenness and ordinariness. This is what Rumi means when he says:

The road to Mecca is hard. If you're a mama's boy
And dislike pain, stay at home. [6]

The Lord gave and the Lord hath taken away. He smote Job with sore boils from the soles of his feet to the crown of his head. Creative work activates something else, dark, which eventually rises and destroys. We should warn our children when they say they want to be creative and tell them to read Job carefully. Whoever is creative will eventually be nailed to a tree.

Goethe refers to this sorrow in his poem called "Holy Longing":

Tell a wise person, or else keep silent,
because the massman will mock it right away.
I praise what is truly alive,
what longs to be burned to death.

In the calm water of the love-nights,
where you were begotten, where you have forgotten,
a strange feeling comes over you
when you see the silent candle burning.

Now you are no longer caught
in the obsession with darkness,
and a desire for higher love-making
sweeps you upward.

Distance does not make you falter,
now, arriving in magic, flying,
and, finally, insane for the light,
you are the butterfly and you are gone.

And so long as you haven't experienced
this: to die and so to grow,
you are only a troubled guest
on the dark earth.[7]

The fifth companion on the journey I would call *art in defiance of nature*. In Latin it is *opus contra naturam*. I do not believe this is a quality of the young artist's journey. Before a person can create art "in defiance of nature" it makes sense that he or she would have to have co-operated with nature for many years. This cooperation with the principles of nature, even the worship of the principles of nature, is what the Taoists teach, what St. Francis teaches, and what Wordsworth and Blake teach.

Nature, however, does not like art. Why should it? Nature gets along very well without art. If one gives a poetry reading outdoors, the wind and the leaves will take the poems and throw them away. The invention of tragedy is attributed to Dionysus; his intensity amounted to a discipline more intense and more directed than the grandiose and carefree disasters of nature.

We now know that vast areas of apparently natural countryside in China were altered at an earlier date by artists, architects, and garden-ers. If the Chinese preferred three hills where only two were standing, they added a third. It is a matter of form. The fifth quality then is an orderliness that expresses spirit more than nature, discipline more than impulse. Rilke's poems embody a discipline that seems to go beyond that of nature. Although we miss the form of the original German in my translation, the content of the following poem conveys a sense of that discipline. In the poem, called "Buddha Inside the Light," Rilke contemplates a statue of Buddha in Rodin's garden:

The core of every core, the kernel of every kernel,
an almond! held in itself, deepening in sweetness:
all of this, everything, right up to the stars
is the meat around your stone. Accept my bow.

O yes, you feel it, how the weights on you are gone!
Your husk has reached into what has no end,
and that is where the great saps are brewing now.
On the outside a warmth is helping,

for, high, high above, your own suns are growing
immense and they grow as they wheel around.
Yet something has already started to live
in you that will live longer than the suns.[8]

# Notes

---

1. Robert Bly and Coleman Barks, unpublished translation of Rumi.

2. Gerard Manley Hopkins, *Poems and Prose*, ed. W. H. Gardner (Harmondsworth, England: Penguin Books), p. 30.

3. William Blake, *The Complete Poetry and Prose of William Blake*, ed. David V. Erdman (Garden City, N.Y.: Anchor Doubleday, 1982), p. 36.

4. As translated by Robert Bly in his *News of the Universe* (San Francisco: Sierra Club Books, 1980), p. 46.

5. Robert Bly, *Silence in the Snowy Fields* (Middletown, Conn.: Wesleyan University Press, 1962), p. 21.

6. Robert Bly and Coleman Barks, unpublished translation of Rumi.

7. As translated by Robert Bly in his *News of the Universe*, p. 70.

8. Rainer Maria Rilke, *Selected Poems of Rainer Maria Rilke*, trans. Robert Bly (New York: Harper and Row, 1981), p. 151.

# Creative Shadows     Lucio Pozzi

It appears that creativity is on the wane, but what really might be happening is that the mental forms that have traditionally constituted the creative mechanisms of our culture have become inadequate in the light of today's experience.

The Modern Movement was our first attempt to destroy the orders of the past and to replace them with methods corresponding to the new scientific and cosmopolitan mass society we live in. But now we are becoming aware that modernization has led us into the trap of formulas that are even less regenerative than the ones it tried to transform. Consequently, we are faced with the unprecedented task of overcoming both the progressive academy of transgression and the regressive academy of conservatism.

The arts are an indicator of what has happened. I am certain one can find parallels in most other activities as well. We artists have tried it all. We have defamiliarized most information, and we have embraced discontinuity, rejecting what we perceived to be the artificial continuities of the past. In the process, quite a few developments have taken place. What is most interesting, however, is that the expected liberation has not materialized. Defamiliarization, breaking down conventions, seeking novelty, parodying this and that, appropriating ever new codes not yet considered to fall within the realm of art, have all resulted in the issuance of norms that have turned out to be equally restrictive, precisely because artists can "dial" any of them as if selecting soda or candy from a vending machine.

"Now, what is wrong with that?" someone might ask. "After all, art has always followed restrictive norms, accepting those constraints as the creative conventions imposed by a given culture, that is, as the very provisions for its own production." Are those of us who are complaining simply nostalgic for imagined "good old ways," not unlike those who would persist in traveling by horse and buggy in the age of the automobile? I do not think so.

Let us take a brief look at the word "creativity." Its most commonly accepted meaning is "something that did not exist before is made to be." Creativity is thus profoundly linked to our notion of time and, as such, is a projection of a specifically modern understanding of experience, one grounded in the categories "before" and "after." Creativity then is not absolute, but rather a possibility of historical nature.

If we consider related concepts, such as "invention" and "discovery," the role played by the experience of time in our conception of the creative drive becomes even more obvious. "Invenire," in Latin, means "to come upon"; "discooperire" means "to uncover that which was covered (unperceived) before."

I do not know whether there was any concern for creativity during the past millennia. It was probably regarded as an obvious and self-evident function of life. Why are we so concerned with it today? If creativity is linked to time, why has our endless search for the new become so sterile as to be nothing more than a predictable cycle of ever-more-specialized fashions?

An objecting interlocutor would respond by pointing out that fashion (and its subsidiary, advertising) is indeed the creative convention of our culture. But that is not enough for me, because my experience is that life, love, death, and memory are not compatible with fashion's rigidities. On the other hand, some creativity is indeed possible within any medium, including fashion and advertising; but since these are goal-oriented activities, their creativity is necessarily limited in its scope.

We are faced with two "creativities": one fast, applied to specific purposes and consumable within a short period of time; the other slow, whose function it is to explore the outer fringes of cognition on a long-term basis. The former is clear and the latter obscure, and somehow the former seems to be a by-product of the latter. My sympathies obviously are with slow creativity, even to the point of accepting the Zen Buddhist alternative of purely contemplative creativity, which produces no action whatsoever.

In the future, radical creativity will probably stem from a disengagement from conceptions of linear time, progress and regress, and from an engagement in more circular models. One thing is clear: our concern for creativity encompasses the culture as a whole. And should we ever find out what we actually mean when we talk about creativity—representing it in terms that are less pedestrian than the goal-oriented ones imposed by the applied research of industry and politics—that might be our first step toward the reconceptualization of thought that some of us long for.

These circuitous and grossly generalizing comments can only hint at the "quantum leap" that is needed in our understanding. By way of concluding, let me hazard some possible avenues of research derived from my own artistic practice. First of all, I have dismissed all concern for the *aspect* of what I do. I have shifted my attention to the workings of the mind. I expect the forms—that which is seen—to be traces of the mind that made them and to have the effect of producing analogous (but not coincidental) "mind-work" in the spectator.

I have also assumed that my deeper intentions cannot be known to me. I thus find myself unbound from any preliminary program of action. Intentions accordingly become instruments, mere operational methodologies. This might mean that I operate as much as possible within the realm of events, leaving all interpretation open to the fluctuations of discourse, which changes again and again, depending on when and where it happens.

In the seventeenth century, such an attitude was considered diabolical in its articulation of alternatives to all orthodoxies and in its flexible, conciliatory, and ambiguous results. As the Italian scholar Elemire Zolla stated so well in a recent essay,[1] syncretism is forever unacceptable to the bigots of all societies, precisely because it is the philosophy of integration. There have been and there remain many proponents of syncretism, from Giordano Bruno, the late-Renaissance thinker who was burned at the stake for his advocacy of this philosophy, to Walter Gropius, the Bauhaus architect, Lewis Thomas, the biologist, Meyer Shapiro, the art historian, Jonas Salk, the scientist, Felix Guattari, the anti-psychiatrist, and others in this century.

Creativity, in our time, might well be found in the renewed use of conventions, but conventions understood as flexible instruments whose deployment avoids a rigid conformity to both the rules of the past and the rules of breaking with the past. Finally, to achieve creativity one would do well not to speak of it. Paradoxically, we should not be discussing it here.

# Note

---

1. Elemire Zolla, "Archetypal Politics in European History: The Myths of Rome and Byzantium" (Paper presented at the "C.G. Jung and the Humanities" conference, Hofstra University, November 1986).

|                        | Robert Bly      |
|------------------------|-----------------|
|                        | Joseph Campbell |
| Creativity             | James Hillman   |
| Symposium              | Lucio Pozzi     |

---

*Hillman*: I want to ask Mr. Pozzi about the rules of the past and about the rules of breaking with the past. According to Mr. Pozzi, breaking the rules is not enough. Evidently, you have to learn the rules of breaking the rules. For example, we know the story of the little kid who went to an experimental "creative" school and asked, "Is this the school where I have to paint what I want, or is this the school where we have to paint three-legged purple cows because that breaks the rules?" We think that if we are doing it differently, we are doing it creatively. Whereas we are trapped again in another set of rules.

*Pozzi*: Forgetting the rules is what the contemporary artist is faced with. The problem arises when the breaking of rules is prescribed. We have the instruction manual in our mental library. As a result, we are caught between the fires that are equally powerful and equally binding. In order to break the rules and to break the rules of breaking the rules, there must be some assumptions behind both attitudes that we take for granted and that we might want to reform or take a new look at. I personally do not know how to do it, especially since I am working in the nonverbal field of making images and paintings. I and most people I know have become very skillful at playing both the game of the rules and the game of forgetting the rules, and this worries me.

A psychiatrist friend of mine in France, Felix Guattari, speaks of the need to reconceptualize thinking. I now approach the problem in a very pragmatic way, maybe even in a pedestrian or childish way, by taking the concept of inspiration literally. The study of etymology is useful for finding the concepts behind the words that we use. The word, inspiration, in Latin is *inspirare*, to inspire, to breathe in, and to expire after. Remembering what I knew about the Oriental ways, about yoga, Zen Buddhist and Taoist techniques, and what I knew of Renaissance hermetic thinking and practices, as they have come down through the centuries to people like Goethe and to Ouspensky and Gurdjieff in Russia—remember that Constructivists gave "breathing lessons" to workers in Red Square every morning before they went to work—I thought maybe one way out of my disarray, my discontent, my feeling that our culture has become inert, would be to start "inspiring" literally. And so I do breathing exercises. I spend hours on my floor, breathing, trying to put myself into a state that will send me on "fishing trips" into images that appear in my mind. Their nature is really unknown to me, because I am one of those on whom mythologies of the past, no matter how well explained, are really lost; on whom even the memories of the lost memories of mythologies are lost. I am trying to retrieve that which comes, without explaining it to myself, and trying to trace it as much as I can on canvas and paper. Of course, when I do it, culture floods in and conditions my time and heritage. I try very tentatively to rebuild from that.

*Bly*: You said that you were upset by the increasing bureaucratization of American art. Would this bureaucratization be an example of thinking that is not rethought?

*Pozzi*: Yes. America is in the forefront of the bureaucratization of culture, which is observable in most industrialized countries and which is rapidly expanding to the nonindustrialized ones as we export our technologies. This is a good place to begin to reconceptualize thought, if it is at all possible.

*Bly*: What do you mean by the bureaucratization of art?

*Pozzi*: The single analogy of bureaucracy for me would be the form letter, the form. Bureaucracy (bureaus, offices) is necessary for the organization of society, but bureaucracy, that is, the dominance (-cracy) of the office, is unnecessary for culture. The bureaucratization of culture has brought about the predictability of conception and the predictability of invention. We have ideal form letters with multiple choices, which appear to be free but are not, because you are given little boxes in which to put crosses.

What I am striving for, at the cost of perhaps stopping the making of art if necessary, is for something else, which I am sure will come because of the discontent many of us feel. My very modest first attempt is to deal with techniques such as inspiration. I am in a deep fog. I prefer my fog, though, to the boring competent yawn of the clarity that surrounds me in our art.

*Hillman*: I am still speaking to what you started with, that you work with the assumption: "My deeper intentions cannot be known to me."

Now this is the place where I think psychology gets it wrong, because psychology assumes that my deeper intentions *can* be known to me— the whole idea of making the unconscious conscious in Freud's sense: where there was id, there ego shall be. Psychology is driven by the urge to make the deeper intentions known. So, I wonder if psychology is not part of the conspiracy against the trusting of what comes forth.

*Campbell*: There is a proverb that I learned in Hawaii, a Polynesian proverb, that seems to characterize the activity of psychologists as you have described them: "Standing on a whale, fishing for minnows."

*Hillman*: It is not just catching the minnows; it is as if the minnows could swallow the whale, or as if this little tip could embrace the iceberg. Psychology works that illusion, that delusion, all the time. Now there is nothing wrong with minnows: they are lovely little insights and discoveries; but they do not explain whales. And what I want to do in my practice is give us, the patient and myself, the sense of being on the slippery old barnacled back of a giant dark moving thing, the psyche or the unconscious or imagination, a living animal that is carrying us "on the foam/ Of perilous seas." Maybe we are not on its back at all but are inside the whale, and the minnows are inside, too.

*Bly*: One of Mr. Pozzi's students told me that at the art school, the teachers require the students to make a statement of intention for their planned artwork. That is madness, is it not? James thinks that psychology may have increased the arrogance of administrators who believe an artist could do such a thing.

*Pozzi*: It could be instrumental. You cannot start in a void. In my teaching and for myself, I use the intention as a springboard. You want to work with something to start with, even if it is a false target. You can start in a direction, and as soon as you leave the "island" of your knowledge and your equipment and everything you have in you, you find yourself working in leaps that do not lead you at all toward the target, which becomes like a mirage. So intentions in that respect could be interesting. The intention could be an instrument that one uses to start.

This is where you distinguish between the superficial intentions and the deeper intentions. Deeper ones are something so complex that we probably are only beginning now to know something about them. Psychology could be one of the methods of inquiry. There are also other methods of inquiry, the ones that come from the Orient, methods of deep introspection, of trance, of parapsychology, which has been so laughed at by the scientific community. I think our situation is culturally so desperate that every avenue of research is useful. Maybe the psychology that you are talking about is one we all disagree with, but are there not other psychologies that could help us in exploring the realm of will and chance and event?

*Hillman*: There is one more place where psychology bothers me. Robert spoke of grief as a necessary characteristic of creativity. There is a good deal of talk in psychology about grief and mourning, but it is something to be "worked through" and it is tied in with depression. Depression is a cover word, whereas grief is something in itself, something to do with ceremonies and rememberings and moving on and losing and dying. It is not "depression" as a pathological condition. This grief is a permanent state of soul. Grieving in T. S. Eliot's sense of grieving for Western European culture and history, it seems to me, is not valued enough by psychology. Grieving is a living nerve in us, there in the soul, asking to be felt—a source of images. So to my mind, psychology is anti-art or anti-imagination in "working through" grief. The deeper cultural possibilities of grief do not get explored as long as we never get out of someone's personal grief, which is being "worked through."

*Bly*: I like that tremendously, because the image of Dionysus implies that his grief is a permanent and natural state for him. Contemporary psychology could also be criticized for emphasizing the human side of the work of art. I am thinking, by contrast, of Mr. Campbell's work, specifically, *The Way of the Animal Powers*, in which he shows that the first gods were animals. In those early hunting cultures, which may have lasted for three hundred to four hundred thousand years, the veil between human beings and animals was thinner than that between human beings and human beings. The early human being then passed through the border into the animal and back again. That is how those great paintings in the caves were done. Later European art can do the same thing. Dürer passes through that veil when he paints the rabbit and the crab.

Psychology concerns itself with communication between human beings. A problem with art now is that the only veil most artists want to pass through is that between human beings, and the psychologists, as we have mentioned, keep to this narrow view. If psychologists really understood the idea, they would have a wolf or a crow in the room where you go for your therapy, and they would say, "Stop talking about the 'significant other' for a while. Pass through that veil. See what you can do with the wolf!"

James said once that there is this "requirement" that when people want to get close, they are always supposed to talk, face to face. I think that is the way women recommend doing things. There is also another way, which is somewhat more male, that was described by a man, in which he and his father went for a walk every Sunday for four hours, over many months. They walked shoulder to shoulder, not saying a word, and came back with tremendous closeness, because to some extent both of them had passed through the veil and back again, and that brings closeness.

*Hillman*: Joseph, add psychology to your remark about sociology the next time. It is not just sociology that frustrates the bringing forth of art, it is also psychology.

*Campbell*: What Robert has said reinforces my whole thought, that by letting the veil of society be the thin veil, you lose touch with nature. This talking business is sociology. The two walking together in silence is getting in touch with nature. The "mysterium tremendum et fascinans" will never be found at a meeting. It is in nature. It is in the sunset. It is in suddenly seeing a deer standing in the forest.

*Bly*: Blake said, "Great things are done when men and mountains meet./ This is not done by jostling in the street."[1] I will give you a Chinese poem, Tang dynasty, translated by Jonathan Chaves:

> Pines and cedars, a hundred feet
> Of green, clinging to the earth.
> The desolate forest is silent—
> No human voices here.
> The hermit's robe is ragged;
> His hair is spotted with gray.
> Among the wolves and tigers
> He reads the *Tao Te Ching*.[2]

*Question*: Is it possible that creativity is, in a sense, getting in touch with something that is bigger than oneself? I am thinking of the problem of ego, and the fact that so many people are concerned with "claiming" what they have done, with having it "belong" to them, rather than realizing that when you create something that is in touch with universal qualities, it really does not belong to you.

*Bly*: I think Mr. Pozzi implied that in his statement. One of the griefs is that art is following fashions with such astounding regularity and slavishness that there is no time to create the deep artwork that belongs to no one. So I agree entirely with this problem of the ego's claims. Capitalism does that.

*Pozzi*: It is even worse. The artist's unconscious has been invaded by the distribution system; that is, the artist invents art on purpose to be compatible with the distribution system. Therefore the artist surrenders or censors the impulses that are contradictory to what he or she believes the distribution system to require.

*Hillman*: I am in an awkward spot, but I better say it right out: I do not like the word "creativity." It has been banned from my vocabulary along with "growth," "commitment," and "acceptance." These words are virus words, infiltrating us with vague idealizations. They infect us with unreflected ideals that we strive to attain, and cannot, and then we fall flat, becoming more dull and ordinary than ever. There is a dreadful disguised moralism in the word creativity: it says we are *supposed* to be creative; each person has a creative node, a true inner self that wants to express itself creatively, in art. It evokes Mozart and Van Gogh as examples and contrasts them with ordinary people. We have a psychology of creativity, and so forth. Genius, okay—each one of us has a genius or a daimon—but let us leave creativity to nature or to the gods and instead feel ourselves as creatures rather than creators. We might not have extinct animals and the bomb had we thought less about creating and more about creatureliness.

*Gilles Quispel*: I think art has a function. What Jung says about the function of art is that in every person there is a sort of desire, to be in tune with the infinite. That is Jung's real discovery: a mysticism that is not something medieval and of the past, but something of the future.

*Hillman*: It is interesting that the conversation keeps moving from art to religion . . . as if there were some connection . . . and there *is* a connection. I think the connection lies in that sense of "otherness" going on when one is actually making something. The material is intractable. It will not submit. The words will not come. You have to wrestle, or you have to put yourself into a kind of empty concentration. You have to surrender in some way and that honors the "other," whether you call this "other" the work, or God, or the unconscious, or the imagination, or the muse, or inspiration. The honoring or surrendering or serving the "other," whether it be a god or an idea or a line of verse or ink, seems to be what keeps art and religion psychologically linked.

*Bly*: Joseph mentioned that whenever material starts to come up from underneath, whenever you are painting or when you are writing a poem, there is some kind of an inherent form in it, and if you can stay with it long enough, the form will absolutely appear. Now, if that is so, why is so much of contemporary art and poetry so formless? Mr. Pozzi?

*Pozzi*: Probably because contemporary artists are not after those inherent forms. Maybe we have become too suspicious of the sterile renditions of such forms, as they have come from the millennia of the past and that are so different from the experience of life that we have. Maybe in order to get rid of the conditions within which those forms were revealed, which we feel are crippling conditions, we have tried some other avenue of thought, and this has landed us in even more formulaic sterility than the one that we are trying to provide an alternative for. Now, after this kind of cleansing and confusing period—perhaps healthily confusing period—the question becomes how to regain access to such formations that we do not even have the memory of the memory of. You are burdening me with a big answer. I wish you would answer your own question, Mr. Bly.

*Bly*: Do you believe in doing figure drawing and going back to representational painting?

*Pozzi*: Well, I have done all kinds of art, and I am now doing paintings that have figures in them with eyes, noses, and smiles, and I am even trying to put expressions in them. I am sort of relearning everything. We have praised artists for being unconventional for so long, which is why the "new" thought has come to me that maybe conventions can be useful instruments, as long as we do not conform to them. What we have reacted against is conformity to conventions. Conventions themselves can be very useful. So a new and helpful word for me is "reconventionalizing." Does that sound reactionary? To me it is liberating. But I would like to hear from you, Mr. Bly. What do you think about your question with respect to your poetry?

*Bly*: It is more fun to talk wildly about other art forms. I would say in contemporary poetry, certain guidelines have been laid out. They are like fences along the road so that horses do not go off into the ditch even if they are blind. One finds poems, called "workshop poems," that are written by blind horses going down the road, a big ditch on either side. The poems require a little about your grandfather, but not too much. And if you are a woman, you always write about your

159

grandmother, who resembled the Great Mother. That is required. This gives you an "A." This is so awful, that if I did not love poetry, I would give up writing immediately. It must be that people are not content to wait for the really dangerous and wild material to come up. Maybe that is because the universities are supporting the education of these young poets, and the atmosphere in universities is quite calm, quite rational, quite unlike our disturbed mood actually. T. S. Eliot never went to a poetry workshop in his life. That is something to think about! The old tradition was either to write or to starve to death, it did not matter too much which.

The idea of "too-easy-art," the connection of art with getting a degree, is somehow an awful, awful thing. I think we are being mothered and fathered to death by the universities.

*Hillman*: There is one more thing I would like to talk about. We were talking about rules, but we also talked about Dionysus and spontaneity, as if only good could come from spontaneity. Most of the murders in America are done in households, "spontaneously." Most of the acts that you may look back at regretting were "spontaneous" acts. Spontaneity, in itself, is not anything more than spontaneity. It is not necessarily making something good, lasting, beautiful, or arresting. Spontaneity should not become a new god, because we don't know what we are talking about if we do not think about what form it takes and in which moment and context the spontaneity occurs. Who is being spontaneous is extremely important; in other words, what figure of the psyche is being spontaneous, and so on. There are many kinds of spontaneity. I want to sound this warning, this caution, because I feel the word is a New Age cover-up for what can be ruthlessness and carelessness, for the general American vice of naïveté and self-indulgence.

*Bly*: Does art spring from discipline or from spontaneity? I know that James has complained in the past that our whole culture is dominated by the child archetype. Everything is growth. Everyone is "growing like a tree" and you are "putting out new branches, and new leaves," etc., etc. In one of his essays he says, "The notion of creative vision and the notion of the child are identified by many critics and painters, as George Boas shows. . . . In our view of imagination, play is given a disproportionate place, as if imagination were not a discipline, not an art, and not a work."[3] We imagine, being Americans, that imagination *is* play. I add that the Europeans are more likely—Kafka, for example—to envision imagination as a discipline, as art, and as work.

*Campbell*: All these rules! I knew that somebody would make you afraid to be spontaneous. The main thing is to get to be spontaneous, and pull it together later. The main thing is to live, to be alive. People say we are all looking for the meaning of life. No one is looking for the meaning of life. We are looking for an *experience* of life. And if you are living by rules and praying by rules, then you are not going to have an experience of life. Somewhere Jung says that theology and religion protect one against an experience of God. That is the final word, I think, with respect to all these rules. God may blow you apart, but it is better to have that experience than to go on through as a shell of a clam that never did anything but clam up. So spontaneity is the word of the day!

# Notes

---

1. William Blake, "The Roaring of Lions," in *The Complete Poetry and Prose of William Blake*, ed. David V. Erdman (Garden City, N.Y.: Anchor/Doubleday, 1982), p. 511.
2. T'ang Yin, "Poems Inscribed on Paintings," in *The Columbia Book of Later Chinese Poetry*, ed. Jonathan Chaves (New York: Columbia University Press, 1986), p. 212. Used by permission.
3. James Hillman, "Abandoning the Child," in *Loose Ends: Primary Papers in Archetypal Psychology* (Dallas: Spring Publications, 1975), p. 34.

# On
# William Blake
### Reason Versus
### Imagination    June Singer

My admiration for William Blake goes back a long time. He has been
for me a major carrier of an image for the creative spirit that I have
come to know in many guises over the years. Blake's struggle to find
a path between imagination and reason is everyone's struggle. He
marked the trail for us well, with poems, pictures, and phantasmagoric
visions of the night. His is a difficult trail to follow, for it is filled with
stumbling blocks, wrong turns, and many surprises. But the rewards,
in terms of a mythology of creation that is gleaned from the misty past
and the apocalyptic future, make it worth the effort required to pursue
it.

Blake was an eccentric by any standards in his own day and in ours,
and he was an extreme introvert as well. He felt little need to conform
to the demands of the world outside himself; for him, the inner world
was all-important as the source of truth, of meaning, of comfort and
support. It is this independence of spirit from the imposition of values
by the external world that characterizes Blake. I believe this inner freedom is the *sine qua non* of all creativity. It is a "tyger," too, because if it
is not appeased, it can be a killer.

William Blake has been called poet, painter, and prophet. Living in
London at the time of the American and French Revolutions, he proclaimed the virtues of freedom; but for him political freedom was important only because it opened the way for freedom of the spirit and
the offspring of that freedom—imagination. Early in his career, in a
long prose poem called "The Marriage of Heaven and Hell," he personified the struggling forces of good and evil in the human soul as
angels and devils. This work was a vehicle for his own inquiry into the
nature of the passions that imprison a person and those that set one
free.

Blake found his inspiration in the work of that earlier visionary,
Emanuel Swedenborg, who had written a book titled *Heaven and Hell*.
Here Blake found support for recognizing the level of reality that exists
beyond the door that can be unlocked only with the key of imagination. Blake eventually repudiated Swedenborg, like so many creative

people who learn from a master and then must go beyond that master to find their own way. The most crucial area of agreement between Blake and Swedenborg has to do with the perception of a relation between the world of nature and the world of spirit, and a sense of the unity underlying both. This is the more remarkable when we note that these two men were living at a time when the influence of the seventeenth-century Enlightenment was at its strongest, and its leading spokesmen—Locke, Descartes, Newton, and Voltaire—had made a clear separation between the rational and the imaginal. Blake regarded their efforts to replace fantasy with their own particular version of reality as pointless. He wrote:

> Mock on, Mock on, Voltaire, Rousseau:
> Mock on, Mock on: 'tis all in vain!
> You throw the sand against the wind,
> And the wind blows it back again.[1]

The schism between the rational and the imaginal went right through the hearts of both Swedenborg and Blake, but in the end Blake had to find his own way to the resolution of the opposites, saying,

> I must Create a System or be enslav'd by another Man's.
> I will not Reason & Compare: my business is to Create.[2]

William Blake was buried in an unmarked grave. Although he never achieved recognition in his own day, his legend and work had been kept alive over the years by a small band of Blake enthusiasts. One of their number, Herbert Jenkins, searched out and found the burial site in a cemetery at Bunham Fields in an obscure part of London. There in 1827, according to Jenkins, Blake had been buried in a pauper's grave, in a plot that had been used on eight occasions, three times before and four times after Blake's interment. Today a simple stone marker carries the legend, "Somewhere in this cemetery lie the bodies of William Blake and his wife Catherine." Creativity does not necessarily result in fame and fortune, or even recognition. But the spirit lives, if not in the public eye, then in the hearts of those whom it inspires.

Despite the fact that Blake was scarcely noticed by the literati while he lived, much scholarship has grown up around him since his death. This is not the matter I intend to take up here. Rather, I want to use the figure of William Blake as an exemplary incarnation of the impulse that most of us experience at times. I want to suggest how the creative spirit (what Jung has called the "daimon") has its way with us, "whether we will or no." This phrase, "whether we will or no," comes straight from Blake's own description of his work: "I also have the

Bible of Hell, which the world shall have whether it will or no."[3] This phrase inspired the title of my book, *The Unholy Bible*, in which I tried to say that the creative spirit often turns everything upside down and looks at the world from an "infernal" perspective.

Most famous of Blake's poems is "The Tyger":

> Tyger! Tyger! burning bright
> In the forests of the night,
> What immortal hand or eye
> Could frame thy fearful symmetry?
>
> In what distant deeps or skies
> Burnt the fire of thine eyes?
> On what wings dare he aspire?
> What the hand dare sieze the fire?
>
> And what shoulder, & what art,
> Could twist the sinews of thy heart?
> And when thy heart began to beat,
> What dread hand? & what dread feet?
>
> What the hammer? what the chain?
> In what furnace was thy brain?
> What the anvil? what dread grasp
> Dare its deadly terrors clasp?
>
> When the stars threw down their spears,
> And water'd heaven with their tears,
> Did he smile his work to see?
> Did he who made the Lamb make thee?
>
> Tyger! Tyger! burning bright
> In the forests of the night,
> What immortal hand or eye
> Dare frame thy fearful symmetry?[4]

Fearful symmetry is the key here. If symmetry is "the beauty of form arising from balanced proportions," the tyger is surely the perfect image for symmetry. The tyger is "fearful." How awesome is the balance of beauty and grace, the marvelous lithesome walk and the fierceness in the tyger's eye! The forests of the night are the places of dreams and all the other mysteries that the psyche withholds from the light of consciousness. There the tyger's burning spirit lights up the darkest places with its powerful energy. It brings us to ask the enduring question, "What immortal hand or eye?" For what is it, who is it, that is the author of such grace? Who is able to frame that fearful symmetry? Where does the creative spirit come from, defying reason and having its own unique way of proceeding? What or who is behind it? Is it above or below? "In what distant deeps or skies/ Burnt the fire of thine eyes?/ On what wings dare he aspire?/ What the hand dare sieze the fire?"

One feels the awesome power in the maker, the creator, the hand of God, in the lines: "And what shoulder, & what art/ Could twist the sinews of thy heart?/ And when thy heart began to beat,/ What dread hand? & what dread feet?" The image takes shape in the darkness and the mystery. And when there is shape, miracle of all miracles, the heart begins to beat! How precious, how familiar this moment to the one who waits and waits and then feels the spirit stirring within. It is not a gentle process. Not alchemy, but the blacksmith's shop is the image here: "What the hammer? what the chain?/ In what furnace was thy brain?/ What the anvil? what dread grasp/ Dare its deadly terrors clasp?"

Then comes the sweetest verse of all, at the moment when the torturous tempering is over: "When the stars threw down their spears,/ And water'd heaven with their tears,/ Did he smile his work to see?/ Did he who made the Lamb make thee? Here is the recognition that there is not only the tyger but also the lamb. The tyger is that fierce and ruthless spirit that seeks only its own expression, its own identity. But the lamb is another image entirely. It is all gentleness; it is love; it is relationship. It has no will of its own but follows the will of the one who leads it. Yet the lamb is a manifestation of the highest power, as much an incarnation of the divine creative power as is the tyger. The lamb is Jesus Christ; no less so is the tyger. Clearly, the images of the divine are often contradictory for Blake. The poet says, "Without Contraries is no progression. Attraction and Repulsion, Reason and Energy, Love and Hate, are necessary to Human existence."[5]

Sometime between childhood and what is called maturity, most of us lose sight of the visionary world of childhood. We become involved with learning all we need to know to get on in the world and take our place among our peers. We are educated, trained, formed, conditioned. Our minds become cluttered with the residues of rote learning. We forget to remember our tygers. Often this forming into a mold comes about in the wake of our initiation into sexuality. To find a mate, to please a mate, to learn to relate in the expected ways, to incorporate intimacy into our behavior, all require certain skills. It is a different kind of learning from the kind that emerged from the intimacies of parent-child, sibling, or childhood-friend relationships, because all these were relatively innocent. It is when that childhood innocence is breached that we find ourselves face to face with the rules and the laws, the approval and the disapproval, that intrude upon our inclinations to be spontaneous. Blake says it well in his poem "The Garden of Love":

> I went to the Garden of Love,
> And saw what I never had seen:
> A Chapel was built in the midst,
> Where I used to play on the green.
>
> And the gates of this Chapel were shut,
> And "Thou shalt not" writ over the door;
> So I turn'd to the Garden of Love
> That so many sweet flowers bore;
>
> And I saw it was filled with graves,
> And tomb-stones where flowers should be;
> And Priests in black gowns were walking their rounds,
> And binding with briars my joys & desires.[6]

Many people, on entering into mature adulthood, lose sight of the tyger and the lamb and, indeed, of the forests of the night. They become deeply involved with the ego world, for better or for worse. At a certain point, they may find that something is lacking in their lives. It may be that they have not tended the creative spirit. Blake's poem "My Pretty Rose-tree" could have been written for them:

> A flower was offer'd to me,
> Such a flower as May never bore:
> But I said, "I've a Pretty Rose-tree,"
> And I passed the sweet flower o'er.
>
> Then I went to my Pretty Rose-tree,
> To tend her by day and by night;
> But my Rose turn'd away with jealousy,
> And her thorns were my only delight.[7]

Does not the jealousy of the rose resemble the fierceness of the tyger? One can easily forget the tyger, much as one passes over the rose! As time goes on, the need to satisfy the demands of the world around us takes precedence over the need to satisfy the world within us. The tyger retreats into his den; the creative spirit goes into the caves of the unconscious.

I suspect that we all have within us an animal soul that has its own needs and its own desires and will have its way, "whether we will or no." Often enough, that part appears first in dreams or in visions of the night. So it was with me when I was led to write my analyst's thesis on William Blake's prose poem "The Marriage of Heaven and Hell." I discovered a facsimile edition of the volume with its hand-colored etchings in the English Library in Zurich as part of a collection of works by and about William Blake. I had been reading extensively in Blake as well as in Nathaniel Hawthorne. I had determined to write my thesis on one of these two, both of whom wrote with great ardor and vehemence of the repressed dark side that vies with the adapted bright side for possession of the souls of most "good" people. One morning at about three o'clock I awakened with a start from a deep sleep. In my head was the complete outline of a thesis on Blake's "The Marriage of Heaven and Hell." Fortunately, I had my dream notebook at my bedside and I hurriedly wrote it down, knowing that if I did not, I would surely forget it by daylight. Then, when I awoke at the usual time, I said to myself: "What a lovely dream, to have my thesis totally and perfectly outlined for me. Too bad it was only a dream." But, when I looked at my pad, there it was, nearly perfect from start to finish.

In beginning a book, one often finds a quotation serves as a leitmotiv for the work that is to follow. The phrase that guided me in my work came from Jacob Boehme, the German mystic and theosophist, whom Blake greatly admired: "Every man carries heaven and hell with him in this world." Boehme, like Blake, was an eccentric. He cared not a whit for what the world thought but trusted implicitly his own inner knowledge, what is called "gnosis." By this time, Blake was no longer following in the footsteps of Swedenborg. In fact, he ridiculed Swedenborg, writing in "The Marriage of Heaven and Hell":

> I have always found that Angels [at this point he classifies Angels with the collective idea of what is good] have the vanity to speak of themselves as the only wise; this they do with a confident insolence sprouting from systematic reasoning.
>
> Thus Swedenborg boasts that what he writes is new; tho' it is only the Contents or Index of already published books.
>
> A man carried a monkey about for a shew, & because he was a little wiser than the monkey, grew vain and conciev'd himself as much wiser than seven men. It is so with Swedenborg: he shews the folly of churches, & exposes hypocrites, till he imagines that all are religious, & he himself the single one on earth that ever broke a net. . . .
>
> Have now another plain fact. Any man of mechanical talents may, from the writings of Paracelsus or Jacob Behmen, produce ten thousand volumes of equal value with Swedenborg's, and from those of Dante or Shakespear an infinite number.

But when he has done this, let him not say that he knows better than his master, for he holds only a candle in the sunshine.[8]

So, in searching for the roots of Blake, one must go to Boehme, who seems to have discovered secrets of true creativity. Boehme has been a penniless shoemaker, given to philosophical speculations. One day he was struck by a sudden illumination that occurred as he watched a beam of light bouncing off the edge of a pewter plate. The light clarified something within him, a glimpse of a mystery that he would spend the rest of his life recapturing and explicating. An inward, introverted person, he isolated himself from the world. In his spiritual cave, his tyger's den, he asked and attempted to answer the question, "Where will you seek for God?" It could as well have been Parzival's asking, "Whom does the Grail serve?" or Jung, searching for the symbols of the self. Boehme had written in his *Confessions*: "Seek for him in your soul, that is proceeded out of the eternal nature, the living fountain of forces wherein the divine working stands."[9]

Boehme then proceeds to expound from his own experience a message that can well be heard by every person who undertakes a creative task. If we could only assimilate this, we would not need to battle that well-known creative block that constantly taunts us with the concerns of "Will it be good enough?" and "Will people like it?" Here is what Boehme writes:

> My beloved Reader, I tell thee this, that everything has its impulse in its own form. It always makes that very thing with which the impulse is impregnated, and the body must always labor in that wherein the spirit is kindled. When I consider and think why I thus write many wonders and leave them not for sharper wits, I find that my spirit is kindled in the manner whereof I write, for there is a living running fire of these things in my spirit, and thereupon (let me purpose what I will) yet they continually come uppermost, so that I am made captive thereby, and it is laid upon me as a work I must do. Therefore, seeing it is my work, wherein my spirit drives, I will write it down for a memorial in such manner as I know it in my spirit and as I attained to it; I will set down no other thing than that I myself have tried and known, that I not be found a liar before God.[10]

In his reading of Boehme, Blake acknowledged that the creative spirit that heeds the inner voice can also learn from others. The creative person, however, will not be enslaved by teachers or by anyone who attempts to enforce upon another person a path that is alien. Therefore, the attachment to a teacher must always be provisional, even as the attachment to a parent, to a belief system, to any image that is all-powerful, must be provisional. Sooner or later a creative person out-grows all attachments. Imagination shows us what is possible, what may lie ahead, and where the path may be. But for imagination to flower, there must be an open space wherein it may grow.

Whenever I return to my study of William Blake, working my way through his difficult and abstruse writings, a bit more of his meaning is revealed. In some respects, reading Blake is like reading some of the more difficult works of Jung. In both, there are many levels of mean-ing, and each level makes itself known to the reader when he or she is ready to receive it. I recently began to wonder about Jung's gnosis, Jung's inner and secret knowledge. He often referred to it but never made it explicit as to what his interest in gnosticism really was about. In my own reflections, I believe I may have found a missing link con-necting Boehme, Blake, and Jung, something of which Jung himself may not have been aware.

This missing link was gnosis, a form of knowing that is not intellec-tual and that is not imposed from outside the individual. It is knowl-edge that springs from within, that is recognized, re-cognized, rather than learned. It comes through the channel of intuition and may bypass the thinking process entirely. This commitment to gnosis, the knowl-edge of the heart, is what shines through Blake's work and is what drew Jung to him. To go back even further, I believe it was this gnosis that brought Blake to Boehme. Jacob Boehme, William Blake, and Carl Jung are links in the chain of gnosis that has been carried forward from the beginning of recorded time, when human beings first artic-ulated their thoughts about the creation of the world and the people who dwell upon it. Perhaps Eve was the Great Mother of gnosis, for she was the first—at least in our Judeo-Christian cultural myth—who made the fateful decision for inner knowledge as over and against re-ceived knowledge.

Much gnostic literature was written at about the same time as the books of the Bible, but it was not included when the Bible was can-onized, for reasons that will become immediately apparent. According to a gnostic book, *The Hypostasis of the Archons*, an anonymous tractate presenting an esoteric interpretation of Genesis 1-6, a jealous god tells the first couple on earth that they are not permitted to eat of the tree of knowledge of good and evil, that is, the tree of gnosis, for if they do they will die.[11] But Satan, who is really the Wise Instructor in the guise of the serpent, tells Eve that she will not die: "for God knows that when you eat of it your eyes will be opened, and you will be like God, knowing good and evil" (Genesis 3-5, R.S.V.). The Wise In-structor does not tell Eve to eat of the tree. The decision to eat or not to eat must be her own responsibility. A wise instructor does not give orders but rather sets forth the possibilities. Eve sees that the tree is good for food and that the tree is to be desired to make one wise. Eve, faced with the choice, chooses to know rather than to do as she is told.

Boehme, like the Wise Instructor, also cries out against blindly accepting authority. Listen to the inner voice, he says:

> Dost thou suppose again that I speak from hearsay? No, I speak the very life in my own experience; not in an opinion from the mouth of another, but from my own knowledge. I see with my own eyes, which I boast not of, for the power is the Mother's. I exhort thee to enter into the bosom of the Mother, and to learn also to see with thine eyes: so long as thou dost suffer thyself to be rocked in a cradle and dost desire the eyes of others, thou are blind. But if thou riseth up from the cradle and dost go to the Mother, then shalt thou discern the Mother and her children. [12]

Boehme seems to be saying here that we must listen to the voices of wisdom and authority but not identify with them or with their ideas. If we are caught up in the mother archetype or, for that matter, the father archetype, we cannot discern it, nor can we see the extent of our own involvement. So every belief, every assumption, must be measured against the inner vision. Boehme reminds us:

> O how good it is to see with one's own eyes! We are all asleep in the outward man, we lie in the cradle and suffer ourselves to be rocked asleep by outward reason; we see with the eyes of dissimulation of our play-actors who hang bells and baubles about our ears and cradles, that we may be lulled asleep or at least play with baubles, and they may be lords and masters in the house.
>
> Rise up from thy cradle: art thou not a child of the Mother, and moreover a child and lord of the house, and also an heir to its good? Why suffer thy servants thus to use thee? [13]

Our political leaders give us reasons, our employers give us reasons, the media give us reasons, all the authorities in our lives tell us what to think. Some of their reasons may be good and true, but one gets the uneasy feeling that hidden purposes lie behind many of the reasons given. In the struggle between reason and imagination, creative people do not accept the reasons without subjecting them to the test of imagination or the inner vision.

Two hundred years ago when he walked the streets of London, William Blake commented upon this tendency to follow leaders unquestioningly. He wrote of the "mind-forg'd manacles," an apt phrase to describe how we ourselves lock up our minds against the new, the daring, the creative thought:

### LONDON

I wander thro' each charter'd street,
Near where the charter'd Thames does flow,
And mark in every face I meet
Marks of weakness, marks of woe.

In every cry of every Man,
In every Infant's cry of fear,
In every voice, in every ban,
The mind-forg'd manacles I hear.

How the Chimney-sweeper's cry
Every black'ning Church appalls;
And the hapless soldier's sigh
Runs in blood down Palace walls.

But most thro' midnight's streets I hear
How the youthful Harlot's curse
Blasts the newborn Infant's tear,
And blights with plagues the Marriage hearse.[14]

In Blake's symbology, London is the human soul and Albion, the ancient name for Britain, is the whole being of every person. London, the soul, is sunken in the morass of collective thinking. Its redemption can come only through imagination: imagining what could be and must be, and then living in accord with the wisdom that has been gleaned from the imagination. "Jerusalem" is the name of the city that symbolizes the feminine aspect of London, or "London's emanation," in Blake's language. Jung would have said that "Jerusalem" is the "anima" of London. Blake's last great prophetic poem, called "Jerusalem," tells of how the feminine aspect was separated from the masculine aspect of the psyche during the so-called Age of Reason, and how the feminine must now be restored through imagination so that Albion, now divided, can be made whole again. Blake has a vision, one that may inform our own times as well as his:

Albion! Our wars are wars of life, & wounds of love
With intellectual spears, & long-winged arrows of thought.
Mutual in one another's love and wrath all renewing
We live as One Man; for contracting our infinite senses
We behold multitude, or expanding, we behold as one,
As One Man all the Universal family . . .
I behold London, a Human awful wonder of God!

He says: "Return, Albion, return! I give myself for thee.
My Streets are my Ideas of Imagination.
Awake, Albion, awake! and let us awake up together.
My Houses are Thoughts: my Inhabitants, Affections,
The children of my thoughts walking within my blood vessels,
Shut from my nervous form which sleeps . . .
In dreams of darkness . . ."[15]

If reason is the hallmark of the mundane self, the earthly self, then imagination is the hallmark of the spiritual self, the divine self. The whole person can be nothing less than an integration of the two, reason and imagination. Creativity does not lie alone in the production of great works of art or in achieving scientific breakthroughs. It lies, essentially, in freeing the mind from its shackles, so that we create our world and ourselves anew, over and over again, in every moment.

*Acknowledgment*

The author gratefully acknowledges permission granted by Random House, Inc., for reprinting Blake's poetry from *The Complete Writings of William Blake*, ed. Geoffrey Keynes.

# Notes

1. William Blake, *The Complete Writings of William Blake*, ed. Geoffrey Keynes (London: The Nonesuch Press, 1957; New York: Random House/Alfred A. Knopf), p. 418.
2. Blake, *Complete Writings*, p. 629.
3. Ibid., p. 158.
4. Ibid., p. 214.
5. Ibid., p. 149.
6. Ibid., p. 215.
7. Ibid., p. 215.

8.  Ibid., p. 157-58.

9.  See Jacob Boehme, *Confessions of Jacob Boehme*, compiled and ed. Scott Palmer (London: Methuen, 1920), p. 48.

10.  Ibid., pp. 63-64.

11.  See James M. Robinson, ed., *The Nag Hammadi Library* (New York: Harper and Row, 1988), p. 164.

12.  Boehme, *Confessions*, p. 85.

13.  Ibid., pp. 85-87.

14.  Blake, *Complete Writings*, p. 216.

15.  Ibid., pp. 664-665.

# Meaning
## in Art   Stephen A. Martin

C. G. Jung was a psychologist of the symbolic image. He cared little for whether an image was "artistic" or not. For him, all images were equally valuable expressions of psychological meaning revealing something of the mysterious working of the human psyche. Art historical and formal considerations were secondary, if not extraneous, to the image's symbolic and psychological import.

Given this distinctly psychological perspective, Jung was attentive to the inner experience of the artist and of his creative process. Outlining his thoughts in two essays written in 1922 and 1930 (*CW* 15), he divided artists into two groups that he labeled the "psychological" and the "visionary." The domain of the psychological artist is the world of conscious cognition and ordinary awareness. Nowhere does the artwork transcend the boundary of psychological intelligibility, remaining eventually explicable in terms of personal associations and decipherable intentions.

For the visionary artist, creation is quite different. It is not the known and ordinary that are compelling, but the strange and primordial that arise from deep within the timeless, archetypal depths of the unconscious. Whereas the psychological artist creates in accordance with canons of style or beauty and personal preference, the visionary artist has no choice but to express what the unconscious wishes, gripped by a numinous impulsion that, if resisted, can split the personality. The visionary artist does not so much make art as be seized by the daimonic force of the artmaking process.

Reflecting the prevailing cultural realities of the known world, the experiences of the psychological artist enhance the artist's sense of identity and well-being. The visionary artist is not so fortunate. Such an artist is forced into a painful, fragmenting dialogue with the unconscious depths, yet it is a dialogue that, if endured and if successful, has the possibility of compensating and healing the one-sidedness of culture like the dream that heals the imbalance of the ego in the individual personality. Being the conduit for this transformation was, for Jung, the artist's highest calling.

A similar preference is present in the work of Erich Neumann, Jung's only student to have written extensively on art and artists. He directly states that in the "creative man's life the emphasis is always on the transpersonal,[1] and that the creative individual is different from other personalities. The creative person is deeply enmeshed, like a child, in a maternal archetypal world that he or she cannot escape but must tolerate and creatively transform in order to remain psychologically balanced. Neumann's clear-cut bias is for the feminine in the archetypal constellation of the creative individual, the unconscious as ground of being, source of all life and creativity. This overemphasis of the mother, or feminine, principle displaces the father principle into a psychological hinterland as the ideal self or as the dominant stylistic conventions of the prevailing collective consciousness.

Being exceptionally open to the unconscious, the creative personality remains perilously close to psychological imbalance. In order to maintain psychic equilibrium, the creative person makes art. By synthesizing the personal and the transpersonal elements of the psyche in the symbolic image, the creative personality overcomes the danger of psychological dissolution in the onslaught of the archetypal world. Neumann's outstanding capacity to empathize with the creative struggle does not compensate for his dependence on a kind of Jungian reductionism to such archetypal categories as the Great Mother, the feminine, the anima, or the self. Yet in fairness to him and to Jung, both men allude to the importance of the personal equation, the individual's particular personality, in the creative process, even if their preference is for the visionary, compensatory, and healing aspects of the artist's work. Perhaps this preference for the archetypal over the personal compensates the psychoanalytic perspective that champions the personal constellation to the exclusion of all else. It is clear, however, that a synthetic approach is needed that values these two important lines of reasoning. That is the purpose of these present reflections.

Before proceeding further, we need an operational definition of "meaning": it is the felt experience of connection to the larger background of human existence that integrates one's uniqueness and personal identity, a sense of belonging to a greater whole, and an appreciation of life's numinosity and mystery. Meaning is like a braid in which culture, personal history, and archetypes are interwoven. Understanding meaning in art therefore demands that these three components or developmental strands be fully and completely illuminated. These developmental strands of meaning are not separable and distinctive but overlap. Their basic shape nonetheless may be hypothetically outlined. The first of these I would call the *collective cultural context*. Its focus is the external aesthetic and socio-cultural conditions that inform the artist's world. The second is the biographical or psychodynamic aspect, which I would call the *autobiographical context*. Its province is the personal unconscious and semi-conscious material that motivates the artist to create. The final strand I would call the *mythic context* in which are brought to light the archetypal underpinnings that act as formative principles in the personal life of the artist and may compensate or balance the prevailing collective *zeitgeist*. Let us look at each in greater depth.

No artist creates in a cultural vacuum. He or she is born into and comes to maturity in a specific time and place, the megarules of which condition and guide his or her psychological and artistic evolution. Even if an artist elects to oppose the prevailing values, that artist still stands in relation to and is responsive to them and is a member of the *collective cultural context*. The vastness and complexity of these conditions are obvious to any student of art history who has ever attempted to determine the influence of politics, social values, aesthetic conventions, and external events on the artist and the artwork. In fact, it is primarily the analysis of these complexities on which the field of art history has chosen to concentrate.

Depending on the circumstances of the artist's life, certain conditions may be more formative than others, such as the cataclysmic effect of the First World War on so many major European artists, or the influence of papal patronage in the Renaissance. Of central importance, however, to this development are the aesthetic advances of the artist's cultural context. The artwork emerges from what has come before and what is in the process of being formed, for it is against or within the context of the prevailing stylistic, formal, and theoretical constructs that the dialogical relation of the artist to the work evolves. The discernment of the specific conditions, the collective realities, that mold a culture and the exploration of the details of the artist's world are the working material of this development. Such realities are quite visible to the critical eye, and solid investigative work can unravel those specific characteristics that have contributed to this process. By way of examples, we could say that cubism did not spring out of a void but was the natural evolution of the shifting scientific, social, stylistic, and art historical perspectives of the last century. Nor were Goya's paintings of war and torment solely the result of his deaf, paranoid state; they were also the objective reflections of the *zeitgeist* of eighteenth-century Spain.

Whereas in the collective cultural context, the larger social and art historical realities were the autonomous conditioning agents, in the *autobiographical context* the world of the family, individual psychology, and personal experience—the "actual life" of the artist—are the principle determinants. It is the psychoanalyst who has excelled in the clinical distillation of and insight into the concrete facts of life that affect an artist's creative production and influence this level of meaning in the artwork. Psychodynamics refers to the nature of the artist's ego, his or her defenses, relationships to important people, life events, and conscious and unconscious traumata. This is the world of the artist's personal complexes. When considering this dimension, the analysis of idiosyncratic content and style may take precedence over subject matter and formal considerations that are dictated mainly by specific cultural conventions and that belong to the meaning of the collective cultural context. Instead, what is important here are the personal twists, emendations, embellishments, or distortions that the artist makes as a response to the inner personal pressures of his or her collection of complexes and conflicts. Thus it comes as no surprise that Michelangelo sculpted and painted Madonnas or Holy Families because of their iconographic importance in the Renaissance. But in what fashion did he envision them, and how do they, in their specific way, express who he is and the struggles he faced? And is it not worthwhile to go beyond simply noting that Picasso, Kirchner, Munch, or even de Kooning have all painted the female form, and recognize that their experience of women and the feminine contributes to the way in which they paint this form? The autobiographical context is a reflection of the unique way in which the artist has assimilated and transformed his or her life history through art. At its worst, such art can be sterile neurotic repetition. But at its best, it can embody what is quintessentially individual in the artist and break through to a mythic dimension that expresses the deepest and most universal qualities that characterize the human condition.

The touchstones of the *mythic context* are those collective formative patterns Jung called "archetypes." They make themselves known by way of prototypical subject matter and gripping emotional valency as expressed through particularities of form and style. No subject is solely archetypal or solely personal, because a given image or subject may reflect basic commonality of experience that can just as well appear quite autobiographical or archetypal. What first tips the scale in favor of the archetypal is the experience by the art viewer of powerful feelings of timelessness and truthfulness that seem to emanate from the work itself. They are not attributable to specific subject or style but appear to belong to the very essence of the work and endow it with a living presence. Our response to this intrinsic aliveness is the compulsion to look again and again, as if enchanted by the work in some inexplicable way. This is the felt experience of the numinous, the hallmark of the presence of archetypal meaning in art. Undoubtedly, such an indefinite manner of discernment opens the attribution of "archetypal" to much criticism because of its subjectivity. Nevertheless, this kind of intuitive, profound empathy inheres in the masterworks of every period, whether it be one of the immensely moving garden studies of the late Monet, or a mature color field study of Rothko in all its preternatural magnificence. In the contemplation of such works, their sense of deep meaning seems self-evident.

The second component of archetypal meaning has to do with the particular archetypal pattern or story that may underlie the work's content. Every creative act, indeed every human act, is informed by these archetypal patterns and can be differentiated when compared to the basic mythemes that illustrate human existence. Even an abstract work speaks of the archetypal mythemes that have enabled it to come forth, just as Neumann so ably illustrated with the work of Henry Moore.[2] Thus in order to discern the archetypal patterns particular to a given work, it is necessary to be familiar with the rich mythologies and symbolic systems, and their depiction in imagery, that have always expressed the eternal in human existence. It is in comparison with these mythic patterns and their images (a process called the "amplification" of the symbol or image) that an approximation of archetypal meaning can be deduced—a meaning that at first lay undifferentiated in those powerful, numinous feelings.

The final point to be considered from within the mythic context is how an artist's work heals or balances the one-sidedness of a culture by bringing to it those psychological values and meaning that have been excluded because of natural cultural development. Like the individual psyche, the psychological life of a culture is selective, promoting and encouraging aesthetic, social, and political developments that seem consistent with established traditions. This is not to say that culture and the collective consciousness are purposely rigid; rather, like all systems, they strive to maintain the status quo, avoid the destabilization of revolutionary ideas, and operate at the minimum level of discord. Under these circumstances, however, cultures, and the symbols that represent their greatest meaning, eventually lose depth and psychological versatility when there is not periodic renewal from the archetypal level of the collective psyche. Compensation in the form of innovative and dramatically new images of aesthetic or physical reality, theoretical constructs that challenge old ideas and renewed spiritual meaning, must come by way of those whose work allows them to touch the depths, be they artists, scientists, or other creative personalities. Such individuals are iconoclasts, whether they desire to be or not, because in bringing new psychological realities to the surface of life, they threaten that precarious collective status quo.

In the same way that dreams, visions, and unconscious fantasies provide the necessary archetypal material to challenge and eventually rebalance the psychic life of an individual, the artist's work—when it carries meaning from the archetypal level of inner experience—expresses the fundamental imperative in all psychic functioning toward eventual dynamic equilibrium. Cultures, like individuals, owe their health to the dynamic relation between the forces of what is consensually acceptable, the collective conscious values, and that which is not, the hidden unconscious potential that, usually perceived by the culture as only destructive, is really the source of renewal. We can therefore appreciate the impact of a work like *Les Demoiseiles d'Avignon*, painted by Picasso in 1907. As an image, it appalled friends and critics and remained rolled up on Picasso's studio floor for years before being purchased sight unseen by the French collector Jacques Doucet, in 1920, because he realized its artistic importance.[3] Yet not long after this, the work has come to be recognized as the harbinger of cubism, one of the single most revitalizing influences in modern art. It is a monumental image whose spatial and volumetric distortions and stylistic innovations were expressive of—among many cultural, scientific, and social changes—the new developments in painting, including Cezanne's redefinition of space and Matisse's dramatic infusion of emotive color into mundane existence. These five harpies, symbolizing on a personal level Picasso's own profound anxiety about and fear of women, are the collective shadow compensations for an age that sentimentalized and devalued the dark power of the feminine. One has only to compare them with the rosy-cheeked women of Renoir or the wistful, ethereal princesses of the Pre-Raphaelites to appreciate the difference. By creating *Les Demoiselles d'Avignon*, Picasso broke open the door for the natural compensatory movement toward greater appreciation of the dark side of life. It stands as a companion achievement with expressionism in every form, be it surrealism, the innovative and iconoclastic developments in modern literature and music, or even the great theories of the unconscious.

Picasso's *Les Demoiselles d'Avignon* was probably conceived in late 1906, and completed in the summer of 1907. This depiction of five prostitutes from the Calle d'Avignon, or red-light quarter, of Barcelona, with its primitive spatial and figural distortions, was a departure from Picasso's more romantic and melancholic blue and rose period imagery. As a personal statement, it exposes a central painful complex in Picasso's personality. It is no wonder that he labeled the painting his "first exorcism picture."[4] What makes *Les Demoiselles* so important on the artistic stage is its "barbaric, dissonant power,"[5] rivaled only by some of Matisse's work of this period or by paintings from Munch, Kokoschka, Schiele, and Kirchner. Reflecting upon the impact of this painting, Robert Rosenblum states that *"Les Demoiselles d'Avignon* marks . . . a shrill climax to the 19th century growing veneration of the primitive."[6] The innovative vitality of this work echoes dramatic contemporary developments in other fields. Just two years previously, in 1905, Einstein altered modern physics with the publication of his *Special Theory of Relativity*; the same year as *Les Demoiselles d'Avignon*, 1907, Freud's milestone, *Three Contributions to a Theory of Sex*, appeared; and the age of electricity, flight, the atom, and plastics dawned with the work of Marconi, Planck, Rutherford, Curie, the Wright brothers, and L. H. Bakeland. Traditional conceptions of distance, size, physical reality, and the nature of the psyche were being pulled apart and turned in upon themselves like these five masked women. The spirit that evoked *Les Demoiselles d'Avignon* came therefore not only from Picasso's artistic imperative but also from a collective trend toward seeing beyond ordinary everyday reality in order to determine its inner workings.

The turn of the nineteenth century brought tremendous emotional energy into the art of painting. Picasso and his contemporaries were breaking through the stifling barriers of bourgeois propriety and capturing a less sophisticated, more primitive side of life in their work. Certainly, their way had been prepared by their predecessors; by Gauguin and his Breton peasants and South Sea nymphs with their flat, strangely lyrical color areas; and by the almost hallucinatory style of his erstwhile friend, Van Gogh. Even Toulouse-Lautrec, gentlemen that he was, focused on the lower levels of life and experience. These men penetrated below the surface, revealing to those who followed the archaic and more magical infrastructure of ordinary life. Their work encouraged painters like Munch to explore an inner world peopled by sepulchral women—seductive, overripe, and dangerous; like Kirchner to ennoble his angulated city witches; like Schiele to obsess over pornographic village maidens; and like Kokoschka to immortalize his angel of despair, Alma Mahler. Picasso seems to have brought together a variety of artistic and cultural trends with *Les Demoiselles d'Avignon* to create a complex, bivalent image of feminine power that related as much to the psychological painters and their prophets as to formalists like Cezanne and Matisse.

Prior to 1906, Picasso's women were more victims than victimizers. Frail and enigmatic, they were creatures who appeared either childishly seductive or old and careworn. This ambivalence about women must have been in part a statement about Picasso's anxiety in the world and his own uncertain masculinity. Upon his return to Paris from Barcelona and the establishment of his permanent residency there in 1905, Picasso seemed "steeped in compassion for humanity and concern with morality and emotion in his work."[7] When filtered through what is known about his psychology at the time,[8] it is probable that, like his characters, Picasso was having a profound difficulty making the transition from adolescence to independent adult life. He felt personally and professionally displaced—an outsider. Not surprisingly, then, are his women frequently bonded with all manner of outcasts, beggars, circus performers, and other examples of dejected, lowly humanity, for Picasso himself felt the victim, mired in an uncertain sense of his own agency and personal direction.

By 1906, Picasso was more settled in Paris. His relationship to Apollinaire had solidified, and he became close friends with Gertrude and Leo Stein, soon to be among his most loyal and influential patrons. In addition, a profound love relationship brought him some measure of rootedness and emotional comfort. Paralleling these positive developments was a more classical, objective style in which female figures assumed monumental, goddess-like proportions. Gone were the pathetic figures of the demimonde and replacing them was this other kind of woman—self-possessed, mysterious, and powerful—executed in warmer earth tones. A series of self-portraits done at the same time and in similar style again suggests how, concordant with this revised image of the feminine, Picasso himself was feeling more substantial, self-confident, and nourished by his increasing success.

It was perhaps because Picasso was growing stronger as an artist that he was more able to express directly his complex experience of the feminine. There is no doubt that the five prostitutes of *Les Demoiselles d'Avignon* were an extremely personal appraisal of the potentially destructive and fearsome power of women and sexuality and, by extension, of the world. We can surmise the personal meaning from anecdotal reports that Picasso and his friends, Guillaume Apollinaire and Max Jacob, named some of the figures; one was called "Fernande" after Picasso's beloved mistress, another was dubbed "Marie" after Apollinaire's future love, Marie Laurencin; and a third bore the same name as Max Jacob's grandmother allegedly from Avignon, France.[9] With regard to the meaning of this action, Mary Gedo writes: "The conscious associations Picasso forged between his demoiselles and his closest friends indicates his allegiance to other men who also suffered greatly at the hands of women."[10] Confirming this supposition that *Les Demoiselles d'Avignon* is a personal statement[11] of Picasso's ambivalence toward and fear of women is his inclusion, in earlier sketches of the composition, of patently self-representative figures. One was supposed to be a medical student and another a sailor. Gedo and other authors argue quite convincingly that these two male figures, eliminated from the final work, are references to Picasso's personal history. The sailor is Picasso as a child, when he too wore a sailor suit and was fussed over and cared for, if not suffocated, by five women (his mother, grand-

mother, two aunts, and a maid). The medical student is Picasso as fre-
quenter of the brothels in Barcelona, where, it was said, he was sexu-
ally initiated and where he contracted a venereal disease. The medical
student persona is also Picasso the observer, who years later in Paris
spent time in the St. Lazare Hospital sketching prostitutes who themselves were being treated for venereal disease.[12] Constellated in *Les
Demoiselles d'Avignon* was Picasso's decided ambivalence about the
feminine: his attraction to its nurturant aspect and his vulnerability to
its destructive, castrating side.

Knowing as we do that archetypal patterns underlie personal emotional experience, *Les Demoiselles d'Avignon* is also an image of the
mythic dimension of the eternal feminine. Even though the painting
has unequivocal personal reference for Picasso, its symbolic force derives from the portrayal of the devouring, emasculating side of the
feminine principle. It is analogous to other such projections of this archetypal reality. The explicit aggressiveness of ancient Medusa is one
example; Kali, the seductive goddess of death, is another. Closer to
home, Picasso's prostitutes bear a symbolic resemblance to the archetypal image of incubi or witches, the demon women who, in concert
with Satan, steal goodness from men's hearts and strength from their
loins. Goya, one of Picasso's great compatriots, was also sensitive to
this archetypal reality and rendered it several times in his paintings of
the witches' Sabbath, as did another Latin artist, the Mexican Outsider
artist Martin Ramirez, who was himself overwhelmed by dark mono-
lithic Madonnas and rapacious, grinning maidens. The imagery of all
three men derives from the same archetypal source.

Although there is little in the painting itself to moderate the loath-
someness of the women, we are aware that the prostitute was not a
solely destructive figure for Picasso and others of his time. Frequently,
she offered sexual solace and emotional acceptance to the artist outcast
during this period in history, inspiring many remarkable works of art.
Contained within the dynamic of this archetypal image is a muselike
quality that enabled Picasso to break through the strictures of conventional morality and confront his own darker, often more spontaneous
and emotionally authentic, shadow side. The prostitutes compensate a
Victorian femininity; they carry the sensual and irrational possibility
of life for an age in which order and propriety were the highest values.
Through them, the artist and the time could eventually become more
consciously integrated and whole. Picasso's muses are incongruent
with the charming, genteel figures of Maurice Denis and are more sin-
istrally alive than the mysterious nymph muses of Puvis de Chavannes.
*Les Demoiselles d'Avignon* is the recollection, for a decadent time, of its
kinship with the primitive, tribal beginnings of all things and how the

feminine principle is the irrational ground of all being. It may also be a recognition of how dependent the life of culture is on this primordial feminine energy not only to make conscious the archaic forces underneath the surface, but to renew ailing psychological and artistic perspectives. This may in part account for some of this painting's "affinity" to certain tribal artworks that also embody this fundamental energy. As "the" proto-cubist painting, *Les Demoiselles d'Avignon* introduced the need to step outside conventional reality with its repressed fears and anxieties in order to touch a more fertile, though frightening, level of personal and cultural expression. After this painting, which symbolizes the turning point, no area of life would be left untransformed.

In the end, the work of art is the container in which the voice of the culture and the artist's personal equation merge with and are suffused by the archetypal energy that moves through both. It is not simply a cultural artifact, neurotic distortion, or archetypal image. Rather, it is truly symbolic, conjoining these various dimensions of reality to produce a living experience that is greater and deeper than all its component parts. Without a thorough understanding of these three aspects, we cannot hope to appreciate the fullest possible meaning of the artwork or to avoid compromising its integrity.

# Notes

1. Erich Neumann, "Leonardo and the Mother Archetype," in his *Art and the Creative Unconscious*, Bollingen Series (Princeton: Princeton University Press, 1959), p. 17.

2. Erich Neumann, *The Archetypal World of Henry Moore*, Bollingen Series (Princeton: Princeton University Press, 1959).

3. Roland Penrose, *Picasso: His Life and Work* (New York: Schocken Books, 1966), p. 130.

4. William Rubin, *Primitivism in 20th Century Art*, vol. 1 (New York: The Museum of Modern Art, 1984), p. 73.

5. Robert Rosenblum, *Cubism and Twentieth-Century Art* (New York: Harry N. Abrams, 1966), p. 12.

6. Ibid.

7. Rosenblum, *Cubism and Twentieth-Century Art*, p. 10.

8. Mary Mathews Gedo, *Picasso: Art as Autobiography* (Chicago: University of Chicago Press, 1980). Gedo's book is a remarkably balanced and insightful work that was the source of much of the information here about Picasso's personal psychology.

9. Ibid., p. 77.

10. Ibid., p. 79.

11. Ibid., p. 78.

12. Rubin, *Primitivism in 20th Century Art*, 1:254.

# Jung and Abstract Expressionism

Terree Grabenhorst-Randall

If the strangest things come together in one place, at one time, in a strange similarity, wonderful unities arise.     —*Novalis*

One of the more fascinating conjunctions in the history of modern art is that between Jungian psychology and abstract expressionism. Many of Jung's ideas played a significant role in the development of abstract expressionist art.[1] Yet the impact of Jung's philosophy on this art lies not so much in the unraveling of the psychological foundation of artistic creation as in its inclusion in a system of interrelationships, mutual dependencies, and metamorphoses that informed and influenced the development of abstract expressionism. Indeed, an attempt to make a literal correlation between Jung's theories and the formal elements in these paintings, drawings, and sculptures, or to content that abstract expressionists painted and sculpted as they did solely because they followed Jungian dictates, would be missing the point. Jung himself stated: "Only that aspect of art which consists in the process of artistic creation can be a subject for psychological study, but not that which constitutes its essential nature" (*CW* 15: par.97, p. 65).

The abstract expressionists' receptivity to Jungian psychology is due in significant part to a rejection of the social realism of the 1930s, which with its graphic depiction of societal ills was seen as too restrictive in form and content. The abstract expressionists searched for forms of expression that would break through individual boundaries of experience in order to create a universal humanistic art out of the collective life of the human species. They sought to accomplish this by developing themes and an iconography that drew on mythology, on primitive art, and particularly on Jung's concept of the collective unconscious.

In Jung's definition, the collective unconscious is a "psychic system of a collective, universal and impersonal nature which is identical in all individuals" (*CW* 91: par.90, p. 43). Moreover, "this collective unconscious does not develop individually but is inherited. It consists of preexistent forms which can only become conscious secondarily and which give definite form to certain psychic contents" (ibid.).

The earliest symbols appearing in the psychological lexicon of the human family are the simplest ones: the circle, the cross, and the triangle. They are closest in meaning and form to what Jung identified as the archetype and are best understood as preconcrete and prepictorial forms imprimis. Jung postulated that archetypes are innate structures in the collective unconscious that form the basis of the human psyche. He also held that images emanate from the unconscious structures and move into the realm of the conscious mind to form the basis of religious experience and often of artistic creativity as well. According to Jung, archetypes are innate symbolic, character/energy patterns within the psyche; one may be either in harmonious accord with them or overwhelmed and dominated by them. The archetypal symbols and images put forth by the unconscious translate into emotional experience, revealing the deeper dynamics of our outer lives.

For Jung, it was no coincidence that such signs and symbols were used by primitive peoples to articulate an indistinct, unshaped multiplicity through abstracted conceptions of reality. Nor is it coincidental, considering the power of the collective unconscious, that cultures as different as the Aztec and the Oceanic developed cult figures that bear a striking similarity. Indeed, death cults, the rite of the magna mater, totemism and mask forms, idols of fertility and symbols of taboos, the cycle of the seasons, genesis, decay and resurrection, are universal themes and motifs found in folk tales, legends, and mythology that transcend time or place.

One finds a similar unity of vision in the formative works of the abstract expressionist painters and sculptors. According to Jung, archetypal, collective images will find a place in art regardless of what one does or does not do, simply by the fact of their existence. Certain motifs do, in fact, recur in the works of the abstract expressionists, such as the mandala, the bird, the single eye, and the mask.

The climate in which the abstract expressionists produced their early works was characterized by a sudden, remarkable synthesis of numerous revolutionary ideas and events. Jungian and Freudian psychology and the new secular philosophies of nihilism and existentialism were enthusiastically embraced by these artists in the 1940s and 1950s. The new literature, epitomized by Joyce's *Ulysses*, fused Freudian ideas of the unconscious with Einstein's theory of relativity. In modern dance, Martha Graham used archetypal myths—and not coincidentally, mythic sets designed by sculptor Isamu Noguchi—to formulate a new and powerful expression. At the same time, Herbert Read's books on the history and theory of art, particularly *The Meaning of Art* (1931) and *Art and Society* (1937), encouraged artists to explore the unconscious for visual forms of expression. Sir James George Frazer's *The*

*Golden Bough: Study in Magic and Religion* was an important source for visual material. Articles on myth and ancient art and exhibitions at the Museum of Modern Art such as "African Negro Art" (1935), "Prehistoric Rock Pictures in Europe and Africa" (1937), and "Ancestral Sources of Modern Painting" (1941) were additional sources of both information and inspiration.

With its psychological orientation and emphasis on dreams and the subconscious, surrealism was yet another source of inspiration and was colonized on these shores in the early 1940s after its proponents fled the ravages of World War II in Europe. Surrealism was a major influence on American artists who were searching for a content in their art that would transcend the traditional boundaries of rationality and logically discoverable reality. Biomorphic images used by many of these artists incorporated amoebic forms that were perfect formal devices for symbolizing psychological states. Automatism, both in writing and in painting, developed as an antithesis to external, rational, and conscious ways of recording reality. It, too, broadened the artists' field of vision.

David Hare's *Dinner Table*, 1950, a quasi-figurative welded steel sculpture, is an example of a surreal work in which the sculptor relies on the principle of free association, what he calls the "spaces of the mind"[2] to develop an imagery associated with the unconscious. Herbert Ferber's bronze sculpture, *Surrational Zeus I*, 1947, subsumes surrealism and mythology in a biomorphic rendering of the human form. Its head is supported by a phallic shaft that seems to "grow" from gaping sharklike teeth. The result is a frightening, totemistic image. The work, moreover, is aptly named. Its "surrationality" is implicit in its form, and Zeus of course is a prime mythic figure, the "king of the gods," that appears in Roman mythology as Jove. Ferber acknowledges that undercurrents of surrealism and existentialism as influences on the work were "immeasurable."[3] These works, and many other abstract expressionist works produced during the 1940s, such as Adolph Gottlieb's *Oedipus*, 1941, Isamu Noguchi's *Monument to Heroes*, 1943, Seymour Lipton's *Prehistoric Birds*, 1946, and Ferber's *Hazardous Encounter*, 1947, were meant to stand as visual metaphors of the human condition.

The single most important event of the period, however, was World War II. In his essay "The Spiritual Problem of Modern Man," Jung analyzes one of the fundamental issues of the twentieth century: the spiritual malaise of modern times. In this essay, he expresses despair over materialism, runaway science, destructive technology, amoral politics, and most especially war. War, Jung believed, had produced a psychological pathology: "I believe I am not exaggerating when I say that modern man has suffered an almost fatal shock, psychologically speaking, and as a result has fallen into profound uncertainty" (*CW* 10: par. 155, pp. 77-78). This sentiment was shared by many artists and writers of this period. Herbert Read saw the destructiveness of World War II generating a state of mind similar to "the same feelings which overcome primitive men, but which they can only express in emotive symbols."[4] Many artists were disillusioned with the past and fearful of the future because they felt that there was an inherent predilection to an annihilation of the species. The mushroom cloud of the atomic bomb hovered, both figuratively and literally, over their lives and had a profound impact on their work. Jeffrey Weiss has commented that "In the case of the atom bomb, nuclear physics was not denied or denounced. . . ." Rather, "The nuclear blast projected contemporary science onto the primordial past. . . . By demonstrating this underlying affinity between the primitive and that which was acutely of their own time, the New York painters rendered tribal truths inevitable and inescapable."[5]

Adolph Gottlieb expressed a similar attitude in 1943, two years before Hiroshima and Nagasaki:

> If we profess kinship to the art of primitive man, it is because the feelings they expressed have a particular pertinence today. In times of violence, personal predilections for niceties of color and form seem irrelevant. All primitive expression reveals the constant awareness of powerful forces, the immediate presence of terror and fear, a recognition of the brutality of the natural world as well as the eternal insecurities of life. That these feelings are being experienced by many people throughout the world today is an unfortunate fact and to us an art that glosses over or evades these feelings is superficial and meaningless. That is why we insist on . . . a subject matter that embraces these feelings and permits them to be expressed.[6]

Myths, especially those of rebirth and renewal, transformation and rites of passage, were important themes used by these artists in their early works and, in some cases, in later works as well. Like Jung, these artists regarded myth as a vehicle to explore the symbolism of the human psyche and as a means of making contact with the collective unconscious. Like Jung, they also believed that the pragmatic identification of myth as a part of one's daily life would help answer fundamental questions that have always troubled humanity: Who are we? Where are we? How did we get here? For the abstract expressionists, the use of myth gave perspective and order to forces that were inexplicable and fearful. Summing up the artist's position on myth,

William Troy wrote in 1946: "We have today reached the point at which we are interested not so much in the substance of particular myths as in the essential pattern or structure of myth in general . . . . [Our purpose is] to make at least practically available . . . that complex of human problems which are embedded, deep and imponderable, in the Myth."[7] It was this search for "the essential structure of myth" that both informed and enlightened the early art of Adolph Gottlieb and Mark Rothko and laid the foundation for later works that came to be regarded as hallmarks of abstract expressionism.

When Gottlieb decided on primitive and mythic themes for his pictographs, he discovered that "by shift in subject matter, we Rothko and Gottlieb . . . suddenly found that there were formal problems that confronted us for which there was no precedent. We were in unknown territory."[8] The desire to explore and chart "unknown territory" was, for these artists, a means of probing the unconscious in the belief that this would push their art forward and would generate new ways of looking at art as well as new ways of responding to it. In Gottlieb's case, the formal solution was to divide his canvasses into compartments, each of which contained a part of the human body, symbols, schematized fish, birds, reptiles, or abstract signs. (See Figure 1.)

For Gottlieb these elements functioned "as a primitive method, and a primitive necessity of expressing, without learning to do so by conventional ways. It puts us at the beginning of seeing."[9] It does precisely that. The symbols take on an almost talismanic quality and collectively generate a mythic whole decipherable by the unconscious. Early works such as *Minotaur*, 1942, and *Persephone*, 1942, epitomize Gottlieb's effort to tap the acausal, instinctual, and prelogical elements of the mythical thought process. *Minotaur*, for example, recalls the myth in which Theseus enters the labyrinth with a "thousand turnings" to kill the Minotaur. It has been suggested that Theseus's descent into the labyrinth may be seen as an analogy to Gottlieb's "search within his own mind for the unknown."[10] This inner search is frequently referred to by Jung in various writings and is regarded as a method for uncovering or making contact with one's own unconscious. Gottlieb was aware of and receptive to Jung's concept of the collective unconscious and has stated: "It was Jung who came out with the idea of the collective unconscious . . . . It just corroborated my idea that . . . if I decided to use certain symbols in my painting, for example, an egg shape, I did this without intending it to be a symbolic reference. Why couldn't I come up with the idea of an egg signifying fertility just as well as some aborigine in Australia? There are symbols which are universal."[11]

Although Gottlieb's early pictographs may at first seem to lend

Figure 1.    Adolph Gottlieb, *Augury*, 1945.

themselves to an interpretation arrived at by means of identifying the myth and the various images, he was more interested in the conception of a form and the expression of the nuances and subtleties of an image as it emanates from the unconscious. As the pictographs develop, formal changes take place. Most notably, more compartments are filled in and the diversity of imagery and its abstract and mythic quality increase. So although in a work like *Augury*, 1945, the title indicates mythological content, the meaning of the work—its unconscious resonances—is implicit in the progression of pictographs that have evolved into a complex symbology. Indeed, the power of these images to transmit information—in this case, foreboding, perhaps death—presents a parallel in painting to Jung's assertion that "Myth is the primordial language natural to these psychic processes. . . . Such processes are concerned with the primordial images, and these are best and most succinctly reproduced by figurative language" (*CW* 12: par. 28, p. 25).

Gottlieb's archetypal motifs could not be more different from the biomorphic imagery used by Mark Rothko, but both artists shared similar concerns. Rothko also professed a "spiritual kinship with primitive and archaic art"[12] and made a conscious decision to employ subjects of archaic myth: "They are the eternal symbols upon which we must fall back to express basic psychological ideas. They are both symbols of man's primitive fears and motivations, no matter in which land or what time, changing only in detail but never in substance. . . . And modern psychology finds them persisting still in our dreams, our vernacular, and our art, for all the changes in the outward conditions of life."[13] The titles of some of his works, which offer clues to these ideas, are reinforced visually. For example, *Archaic Phantasy* 1945, with its dense piling of abstract images, evokes that part of the consciousness Rothko characterizes as "fancy free and violently opposed to common sense."[14] *Memory*, 1944-1946, both in its title and in its formal elements, evokes a primitive, archaic past, reflecting Rothko's belief that myth is the embodiment of our earliest memories of our own origin as well as a reflection of a human interest in prehuman, primordial existence. Apparently, Rothko's search for a more perfect psychic state through the understanding of the genesis of life yielded formal innovations in his art centered around the iconography of water that neatly wedded themselves to some of Jung's ideas.

Water, probably because of its omnipresence, has long been considered by many ancient cultures to be primeval and eternal, the source of all things. According to Stephen Polcari, "For Jung and Rothko, the sea and the ritual use of water symbolized the spiritual rebirth of the individual through the change into a new individual."[15] Polcari has suggested that the choice of an aqueous environment for Rothko's hybrid forms as well as the translucent luminosity of many of his works from this period may be related to Jung's "idea of water as a symbolic means of transformation."[16] Several of Rothko's *Untitled* oils and works on paper from the 1940s[17] consist of ambiguous, compound hybrid forms that seem capable of imminent metamorphosis and that emerge from a shallow, watery background that resembles a primordial sea. An important aspect of their works is their luminosity. Rothko used watercolors to create a pictorial surface that shimmers and floats on a sea of muted colors. His oils, which he thinned to the consistency of watercolor and applied in overlapping glazes,[18] took on the same luminosity as the watercolors.

The most striking, insistent feature in all these works is their extreme fluidity. Though the biomorphic forms are drawn with precision, the total image dissolves at every attempt to grasp it on a conscious, visual level. Water, used by Rothko as a symbolic, iconographic device, is a perfect visual equivalent of the "watery chaos" stage found in so many creation myths. Rothko evidently regarded water as a suitable formal element for identifying the sources for the existence of certain psychic forms, that is, archetypes that Jung believed were accessible through dreams.

Of all the abstract expressionists, Jackson Pollock was the most familiar with the practical application of Jungian theory of art, due to its use as therapy while he was undergoing treatment for alcoholism. From 1939 to 1941, Pollock worked with a Jungian analyst, Joseph L. Henderson, and during this time produced several paintings, drawings, and sketches that were used for analysis by Dr. Henderson. Pollock later worked with Dr. Violet Staub de Laszlo for at least two more years, and again art was used as a therapeutic tool. Because of this close relation to Jungian therapy, Pollock apparently made conscious decisions to apply some of Jung's most important theories—in particular, alchemy and the process of individuation—to the making of his art. Pollock had access to Jung's writings from the mid-1930s on, was well versed in Jungian theory, and has stated that he considered himself a "Jungian artist."[19]

It is not clear whether Pollock formulated his understanding of Jung through the reading of primary materials or secondhand. He was familiar with fellow artist John Graham's book, *System and Dialetics of Art* (1937), a transposition of several of Jung's ideas. It is likely that this book had a significant impact on Pollock, particularly that section of the text in which Graham declares: "The purpose of art in particular is to re-establish a lost contact with the unconscious . . . with the primordial racial past and to keep and develop this contact in order to bring to the conscious mind the throbbing events of the unconscious mind."[20]

Another Graham essay, "Primitive Art and Picasso," was also familiar to Pollock. Published in 1937,[21] it influenced many artists of the period and asserted the validity of primitive art as a course of imagery that would facilitate the use of the unconscious contents of the psyche. In Pollock's *Mask*, 1938-1941, the looming, one-eyed shape that dominates the composition is very similar to the kind of primitive imagery described in Graham's essay. Pollock may have borrowed images in *Mask* from other obvious sources, such as Picasso's "African" works, or directly from Native American art At any rate, *Mask*, like Gottlieb's *Masquerade*, 1945, evokes the art of tribal cultures that are themselves archetypal in their use of form as symbol.

The historical function of the mask, in most cultures, has been to enable the masked person to assume another role or persona in order to achieve a different psychological state through the submersion of his or her own persona. Many primitive societies employed the mask in initiatory rites and rites of passage in order to achieve a state of transformation and liberation. *Mask* is significant in Jungian terms because it includes at least two specifically Jungian archetypes, both related to psychic liberation: the single eye, which connotes self-awareness in Jungian literature, and bird forms, which symbolize liberation or transcendence. These symbols are found in dreams during what Jung calls the "process of individuation." Individuation is the process whereby one seeks a total integration of the psyche. This was the goal of all Jungian therapy and was Pollock's personal goal as well. Therefore, Pollock either consciously or unconsciously referred to symbols that have been identified in Jungian literature as those that appear in dreams in the course of psychic integration.

Ultimately, individuation should lead to the totality of the psyche. This higher stage of consciousness has a set of images discrete to it and is referred to by Jung as mandala symbolism. According to Jung, mandalic symbols are archetypal "images that refer directly and exclusively to the new centre as it comes into consciousness" (*CW* 12: par. 45, p. 41). He defines the mandala as a "circle" or a "magic circle" that is "always an inner image, which is gradually built up through active imagination . . . at such times when the psychic equilibrium is disturbed" (*CW* 12: par. 123, p. 96). Significantly, Jung theorized that the action of drawing the mandala both symbolized and promoted psychic unity.

Pollock's *Circle*, 1938-1941 (Figure 2) qualifies as a classic textbook illustration of mandalic symbolism. Encased in a circular shape are writhing serpents painted in lurid oranges, reds, greens, blues, and

Figure 2.    Jackson Pollock, *Circle*, ca. 1938-1941.

yellows. One serpent is two-headed, linked to a common abstracted body. This image may refer to the reconciliation of opposites. According to Jung, psychic health requires a resolution or integration of unresolved opposites. Pollock's *Circle* may represent just such an effort.

Jung's theory that the processes of alchemy were similar to the creative process was embraced by many artists of the period. Alchemy is the art of transformation. The transmutation of lead into gold is a metaphor for the evolution of the lead of personality into the gold of spirit. Pollock effected the transformation of the self by becoming part of his work. In his mature works of the 1950s, Pollock abandoned the traditional technique of painting a canvas on an easel or upright against a wall. Instead, the canvas was laid on the floor so that he could, literally, "get into the painting," dripping and splattering paint on it from loaded brushes while walking rapidly around it. This all-over, spontaneous effect is an example of how, in Peter Busa's words, "Pollock created a new basis for physical involvement, one which is psychic, one in which there was real involvement with the idea of where man's space is."[22]

As a logical progression in Pollock's artistic development, this technique—very probably influenced by Jungian theory—became one of the most significant formal techniques in the history of modern painting. Clearly then, for Pollock, art provided an effective means of expressing the unconscious. Although Jung's theories were not the only sources for Pollock's imagery and iconography, his ideas at the very least validated the impulses of mystery, violence, and eroticism quickening in Pollock's art at that time.

In his essay "The Spiritual Problem of Modern Man," Jung contends that the pathology of modern life has caused men and women to fall "back on the reality of psychic life and [expect] from it that certainty which the world denies [them]" (*CW* 10: par. 182, p. 89). Jung posits:

> If [modern man] turns away from the terrifying prospect of a blind world in which building and destroying successively tip the scales, and then gazes into the recesses of his own mind, he will discover a chaos and a darkness there which everyone would gladly ignore. . . . And yet it is almost a relief to come upon so much evil in the depths of our own psyche. Here at least, we think, is the root of all evil in mankind. Even though we are shocked and disillusioned at first, we still feel, just because these things are part of our psyche, that we have them more or less in hand and can correct them or at any rate effectively suppress them. We like to assume that, if we succeeded in this, we should at least have rooted out some fraction of evil in the world. (*CW* 10: pars. 164-165, p. 82)

These ideas helped spark the development of themes of monsters, nocturnal subjects, and a color symbology associated with fear and death in the work of many of the abstract expressionist painters and sculptors.

The abstract expressionists used monsters drawn mostly from Western mythology as mythic beings who violate the accepted boundaries of the world and thus open the world to the threat of chaos. For example, *The First Cyclops II*, 1947, a painting by Theodoros Stamos, evokes by its very title the horrific one-eyed monster of Greek myth. The chaos and disintegration of order wrought by World War II, along with the mythological tales told him as a child by his parents, helped shape this and other works that are saturated with myth and ritual. *Cyclops* is an amorphous one-eyed figure, painted like most of Stamos's other works from this period, at night, in hazy, fuscous colors laid on a gravely surface. The overall effect is of something prehistoric, even preconscious, that evokes primal emotions of fear and confusion. Further, the indistinct form of the cyclops, with its feathery outline, suggests the potential of mutability, heightening the sinister quality of the work.

Gottlieb also painted primordial, archetypal images that bear the same disturbing sense of mutability. The title of Gottlieb's 1942 painting, *Minotaur*, refers to a compound monster—one that combines attributes of different species, in this case a bull and a man.

The sculptural counterpart of these paintings is exemplified in one of a series of works begun in 1946 by Seymour Lipton, *Moloch #3*, 1947, which Albert Elsen described as "perhaps the most ferocious image in modern sculpture up to that time."[23] *Moloch #3* is a compact image consisting solely of the head of the beast. Made of soldered sheets of lead, it has a reptilian, crustlike surface, a hollowed eye sunk in a skeletal head, and gaping jaws. Lipton commented that "Moloch, a god of Eastern human sacrifice, is probably . . . related to the war."[24] He additionally stated, "Moloch became important to me in terms of the hidden destructive forces below the surface in man. War always seemed to break out against the logic and necessity of peace."[25] Lipton meant for his monster to stand as a visual metaphor for what is human: "The drive was toward finding sculptural structures that stemmed from the deep animal makeup of man's being. . . . The ferocity in all these works relates to the biological reality of man; they are all horrendous but not in any final negative sense, rather they are tragic statements on the condition of man, thereby ironically implying a courage needed to encompass evil, indifference and dissonance in the world of man."[26]

Ferber's sculpture *Hazardous Encounter II*, 1947 (Figure 3), is a striking bronze in which a barbed phallic shape penetrates a v-shaped "feminine" orifice topped with organic knobs. The overall effect is both monstrous and mythic—an evocation of universal human conflict.

Isamu Noguchi's elegantly enigmatic *Monument to Heroes*, 1943, could not be more visually different from Lipton's or Ferber's violent, aggressive works. These three artists, however, share a similar ethical sensibility. Conceived as a model for an unrealized war monument, Noguchi's sculpture is constructed of a cardboard tube from which "found objects" like wood and bones protrude. The monument was meant to stand as a "dirge for futile heroes who killed themselves—for what?"[27]

Figure 3.  Herbert Ferber, *Hazardous Encounter II*, 1947.

Nocturnal subjects were also popular themes used by the abstract expressionists and were equated with the darkness of the mind or of the unconscious. Jung wrote of the night: "[What] is significant in psychic life always lies below the horizon of consciousness, and when we speak of the spiritual problems of modern man we are speaking of things that are barely visible—of the most intimate and fragile things, of flowers that open only in the night" (*CW* 10: par. 194, p. 93). Baziotes's *Figures in the Night*, 1947, shows misshapen beings on the edge of vision, painted in dark, collapsing hues. For Baziotes, literal meaning was scarcely the point; he sought an almost mystical emergence of forms on the canvas: "As for the subject-matter in my painting, when I am observing something that may be the theme for a painting, it is often an accidental thing in the background, elusive and unclear, that really stirred me, rather than the thing before me."[28]

The weighted symbolism of the color black used as a metaphor for mystery, terror, or death is frequently found in the works of the abstract expressionists. For Barnett Newman, black was associated with death, as in the case of the painting *Abraham*, 1949, named for his recently deceased father.[29] Robert Motherwell stated in 1950 that the *Elegies*, with their massive black shapes, "are funeral pictures, laments, dirges."[30] For Rothko, black represented "darkness and fertility, earth and night."[31] According to Alfonso Ossorio, who knew Pollock, the artist saw the colors black and white as "the sleep and waking of a world where the freedom of private agony and release finds its discipline in the communal basis of these tensions."[32] Hans Hofmann stated that he was interested in "the mystic realm of color."[33] This interest can be seen in *Black Demon*, 1947, an organic, abstract work in which a black form with a gaping mouth lurches across the red and white background, creating a mood of unease and foreboding.

In Herman Cherry's *Night Promenade*, 1954, black is critical to the meaning of the work. The black background imparts a mysterious, meditative mood to this somber canvas and makes the smallish gray square in its upper right corner beckon like a door to the interior of the mind. Cherry has said that "The emotional elements in color are very important to me, and it's really like feeling my way in a dark room.[34] In *Night Promenade*, Cherry's use of black provides an eloquent response to the assertion of his friend David Smith that "Somewhere, Herman, there is an answer mystical and magical" in color"[35]

In Robert Richenburg's large, predominantly black canvas, *Secret Boxes*, 1964, color plays an important role. "For me black is an important color because it has a magical quality. It is a reference point for my subconscious feelings."[36] The way he uses color is almost automatic: "I take a palette knife to punch into the night to find the daylight in the lighter colors beneath the canvas's dark pigment."[37] Emerging from the dark background, the squiggly glyphs in their numerous boxes confound us with their secret and magical messages. The overall effect is that of an enigmatic, crowded landscape simultaneously primal and "modern."

Although the thrust of Jung's general psychological philosophy served to reinforce the general pessimism of the age, not all the artists responded similarly. For some, it was an opportunity to expand their consciousness in a more mystical, joyous way. Alfonso Ossorio recalled that when he began reading Jung in the 1930s, there was an "immediate shock of recognition."[38] For him, Jung's psychology with its larger spiritual and mythological orientation was like a "mystical meeting of religions."[39] Ossorio, who comes from a Roman Catholic culture, agrees that there are religious elements in his art—not of a conventional nature but of a mythic and intensely intellectual kind. Ossorio's wax and watercolor painting *Mother Church*, 1949, is a "mythology of life."[40] The extremely compressed female figure, with its lactating breasts, "is both a symbol of the Mother Church and the crucified Christ. The milk spurting from the breasts of the female figure signifies the source of life and is, at the same time, the blood of the crucified Savior."[41] The dualism, inherent in Christian thinking, is also fundamental to Jungian thinking.

John Ferren has wryly called himself a "Zen Methodist"[42]—a very apt description for an artist whose work, which while founded in nature, has mystical overtones and multiplicitous meanings that are informed by a deeply spiritual attitude grounded in numerous sources. This catholic approach led him not to embrace or reject any particular faith but rather to continue a critical inquiry into the "nature of belief."[43] We see this multiplicity in *The Approach*, 1959. The bright color and transcendent light are used in a symbolic manner that is analogous to Jung's description of the enlightenment of consciousness. Characteristically, Ferren chose this aspect of one's consciousness—the brightness of a developed, critical consciousness rather than the evil, chaotic, and darkened recesses of the unconscious.

There is a suggestion of doors in this work. It may be that the passing through from one side to the other or from one place to the next is not what is implied in the title. Rather, it may be the journey, the "approach," that Ferren chooses to paint. It is likely that given Ferren's deeply mystical approach to his art, and his purposeful decision to live a "life of the spirit,"[44] this journey is meant to be understood as an inner search, as in Gottlieb's search in *Minotaur*, or Ibram Lassaw's search in *Labyrinth V*, 1964 (Figure 4), a rectangular box of welded sheets of brass and copper with ragged orifices that reveal a mysteriously layered interior.

In 1938, Ibram Lassaw saw the function of a new generation of American painters and sculptors in quite unequivocal terms: They would make art by experimenting with new ideas in the sciences, particularly those ideas "influenced by the recent discoveries in psychology and psychoanalysis."[45] Since the 1940s, his work has reflected, in addition, a consistent and highly developed mystical strain, reflecting an avid interest in the German mystic Meister Eckhart, the Zen philosophy of Daisetz Teitaro Suzuki, and a fascination with astrology and science fiction and, finally, with Jung.

Lassaw began reading Jung in the 1930s, and saw Jung's work as having an "immediate impact upon the human psyche."[46] The impact was just as immediate on his own art. He began experimenting with abstract forms in sculpture generated from "automatic" drawings and gradually evolved plastic, biomorphic structures that seem to be a visual articulation of Jungian interior space. *Mandala*, 1949, is a series of vertical interconnected lucite planes, pierced by irregular "organic" openings. The title of the piece is significant, since Jung, as we have seen, believed the mandala to be an "inner image" developed by the imagination. Lassaw affiliated himself with Jung's concept of the collective unconscious in a highly personal, even mystical way. "It seems to me that the muse is one's own instinct, and therefore is the subconscious. Since Jung believed that the male's unconscious is feminine, the

Figure 4.   Ibram Lassaw, *Labyrinth V*, 1964.

anima, it therefore is my own unconscious."[47] Lassaw's unconscious,
guided by a critical, eclectic intellect, has produced a remarkable number of sculptures whose mythological and astronomical titles—*Mandala, Milky Way, Metagalaxy*—reflect a preoccupation with finding
one's place in the universe. He has stated that he finds "a sense of se-

curity in the identification . . . that I am with the process taking place in the universe, and the knowledge that I am always a part of the unknown but wonderful event."[48]

In 1946, Isamu Noguchi made a statement that echoes the views shared by the abstract expressionists of his generation:

> The essence of sculpture is for me the perception of space, the continuum of our existence . . . . Since our experiences of space are, however, limited to momentary segments of time, growth must be the core of existence. We are reborn, and so in art as in nature there is growth, by which I mean change attuned to the living. Thus growth can only be new, for awareness is the ever changing adjustment of the human psyche to chaos. If I say that growth is the constant transfusion of human meaning into the encroaching void, then how great is our need today when our knowledge of the universe has filled our space with energy, driving us toward a greater chaos and new equilibrium.[49]

Noguchi's equating of space with growth, life, and the human psyche and his plaintive cry against the void and chaos have strong Jungian ring to them. They also constitute a point of view that could have been formulated only in the twentieth century. As the classical concept of reality disappeared, opposites were united and other opposing pairs that had been points of origin for pictorial perception began to dissolve. The dissolution and mingling of time and space made it possible to view art in a much broader context.

Noguchi's *The Seed*, 1945–1946, made of interlocking, cast-aluminum sections, is a sculpture of eloquent restraint that epitomizes the mythic quality of elemental forms. It is a distillate symbol, fusing as it does shapes that can be perceived as references to the human body with organic forms just emerged from the earth. In his *Monument to Heroes*, bones protruding from a painted cardboard tube evoke a mythic totem. The smooth, biomorphic shape of *The Seed* offers, in its turn, a mythic harmonium: birth, growth, death—the "eternal cycle." Indeed, Noguchi has said that he became "steeped in the transformation of myth in my sculptures," [50] and that his working method was "to indicate, to catch a fleeting reflection of things to be born from the fringes of consciousness."[51] For Noguchi, *The Seed*, like many of his sculptures, may also stand as a metaphor for aesthetic growth, what he called "change attuned to the living,"[52] that was an imperative concern to him in the nuclear-menaced 1940s.

All these artists were searching for a new artistic vocabulary. Gottlieb, Rothko, and Pollock purposely invoked Jung's concept of the collective unconscious and purposely used myths to reveal important psychological truths. But whether Jung was a specific source for their artistic evolution or not, each of these artists arrived at a similar find: the visualization of an archetype. And whether the archetype took its shape via a grid structure or via biomorphic imagery, its impact was the same. In Jung's words:

> The impact of an archetype . . . stirs us because it summons up a voice that is stronger than our own. Whoever speaks in primordial images speaks with a thousand voices; he enthralls and overpowers, while at the same time he lifts the idea he is seeking to express out of the occasional and the transitory into the realm of the ever-enduring. He transmutes our personal destiny into the destiny of mankind, and evokes in us all those beneficent forces that ever and anon have enabled humanity to find a refuge from every peril and to outlive the longest night . . . . That is the secret of great art, and of its effect upon on. (*CW* 15: par. 129, p. 82).

The importance of Jung's idea of the collective unconscious as a continual source of meaning is that it enabled artists to develop instinctual powers, to fuse the schemes of the intellect and the archaic imagination into a mythic totality. It also helped them realize the unity of dream and reality, of primitive and modern, and strike a balance between private and universal meaning. The ultimate result was a powerful new evocation of art. But it was the effort required to bring abstract expressionism to this fruition that excites and that reminds one of Joyce's Stephen Dedalus, himself a creature who is part myth, who proclaims in *A Portrait of the Artist as a Young Man*: "I go to encounter for the millionth time the reality of experience and forge in the smithy of my soul the uncreated conscience of my race."

# Notes

1. Although the label "abstract expressionist" is imprecise and its usage is not fully agreed upon by artists or scholars, it is a term frequently employed in the literature. For the sake of consistency, it will be used throughout this essay.

2. Robert Goldwater, "David Hare," *Art in America* 44, no. 4 (Winter 1956-1957): 18.

3. Herbert Ferber, conversation with author, New York City, August 2, 1986.

4. Herbert Read, *Art and Society* (New York: Schocken Books, 1966), p. 11.

5. Jeffrey Weiss, "Science and Primitivism: A Fearful Symmetry in the Early New York School," *Arts Magazine* 57, no. 7 (March 1983): 86.

6. Adolph Gottlieb and Mark Rothko, "The Portrait and the Modern Artist," typescript of a broadcast on *Art in New York*, WNYC, October 13, 1943, pp. 1-2.

7. William Troy, "Postlude: Myth, Method, and the Future," *Chimera* 4, no. 3 (Spring 1946): 82-83.

8. Andrew Hudson, dialogue with Adolph Gottlieb, New York City, 1968.

9. Adolph Gottlieb in "New York Exhibitions," *MKR's Art Outlook* no. 6 (December 1945): 4.

10. Sanford Hirsch and Mary Davis MacNaughton, catalogue of an exhibition, *Adolph Gottlieb: A Retrospective* (New York: Adolph Gottlieb and Esther Gottlieb Foundation, 1981), p. 44.

11. Adolph Gottlieb, interview by Dorothy Seckler, New York City, October 25, 1967; transcript, Archives of American Art, p. 17.

12. A response to remarks by the art critic Edward Alden Jewell on Gottlieb's and Rothko's paintings in the Federation of Modern Painters and Sculptors Exhibition held in New York at Wildenstein Gallery, June 1943. The statement was published in Mr. Jewell's column in the *New York Times*, June 13, 1943.

13. Mark Rothko, "The Portrait and the Modern Artist," typescript of a broadcast on *Art in New York*, WNYC, October 13, 1943, pp. 1-2.

14. A response to remarks by the art critic Edward Alden Jewell on the exhibition held in New York at Wildenstein Gallery, June 1943. See n. 12 above.

15. Stephen Polcari, "The Intellectual Roots of Abstract Expressionism: Mark Rothko," *Arts Magazine* 54, no. 1 (September 1979): 127.

16. Ibid.

17. See the checklist in catalogue of an exhibition, *Jung and Abstract Expressionism: The Collective Image Among Individual Voices* (New York: The Hofstra Museum, Hofstra University, 1986).

18. Bonnie Clearwater, *Mark Rothko: Works on Paper* (New York: Hudson Hills Press, 1984), p. 30.

19. Selden Rodman, *Conversations with Artists* (New York: Devin-Adair Co., 1957), p. 82.

20. John D. Graham, *System and Dialectics of Art* (New York: Delphic Studios, 1937), p. 31.

21. Graham, "Primitive Art and Picasso," *Magazine of Art* 30, no. 4 (April 1937): 236-239.

22. Busa quoted in Sidney Simon, "Concerning the Beginnings of the New York School: 1939-1943," *Art International* 11, no. 6 (Summer 1967): 20.

23. Albert Elsen, *Seymour Lipton* (New York: Harry N. Abrams, n.d.), p. 29.

24. Ibid., p. 28.

25. Ibid., p. 27.

26. Ibid., p. 29.

27. Noguchi quoted in Sam Hunter, *Isamu Noguchi* (New York: Abbeville Press, n.d.), n.p.

28. From a statement by William Baziotes, "I Cannot Evolve Any Concrete Theory," in *Possibilities* 1, no. 1 (Winter 1947-1948): 2. See also *Modern Artists in America*, ed. Robert Motherwell and Ad Reinhardt (New York: Wittenborn Shultz, 1951), p. 15.

29. See Evan R. Firestone, "Color in Abstract Expressionism: Sources and Background for Meaning," *Arts Magazine* 55, no. 7 (March 1981): 140.

30. Quoted in ibid.

31. Dore Ashton, *About Rothko* (New York: Oxford University Press, 1983), p. 89.

32. Alfonso Ossorio, introduction to catalogue of an exhibition, *Jackson Pollock* (New York: Betty Parsons Gallery, 1951).

33. Hans Hofmann, "The Search for the Real in the Visual Arts," *Search for the Real and Other Essays*, ed. Hans Hofmann and Sara T. Weeks (1948; reprint, Cambridge, Mass.: MIT Press, 1967), p. 45.

34. Quoted in Sarah M. Lowe, catalogue of an exhibition, *Herman Cherry, Monotypes* (New York: City University Graduate Center, 1985), n.p.

35. Ibid.

36. Robert Richenburg, conversation with author, East Hampton, N.Y., August 12, 1986.

37. Ibid.

38. Alfonso A. Ossario, conversation with author, East Hampton, N.Y.: July 16, 1986.

39. Ibid.

40. Ibid.

41. Ibid.

42. Quoted in Irving Hershel Sandler, "New York Letter," *Quadrum: International Magazine of Modern Art* 14 (1963): 123.

43. Ferron quoted in Craig Bailey, catalogue of an exhibition, *Ferren* (New York: City University Graduate Center, 1979), p. 6.

44. Rae Ferren, conversation with author, East Hampton, N.Y., August 12, 1986.

45. Ibram Lassaw, "On Inventing Our Own Art," *American Abstract Artists Yearbook* (New York: n.p., 1938), section viii.

46. Ibram Lassaw, conversation with author, East Hampton, N.Y., August 12, 1986.

47. Ibid.

48. Ibram Lassaw, "Pespectives and Reflections of a Sculptor: A Memoir," *Leonardo: International Journal of the Contemporary Artist* 1, no. 4 (October 1968): 355.

49. Isamu Noguchi, *Isamu Noguchi: A Sculptor's World*, with a foreword by Buckminster Fuller (New York: n.p., 1968), p. 28.

50. Ibid., p. 29.

51. Ibid.

52. Ibid., p. 28.

# Artists' Roundtable: Jung's Influence

Mark Hasselriis

Ibram Lassaw

Robert Richenburg

Terree Grabenhorst-Randall, *moderator*

*Terree Grabenhorst-Randall:* What aspect of Jung's thinking was most important to your development as an artist, Mr. Lassaw?

*Ibram Lassaw:* The aspect of Jung's writings that interested me at first was the idea of the anima. At a very early stage, I began to feel that the anima must be identified with the classical Greek idea of the Muse— the idea that the artist in the studio invoked the aid of the Muse, which is a kind of spirit or goddess. It seemed to me that was exactly what the anima was. For years it was just an idea in my head and I did not actually experience it, but one day I noticed something. I was working on a sculpture, and I had begun to draw the wire out in three-dimensional space. As I was quickly bending the wire into a predetermined shape, I noticed that it was not quite what I wanted; but before I decided to change it, I looked at it and I found that it was really better than I expected and had determined. This went on all afternoon. It was as if I had caught the anima or the muse in flagrante delicto. There it was, and since then I have not even noticed it, because I do not look at it from any kind of distance. I do not like to see myself working. I just like to plunge into it entirely. But that experience solidified my idea that the unconscious or the anima was actually a living presence.

*Grabenhorst-Randall:* Mr. Richenburg, would you like to comment on the unconscious material in your art?

*Robert Richenburg:* The unconscious definitely plays a large role in my art as it does in all art. I first read Jung in the 1930s, and became more involved with his theories in the late 1940s and early 1950s. His ideas were part of the language and thought prevalent during that period. There is evidently a collective unconscious, which contains ideas that characterize a particular time, and they are important to the artist. How these ideas are transmitted and how they affect people is difficult to discern. Who knows where ideas come from? Jung brings up again and again the complexity of the human personality. People are often asked about who influenced them most. James Michener said it had been some obscure grade-school teacher. Of Jung it is asked which ideas were really his and which ideas came from Freud? And what of Freud's ideas? Did they start with him? Did they go way back? The Greeks, Shakespeare, Dostoyevsky, and others have come up with similar ideas.

Certainly, Freud and Jung were influential all through the 1920s, 1930s, and early 1940s. Both had an enormous effect, not only on art but on a wide range of endeavors and individuals. Existentialism and Eastern thought came in at a certain point. Surrealism, which came out of psychoanalytic thought, was crucial. I do not know of any artist who was not at least familiar with many, if not all, of these concepts.

One of the concepts that influenced me a great deal was the idea that you can work without conscious control. And I found in my own work, again and again, that if I could dispense with the censor, somehow deeper images would appear—at least they seemed so to me. So the big black picture that I have in this show was started by throwing paint on the canvas, with very little conscious control. I was obviously affected by the surrealists, by Jackson Pollock and Willem de Kooning. But many different people played a significant role in my development. Hans Arp was important to me, and Rembrandt, Van Gogh, Mondrian, Klee, Duchamp, Ozenfant, Hans Hoffmann, Pound, Valery, and of course Picasso.

*Mark Hasselriis:* What is important about Jung for us here is not so much his impact on psychiatry and psychology but his impact on artists. He awakened us to ancient traditions, to ancient knowledge, alchemy; to ancient forms, squares, triangles; to the founts of creative imagination, of poetry and art. Remember that the industrialism and materialism of the nineteenth century had practically crushed the mythological soul of modern men and women. Freud opened the door to the rediscovery of mythology, which Jung and others then explored more fully, and which acted like a great leavening of creativity on artists and writers.

*Grabenhorst-Randall:* Jung identified archetypes as preexistent forms in the collective unconscious. You said that when you worked without conscious control, deeper images would appear. Would you identify those as archetypal elements in your art?

*Richenburg:* Yes, I think they were, because I responded to them more deeply, and other people did also. But one of the things Jung mentioned again and again was that we do not really consciously know what these subconscious images are until they finally reveal themselves in different ways, sometimes through complexes.

*Hasselriis:* Jung focused not only on the Western experience of dreams and images, but on the traditions of the East as well. He pointed out that form, which had dominated art in the Western world, was viewed in the East as nothing other than nonform. If you concentrated on form, the realization of the formlessness of form itself would come forth; that is, you would see it as energy or perhaps as something evanescent. You cannot separate one from the other. There is a polarity between form and formlessness, and depending on how an artist approaches the unconscious, he or she sees it as either putting forth forms or shattering and breaking them. Jung draws attention to this duality. This is related to Robert's question about where ideas come from. Different cultural situations or epochs bring forth different things. This is true on an individual level and for society as a whole.

*Grabenhorst-Randall:* Both Freud and Jung had an impact on the abstract expressionists. It is interesting that, apparently, the abstract expressionists found Jung more compatible to their own way of thinking. I might offer the idea that Freud's rather lateral vision of all human drives as being motivated by a repressed libido may not have been much to the liking of the American way of thinking. I wonder if Jung found more receptivity in this country because of that?

*Lassaw:* Well, in his writings, Jung addressed himself occasionally to art, to the history of art, and to the position of the artist. I am not aware that Freud was very much involved in that. He might have touched on it in a peripheral way, but it was in the writings of Jung that I found the artist and art a part of human development. It gave me a much greater feeling of confidence in what I was doing.

*Grabenhorst-Randall:* The abstract expressionists, especially during the 1940s, were very receptive to psychoanalytic ideas in general. I wonder why that happened in the 1940s? What made artists so receptive to Jung's and Freud's ideas?

*Lassaw:* Many of the ideas, as you mentioned, were in circulation around the world. Artists, like other people, picked them up. I have always been very curious about things, and I like to read about science and psychology. In the 1930s, I came across a book called *The Secret of the Golden Flower* in which Jung had written a commentary. That was my first contact with Jungian thought, and it led me to read more of

Jung. I have always had a tremendous interest in science, too, and I try to find parallels in the thinking of psychology and science. For example, in the "Big Bang" theory you have the idea of original pure plasma, pure energy, which begins to expand and then cools down to form hydrogen atoms. Then, through condensation, it forms heavier atoms and creates stars and so on. Eventually, all matter in the universe is formed, and it is still forming. Evolution continues. These atoms all around me have been around for billions of years. As a result of such realizations, Jung's collective unconscious became *real* to me. It was not just a theory or an ideal, but an actual, physical truth. I felt it emotionally—that I am a part of the universe. I was produced by the universe, and I am functioning as an ecological part of it. I imagine the artist as a kind of endocrine gland that secretes hormones for the human race. You know, like one part in 500 million of a certain hormone can drastically change an aspect of life, of living. Throughout history, artists have fulfilled this kind of function, even though they may not realize it consciously. So art has a very important function. It has been around for 20,000 years.

*Grabenhorst-Randall:* The mythic experience was important to many of the artists in the 1930s and 1940s. Was it relevant for all of you, and is it still relevant today?

*Lassaw:* I think it had a freshness back in the 1930s and 1940s. Now, much of it is almost taken for granted. We no longer are conscious of it, at least speaking for myself. We just assume it is true, but it does not seem like a new idea to us.

*Hasselriis:* I think that it is probably true that the newness of Jung and of those discoveries has worn off. Nevertheless, we really have not plumbed the depths of those revelations. The mythic experience is a continually recurring series of discoveries that comes not from changes in the circumstances that life puts upon us but from the deep well of human experience itself. In other words, new technologies are changing society in enormous ways on the surface. Today it is the computer and the laser; in the nineteenth century, it was electricity and the machine. But the mythic patterns that Jung and Freud and Campbell and others describe have a life that does not lie on the surface. Life experiences do not change with the same rapidity as technology. Human beings have been on the planet for some millions of years. Mythic patterns demonstrate that myths today tell the same stories in today's terms as myths in the past told in ancient terms, in Greek terms, in Egyptian terms, in Hindu terms. If you study them carefully, you realize that a human being is a human being, in antiquity as today. The circumstances change, but what does not change—or only very gradually—is our organic humanity. We have not really fathomed the ideas touched upon by Jung. We have not fathomed the psyche. We still do not know what it is.

*Grabenhorst-Randall:* Since the concept of the unconscious is not yet clarified, and since there is a lot yet to be done simply to clarify that concept, how can we apply it to the interpretation of art? How can we discuss the elements of it in art?

*Hasselriis:* Something stirs within the artist. The creative urge is something that pushes the artist from within, no matter how extraverted the artist's self-expression may be. I have heard artists speak about change in their art; it has to come from within. They cannot follow the fashion, either. Art falls apart if it is merely fashion. Artists cannot manipulate their medium.

*Richenburg:* I agree. There is a tremendous mystery to the process of creation. For me, much of my art starts from other work I have done. Many ideas come from ideas that other people have had. A lot happens as I confront the particular work I am creating. One thing moves to the other. I, in general, as most artists, go to my studio regularly and stay there most of the day. If inspiration comes, fine; if it does not, then there is nothing I can do about it. You simply work and sometimes something marvelous happens. But why that time and not another time, I do not have the faintest idea. Sometimes when you think the work is going wonderfully well, nothing has happened. Sometimes you create a work that you think is a total failure, and later you find that it is one of the best works you have done. I have taught a lot over the years, due to the necessity of earning a living, and one assignment I used to give was to have students do the worst painting they could possibly do, or the worst sculpture. I mean, make it really awful. And it almost always turns out to be one of the best things they have done. They are simply violating everything: the artistic convention as well as their own original intentions.

In art, sometimes you run out of ideas. At one point, I ran out of ideas as a painter. I did not know what to do. So I started doing sculpture, and then I started doing photography, and then went back to painting or to drawing. You go to whatever is going to help you. But as to how and why, you do not know. The unconscious and the collective unconscious have to be part of everything we do. Jung has mentioned that maybe a fourth, a third, or even half of what motivates us is submerged below, and I think there is no question about that.

*Lassaw:* I remember a quotation from Jung about projections, which is what we are talking about here. He says, "Such projections repeat themselves, whenever man tries to explore an empty darkness and involuntarily fills it with living form" (*CW* 12: par. 346, p. 245). There is your unconscious at work.

*Hasselriis:* The anima, as Jung points out, is sometimes like a mysterious creature. She brings treasure, like the mysterious figure in a fairy tale who brings treasure, but she cannot be controlled and may even be a menace at times. It is not a matter of seeing it simply as a feminine part of yourself, but as a spirit that moves within, that you do not know too well.

*Lassaw:* That is what I think of the Jungian ideas of the collective unconscious and of the archetypes of the unconscious. The archetypes of the unconscious make me think of the pantheon of Olympus, of the gods and goddesses. The Greeks projected them onto the outside world, but actually they are within us. In other words, all the gods and goddesses are living in our own minds, in our bodies, and we are realizing the wishes and the influences of all these gods and goddesses. The unconscious is nature after all, and we are a form of nature. I do not own these atoms. They have been around for billions of years. So it gives me a great feeling of confidence. The thing that I enjoy most, when I am working, is to be surprised by what happens. Sometimes I am really greatly surprised. I enjoy having my mind boggled. It is the greatest thrill just to work without any particular intentions and to discover suddenly that something wonderful is happening. It is as if I were an instrument of these gods and goddesses, of nature itself, in other words.

*Grabenhorst-Randall:* We seem to keep going back to the idea of the wellsprings of creativity. Where are they? What motivates them? What nurtures them? Many abstract expressionists stated that the process of creation is one in which the transformation of the self occurs as the result of the physical act of creation. There are parallels in Jung's theory of alchemy. Do you see a relation between the two?

*Hasselriis:* Yes, I do. For example, there is a work by Jackson Pollock (*No. 10*, 1951), a picture of a head in black and white. The dynamism in it and the movement around the head give the impression that it was created in a very short time. The head is human and it is exploding, bursting into pieces. There are some other pieces by Pollock that came a little later, that look like a stone to me, like a matrix. Now, in the picture of the head there is a form of a man—perhaps representing Pollock himself or representing humanity—that is exploding into pieces; it is being destroyed. In the other works, he seems to have plunged down into something like a matrix, a matrix in the sense of Jung's notion of the unconscious, of a "mother substance." We see things coming up from it.

We can see parallels in alchemy. The alchemist is an artist; or, it might be more accurate to put it the other way around: the artist is an alchemist. The alchemist, in order to start work, follows a traditional procedure that conforms to certain patterns. A substance, which is called the *prima materia*, and which is usually shown as an absolute black mass, must be transformed by the alchemist to bring about the birth of the philosopher's stone. The philosopher's stone is not a stone in the sense of a diamond or a ruby, even though it is sometimes pictured as such. It symbolizes a human spirit that is androgynous, dual in nature, and represents the evolution of something primordial and chaotic into something transcendent. Jung gives many different descriptions of these alchemical processes as they appear in dreams. They also occur in art. The artist may be moved by something that is completely formless or something that is just a stone, a surface of a wall, an amorphous substance. Out of that, the artist creates something that grows and ceases to be amorphous. It acquires a definite form, and then, ultimately, it may become moribund and be destroyed. Pollock was aware of forms. It shows in his work, especially in his early work, which seemed about to explode. Forms crystallize and are then destroyed. What happens when they are destroyed? In alchemy, you plunge back into the amorphous substance of the source and rebuild. The process of evolution from the black substance, the *prima materia*, to the philosopher's stone goes through evolutionary stages in an upward creative movement, passing through a red phase, a green phase, and finally a peacock blue phase just before the birth of the hermaphrodite or lapis or rhebus. All these names refer to the philosopher's stone. This evolutionary process in Hindu philosophy is the path of bringing life into the world, of becoming involved in the multiplicity of life. Involution, which goes in the opposite direction, from multiplicity back to the simplicity of the source, is the path of the yogi. Interestingly, the gods take humans into the world of form, into multiplicity, and the goddesses take humans out of form, back toward the source. In India, these two paths are called the path of procreation and the path of ascent, that is, back to the source, the path of the divas, the path of the gods. Involution goes from complexity to simplicity, and evolution from simplicity to complexity. It is the same thing in alchemy, which after all, as Jung says, is essentially a branch of Egyptian philosophy. Alchemy means "from Khem," the ancient name of Egypt being Khem. The word "khem" in Egyptian means, "black," the black soil of that country, the black land that brought forth all fertility. So the idea of blackness bringing forth greenness or redness and finally giving birth to the philosopher's stone is very much in keeping even with the landscape of the country itself. The process, therefore, is either evolutionary or involutionary.

I see the same thing in art. For example, in abstract expressionism there is a plunge back to the source, a shattering of forms. Then there is a gradual putting them together again and reemerging. This process is a continuous one. Do you feel that there is an evolutionary and an involutionary process, a creation and a destruction?

*Richenburg:* Yes, I do. My painting in this exhibition is based on a process of construction and destruction, repeated over a long period of time, and as part of that process a movement to and from the unconscious and consciousness, from the sensuous and the intellectual. I placed the painting on the floor and threw large amounts of paint of predetermined colors on the canvas, using very little conscious control. Then the entire canvas was painted black. Afterward, I took a palette knife and scraped much of the black off within the structure of a grid. I did not know what forms or colors would emerge from this scraping process until I actually did it. Then I imposed a different grid of black rectangles over the entire painting and scraped and added other forms and colors again and again.

The grid is an ancient element. You find it in art right from the beginning. The grid was imposed on the canvas, and then over it I added things like circles, squares, and rectangles, but I did not know exactly where they were going to be. I trusted the scheme, the grid, at least in this particular picture, and in many others I did at this time. So it was all a question of destroying the picture to find the picture, and bringing it from night and total blackness to daylight and the multiplicity of forms that came through. Each little form became like a window or box, and each little area became like a picture in itself. Because of this, Marianne Moore named this picture *Secret Boxes*. So there is a whole series of things that come into this painting, and I just have no way of knowing how they got there. It was a question of destroying and then constructing.

*Lassaw:* I do not have quite that experience, because in my work I construct. I start with nothing and develop it from there. When I was young, I took a great interest in the history of art; I read every book I could get a hold of, even when I was 12 or 13. I wanted to know everything that happened in the history of art since the very beginning. I made myself a kind of picture encyclopedia, cutting our illustrations and reproductions of paintings and sculptures from the earliest times to the present. It came to thirty-three volumes of these homemade encyclopedias. Then I began reading the writings of Roger Fry, Wassily Kandinsky, and others on theories of modern art, especially Kandinsky's *The Art of Spiritual Harmony*. In a sense, it was a period of destruction. In the teens of this century, Russian constructivism sought to reduce art to the simplest elements. These artists turned their backs on the history of art and went back to the basics, so they thought. That was a destruction of the old.

*Hasselriis:* Destruction should not be looked at only negatively; it is essential for new life. Life and death are always paired; opposites are always together. That idea runs through the whole of Egyptian philosophy. East and West are shown together in the same picture, paired like twins. The rising sun is indistinguishable from the setting sun. So when we speak of destruction, remember that it makes way for something creative. Things become moribund, old, outdated. The purification of the spiritual life of the times requires a destruction, and something new comes. To me, abstract expressionism, in some respects anyway, is a clearing away of outmoded forms, and it repeats this process again and again. First the form is abstract, and then it begins to take shape and become more concrete and crystallized; then it is shattered again. Do you think this process is going to undergo major changes, or do you think it will be repeated and repeated and repeated?

*Lassaw:* Well, I do not think anything is ever repeated exactly in the universe. I do not see that kind of world. Evolution is in process all the time, and there may be rhythms and spiral developments; nevertheless, nothing, in my opinion, is ever repeated. That would not be creative. Imagine a creator who is somewhere outside the universe, creating. It would be boring to know in advance what is going to happen. An artist would not be able to work. I would hate to work on something if I knew exactly what was going to happen. I want to be surprised. The essence of abstract expressionism is being conscious of the immediate moment, the present moment, now, and not the conceptualization, not having some idea in mind that you want to carry out. Meister Eckhart says: "Where there is no yesterday nor morrow, where it is now and today, there we see God."[1] In Zen Buddhism, the very moment is wondrous and miraculous. *Now* is the sacred moment in which the creation of the universe is taking place. In making a work of art, there is an evolutionary process that is projected by the unconscious, in which one should not interfere with the conscious mind too much.

*Hasselriis:* Coomaraswamy, in a book titled *Time and Eternity*, quotes Meister Eckhart. The whole book is based on the theme that the moment, neither past nor future—the "eternal now," as it is sometimes called—is the divine connecting link between the universe and humanity and that moment is the moment in which we all live. The mystics were very much concerned with that moment and not with the anticipation of tomorrow or with the remembrance of yesterday.

*Richenburg:* I think it has to be that. In terms of destruction, art historians and artists in general—in order to discuss art—first have to kill it. You have to look at it in a totally different way from just experiencing it, which in a sense kills it. The whole development of art has to do with a new movement, like impressionism, which in a way has to kill the art that preceded it. It is like the son who metaphorically has to kill the father. The young artists coming up today want to destroy or at least get away from the artists who have been successful or who have become the establishment. This always goes on.

*Lassaw:* The trickster comes into this development, too. I remember in the early days of Dada and surrealism, during World War I, when many people recognized the enormous madness of the war—the Battle of Verdun, for example, in which three million men were engaged in war and pieces of flesh were flying all around. And they felt what they were doing was somehow justified. This is "civilized" Western culture, you know. It was the artists who pointed out the madness of it. They played tricks of all kinds: at the Cafe Voltaire in Zurich, for example, they decided to abandon the rational thinking of the West that had led to such idiocy, and they decided to laugh at it and make fun of it. That was the trickster side of modern art. It was a revulsion against much of the thinking that spoke of honor and patriotism in the face of the utter stupidity of what was going on.

*Grabenhorst-Randall:* In interviewing the artists for the current exhibition, I found that many referred to World War II, nihilism, existentialism, Hiroshima, and Nagasaki as the ultimate tragic circumstances they were dealing with, especially in the 1940s. They often referred to their own works of art as metaphors of the human condition, tragic metaphors of the human condition.

*Richenburg:* I think there are certain times in history where this kind of thing occurs. I think life in general is tragedy. This is pretty well sustained by history. But there are certain periods where somehow this is accentuated—why I do not know. Abstract Expressionism reflects a more serious, tragic sense of life, whereas op art and Neo-Dada, which came later, seem to be concerned with life's lighter and even absurd aspects. Throughout all these periods and artistic movements, there remains this fundamental thing: that an artist is essentially very much like a child, in front of an easel with certain materials, and is simply making something. We are not so terribly different from the child, painting at an easel and getting tremendous satisfaction from what we create.

# Notes

1. Franz Pfeiffer, *Meister Eckhart*, trans. C. de B. Evans (London: John M. Watkins, 1947).

# Journeys of
# Body and Soul:
# Jean Erdman's
# Dances   Deborah Welsh

with Jean Erdman, Nancy Allison, and Leslie Dillingham

> The dance . . . speaks of potentialities and aspects of humanity that
> are antecedent to words, antecedent even to the spheres of personal
> recollection, and constitute the primary heritage of the human
> spirit.                                                    —*Jean Erdman*

Unlike most primitive cultures, wherein dance is an inherent ritual
experience, in modern times we have severely limited ways in which
to assimilate dance into a larger life context. Like all creative expression, dance arises from unconscious depths. C. G. Jung's work teaches
us to value messages from the unconscious (dreams, myth, art, etc.) as
well as the process of assimilating them. Hence, his work provides
insight into dance as a powerful way of embodying and realizing the
moving potential of the human soul.

Dance, along with dreams and mandalas, can be a most important
means of expressing unconscious content. Jung recognized the power
of movement when he wrote of the transportive quality of rhythm
confirmed by the Sufi dervishes and by many primitive dances (*CW* 5:
par. 481, p. 315). He also mentioned patients of his who danced mandalas rather than drawing them; he later said, "one or two women
danced their unconscious figures" (*CW* 18: par. 400, p. 173). According to Jung, a process in which images are objectified in a creative form
(not just dreamed) quickens maturation because the material is produced from the unconscious into a conscious state of mind (*CW* 18:
399, p. 172).

Today there is an increasing interest in the body and movement in
relation to Jung's work. Jean Erdman, dancer and theater artist, approaches dance much as it is approached in preliterate cultures, that is,
as a means of contact with the unconscious, which is the source of
personal development and power. Erdman and her Theater of the
Open Eye presented a retrospective of her early work (1943-1957) at
the "C. G. Jung and the Humanities Conference" at Hofstra University in November 1986. In the collaborative presentation here, she describes and discusses her experience of these dances to provide a point

of view from which others (whether as performers or audience) may experience dance as a potential path toward individuation.

## Jean Erdman and Modern Dance

Jean Erdman's inheritance from earlier pioneers of modern dance and her legacy to us are a tremendous devotion to expressions of the soul. The medium is body movement that is created anew with each dance. Erdman never utilizes a mechanistic "plugging in" of established dance steps or patterns. Instead, her dances are autobiographical bodily expressions that touch upon the collective human experience. The creative process for her is as Jung describes: "The creative process, as far as we are able to follow it at all, consists in the unconscious activation of an archetypal image, and in elaborating and shaping this image into the finished work. By giving it shape, the artist translates it into the language of the present, and makes it possible for us to find our way back to the deepest springs of life" (*CW* 15: par. 130, p. 82).

Born in Honolulu in 1916, where she studied Hawaiian dance, among other dance forms, Jean Erdman was inspired by the followers of Isadora Duncan. While attending Sarah Lawrence College, she began her formal dance training with Martha Graham at the summer school in Bennington. By the early 1940s, Graham was a major figure in the world of dance, and Erdman became a soloist in Graham's company. The intellectual passion with which Martha Graham approaches dance is also evident in Jean Erdman's work, as is the preoccupation with mythological and literary motifs that she shared with husband Joseph Campbell. In 1944, she left the Graham Company to form the Jean Erdman Dance Group and to develop her own dances, which took the form of personal journeys into both the perils and the delights of the unconscious realm. Erdman suggests that at the core of choreography—beyond any external influence—each dancer has what might be described as a "personal theme" that threads its way through the dances.

At about the same time, another important young dancer, Merce Cunningham, left the Graham Company. Erdman and Cunningham had choreographed dances together at Bennington, and both enjoyed musical collaborations with John Cage. But whereas Cunningham and Cage departed radically from Graham's dramatic style, Erdman created dances somewhat similar to Graham's, both in structure (i.e., soloist/chorus) and in the use of narrative themes. The lyricism and womanliness of her dances, however, are purely Erdman's own. It is her belief that good choreography is based upon the desire to approach, through individual and personal style, in dance, an experience that is inexpressible any other way. Because of this, she maintains an important position vis-à-vis the primarily male rebels and their followers whose battle cry became "movement for movement's sake" in the mid-century revolution in modern dance. Erdman retained the choreographic power of myth, literature, and personal human experience. In later years, she moved even more thoroughly into a dramatic and literary style, especially in her best known work, "The Coach With the Six Insides" (1962), in which she evokes the dream world of James Joyce's *Finnegans Wake*.

## Dance and the Process of Individuation

Historians agree that the origins of dance are among the earliest expressions of the mystery of the universe. In the act of dancing, we bodily approach the unconscious and feel unified with a power and energy that are greater than ourselves. In this experience of unified energy, we are less likely to fear the unknown because it is not something experienced as outside ourselves. Instead, we physically manifest and begin to relate to the contents of the unconscious. This is the central and on-going task of Jung's individuation process. The ego acknowledges and assimilates messages, in the form of symbols, from the unconscious. Because dance is the actual embodiment of unconscious experience, it would seem to be an excellent means of making manifest unconscious material. We have, however, not really learned as yet how to use the dance experience to its full potential in relation to Jung's work.

One difficulty lies in the aesthetic and/or the psychological use of the word symbol. The interpretation of the meaning or existence of symbols is left to the individual, whether it be the choreographer, dancer, or audience. In Erdman's opinion, the symbol, as a work of art, "does not require anything." "Art," she says, "carries connotations of the absolutely unknowable, and through the aesthetic form the symbol can become known to the individual as food for the spirit that goes far beyond the psychological reference. One *knows* something has happened even though it may be unspeakable."

Erdman's understanding of symbol complements Jung's definition. According to Jung, a symbol "lives when it is the best and highest expression for something divined but not yet known to the observer. It then compels his unconscious participation and has a life-giving and life-enhancing effect" (*CW* 6: par. 819ff., p. 476). The process of symbol formation, as Jung describes it, involves both consciousness and the unconscious: a collaboration that depends on the attitude of the observing consciousness. The symbol always remains a mystery. If its meaning is "understood," it ceases to be a symbol and a mystery.

Jung's process of individuation involves the assimilation of symbolic information—the transformation of energy from the unconscious to the conscious. I propose that dance can and does function effectively within this process.[1] First, during the dance, the state of consciousness is ego-diminished and becomes more receptive to the "collaboration" between consciousness and the unconscious. Symbolic content may arise from the unconscious while one is dancing, which I call *evocation*. The Native American Ghost Dance is an example of such dancing, in which one of the primary purposes is to gain ancestral knowledge.[2] Although the dancing is not done solely to produce symbolic information (we do not go to sleep for the express purpose of dreaming), it is done with a mindfulness of this potential.

Second, in the process of assimilating symbolic information into consciousness, dance becomes an *enactment*. In dream work, we do many things to facilitate assimilation, such as writing and talking about the dream images, or attending to bodily responses. Dance can be a powerful and effective means of assimilation. Through the enactment of a symbol in dance, the dancer and audience experience an embodiment of the unconscious content. This is why some dances seem so confusing or difficult, since we are not necessarily privy to a solution, only to a mystery. It also explains why one person finds a particular dance powerful and integrating and another finds the same dance unnerving. It is a matter of the state of the individual psyche. When the Oglala Sioux Black Elk told his story of spiritual transformation in the early 1930s, he said that he was counseled by the great shaman to dance his "big dream" to resolve the psychic difficulties it has caused him through his childhood.[3] Dance can help us confront the unconscious and work with it consciously by giving us a technique, a craft, similar to the shaman's for our journeys of the spirit.

## Jean Erdman's Dances
### (as performed November 20, 1986, at the John Cranford Adams Playhouse, Hofstra University)

Each of the dances represents a stage of Jean Erdman's own dance journey. For her, creating dance means "daring to put yourself into unknown territory . . . to bring into focus and into form that experience, thought, combination, or insight that had not yet been formulated in one's own generation. If you dare to dwell in the unknown realms that are yours, then you are breaking into unconscious content. That's the way I have worked." She uses dance improvisations as well as imagination, intellectual as well as dream experiences, to evoke her dances: "Each dance is a unique thing, just as each person is unique. [The process] was to find out the almost wordless, feeling-toned thought that one wanted to deal with . . . to find out what *it* asked for."

### *"Daughters of the Lonesome Isle"* (1943)
Dancers: Nancy Allison, Leslie Dillingham,
and Dianne Howarth.
Music: John Cage.     Piano: Jerry Benton.

Erdman's fascination with early Cretan culture and the great and powerful goddess religions led to a desire to explore what was female in the absence of the male. This dance presents three aspects of woman: youth, mother, and woman of experience. The last, in her words, is "one who is older and has been through a lot; things have not been great; sort of near the end; hollowed out." She believes that each aspect is in every woman. The dance evolved as she improvised movement styles for each aspect.

The youth moves vigorously, with a kind of skittering joy, whereas the mother's movement is rounded and close to the ground, and the woman of experience is somewhat harsh and brittle. With the dancers costumed exactly alike and moving in unison, the dance begins and ends in a circle, because, in Erdman's opinion,

> We are all one. We had to begin as one. I used to feel it was the realm of the female, as it were, awaiting. The female does wait. She cannot be fertilized without the male, but she can be her complete self. She is there. She goes through all this life experience. And she will keep doing that . . . waiting for a relationship. . . . So that is why the dance goes back to a circle. It is a celebration of the feminine principle.

Dancer Nancy Allison calls "Daughters" the most rhythmically mathematical of Jean's dances:

> You do what you do and the music does what it does and after years, the two come together! What she [Erdman] did, what she is *able* to do, is feel what she calls the "fundamental pulse," and she syncopates her movement off that and that is what makes it so beautiful. . . . Aspects of the character are brought forth from their rhythm, not just the shape of the movement.

Allison dances the youth role, originally danced by Erdman:

> There is one part where the shoulders are going in six even counts and the feet go in 1-and-2, 3-and-4. I didn't even know where my shoulders were! Now it is one of my favorite movements. I love

it. I think it is just brilliant. It gives a little bubbling up from the inside feeling that is just so perfectly youth.

Leslie Dillingham's role in the dance, the Woman of Experience, is quite different. In it, she feels she has an opportunity to evoke the images of a part of herself that is not usually very present. "Most people think of me as a pretty cheerful person," she says. Dancing this woman allows her to be harsh and angry—that ravaged human energy that most of us can empathize with, more or less, even if not in our conscious and ordinary lives.

Figure 1.   Jean Erdman, "Ophelia," 1946.

### *"Ophelia" (1946)*
Dancer: Leslie Dillingham.
Music: John Cage.     Piano: Jerry Benton.
(See Figure 1.)

Joseph Campbell is responsible for the title of this dance. When he saw
the work in progress, it evoked in his imagination the tragic and sor-
rowful figure of Ophelia. For Erdman, the naming came only after she
had developed a dance that dealt with the inability to assimilate the
disintegrating experience that characterizes the second stage of Jung's
individuation process. This stage is the most difficult in that here either
we move toward wholeness, through the symbol, or we do not. For
Erdman, when one crossed a psychic threshold, it is a dismembering
experience that can be worked through and learned from; or alterna-
tively, it can destroy an individual. The dance has the dramatic form
of a failed threshold crossing. And we watch the stages of disintegrating torment, the different "rooms of torture and struggle," through
which she pursues the insight that is unbearable. She has come up
against something she just cannot unify in her experience. Only after
the character became Ophelia, Erdman reveals, did she end the dance
in a movement of floating submission to her disintegration.

Dancer Leslie Dillingham said the dance demanded a great deal of
time for her to internalize it. The movement is so subtle, so simple,
and breath-based that it was "as if someone threw a stone in the pit of
my stomach and a dance came rippling out." At first it was difficult
not to act or emote; but gradually she trusted the physical sensation
and allowed the emotion to be an echo of the motion and momentum
in the movement.

### *"Creature on a Journey" (1943)*
Dancer: Nancy Allison.
Music: Lou Harrison, recorded by John Cage,
Merce Cunningham, and Doris Halpern.

The Creature is a lively, birdlike being that seems to come from paradise but embodies all the wonderful foibles of humankind. It is proud
and at the same time just a little silly in its preening and prancing
about. The dance is a lighter look at life's journey, of which Erdman
says, "There we are, looking at ourselves: having a hard time making
up our minds, backtracking, never getting started, and somehow finally getting there!"

This dance is rooted in pure movement improvisation: a symbolic
evocation that resulted from Erdman's "fooling around" in the studio
one day. It was so powerful in its "rightness" that not only did she
remember it (an unusual occurrence in improvisation), but she showed

it to John Cage, who knew the exact piece of music for it, written by Lou Harrison. Nothing was changed in either movement or the music—synchronicity at its best! The piece is written for three percussion instruments in 3/4, 4/4, and 5/4 time. The dance is performed to rhythmic counterpoint in 2/4. Such a lively dance goes straight to the origins of all dance, which in early cultures were often animal depictions.

### *"Changingwoman" (1951)*
Dancer: Leslie Dillingham.
Music: Henry Cowell.     Piano: Jerry Benton.

Through the use of nature imagery and human sound to suggest the stages of becoming, the dance evolves through the inner transformations that bring one to maturity in harmony and fulfillment. First, there is the Forest Voice, a burning forest, and a great cry of anguish. The movements, Erdman says, are like branches falling from burning trees, ever down, down and pulsing. The dancer, Leslie Dillingham, says that for her the image is one of birthing cries—the experience of simultaneous creation and destruction. Exhaustion gives way to the Wind Voice, as the dancer watches from stage right to left as if something were passing by. The energy shifts now from down to up, but it is still an experience of loss of human control shown through a great deal of movement backward, blowing in the wind, a response to external force. Again, the dancer gives in to the image and falls—to be borne now by the Brook Voice, as if this joyful, bubbling sound releases the tension for awhile. Finally, Part I ends in the Earth Voice, where there is deep silence and repetition of a spatial pattern that forms a triangle—perfect balance. The space now is made magical and alive with harmony.

The second part of the dance reminds us that harmony is short-lived, according to Erdman; "there is something to be tended to." The Sea Voice is one of endless darkness, a place that could swallow you. The waves begin wide and become narrow, catching you, stopping you, holding you down. Then the Desert Voice presents yet another point of view in contrast to the danger and thrill of the deep sea; the desert is ravaging, harsh, and dry. For Dillingham, these images in Part II are similar to the image of Hecate and the role she has in "Daughters." In this part of the dance, the status quo is shattered in a destruction even more violent than in the first. We wonder if harmony can ever be reached again.

From out of the sudden blackout and utter dark, Part III reveals the Moon Voice, with its extremely high vibrating sound. Here is the loving, life-sustaining breath. The moon is "her place," Erdman says. Inspiration for the sweet, Oriental sound that characterizes the moon came from a childhood experience of classical Chinese theater, where Erdman was touched by the otherworldly sounding voices and magical environment. The dance movement is so simple and reassuring. As she describes it: "There is no obstruction, no weight, nowhere to go. Everything is now, right there. And as long as one is in this state, the moon is full." Again, the dance is a journey to fulfillment, an enactment of a dance voyage made by one woman, enacted by another, and available as a source of affiliation for many.

### "Pierrot, The Moon" (1954)
Dancer: Nancy Allison.
Music: Béla Bartók.      Piano: Jerry Benton.

Once, when Erdman was riding on a train, gazing out at the moon, for the first time she saw the face of the "man-in-the-moon" she had heard about so often. To her, he looked just like Pierrot. So she made a classic French Pierrot costume of springy rayon jersey that shows every tiny twinge of a muscle; then she improvised movement for it in order to characterize this man-in-the-moon and ultimately create a story of love and spirit. Pierrot, after playing and singing his heart out, failing to attract the young lady to her window in response, hangs himself in the tree under the window. Immediately, his face appears in the moon. The young lady does respond to the moon and shows her longing for him, but is frightened away when the moon comes down toward earth to approach her. Pierrot, confident now, steps out of the moon to repeat his love song, only to discover the lady is nowhere to be found. Desperate, he decides to hang himself, turns toward the tree, and suddenly sees himself already hanging there. As he slowly raises his finger in amazement to point to himself, his face, once again, shines forth in the moon. The dancer, Nancy Allison, says,

> what Pierrot goes through is very easy for me to relate to—striving for perfection. For him it is striving for his lady love. . . . I had to figure out who she was. I had to put someone in that window (of the set) who was important to me. At first, it was people I had seen dance that I thought I wanted to be able to emulate. Then it became a wider image of unattainable perfection. No matter how hard you try, you are never going to get there. And you are going to keep trying!

At times, Allison has had transcendent experiences in the role of Pierrot, when she experienced the "dance doing her" and she finished with a great sadness for the tragic nature of her character. The ending three-fold image of Pierrot as the human (life), the hanged one (death), and the moon (rebirth) suggests persisting life in the cycles of time.

### "Fearful Symmetry" (1957)
Dancer: Dianne Howarth.
Music: Ezra Laderman.    Cello: Ravenna Helson.
Sculpture: Carlus Dyer.
(See Figure 2.)

Erdman awakened one day with a vision of a costume that would stand up by itself. Several ideas fell into place in relation to the dance: she was reading Blake's "The Tyger" and was transported when she heard a cello solo of Ezra Laderman. The idea of the removable costume/ sculpture was still so vague and wordless that all she could do was bring these things together and experiment. The result is a dance she calls an allegory in six visions: Eye of Fire, The Dare, The Net, The Sword, The Rack, and Burning Bright. This dance is a power struggle. The dancer is at first one with the sculpture, then must define herself separately from it. The task is not easy. She removes a long red flow of fabric from the sculpture, which she plays with at first like a cat its prey. Then she attacks it in a ritual-like attempt to gain enough power to confront the other, awful thing out of which she has emerged. She attacks and is hung on the rack, in evocation of the torture of the night-sea-journey. In the final section, the dancer is born again to the new blood of the red fabric. She handles it with the mouth of her own smaller mask that is the same shape as the sculpture. Then she manipulates it forward and backward until she finds a place on the stage, diagonally opposite and facing the sculpture, balanced in resolution and symmetry.

### "The Perilous Chapel" (1949)
Dancers: Nancy Allison, Leslie Dillingham, Kikilia Fordham, Sara Hook, Miki Orihara, and Susan Tenney.
Music: Lou Harrison, recorded by Peter Schubert.
Mobile: Carlus Dyer.
(See Figure 3.)

> "And I saw a new heaven and a new earth: for the first heaven and the first earth were passed away and there was no more sea."
> —*Revelation*

"The Perilous Chapel" title is taken from Arthurian legend of the Holy Grail adventure. It is simply to suggest that the theme of the dance is one of a soul's adventure in the crisis of a life-transform-

Figure 2.  Jean Erdman, "Fearful Symmetry," 1957.

ing experience, as also the quote from Revelation would indicate. The mobile provides the suggestion of an impact from outside, a revelation from an unsuspected sphere. The dancers are related to it as human beings are related to the creative or destructive power that transforms their world and forces upon them a new orientation. The dance is the visualization of an experience seen through the "individual" in my role and the "group" in that of the other dancers. The appearance of the mobile actually transforms the

227

Figure 3. Jean Erdman, "The Perilous Chapel," 1949.

space and force center of the space.   (Jean Erdman's Notebooks, unpublished)

Both Nancy Allison and Leslie Dillingham described the impact the ritual of this dance had on their lives. The learning process bonded the six young dancers into a group that, in fact, extended beyond ordinary dance action to timeless time, where the dance truly is. Allison says, "each woman had to find herself, what her response was, and you see it very clearly where we all break off. There is a clear separateness that happens after Susan is touched by the sculpture." Each one responds in an individualized way to the conflict and chaos that Erdman very carefully creates. This dance, too, ends in resolution. That is the way Erdman likes it to be: full circle, yet always with the awareness that we end to begin again.

## Conclusion

By living through these dances, Erdman herself and her dancers have matured. Erdman is fiercely committed to what Jung called the objective psyche in her dance. She says: "When I see a dancer who works what I call subjectively, I am embarrassed. People have different tolerance for that subjectivity, but there is no way that it can be freshly

228

experienced the way the original dancer made it, because the dancer's subjective personality is in between. . . . When an artwork is really resolved in aesthetic terms, then it does not refer back to the individual, personal psychology in the same way."

There is a healing quality in performing Jean Erdman's dances because she is not afraid to require herself and her younger dancers to confront frightening and uncontrollable aspects in order to integrate them through the discipline of the dance art. The dances are healing in a profoundly artistic way. Her dancers know that what they do is relevant to their own well-being. Nancy Allison realizes that for each of them, including Erdman herself, the task includes finding the interface between the dance experience and their personal lives. Some people, she says, still think of dance in terms of escapism ("everything's beautiful at the ballet"); but for her, the opportunity to dance is a way to challenge her whole person: body, mind, and spirit. She says, "I think there is such a level of truth about the female existence in Jean's work that you touch into it. . . . I came to it through believing in it." Leslie Dillingham underscores the importance of Erdman's use of cycles and relates her own experiences of the dances to the triple goddess. Erdman herself never loses sight of the art that is her life. None of this "just be spontaneous and thou shalt be healed through movement" for her! Like a powerful shaman, she says, "It is really the discipline of the art that is the medicine. That is the medicine in the art. It must come from discipline."

# Notes

---

1. See my "Symbolic Expression in Dance Experience: Individuation and the Sacred in Three Forms of Dance" (Ph.D. diss., Syracuse University, 1984).

2. See J. Mooney, *The Ghost Dance Religion and the Sioux Outbreak of 1890* (Chicago and London: University of Chicago Press, 1965).

3. John G. Neihardt, *Black Elk Speaks* (New York: Pocket Books, 1959).

# Twelve Dreams by James Lapine: Enactment as Creative Process    Linda Huntington

During the winter of 1981-1982, James Lapine presented his play *Twelve Dreams* at Joseph Papp's Public Theater in New York City. The "imaginal seed" for this production had been a case study outlined by C. G. Jung in *Man and His Symbols*. The case material consisted of twelve dreams experienced by a young girl shortly before her death. The girls' father, an analyst, had received a handwritten booklet of the dreams as a Christmas present from his daughter, which he in turn shared with Jung. These dreams, consisting primarily of images of death and rebirth, were termed by Jung "the weirdest series of dreams I have ever seen."[1] They made a deep impression on him. In *Man and His Symbols*, Jung indicates that their archetypal nature reinforced his theory of the collective aspect of such unconscious images: "They undoubtedly contain 'collective images,' and they are in a way analogous to the doctrines taught to young men in primitive tribes when they are about to be initiated as men."[2]

Jung had been familiar with the sequence long before this essay appeared in 1961. Some of the material had been presented at a private seminar on the "Psychological Interpretations of Children's Dreams" in Zurich during the winter of 1939-1940. Ten years later, Jung mentioned the case in "A Study in the Process of Individuation," referring to the girl's dreams as "exceedingly 'unchildish fantasy' [that] can hardly be termed anything but archetypal" (*CW* 91: par. 624, p. 353). Jolande Jacobi discussed the case in her essay "The Dream of the Bad Animal," in which she disclosed that the eight-year-old girl had died of scarlet fever the year after the Christmas in question. In 1961, shortly before his own death, Jung returned once again to the young girl's dreams, the images of which he had carried with him for over twenty years; he revealed the full sequence for the first time in *Man and His Symbols* in an essay titled "Approaching the Unconscious."

The images of the dream sequence have had a powerful effect on those who are familiar with them. Their transformative energy, probably attributable to their starkly archetypal character, not only sparked

Jung's lifelong interest and inspired Lapine's dramatization, but also in my own experience has generated an extraordinary creativity and introspection among students in my class.

Twenty years after the publication of *Man and His Symbols*, James Lapine produced a play based on the dream sequence. His adaptation of Jung's case study combines the actual staging of the dreams with psychological commentary provided in the narrative. In Lapine's version, a young girl, Emma Hatrick, lived with her father, Charles, a practicing psychiatrist and former student of an unnamed "Professor," a prominent European doctor. During the opening scene of the play, Winter 1936, the Professor has come to Hatrick's university to lecture on his current research. During the Professor's stay with him, Hatrick shows him the Christmas present from Emma, the dream book, which becomes the focus of the play.

Translating the sparse list of images into visually concrete dramatizations must have presented a considerable challenge to Lapine, whose efforts may perhaps have been facilitated by the fact that dreams frequently unfold in a dramatic sequence, as Jacobi reminds us: "The dream—and Jung has found this to be true of most dreams—represents an actual drama in condensed and simplified form and readily lends itself to a breakdown according to the order underlying classical drama."[3]

The dramatizations of the dreams are interpolated into the play at certain intervals and in a set format: the play action freezes while the spotlight focuses on a specific character or image. The dreams are rarely recited; they are enacted, staged with little or no dialogue, but are often accompanied by sounds or music. A word in the dialogue usually triggers the transition from "play-time" to "dream-time." One of the more interesting changeovers occurs at the beginning of the play, which opens with a question–and–answer session at the end of the Professor's lecture. The Professor addresses the theater audience, which of course has not been privy to the content of his talk. He recounts an experience he had during a visit to a Pueblo village: "One day I had to climb a ladder to enter one of their structures. Well, I did so—but while the Indians climb up backwards, I climbed up the normal European fashion, facing the ladder. When I did this, a great shout came forth. A bear! a bear! (*He laughs.*) They thought I was a bear."[4] "Bear," the Professor's animal totem, is the word that cues in the first dream enactment, in which all the characters participate: "Once upon a time there was a bunch of small animals. They came together and frightened me. They grew to a tremendous size and swallowed me up." In this initial tableau, each character is assigned an animal totem with its appropriate sound, which identifies him or her, by association, with certain personality traits.

The most graphic demonstration of co-existing or overlapping time frames occurs at the end of Act I when the Professor, having questioned Emma about her dreams, examines her in her bedroom. Emma recalls her dream: "Once upon a time I was very ill. Suddenly all of these birds came out of my skin and began to cover me completely."[5] As she does so, the stage is filled with a cacophony of bird screams and waltz-tempo music. The Professor proceeds to pull live white mourning doves out from under the white sheet that covers Emma. The birds then fly up to the rafters surrounding the set while Emma's screams gradually drown out the music.

On four occasions (Dreams 4, 7, 10, and 12), the dreams are referred to directly and then staged, bringing about a fusion of the two contexts, play and dream, narrative and experience. For example, the final dream is recited as Hatrick holds his dying daughter in his arms: "Once upon a time, swarms of gnats covered the sun, the moon and all of the stars in the sky, except one. That one star fell from the sky and landed on a pretty little dreamer."[6] At that moment, the reality of the dream and the reality of the play become one. The dream image, concretized by the spoken word, is simultaneously fixed visually by the dramatic enactment.

Lapine recognized the difficulty of presenting material of this nature. He was especially concerned to keep the visual effects restrained enough to be evocative, that is, to go beyond the mere spectacle. The images had to be suggestive but not overwhelming, lest they preclude the viewer's individual and personal relation to them. Jung himself stressed the need to interact in this way with unconscious contents, for example, as Emma did with her dream book. It is Lapine's desire to achieve a similar interaction at a collective level, hoping to move his audience to react and interact with the dream images long after the play is over.

In addition, Lapine is not only concerned with recreating and interpreting the dream sequences. He also attempts to introduce Jungian concepts. In particular, there are a number of alchemical allusions; for example, the Professor, having returned to Europe, refers to a lecture on alchemy he delivered in London. The alchemical transformation of base metal to gold is mirrored by each character's transformation in quest of self. Allusions to the idea of coming to consciousness punctuate the play at regular intervals in the form of the housekeeper's periodic appeals to Emma to "wake up," an appeal that is intended for the other characters and for the audience as well.

Lapine, adhering closely to Jung's interpretation in *Man and His*

*Symbols*, presents Emma as a young girl on the brink of adolescence who is about to undergo a dual initiation, into puberty and into death. In the play, she is regularly reminded of "appropriate" dreams for a preteen girl, such as dreams of getting married, or of being a ballet dancer or some other admired female role. Emma and her friend play "grown up" as they mimic Emma's father with one of his patients, but the two are very young girls again when they giggle uncontrollably over "those ugly bumps" on a nude woman pictured in Dr. Hatrick's medical text.

It becomes apparent in the course of the play that the "normal" dreams of adolescence are not available to Emma. Jung says of them: "Little or nothing in the symbolism of her dreams points to the beginning of a normal adult life, but there are many allusions to destruction and restoration."[7] Indeed, the bird dream—amplified by references to her favorite Christmas present, a book about birds, and to her favorite bird, the owl—suggests a deeper symbolic significance. Her evening prayer, "Spread out thy wings, Lord Jesus mild, and take to thee thy chick, thy child."[8] further supports the impression of a strong internal identification with birds as spiritual symbols rather than as creatures of nature.

As the intensity of dream activity increases, Emma enters a new level of consciousness, one that brings a growing awareness of death as she struggles to prepare for the final initiation of her short life. As Jung points out, "These dreams open up a new and rather terrifying aspect of life and death. One would expect to find such images in an aging person who looks back on life rather than to be given them by a child who would normally be looking forward. . . . Experience shows that the unknown approach of death casts an *adumbratio* (an anticipatory shadow) over the life and dreams of the victim."[9]

The dreams as presented in the play retain enormous power because, as in Jung's original retelling, they give only the sparsest recounting of the images. Lapine never allows Emma to reflect on or analyze her experiences. The images remain unexplored, unfathomed, functioning—to use Jung's words—"like the tales told at primitive initiations or the *Koans* of Zen Buddhism."[10] In this way, the dreams not only present images of death and rebirth, but they are an experiential preparation for death. James Hillman's hypothetical vision of the underworld suggests a preparatory role and value of such dreams: "What one knows about life might not be relevant for what is below life. What one knows and has done in life may be as irrelevant to the underworld as clothes that adjust to life and the flesh and bones that clothes cover. For in the underworld all is stripped away, and life is upside down. We are further than the expectations based on life experience, and the wisdom derived from it."[11]

The attainment of the wisdom of the underworld, of that dark place, is intimated in Hatrick's reading to Emma from *The King and the Corpse*.[12] In Lapine's adaptation, the king finally admits his limitations after being exhausted by the corpse's riddles: "I have no more answers for you. All of my royal knowledge is of no use. I don't have all of the answers to all of the riddles of the world."[13] At the very moment of the king's recognition of the incompleteness of worldly experience and power, the corpse is silenced forever. Emma falls asleep while her father reads the moral of the tale: "And just as one may discover on awakening that what had been obscure the day before is now understood, so the king came from his night of experience, full of wisdom and transformed."[14] It is the awakening to higher consciousness that follows the encounter with the underworld. Hillman adds: "The underworld and its imagery holds the deepest riddles and eventually becomes the prime concern of anyone engaged in soul-making."[15] The moment of illumination as depicted in the tale, along with repeated references to Christmas and the winter solstice in the play, all images of passage from darkness to light, reinforce the sense of expanded consciousness that culminates in Hatrick's telling of Emma's last dream: "The one star fell from the sky and landed on a pretty little dreamer."

The visual and emotional impact of these dreams is profound, even numinous. Each is a tableau, representing an integral part of the drama, but each is also a timeless moment in and of itself. In each sequence, the dream is transformed from a personal to a communal experience, as it draws in all the other characters as well as the audience. Although the immediate focus is on Emma, her initiation is mirrored by the others. Her father, for example, the embodiment of the "wounded healer," struggles to come to terms with the grief over his dead wife and over the impending death of his daughter. Like so many of his patients, he, too, is guilty of sublimating feelings, especially in relation to Emma. When Emma calls her dreams "interesting stories"[16] and says she had them while she was asleep, Hatrick, caught off guard by the ingenuousness of her statement, is unable to question her further, to express his feelings. At the end of the play, the Professor reminds him, "I recall your saying once, shortly after your wife's death, that you wished you could feel less. Unfortunately to do so is simply to bury the moment, the result of which is another kind of death as well."[17] By opening himself to the full weight of his feelings, however painful, Hatrick is finally able to bear the burden of Emma's death, so poignantly underscored by the image of the father holding the dead body of his daughter.

The other characters' initiations are interlaced with Emma's in a similar fashion. There are moments of doubt and subsequent revelation for each. In the final scene, all assemble, transformed, reaching out to Emma in a moment of communion before she dies. In this way, Lapine's drama depicts coming to consciousness as a healing process. From the dark night of *The King and the Corpse*, from the darkness of the winter solstice, grow the seeds of light, of expanding consciousness, which culminate in each character's individual revelation.

The members of the audience are also participants in this process, drawn into the action of the play by its characters, who address them directly and interact with them as though they were characters in the play. It is this kind of participation and degree of interaction that encouraged me to use the play in a class on psychological aspects of contemporary fiction. Although my students were not familiar with Jungian concepts, they were all artists, and it was my hope to bridge the conceptual gap via an experiential grasp of the dream images. Class response was overwhelming. Several students brought in copies of *Man and His Symbols*. Others were eager to share childhood dreams, some doing so for the first time. Still others were fascinated by *The King and the Corpse*, which we read together. We discussed attitudes toward death and shared our fears.

The class response to the play and to the dreams in many ways reinforced Jung's conviction of the abiding power of archetypal images to generate creative energy. Several students illustrated books of dream sequences. Some painted their own interpretations of Emma's dreams. One young woman created a slide performance with music, which she called a "dreamscape," as a eulogy to a friend who had died in her early teens. The play had been an awakening for her, bringing acceptance of the friend's death. Another woman, intrigued by the notion of animal totems, imagined herself reborn from the mouth of a huge golden carp, her personal symbol, and painted a scroll of a woman emerging from the mouth of the fish, holding two green candles to light her way through the darkness.

The most numinous work was created by a young man who outlined a healing circle with a small bundled figure at its center, representing the body of the child. Installed in a black room, lighted only with candles, the sculpture was the focal point of a ceremony intended to help the child on its passage into the next world. The others, awed by this image, were unable to respond at first; but once they entered the "sacred space" of the circle and circumambulated the bundled figure, they were quickly drawn into its mythic aura, participants in an initiation ritual.

Lapine's play *Twelve Dreams* had become a catalyst for this group of young artists, generating a number of creative works and enactments just as Jung's initial documentation and interpretation of the young girl's dreams had inspired Lapine to create the drama. In this way, for almost fifty years, these twelve dreams, profound and prophetic emanations from the unconscious, have deeply affected those who have worked with them. The dreams, as understood by Jung, Lapine, and the students, not only illuminate the unconscious creative source but also demonstrate the power of their collective archetypal images to generate introspection and creativity, reinforcing Jung's view of them as mediators of healing and higher consciousness.

# Notes

1. C. G. Jung, Marie-Louise von Franz, Joseph L. Henderson, Jolande Jacobi, and Aniela Jaffé, *Man and His Symbols* (New York: Dell Publishing Co., 1964), p. 59.

2. Ibid., p. 63.

3. Jolande Jacobi, *Complex/Archetype/Symbol in the Psychology of C. G. Jung*, trans. Ralph Manheim, Bollingen Series (Princeton: Princeton University Press, 1959), p. 141. Cf. C. G. Jung, *Dreams*, trans. R.F.C. Hull, Bollingen Series (Princeton: Princeton University Press, 1974), p. 8off.

4. James Lapine, *Twelve Dreams* (New York: Performing Arts Journal Publications, 1982), I, i.

5. Ibid., I, viii.

6. Ibid., II, vii.

7. Jung et al., *Man and His Symbols*, p. 63.

8. Lapine, *Twelve Dreams*, I, iv.

9. Jung et al., *Man and His Symbols*, p. 63.

10. Ibid.

11. James Hillman, *The Dream and the Underworld* (New York: Harper and Row, 1979), p. 43.

12. Heinrich Zimmer, *The King and the Corpse: Tales of the Soul's Conquest of Evil*, ed. Joseph Campbell, Bollingen Series (Princeton: Princeton University Press, 1948).

13. Lapine, *Twelve Dreams*, II, v.
14. Ibid.
15. Hillman, *The Dream and the Underworld*, p. 202.
16. Lapine, *Twelve Dreams*, II, v.
17. Ibid., II, vii.

# A Survey of
# Jungian Literary
# Criticism
# in English    Jos van Meurs

Jungian literary criticism begins with Jung himself. The first extended
application of Jung's psychology to the interpretation of a literary text
is to be found in his book *Psychology of the Unconscious* (first German
version, 1912; later version retitled *Symbols of Transformation*). In this
work, which marks Jung's break with Freud and gives us the first formulation of his own archetypal psychology, there is a long discussion
of mythical motifs in Longfellow's narrative poem *Hiawatha*. The
events of the hero's life, which include a miraculous birth and battle
with a sea monster, are viewed as symbolizing the transformation of
his life-force in a development toward greater consciousness that Jung
later called the process of individuation. After the publication of the
English translation of this book in 1916, Jung began to acquire a wider
readership in the English-speaking world. Among the creative writers
who in these early years were influenced by Jung are Jack London,
Eugene O'Neill, and D. H. Lawrence. In 1917, the last year of his life,
London wrote some very Jungian short stories.[1] And although it does
not show directly in his work, Lawrence, in a letter written in 1918 to
Katherine Mansfield, tells his correspondent that he was impressed by
"the Jung book."[2] O'Neill was strongly influenced by Freudian psychology, but around 1920, he also wrote some plays that bear witness
to his reading of Jung.[3]

   Around 1920, we also find the first tentative applications of Jung's
psychology to literature and art in essays by literary critics and in a
study by the English philosopher John Thorburn titled *Art and the Unconscious* (1925). It is Jung himself, however, who is the first to theorize
about the relation between analytical psychology and literature in two
lectures delivered in 1922 and 1930 (*CW* 15). The impact of great art,
Jung claims, is due to the artist's tapping of archetypal images: "Whoever speaks in primordial images speaks with a thousand voices"
(*CW*15: par. 129, p. 82).

   Jung distinguishes between two forms of art: on the one hand, psychological or personalistic art that expresses the personal psychology

of the author, consciously developed; on the other, visionary art that is symbolical and archetypal. Goethe, Dante, and Melville are mentioned as striking examples of archetypal art. Jung never wrote a full psychological analysis of a literary work, as Freud did of the story *Gradiva* by the German novelist Wilhelm Jensen. But in 1932, he attempted a piece of practical literary criticism in a long paper on James Joyce's *Ulysses* (*CW* 15: par. 163ff., p. 109ff.). This paper, however, can hardly be called an analysis of the novel, as Jung frankly says that the book bores and irritates him, the only beauty of it being that it perfectly expresses the futility and squalor of modern life.

After these first beginnings in Jung's writings, it took a surprisingly long time for Jungian literary criticism to develop. The English critic Herbert Read commented on Jung in several essays written in the 1920s, but although he knew Jung personally and later lectured at Eranos conferences, he makes only occasional reference to Jung in his criticism. The two pioneering works in Jungian literary criticism were published by two English women, Maud Bodkin and Elizabeth Drew, in 1934 and 1949. Neither book had any real critical follow-up. It is only in the 1960s, and then for different reasons, that Jungian literary criticism began to catch on.

Maud Bodkin, in some articles published in the 1920s, was the first to begin a more systematic investigation into the relevance of the new psychology of the unconscious for art criticism. This resulted in her book *Archetypal Patterns in Poetry* (1934), which for many years remained the only extensive Jungian literary study. Her aim was to test Jung's hypothesis that the emotional significance of great works of art is due to the "stirring in the reader's mind . . . of unconscious forces . . . or archetypes."[4] She discusses her own responses and those of some well-known critics to archetypal patterns such as rebirth, heaven and hell, devil, and hero and God, in great European writers like Homer, Virgil, Dante, Shakespeare, Milton, Goethe, and T. S. Eliot. Bodkin's book in rich and sensitive, full of suggestive insights that might have been taken up and developed by other critics. But her study actually seems to have had little immediate influence. One of the reasons for this neglect is no doubt that her frankly subjective method clashed with the current movement toward objective methods in literary studies. Bodkin's laudable attempt to base her psychological analysis of poetry on a full awareness of "the emotional and intuitive experience communicated" had as its aim the appreciation of poetic suggestiveness rather than abstraction and scientific exactitude. I suspect, moreover, that the academic world was shy of an amateur student of literature who was neither a professional psychologist nor a professional literary scholar, and, equally bad, who made eclectic use of Freud, Jung, and other psychologists.

Symptomatic of the general reaction in the scholarly world is the case of a young professional critic, Stanley Edgar Hyman. In 1948, he published a well-known survey of the methods of literary criticism, titled *The Armed Vision*. More than half of the chapter on psychological criticism is devoted to an enthusiastic discussion of Bodkin's book. Hyman wonders why nothing had so far been done with the possibilities Bodkin opened up, and why she remained unknown; after all, he says, "it is Maud Bodkin's distinction to have made what is probably the best use to date" of psychology in literary criticism. Furthermore, he adds: "in a number of respects Jung's analytical psychology might seem more fruitful for literary analysis than Freudian psychoanalysis."[5] Ironically, he later changed his mind. In the 1940s and the 1950s, it was possible to make use of both Freud and Jung, but wherever depth psychology established itself at the universities, it had to be Freudian only. Consequently, we find that Hyman reverts to a strictly Freudian position, from which in 1957 he completely retracts his praise of Bodkin and Jung, and even attacks the neo-Freudian revisionists for having abandoned Freud's key insights.[6]

In spite of the lack of interest on the part of the scholarly world, Jungian literary criticism slowly began to gain ground after the Second World War, much more so in America than in England and in Europe. If we look at England first, we notice that very little psychological criticism was written there, although the Analytical Psychology Club in London flourished, and some Jungian analysts ventured into the literary field. In the lecture series of the Guild of Pastoral Psychology in London, for instance, analysts regularly turned for their popularization of Jungian notions to examples from myth and literature, but we find few extended literary studies. In the universities, there seems to have been hardly any reaction to Jung. There were, however, some idiosyncratic amateurs who wrote interesting Jungian books, perhaps after they had profited from personal analysis. The literary application of Jung is related to enthusiastic pleas for Jungian depth psychology and personal individuation as the best answers to the need for psychological progress in a divided and chaotic postwar world. Examples include Percival Martin's book *Experiment in Depth* (1955), which studies common themes in the work of the historian Toynbee, the poet T. S. Eliot, and Jung; and David Streatfeild's lengthy archetypal analysis of the best-selling hard-boiled police novel *No Orchids for Miss Blandish* by James Hadley Chase (1959).

Among the literary scholars interested in Jung there is the well-known poet-scholar Kathleen Raine, who in her early work was considerably influenced by Jung. Her studies of the background of William Blake's work led her to investigate, however, the hermetic, occult, and Neoplatonic traditions (*Hermetica*, Paracelsus, Boehme, Swedenborg) that influenced both Blake and Jung rather than to apply Jungian psychology to the interpretation of Blake's poetry.[7] One of the few university teachers who acknowledged Jung's influence was Graham Hough, professor of English literature at Cambridge, who lectured at the Zurich Jung Institute and at Eranos conferences.

Some years ago I started making an inventory of all Jungian literary criticism written in English. My information about European countries other than England is not precise enough to permit confident generalizations, but it would seem that the scarcity of Jungian literary criticism in Europe is due to the general dismissal of Jung by the academic world. The positivist bias of academic science keeps Jung's name out of most psychology courses even today, with the occasional exception of a professor who developed a personal interest in Jung.

In America before and after the war, the situation was rather different. The Jungian archetypes found a greater response. I suppose one of the reasons is that more Americans had the money to have themselves analyzed by Jung; another may be the greater flexibility and openness of the American university system compared with the more rigid academic traditions in Europe.

Among the first generation of those who had personal analysis with Jung and who went back to the United States to become analysts themselves, there were several who attempted psychological interpretations of literature. These pioneers of the Jungian movement were mostly women. Of these, Esther Harding was the first to write on the poetry of T. S. Eliot in her 1935 book *Women's Mysteries*. After the war, she published an article on Rider Haggard's novel *She* (one of Jung's own pet examples of anima description),[8] and she wrote a book on Bunyan's *Pilgrim's Progress* titled *Journey into Self*. Among the men who discovered Jung and wrote on literature, the best known are James Kirsch on Shakespeare, Joseph Henderson on T. S. Eliot, and later Edward Edinger on Melville.[9] Analysts naturally tend to look at literature through psychological lenses, so their interpretations are often more Jungian than literary. Henderson's essays on Eliot's poetry are perhaps the best literary discussions written by an analyst that I have come across.

If we turn to the literary scholars and teachers in America who made use of Jung, we reach the second landmark in Jungian literary criticism: the study of Elizabeth Drew titled *T. S. Eliot: The Design of His Poetry* (1949). It was her book that sent me off on my own Jungian quest. Her excellent discussion of Eliot's work aroused my curiosity about the psychological theory she cautiously and tactfully applies, and about the surprising fact that in Eliot scholarship, Drew gets little notice. The book still seems to me a model for an analysis that does not reduce the work of art to something else but provides illuminating, sensitive, and sensible interpretation. At the same time, it is an example of what is possibly the most fruitful way in which Jung's psychology can be applied to literature. Drew traces parallels between the symbols and patterns in Eliot's poetry as it develops over the years, and the progression of dream symbols and mythical archetypes Jung discovered in the individuation process.

In his early poems, Eliot projects the shadow side of his own sophisticated intellectuality into the brutal figure of Apeneck Sweeney. While going through a severe depression in 1920, he wrote *The Waste Land*, his famous long poem full of archetypal symbolism about the quest for life's meaning amidst the spiritual aridity of modern society. The female figures here are threatening and destructive, or boring and negative; but when Eliot found his way back to orthodox religion, he described a series of meetings with powerful positive anima figures in the poem "Ash Wednesday." In the philosophical *Four Quartets*, which close Eliot's poetic career, the achievement of psychic wholeness, the glimpsing of God's grace in this life, is expressed in symbols of quaternities and of the centering mandala in the image of the "still point of the turning world." Comparison with the archetypes of the individuation process illuminates the meaning of these symbols.

As happened with Maud Bodkin's book in the 1930s, Elizabeth Drew's work had no immediate follow-up in the 1950s. In the therapeutic field, the Jungian school was establishing itself in various parts of the U.S., notably in New York and California.[10] The Bollingen Foundation in New York for many years supported Jungian and archetypal studies that spread the knowledge of Jung's psychology and of related fields of mythology, Eastern religion, and art by means of its splendid series of Bollingen publications. Yet in spite of this groundwork, we still find in the 1950s only an occasional article of Jungian literary criticism.

It should be emphasized that the Jungian literary criticism I am discussing must be distinguished from other types of "myth criticism" or "archetypal criticism" with which it is often grouped. After 1945, "myth" became for a time a popular, though often confusing, term in literary analysis. The impact of Frazer's great comparative studies of the world's folklore, magic, and rituals in *The Golden Bough* (rev. ed. 1911), and, to a lesser extent, of Jung's combination of psychology and myth in his *Psychology of the Unconscious* (1912), is clear in the work of literary critics like Richard Chase (*Quest for Myth*, 1949), Francis Fergusson (*The Idea of a Theatre*, 1949), Philip Wheelwright (*The Burning Fountain*, 1954), and the influential "archetypalist" Northrop Frye (*Anatomy of Criticism*, 1957). Their studies of the recurrence of mythic formulas and archetypes apply to plot patterns, genres, and literary conventions rather than to the psychology of character. Northrop Frye acknowledged the influence of Jung on his theory of literary myths, and he borrowed the term "archetype" from him. But symbols, myths, and archetypes are for Frye strictly literary concepts. He means by an archetype "a typical or recurring image . . . the symbol which connects one poem with another and thereby helps to unify and integrate our literary experience."[11]

The Jungian criticism I am concerned with uses "archetype" in the specific sense of Jung's depth psychology—as a structuring element in the human psyche. Jungian literary critics study the psychological aspects of the characters and their relations, as well as the mythical and archetypal symbols of literary works, in themselves and as expressions of the author's "inclusive" psyche. They apply to literature not only Jung's but also extensions of Jung's ideas in the works of his most influential followers: Erich Neumann (*The Origins and History of Consciousness*, 1949, and *The Great Mother*, 1955), Joseph Campbell (*The Hero with a Thousand Faces*, 1949, and *The Masks of God*, 4 vols., 1959-1968), and James Hillman (*Re-Visioning Psychology*, 1975; *The Dream and the Underworld*, 1979; and *Healing Fiction*, 1983).

The great stimulus for the more widespread study of Jung and for the literary application of his ideas came in the 1960s with the counterculture of the younger generation that, for a variety of reasons, started a radical questioning of the effects and the foundations of our rational, scientific thinking and our technological society. It was not only the political disasters of those years that made the need for cultural self-criticism so strongly felt. Among all the cultural, social, and political factors that contributed to the rise of the counterculture, alongside the general interest in myth, in feminine-oriented psychology, and in non-Western religions, Jung's psychology became a popular subject for study. Though archetypes and the individuation process will seldom be given a place in official American university courses, Jung must have been widely read by the students of the arts and humanities. For in the 1960s, articles began to appear in university periodicals, and in the 1970s, we begin to have the first of many doctoral dissertations that draw on Jung's work., These studies were followed in the late seventies and early eighties by monographs that view the totality of an author's work from a Jungian perspective. We already have a number of Jungian studies of Shakespeare, and two or more each of Blake, Melville, and Doris Lessing.[12] In addition, there is a pleasant and witty book on

Tolkien, and a brilliant study of the writer of horror fiction H. P. Lovecraft.[13] Furthermore, there are Jungian books on, among others, Bunyan, Keats, the Brontë sisters, Lawrence, Yeats, Forster, Norman Mailer, Charles Olson, Patrick White, and Robertson Davies.

This growing interest in Jung may be illustrated from a count of the American dissertations that apply Jung's psychology to various disciplines. The *Comprehensive Dissertation Index*, section Humanities, lists some 320 dissertations written between 1955 and 1982 that make substantial use of Jung.[14] There are occasional Jungian dissertations before 1960, an average of about 5 per year in the sixties; the yearly totals swell in the early seventies to about 20 per year, and in the peak years of 1977, 1978, and 1979, they mount to 31, 33, and 35, respectively. In the early eighties, the figure falls below 20 again.

Another way in which Jungian concepts have made their mark in colleges and universities is in the appearance, since 1970, of a number of anthologies for literary survey and writing courses in which the texts are arranged to illustrate the major archetypes. Most notable among these are two anthologies edited by Harold Schechter and Jonna Gormely Semeiks. One is a sourcebook for a writing course, titled *Patterns in Popular Culture* (1980), a most attractive collection of a variety of pieces ranging from classical myths and epics, fairy tales, poems and prose, to pop songs and comic strips, with stimulating commentary and questions, that makes an excellent popular introduction to the world of Jungian archetypes. The other is the anthology published in 1983 by the same authors, *Discoveries: 50 Stories of the Quest*, in which the stories are arranged according to the stages of Joseph Campbell's hero quest to give an idea of the individuation process.

Jungian criticism works well with literature that has strong symbolical and mythical elements. That is why nineteenth-century Romanticism has been a fruitful subject. Judging from the reviews by the specialists in the annual surveys of the bibliographical series *American Literary Scholarship*, it may well be argued that a number of studies written in recent years from Jungian perspectives have made real contributions to the interpretation of the work of Poe, Emerson, Whitman, Dickinson, Hawthorne, and Melville. One notable aspect of this development is that, however brief the tradition still is, Jungian criticism of the American Romantics is cumulative. Martin Bickman's excellent book, *The Unsounded Centre: Jungian Studies in American Romanticism* (1980; rev. ed. with new title, 1988), summarizes and extends work done by a number of critics in the preceding decade. In his chapter on Poe, for instance, Bickman acknowledges essays written in the 1970s by four different critics who treated Poe in the context of the psychological theories of Jung and Neumann. One of these critics,

Barton Levi St. Armand, opened up new approaches to Poe when he related Poe's known interest in hermeticism and alchemy to interpretations of some of the stories as journeys toward a stage in which psychological opposites are reconciled. Bickman himself used Jung's and Neumann's anima theories to explore the feminine elements in Poe's work and to argue that the theme of psychic dissolution in many of Poe's stories includes a complementary vision of psychic expansion.

Psychological contrasexuality is also examined in the work of other writers when Bickman discusses the imagery of widening consciousness and the theme of psychic growth in the poetry of Emily Dickinson and Walt Whitman. And Bickman is not the only critic who made good use of Jung in a book-length study of the American Romantics. In 1975, the poet-critic Albert Gelpi published a fine study of the five major poets of American Romanticism: Taylor, Emerson, Poe, Whitman, and Dickinson titled *The Tenth Muse: The Psyche of the American Poet*. Although Gelpi does not write from an exclusively Jungian point of view, the bias is Jungian. He sees a poem especially as the poet's effort to integrate the conscious and unconscious aspects of his or her psyche. Gelpi's sensitive readings of the poems find fruitful support in the archetypal psychology not only of Jung, but also of his followers Neumann, von Franz, and Hillman.

It stands to reason that the most mythical and symbolical of American authors, Herman Melville, has also been the subject of numerous Jungian interpretations. I have found some twenty titles of books and articles. Comparing four book-length Jungian studies of Melville may give an instructive picture of the insights to be derived from, as well as the limitations inherent in, the psychological approach. At the time of the *Moby Dick* centenaries in 1951, the Harvard psychologist Henry Murray wrote a brilliant essay.[15] Drawing on both Freud and Jung, and freely linking up his interpretation of the novel with conjectures about the author's personal psychic development, he offered a reading that pertinently unites psychoanalytical, archetypal, religious, and sociocultural viewpoints. Ahab is seen as the embodiment of the satanic Antichrist who captains the forces of the id in their rebellion against the white whale, symbol of the repressing superego of New England conscience. At the same time, viewed archetypally, Captain Ahab is the protagonist of the Great Goddess of Oriental and so-called primitive religions, the feminine principle dismissed by the Biblical mythmakers and the whole Hebraic-Christian and, particularly, the American Calvinist tradition. Melville, as a true poet, was "of the Devil's party" and fully aware that he had written what he called in his letter to Hawthorne "a wicked book." Henry Murray established his reputation as a Melville critic with his hundred-page introduction to the

1949 edition of Melville's novel *Pierre*, in which he gives an uncommonly thorough and perceptive analysis of the psychological complexities of Melville's wildly uneven novel.

Another fine Jungian study of Melville is James Baird's *Ishmael* (1956). Baird sees Melville as an essentially religious artist who, on the basis of his experiences of "primitive" life in Polynesia, created in his books new symbols for the human relation to God to replace the Christian symbols impoverished by what he calls "the cultural failure of Protestantism." Of the six archetypal symbols Baird distinguishes, the most striking is, of course, that of the white whale, the mythic "chaos-dragon," Melville's supreme symbol of life and death and of the ambiguity of the unknowable God.

Compared with the scope and the subtlety of Murray's and Baird's interpretations, the later Jungian books on Melville are disappointing because they tend to reduce the complexities of Melville's art too much to the psychological schemata. This criticism holds, I think, for the expansive book *The Melville Archetype* (1970) by the literary critic Martin Pops, who examines the symbolism in Melville's work "as a quest for the Sacred," and for the concentrated study of *Moby Dick* (1975) by the Jungian analyst Edward Edinger. However penetrating some of Edinger's insights may be, his overall interpretation of Ahab's voyage as an ongoing individuation process leads to distortions of both psychological meanings and literary effects.

It is important to keep in mind the limitations of all psychological literary criticism. Depth psychology, whether Freudian or Jungian, post-Freudian or post-Jungian, works with a unifying and simplifying scheme to explain and analyze the intricate workings of the psyche. Literature, it can be argued, and certainly great literature, tries to grasp and embody in words the concrete complexity of human experience. The critic who uses psychological notions to bring out aspects of this complexity may provide insights; the critic who imposes a psychological scheme on the literary test will in all likelihood limit and distort.

It is obvious that some kinds of literature lend themselves better to the Jungian approach than do others. Jung's archetypes and individuation process find their analogues especially in literature and other art forms of a symbolical and mythical character, in which images and events function to a greater or lesser extent as symbols. Although there are several Jungian books and some forty articles attempting archetypal interpretations of Shakespeare's plays, most of them are disappointing. I suspect that with the exception of *A Midsummer Night's Dream* and *The Tempest*, the psychological realism, the moral reference of themes and images, and the complex interrelations between characters and situations make Shakespeare's plays a form of literature for which interpretation through Jungian symbolism is less relevant. On the other hand, Jungian concepts can be applied fruitfully to the interpretation of the strong symbolist and mythical elements in many nineteenth- and twentieth-century writings, from the symbolic density of T. S. Eliot's poetry to the mythological simplicity of Rider Haggard's romances. Superman cartoons, and Star Wars films.

What has already been achieved in Jungian criticism of some of the current century's authors is well expounded in an article written in 1982 by two Canadian scholars, F. L. Radford and R. R. Wilson, who wrote on Jung's influence in modern literature.[16] They argue that characterization in modern novels, without necessarily being subtler than that in nineteenth-century fiction, clearly incorporates important elements from the concepts of unconscious motivation developed by Freud and Jung. Building on a considerable number of earlier Jungian studies of D. H. Lawrence, Patrick White, and Robertson Davies, Radford and Wilson show how the acquaintance of these authors with the theories of Jung lends archetypal significance to the characters in Lawrence's novels as well as to those in several of White's novels, and how it informs the patterning of the novels of Robertson Davies, who is in a direct line of descent from the Jung-influenced German novelists Herman Hesse and Thomas Mann.

Surveying the whole field of Jungian literary criticism written in English, we find that, besides a number of disappointments, a great many stimulating articles and books have been written during the past twenty-five years, and that a surprising variety of authors from the past and present have already been studied from a Jungian point of view. The boom in Jungian literary studies of the seventies may be over. Yet a working knowledge of Jungian and Freudian psychology will no doubt in future be part of any good critic's equipment. To put it more strongly, much more may be expected if we take into account the quality of the excellent psychological commentary in Theodora Ward's book *The Capsule of the Mind: Chapters in the Life of Emily Dickinson* (1961), and Allegra Stewart's study, *Gertrude Stein and the Present* (1967), two critics who unobtrusively included a Jungian perspective in their sensitive analyses of the works and the inner lives of their authors. It is worth noting that throughout the years, women writers have done particularly well in this field. Among present-day literary scholars who write excellent Jungian criticisms, there are Evelyn Hinz, Lorelei Cederstrom, Nancy Bailey, Annis Pratt, and Stephanie Demetrakopoulos. Furthermore, feminist literary critics have contributed significantly to the debate about the need for revising and developing some of Jung's theories, notably his conception of the anima/animus archetype. For this, see the volume of essays *Feminist Archetypal The-*

*ory: Interdisciplinary Re-Visions of Jungian Thought*, edited by Estella Lauter and Carol Schreier Rupprecht (1985).

A promising new development in the 1980s is the increasing use that critics have been making of James Hillman's "re-visioning" of Jung's psychology. With its emphasis on images as the "poetic basis of mind," Hillman's archetypal psychology has obvious relevance for literary interpretation. Ralph Maud's essay "Archetypal Depth Criticism and Melville"[17] suggests how Melville may be viewed in the light of Hillman's "imaginal" psychology with its notions of depression and the need to confront death as necessary elements in human "soul-making."

Among the most remarkable Jungian criticism of the 1980s is the work that has been done on Patrick White by the Australian critic David Tacey, who was profoundly influenced by Hillman. In his lucid study *Patrick White: Fiction and the Unconscious* (1988), Tacey argues that there is a radical discrepancy between the genuine unconscious symbolism in White's novels and the author's superimposed intellectual constructs and interpretations. This thesis is persuasively developed on the basis of what Tacey sees as the starting point for archetypal criticism, namely, the critic's complete imaginative receptivity to the symbolic material in the novels.

In conclusion, it may be said that Jungian literary criticism is mostly what has been termed "expressive criticism," which holds the view that literature expresses the conscious and unconscious mind and feelings of the author, and thereby, in the Jungian archetypal view, the thoughts and feelings of men and women in general. This criticism has been opposed to the more intellectual and abstract pursuits of recent linguistic, structural, poststructural, and deconstructionist schools of criticism. Jungian criticism as employed so far belongs to that more traditional type of literary analysis and interpretation that focuses on the human content of texts. It is a psychological criticism that tries to unravel further strands in the "imaginal" life of images, symbols, and themes of literary works by using the insights and concepts of depth psychology and the analogies with dreams and myths.

*Acknowledgment*

The material presented here is part of the introductory survey in my book, *Jungian Literary Criticism, 1920-1980: An Annotated, Critical Bibliography of Works in English* (Metuchen, N.J.: Scarecrow Press, 1988).

# Notes

1. See the collections *The Red One* (1918) and *On the Makaloa Mat* (1919). See also James McClintock, *White Logic: Jack London's Short Stories* (Grand Rapids, Mich.: Wolf House Books, 1975).

2. Lawrence to Katherine Mansfield, December 5, 1918, *The Letters of D. H. Lawrence*, vol. 3, ed. James T. Boulton and Andrew Robertson (Cambridge: Cambridge University Press, 1984), p. 301.

3. See *The Emperor Jones* (1921) and *The Great God Brown* (1925). See also Doris V. Falk, *Eugene O'Neill and the Tragic Tension*, 2d ed. (New York: Gordian Press, 1982).

4. Maud Bodkin, *Archtypal Patterns in Poetry: Psychological Studies in Imagination* (London: Oxford University Press, 1934), p. 1.

5. Stanley Hyman, *The Armed Vision: A Study in the Methods of Modern Literary Criticism* (1948; New York: Vintage Books, 1955), pp. 132-134.

6. Stanley Hyman, "Psychoanalysis and the Climate of Tragedy," in *Freud and the 20th Century*, ed. Benjamin Nelson (Cleveland: World Publishing Co., 1957), p. 174.

7. See, e.g., Kathleen Raine, *The Human Face of God: William Blake and the Book of Job* (London: Thames and Hudson, 1982). See especially the chapter titled "Blake's Job and Jung's Job."

8. See Esther M. Harding, "*She*: A Portrait of the Anima," *Spring* (1947): 59-93.

9. James Kirsch, *Shakespeare's Royal Self* (New York: G. P. Putnam's Sons, 1966); Joseph Henderson, "Stages of Psychological Development Exemplified in the Poetical Works of T. S. Eliot," *Journal of Analytical Psychology* 1, no. 2 (1956): 133–144, and 2, no. 1 (1957): 33-49; Edward F. Edinger, *Melville's Moby Dick: A Jungian Commentary* (New York: New Directions, 1978).

10. See Joseph Henderson, "Reflections on the History and Practice of Jungian Analysis," in *Jungian Analysis*, ed. Murray Stein (La Salle: Open Court Publishing, 1982), pp. 3-26.

11. Northrop Frye, *Anatomy of Criticism* (Princeton: Princeton University Press, 1957), p. 99.

12. On Shakespeare, see Kirsch, *Shakespeare's Royal Self*; and Alex Aronson, *Psyche and Symbol in Shakespeare* (Bloomington: Indiana University Press, 1972). On Blake, see Christine Gallant, *Blake and the Assimilation of Chaos* (Princeton: Princeton University Press, 1978); and June Singer, *The Unholy Bible: A Psychological Interpretation of William Blake* (New York: G. P. Putnam's Sons, 1970). On Melville, see James Baird, *Ishmael* (Baltimore: Johns Hopkins University Press, 1956); Martin L. Pops, *The Melville Archetype* (Kent, Ohio: Kent State University Press, 1970); and Edinger, *Melville's Moby Dick*. On Lessing, see Roberta Rubenstein, *The Novelistic Vision of Doris Lessing: Breaking the Forms of Consciousness* (Urbana: University of Illinois Press, 1979); and

Mary A. Singleton, *The City and the Veld: The Fiction of Doris Lessing* (Lewisburg, Penn.: Bucknell University Press, 1977).

13. Timothy R. O'Neill, *The Individuated Hobbit: Jung, Tolkien and the Archetypes of Middle-earth* (Boston: Houghton Mifflin, 1979); Barton L. St. Armand, *The Roots of Horror in the Fiction of H. P. Lovecraft* (Elizabethtown, N.Y.: Dragon Press, 1977).

14. Of these 320 dissertations, about half are on literary subjects. The others are in psychology (77), education (61), religion (31), philosophy (9), and a few in fine arts and sociology.

15. Henry Murray, "In Nomine Diaboli," *New England Quarterly* 24 (1951): 435-462.

16. F. L. Radford and R. R. Wilson, "Some Phases of the Jungian Moon: Jung's Influence on Modern Literary Studies," *English Studies in Canada* 8, no. 3 (1982): 311-332.

17. Ralph Maud, "Archetypal Depth Criticism and Melville," *College English* 45, no. 7 (1983): 695-704.

# Descent to the Underworld
## Jung and His Brothers     Evans Lansing Smith

The descent to the underworld (*nekyia*) is the single most important myth for the modernist authors who wrote during C. G. Jung's lifetime. Serving as a central allusion in their writings, the myth gives to these works that "shape and significance" that T. S. Eliot saw to be the consequence of the "mythic method." Furthermore, the composition of these works tends to coincide with a psychological or physical crisis in the writers' lives, and this breakdown in the inner sphere is reflected outwardly by the cultural catastrophe of World War I. Hence, the myth of the descent to the underworld can be seen as the Ur-myth of modernism (what Wallace Stevens described as the myth before the myth began), giving shape and significance to its major works, life histories, and historical events.[1] Jung's breakdown of 1912-1916, which he regarded as a descent to the underworld, illustrates this pattern precisely and should be discussed with reference to his literary contemporaries.

Writers of this period for whom the descent to the underworld was a focal myth include Joseph Conrad, who wrote *Heart of Darkness* after turning forty, when he faced a serious illness, severe financial strain, and the death of his last surviving Polish relative. He refers to this period as "a taste of hell"[2] and incorporates many elements of the classical and Christian descent to the underworld in the story. Another example is Thomas Mann, who composed *Death in Venice* after the suicide of his sister Carla, perhaps the most devastating blow of his early career.[3] In an effort to recover, he vacationed in Venice, where many of the details of the descent to the underworld employed in his famous novella synchronistically presented themselves (such as the illegitimate gondolier who ferries Aschenbach to the Lido, and the pomegranate juice service on the veranda of his hotel). W. B. Yeats, whose Byzantium poems recount a journey across the water to a mythological underworld, composed *A Vision* in 1916, after the tragic Easter Rising in Dublin, during which Maud Gonne's husband was killed. Chapter 3 of that work concerns information about the soul in the underworld that Yeats received from his wife's spirit communications. D. H. Lawrence experienced the nightmare of political persecution and censorship during 1912-1916, the period when *Sons and Lovers, The Rainbow,* and *Women in Love* were written, all of which use the myth of the underworld in diverse ways. T. S. Eliot incorporates many elements of the descent to the underworld in *The Waste Land,* which took its final shape after the poet's "full-scale breakdown" in 1921,[4] and later in *Four Quartets,* begun during a "depression of spirits so different from any other experience of 50 years as to be a new emotion."[5] Similarly, Hermann Broch began work on the magnificent *The Death of Virgil* in a climate of political and personal catastrophe: in 1938, after a period of familial crises, wandering, and doubts about his literary vocation, he was briefly imprisoned in Vienna by the Nazis, and this recognition "of the possibility of his own death not far off" led to the germination of the novel.[6] These and other important modernists (James Joyce, Marcel Proust, Ezra Pound, Malcolm Lowry, and later Doris Lessing, Eugene Ionesco, and Thomas Pynchon) also use the myth of the descent to the underworld in later works, and often in similar conditions of personal and social crisis.

The stress of such conditions precipitates the descent, during which the patterns that give shape and significance to the lives and works of the modernists are revealed. James Hillman has outlined the relation between Hades and *eidola,* those "ideational forms and shapes, the ideas that form and shape life."[7] The modernists develop their own terminology to express this relation. Yeats calls the shaping power behind an artist's life and work the "daimon," which he understood as spirits of the dead that come alive in the images of great poems.[8] Similar spirits of the dead dance through Eliot's lines in *Four Quartets,* where he repeatedly uses the simple word "pattern" to express the shaping powers discovered by the poem. Broch uses a variety of terms for the *eidola* revealed during Virgil's descent into the underworld: the "dream-form of all images," the "seed of every symbol" in the depths of Hades, the "form which is the pattern of all forms," the "archetype," and "the arch-image."[9] All these terms express Broch's notion of the "archimage of all images."[10]

Jung's experience and use of the descent to the underworld follows a similar pattern of crisis and revelation. *Symbols of Transformation* was completed in 1911, when Jung was thirty-six. It was a "critical" time in his life, marking "the beginning of the second half of life, when a metanoia, a mental transformation, not infrequently occurs" (*CW* 5: xxvi). He was "acutely conscious, then, of the loss of friendly relations with Freud" caused by the publication of the book, after which he felt extreme inner uncertainty and severe disorientation. Feeling that he had reached a "dead end," Jung set out to find "what unconscious or preconscious myth was forming me, from what rhizome I sprang" (*CW* 5: xxv). On a four-day cruise on Lake Zürich, his friend Albert Oeri "fell into the habit of reading aloud the Nekyia episode of Homer's *Odyssey*, the journey of Odysseus to the Sojourn of the Dead. It was significant because Jung now approached perhaps the most shattering experience of his life, and later frequently referred to it as his own Nekyia."[11]

Jung's anxiety and breakdown, then, began with a synchronistic clue about the myth he was living: it was the descent to the underworld. This should not be surprising: *Symbols of Transformation* is primarily concerned with the regression of libido into the depths of the unconscious, a process understood as a descent to and return from the underworld. Throughout the book, Jung traces the libido as it retreats beyond "the presexual stage of earliest infancy" to "the intra-uterine, pre-natal condition" and finally "irrupts into the collective psyche where Jonah saw the 'mysteries.' " Here in the depths, the libido "reaches a kind of inchoate condition in which, like Theseus and Peirithous on their journey to the underworld, it may easily stick fast. But it can also tear itself loose from the maternal embrace and return to the surface with new possibilities of life" (*CW* 5: par. 654, p. 420).

In this passage, Jung equates the regression of libido with the descent to the underworld, which is conceived of as maternal. The entire book, in fact, is concerned with this struggle to return to and be redelivered from the mother, who, as the underworld, symbolizes the matrix of those "collective images (archetypes)" that are activated by the libido's descent. Thomas Mann establishes the same equation in *Joseph and His Brothers*: the well into which Joseph is thrown by his brothers is both the underworld tomb and the mother womb from which Joseph is reborn as Osarsiph. This correlation of underworld and mother becomes a central leitmotiv in the work.[12]

Jung's personal descent, following the publication of *Symbols of Transformation*, closely parallels the pattern of abduction and revelation discussed by James Hillman: like Persephone, whose abduction by Hades precipitates the revelation of "the ideas that form and shape life," Jung journeys to the "land of the dead" and returns with the "pattern" that gives shape and significance to his life and work.[13] Furthermore, Jung's breakdown of 1912–1916 coincides with World War I, so the myth of the descent to the underworld, which he shares with the great literary artists of the period, can be seen as the myth he lived by.

Many details of the descent to the underworld surface in Jung's dreams and fantasies during this period. In one dream, a female dove with a human voice spoke of "the twelve dead" whom she needed to absorb before she could become human.[14] Around Christmas of 1912, he dreamt of a lane of Merovingian sarcophagi, each one with a knight carved on it that came to life under Jung's scrutiny. At this point, he resolved to submit to "the impulses of the unconscious" by paying close attention to its spontaneous productions.[15] By October of 1913, the pressure built up to a vision of a "monstrous flood" covering Europe and turning to a sea of blood. The outbreak of war in August 1914, relieved Jung's fear of imminent insanity by establishing the objective meaning of this vision. As with Lawrence, who used the image of the flood and the underworld in *The Rainbow* (1915), and who also endured a private nightmare at this time,[16] Jung's collapse synchronistically reflects the outer events of the period.

Jung's *nekyia* led to a "pandaemonium of images" (to use Hillman's phrase): he records an "incessant stream of fantasies" let loose by an emotional tension so severe that "certain yoga exercises" were required to allay it. Like Persephone, he felt a "violent resistance" to and "distinct fear" of the impulse to "plummet down into" the fantasies stirring "underground." Yet on December 12, 1913, Jung resolved "upon the decisive step" and let himself be swept under by the flood. He describes his descent as a plunging "down into the dark depths" of a deep twilight. Then he imagines removing a crystal from the mouth of a hollow fountain, which erupts in blood after he sees a dead blond youth float by on an underground stream with a scarab beetle behind. A few days later, he had his vision of Siegfried murdered while riding "a chariot made of the bones of the dead."[17] Then "an inner voice told him that he must understand" the dream or shoot himself.[18]

The recurrence of the "steep descent" to "the land of the dead" sets the pattern for Jung's active imagination during this time and ultimately moves beyond death and abduction to revelation: first Salome and Elijah, and then Philemon, whom Jung calls his "ghostly guru," appear as *psychopompoi*, his guides to the underworld.[19] Although Vincent Brome suggests that the dream of the murdered Siegfried (Sigmund Freud) and affair with Toni Wolff (the mother figure) point to Jung's living out "one of the oldest myths of all—parricide,"[20] one can see the outlines of a still older myth in these imaginal events: Toni Wolff is not the apex of an Oedipal triangle; rather, she is Jung's Persephone, the Queen of the Underworld who personifies, as Anthony Storr puts it, the "matrix of a mythopoetic imagination which had vanished from our rational age," and which Jung rediscovers as a result of his descent.[21]

In 1916, Jung felt the crisis begin to reveal the "outlines of inner change," and he felt "compelled from within to formulate and express what might have been said by Philemon." Then the hauntings came as the underworld began its ascent: the front doorbell rang loudly several times with no one there, a white figure passed mysteriously through the rooms, and Jung felt the house "crammed full of spirits . . . so thick it was scarcely possible to breathe." They cried out in a chorus, "We have come from Jerusalem where we found not what we sought," and for the next three evenings Jung wrote his *Septem Sermones ad Mortuos*, the title of which shows that the events of this period in his life are more coherent when seen under the aegis of Hades than of Oedipus. As with Mann and Lawrence, collapse led to composition, though Jung feared and rejected the imaginal figure of Salome suggesting that what he was doing had anything to do with art.[22]

Following this climax of Jung's descent, he identified the unconscious as "the mythic land of the dead" to which his soul or anima had flown a few days before writing the *Seven Sermons*. He writes that "these conversations with the dead formed a kind of prelude to what I had to communicate to the world about the unconscious: a kind of pattern of order and interpretation of its general contents."[23] That is to say, the descent to the underworld moved Jung through breakdown to a revelation of that which gave shape and significance (a "pattern of order and interpretation") to his life and work. All subsequent creative activity came from the initial dreams and fantasies (the riches spilled from Pluto's cornucopia), which began in 1912, and ended with the drawing of his first mandala in 1916. As "an expression of the self" and representation of the "microcosmic nature of the psyche," Jung saw the discovery of the mandala as the ultimate achievement of this period. Like the circles and squares of Kandinsky's *microcosmoi*, painted at the same time, Jung's mandalas expressed the dynamic of "Formation, Transformation, Eternal Mind's eternal recreation."[24]

The descent to the underworld becomes the myth Jung lived by, and the myth of analysis as he saw it. In his "Psychological Commentary on 'The Tibetan Book of the Dead,' " Jung writes that the revelation of the basic forms of the imagination at the time of death corresponds to the "transformation of the unconscious that occurs under analysis" (*CW* 11: par. 854, p. 523). In the Tibetan system, the underworld has three levels: the *Sidpa Bardo*, a realm of sexual fantasies leading to rebirth and renewed imprisonment of the soul; the *Chönyid Bardo*, replete with the karmic illusions of psychic inheritance recorded in the imagery of the archetypes; and the *Chikhai Bardo*, where the pure light of liberation from attachment to thought shines. A Freudian psychology is appropriate to the first, a Jungian to the second, and perhaps some version of a transpersonal psychology to the third.[25]

Jung interprets the psychic residua of previous existences (the karmic illusions of the *Chönyid Bardo*) as a psychic heredity not "confined either to family or to race. These are the universal dispositions of the mind, and they are to be understood as analogous to Plato's forms (*eidola*), in accordance with which the mind organizes its contents." He then points out that "in the case of our 'forms,' we are not dealing with categories of reason but with categories of the *imagination*" (*CW* 11: par. 845, pp. 517-518), that is, the archetypes. The experience of these "transsubjective psychic realities" becomes possible only when we move beyond the *Sidpa Bardo* (of fear and desire), thereby giving up "the supremacy of egohood, regarded by reason as sacrosanct. What this means in practice is complete capitulation to the objective powers of the psyche . . . a kind of figurative death, corresponding to the Judgment of the Dead in the *Sidpa Bardo*" (*CW* 11: par. 846, p. 519).

Here then is one source of Hillman's interpretation of Persephone's abduction by Hades as a rape of the ego leading to the revelation of the psychic forms of the imaginal (*eidola*). Jung also calls these forms *eidola* and argues that their revelation is experienced as a flood of "uninhibited imagination" overwhelming consciousness with a "chaotic riot of phantasmal forms" (*CW* 11: par. 849, p. 521). This description recalls his own personal *nekyia* of 1912-1916, and anticipates his near-death experience of 1944, during which the archetypal motifs of the descent to the underworld again emerge as the informing pattern of Jung's imagination.

After breaking his foot, Jung collapsed into an unconscious delirium on the edge of death, during which he experienced a series of visions. He felt himself "on the point of departing from the earth" and encountered a huge block of granite hollowed out into a temple with a yogi by the entrance. As he walked toward the inner chamber, he felt the "whole phantasmagoria of earthly life stripped away," as if he were on the verge of meeting those who could explain all. But the image of his doctor appeared and called him back to earth, putting an end to the vision. Jung found it difficult to forgive the doctor this favor and sunk into a deep depression by day that was blessedly relieved by ecstatic visions at midnight, when he felt himself "floating in space, as though I were safe in the womb of the universe—in a tremendous void."[26]

Here the underworld, imagined once again as maternal, holds the promise of ultimate knowledge and union with the matrix of fate. Explicit motifs of the Hades or Persephone complex surface in Jung's vision of his nurse as an ancient partner in the kabbalistic marriage of Malchuth and Tifereth. Other instances of the *hierosgamos* are then celebrated in a magnificent "green landscape," which Jung refers to three times in two pages as the "garden of pomegranates." It is therefore odd that Persephone, who eats of the pomegranate and is married to Hades in the underworld, is left, perhaps apotropaically, unmentioned. It is as if Jung instinctively followed the folkloric command not to utter the names of the lords of the dead. Nevertheless, the outlines of the myth are clear in this vivid description of Jung's second *nekyia*, which reveals the eternal aspects of the soul, now seen not as projections of the imagination but as absolute objective realities.[27]

To turn now to Jung's "brothers," several of the modernist writers mentioned earlier who shared this interest in the myth of the descent to the underworld had some contact with or knowledge of Jung. James Olney tracks down allusions to Jung in W. B. Yeats's conversations and notes that Jung had a signed copy of *A Vision* in his library. Although he finds these connections a blind alley, he provides ample evidence of central ideas shared by Jung and Yeats, which he derives from their common heritage of Platonic thought.[28] Perhaps the most important of these is Yeats's notion of a universal consciousness, which he called *Anima Mundi*. Richard Ellmann describes this as "a storehouse of images which the poet does not invent but receives,"[29] and Yeats called it "a great memory passing on from generation to generation" that is activated in the images appearing "before the mind's eye, whether in sleep or waking."[30] The analogies to active imagination and the collective unconscious are clear, suggesting a deep affinity between Yeats and Jung, even if there was no direct influence either way.

James Joyce, who met Jung to discuss his daughter Lucia, seemed to share her sarcastic judgment of Jung, yet he accepted Jung's introductory essay to the German edition of *Ulysses*. At any rate, Sheldon Brivic convincingly discusses evidence of Jungian and Freudian elements in Joyce's work. These are perhaps most clear in *Finnegans Wake*, an immense repository of archetypal themes activated by the sleep-death of its main character, Finnegan-HCE (whose descent into the underworld of dream and myth John Bishop sees as based on the *Egyptian Book of the Dead*).[31] In fact, the book seems a dramatization of a sentence from Joseph Conrad's *Heart of Darkness* that is very congenial to a Jungian viewpoint: "The mind of man is capable of anything—because everything is in it, all the past as well as all the future."[32]

In his *Fantasia of the Unconscious* (1922), a book that would appear to owe a great deal to Jung, D. H. Lawrence complains that Jung exchanges his university gown for a priestly surplice so often that we do not know where we stand. Further, he expresses his preference for "Freud's *sex* to Jung's *libido* or Bergson's *élan vital*" because it is a more "definite reference."[33] In one of several of Lawrence's letters that mention Jung, he writes that "Jung is very interesting, in his own sort of fat muddled mystical way."[34] Harry Moore notes several occasions when Lawrence could have had contact with people influenced by

Jungian thought, including a visit in the summer of 1919 with Rosalind Baynes, whose husband, Godwin Baynes, was a Jungian analyst who translated *Psychological Types*. Perhaps this visit explains the close parallel between Jung's notions of individuation and typology and Lawrence's description, in *Psychoanalysis and the Unconscious* (1921), of "vital self-realization" as the human psyche's acceptance of the "whole fourfold nature of its own creative activity."[35] Moore also mentions a stay at Mabel Luhan's ranch in March 1924, when Lawrence may have met fellow guest Jaime de Angulo, a serious student of Jung and of American Indian mythology. In addition, one of Lawrence's less appreciative eulogists charged Lawrence with "a paranoid belief to the effect that his theories about psychoanalysis had been stolen by C. G. Jung."[36] Although Moore dismisses this charge as ridiculous, it does indicate points of contact between the two men. Lawrence, after all, was as fascinated as Jung was by the power of the unconscious to produce mythic energies and patterns that could transform and revitalize lives gone astray.

Other modernists were more generous (if often ambivalent) in their acknowledgment of Jung. Malcolm Lowry wrote that though Jung's *Modern Man in Search of A Soul* was "more or less popular and dry half-gobbledegookery," it was nonetheless full of the "wisest sort of speculation."[37] Richard Costa calls Geoffrey Firmin, the main character of *Under the Volcano*, a "Jungian conductor" for the many archetypal symbols in the novel, and he suggests generally that Lowry's life and fiction were "archetypal in the Jungian sense." Jung himself, Costa notes, was interested in the novel (which had been sent to him by Lowry's wife) and invited Lowry to come to Switzerland for treatment.[38] Likewise, Hermann Broch met Jung in 1932, and incorporated archetypal themes into his "Zodiac Stories" written shortly thereafter. His correspondence with Jung indicates continued interest and influence, perhaps most clearly found in Broch's notion of the "epistemological unconscious" as a vast reservoir of knowledge and archetypal imagery.[39] Broch's *The Death of Virgil* is replete with eloquent evocations of such symbolism.

Perhaps most openly appreciative, however, was Thomas Mann, who recognized and honestly acknowledged Jung's importance. In *The Magic Mountain*, Hans Castorp, whom Settembrini compares to "Odysseus in the kingdom of the shades," delivers this essentially Jungian soliloquy at the climax of the novel, after a dream vision of terrible hags devouring children in a cave beside the sea: "Now I know that it is not out of our single souls we dream. We dream anonymously and communally, if each after his fashion. The great soul of which we are a part may dream through us, in our manner of dreaming, its own secret dreams."[40] Although analogies to the collective unconscious remain implicit in this passage, Mann is later quite explicit in his tributes to Jung.

In a letter written to Karl Kerényi in 1941, Mann commends the mythologist's discovery of common ground with Jung as "a most remarkable, propitious achievement." He calls *The Divine Child* "an extremely interesting book" and comments that "no wonder that something so wonderfully interesting results when two initiates of such stature join forces. It would amuse you to see how profusely marked and underlined the pages of my copy are." Mann then remarks that "the principle that lies behind" the collaboration of Jung and Kerényi is important to him, and that it had produced a book "which is rich and fascinating, and which, incidentally, has confirmed for me, through many details, that there is a very correct instinct behind my own unscholarly mythological musings." He is particularly delighted to find that the *psychopompos* is essentially a child divinity, thinking of Tadzio in *Death in Venice*, and he notes that "the absence of a 'unity of the individual' in primitive thought of which Jung speaks is something I have treated quite on my own as a humoristic element in *The Tales of Jacob* (Eliezer)."[41]

Other letters witness a synchronistic connection between Mann and the cooperative work of Kerényi and Jung that may in some instances have contributed to direct and quite specific influences: Mann writes that he received Kerényi's *Mysteries of Eleusis* when he was working on the use of the "Demeter-Eleusinia" mystery rite as background to the marriage of Joseph and Asenath in *Joseph the Provider,* and he received Kerényi's contribution to *The Trickster* just as *Felix Krull,* whose main character represents Hermes, was appearing in print. In addition, Mann continues to emphasize his support of Kerényi's "highly fruitful and fortunate scholarly collaboration with Jung. This cooperative labor is a most gratifying phenomenon. It is essential that myth be taken away from intellectual Fascism and be transmuted for humane ends. I have for a long time done nothing else."[42]

Mann discusses this debt to Jung most openly in his essay "Freud and the Future," which is concerned with "the perception of the apparently objective and accidental as a matter of the soul's own contriving." He calls this insight "the alpha and omega of all psychoanalytic knowledge," and he finds the clearest expression of the idea in Jung's "significant introduction to the Tibetan *Book of the Dead.* 'It is so much more direct, striking, impressive, and thus convincing,' [Jung] says, 'to see how it happens to me than to see how I do it.' " Although Mann concedes that this "bold even extravagant statement" would not have been "conceivable without Freud," the essay proceeds with a focus on

Jung: "Nobody has focused so sharply as he [Jung] the Schopenhauer-Freud perception that 'the giver of all given conditions resides within ourselves—a truth which never becomes conscious, though it is only too often necessary, even indispensable that it should be.' A great and costly change, he thinks, is needed before we understand how the world is 'given' by the nature of the soul."[43]

Mann takes up the conception found in the Tibetan *Book of the Dead* that "even the gods [are] among the 'given conditions' originating from the soul." He illustrates this idea with reference to *Joseph and His Brothers*, in which Abram is seen as the "father of God" who "perceived and brought Him forth" by the "power of his own soul," so that the covenant is simply the outer expression of a previously achieved inner truth. Jung's formulation of "the soul as 'giver of the given' " is cited as the central conception of the novel, in which it reaches "an ironic pitch which is not authorized either in Oriental wisdom or in psychological perception." Taking this insight as the basis of his discussion, Mann develops his notion of the "lived myth" as a "celebration" in which one becomes conscious of the soul projecting a mythic identity through the vehicle of an ego. Joseph is cited as an example of such a "celebrant of life," who "with charming mythological hocus-pocus enacts in his own person the Tammuz-Osiris myth, 'bringing to pass' anew the story of the mangled, buried, and arisen god, playing his festival game with that which mysteriously and secretly shapes life out of its own depths—the unconscious."[44]

Mann then repeats Jung's phrase for the fourth time: "The mystery of the metaphysician and psychologist, that the soul is the giver of all given conditions, becomes in Joseph easy, playful, blithe—like a consummately artistic performance by a fencer or juggler." His essay might therefore just as logically be called "Jung and the Future": it reveals the myth of the descent to the underworld (Joseph as Tammuz-Osiris) as that which "mysteriously and secretly shapes life" in the *Joseph* novels, and it takes its starting point from Jung's own discussion of the underworld in the Tibetan *Book of the Dead*. For both novelist and psychologist, the underworld is conceived as the place where the soul generates the supreme fictions that give shape and significance to life. "Freud and the Future," therefore, avows a clear debt to Jung and celebrates the "meeting of psychology and myth, which is at the same time a celebration of the meeting between poetry and analysis."[45] Furthermore, since Jung saw the descent to the underworld as the myth of analysis, this celebration suggests the parallel between *poesis* and *nekyia* discussed at length in the prelude to *Joseph and His Brothers*, in which the writer is seen on a journey into the lower world of the past.

In the essay, Mann ends with the hope that a new "humanism standing in a different relation to the powers of the lower world, the unconscious, the id" can emerge as a result of the revolutionary force of the "analytic revelation" of the soul as the "giver of all given conditions." In this vision of what Jung called the "symbolic life," the ego's relation to the underworld would be "bolder, freer, blither, productive of a riper art than any possible in our neurotic, fear-ridden, hate-ridden world."[46] This promise of a riper artistic covenant with the underworld was one Jung contributed immeasurably to bringing about. After all, he began his own encounter with the unconscious in a spirit of serious play, building castles and altars along the shores of Lake Zürich, and his techniques of active imagination have spread beyond the consulting room in the form of guided fantasy, waking dream exercises, and sand tray therapies for children.[47] Yet like his brothers (all of whom were thrown, like Joseph, into the well), Jung established this "bolder, freer, blither" covenant through the immense suffering of his own personal *nekyia*.

# Notes

1. John Vickery quotes Stevens to this effect and discusses more recent uses of the descent to the underworld in allusions to Persephone and Orpheus in works by Lowell, Raine, Rilke, Muir, and Valery. See John Vickery, "*The Golden Bough*: Impact and Archetype," in *Myth and Symbol: Critical Approaches and Applications*, ed. Bernice Slote (Lincoln: University of Nebraska Press, 1963). Hugh Kenner also considers the *nekyia* as perhaps the most primal of all myths in his discussion of Ezra Pound's notion of the vortex. See Hugh Kenner, *The Pound Era* (Berkeley: University of California Press, 1971), pp. 147-149. Other myths have been proposed as the Ur-myth of modernism: Vickery offers the "displaced quest romance" ("*The Golden Bough*," p. 187). Rick Tarnas discusses Prometheus in the lives and works of the modernist as well as previous revolutionary periods. See Richard T. Tarnas, "Uranus and Prometheus," *Spring* (1983): 59-86. John Foster, in *Heirs to Dionysus: A Nietzschean Current in Literary Modernism* (Princeton: Princeton University Press, 1981), focuses on Dionysus in Nietzsche, Mann, Gide, and Lawrence.

2. Quoted in Ian Watt, *Conrad in the Nineteenth Century* (Berkeley: University of California Press, 1979), p. 129.

3. See Thomas Mann, *A Sketch of My Life* (New York: Alfred A. Knopf, 1970), pp. 37-42.

4. Ronald Bush, *T. S. Eliot: A Study in Character and Style* (Oxford: Oxford University Press, 1983), p. 68.

5. Ibid., p. 210.

6. See Ernestine Schlant, *Hermann Broch* (Boston: Twayne Publishers, 1978), pp. 92-95.

7. James Hillman, *The Dream and the Underworld* (New York: Harper and Row, 1979), p. 51.

8. See James Olney, *The Rhizome and the Flower: The Perennial Philosophy: Yeats and Jung* (Berkeley: University of California Press, 1980), p. 191. Cf. Robert Langbaum, *The Mysteries of Identity: A Theme in Modern Literature* (New York: Oxford University Press, 1977), p. 173.

9. Hermann Broch, *The Death of Virgil*, trans. Jean Starr Untermeyer (San Francisco: North Point Press, 1983), pp. 81, 159, 212, 444, 472, and 477.

10. See Schlant, *Hermann Broch*, p. 115. For a detailed discussion of the descent to the underworld in the lives and works of these writers, with more complete references, see my "Descent to the Underworld: Towards an Archetypal Poetics of Modernism" (Ph.D. diss., The Claremont Graduate School, 1986).

11. Vincent Brome, *Jung* (New York: Atheneum, 1981), p. 157.

12. Thomas Mann, *Joseph and His Brothers* (New York: Alfred A. Knopf, 1976), pp. 396-397.

13. C. G. Jung, *Memories, Dreams, Reflections*, ed. Aniela Jaffé, trans. Richard and Clara Winston (New York: Vintage Books, 1965), p. 192.

14. Brome, *Jung*, p. 157.

15. Jung, *Memories*, p. 173.

16. See Paul Delany, *D. H. Lawrence's Nightmare: The Writer and His Circle in the Years of the Great War* (New York: Basic Books, 1978).

17. See Jung, *Memories*, pp. 177, 178, and 180.

18. Brome, *Jung*, p. 163.

19. Jung, *Memories*, pp. 181-182 and 184.

20. Brome, *Jung*, p. 161.

21. Quoted in ibid., p. 164.

22. See Jung, *Memories*, pp. 190, 191, and 185-188.

23. Ibid., pp. 191 and 192.

24. Ibid., p. 196.

25. Stanislav Grof is the most rigorous and articulate practitioner and theoretician of the transpersonal psychologists. Ample evidence for a Jungian level of the unconscious analogous to the *Chönyid Bardo* is recorded in his books on LSD psychotherapy. The technique he calls "holonomic integration" in *Beyond the Brain: Birth, Death, and Transcendence in Psychotherapy* (Albany: State University of New York Press, 1985) offers a holistic approach to ther-

apy that orients Freudian and Jungian concerns toward the goal of spiritual liberation.

26. See Jung, *Memories*, Chapter 10, esp. pp. 290, 291, 292, and 293. Jung's experience closely follows the pattern of the near-death experience analyzed in the research of Dr. Kenneth Ring. See especially his *Heading Towards Omega: In Search of the Meaning of the Near Death Experience* (New York: William Morrow, 1984), which provides an experiential and developmental perspective on the idea that the descent to the underworld reveals the archetypal patterns governing life.

27. See Jung, *Memories*, pp. 294-295 and 295-296.

28. See Olney, *The Rhizome and the Flower*, pp. 4-5 and 6-7.

29. Richard Ellman and Robert O'Clair, eds., *The Norton Anthology of Modern Poetry* (New York: W. W. Norton, 1973), p. 131.

30. W. B. Yeats, *Essays* (London: Macmillan, 1924), p. 510.

31. John Bishop, *Joyce's Book of the Dark: Finnegans Wake* (Madison: University of Wisconsin Press, 1986).

32. Joseph Conrad, *Heart of Darkness*, ed. Robert Kimbrough (New York: W. W. Norton, 1963), p. 37. Frederick Karl in *Joseph Conrad: The Three Lives* (New York: Farrar, Strauss, Giroux, 1979), discusses a network of archetypal imagery (which he boils down to a conflict between Prometheus and Orpheus) in Conrad's works.

33. D. H. Lawrence, *Psychoanalysis and the Unconscious and Fantasia of the Unconscious* (New York: The Viking Press, 1960), p. 61.

34. Quoted in Harry T. Moore, *The Priest of Love: A Life of D. H. Lawrence* (New York: Penguin Books, 1974), p. 938.

35. Lawrence, *Psychoanalysis and the Unconscious*, p. 41.

36. See Moore, *The Priest of Love*, pp. 493 and 645.

37. Malcolm Lowry, *Selected Letters of Malcolm Lowry*, ed. Harvey Breit and Margerie Bonner Lowry (Toms River, N.J.: Capricorn Books, 1965/1969), p. 250.

38. See Richard Costa, *Malcolm Lowry* (New York: Twayne Publishers, 1972), pp. 166, 162, and 158.

39. See Schlant, *Hermann Broch*, pp. 73 and 100.

40. Thomas Mann, *The Magic Mountain*, trans. H. T. Lowe-Porter (New York: Random House, n.d.), pp. 57 and 495.

41. Thomas Mann, *Mythology and Humanism: The Correspondence of Thomas Mann and Karl Kerényi* (Ithaca: Cornell University Press, 1975), pp. 100 and 101.

42. Ibid., p. 103.

43. See Thomas Mann, "Freud and the Future," in his *Essays of Three Decades* (New York: Alfred A. Knopf, 1976), pp. 418, 412, 418, and 419.

44. Ibid., pp. 419, 420, and 421-426.

45. Ibid., pp. 426 and 427.

46. Ibid., p. 427. James Hillman's notion of the "imaginal ego" follows from a similar aesthetic stance in relation to the unconscious. He imagines an ego more open to the archetypal realities of the psyche through an awareness

of the connections between death and dream. See Hillman, *The Myth of Analysis* (Evanston: Northwestern University Press, 1972), pp. 188–190.

47. Examples of such "playful" approaches to the unconscious include Robert Masters and Jean Houston's *Mind Games* (New York: Dell Publishing Co., 1972) and Mary Watkins's more scholarly *Waking Dreams* (Dallas: Spring Publications, 1984).

# Part III
## Post-Jungian Contributions

# The Feminine

## Pre- and Post-Jungian    Beverley D. Zabriskie

Gender has been a constant through the ages. Nearly all races and tribes, seeking to describe the universe and to find their place in it, have been informed and inspired by the perceived differences of the sexes in their attempts to render the world and its workings psychologically comprehensible and emotionally accessible.

Our early mythopoeic ancestors discerned and described similar parts and patterns in nature itself and in its creatures. To them, earth and sky seemed to come together and touch, much as women and men. In the cycles of the seasons, of the moon and the tides, and of the female body, they felt similar rhythms. To most races, the earth seemed female as it received, contained, bore, and brought forth; as did the caves and crevices that embraced, enclosed, and hid; the branches of spreading trees that shaded and sheltered; and those large-winged birds that brooded over their young. The swiftly moving streams; the swelling, invading, and receding rivers; the urgency and intensity of the rising sun, seemed a contrast. These had the qualities of the male member as it rose, thrust, and fell; as did the shoots of grain pushing through the soil; and the flights of high-soaring birds rising to the sun as they pierced the ever-present yet distant sky.

The receptive and the penetrating, the near and the distant, the cyclic and the linear, the containing and the moving, were manifest pairs, complements, contrasts, opposites, in both the elements and creatures of nature. They were assigned gender, the most apparent carrier of difference. Gender was thus projected onto, and seen in correspondence with, humankind's external surroundings: with particular areas of the earth; with discrete reaches, specific planets, and configurations in the sky; with times of day or night or of the year. Gender informed and shaped the understanding of the universe—of geography, astronomy, and cosmology—and was then extended into mythology, theology, philosophy, history, sociology, and psychology.

When societies were primarily agricultural, when women were obviously significant participants in the valued aspects of existence and work, their life-giving and life-enhancing capacities were seen as particularly numinous. Figurines from archaic times attest to a fascination with the female body, and the practical objects of beginning civilizations imitated the forms and functions of the sexual, birth-giving and nurturing female: urns that received, vases that held, pitchers that brought forth, storehouses and treasuries that contained, enclosed spaces that encircled, and thrones that supported. Female attributes were celebrated in artistic and religious forms, and feminine energies were personified and deified. The Great Goddess, worshiped in many guises and names, expressed the numinosity of a range of feminine powers: the biological and the spiritual, the creative and the procreative. A Great Mother from whom the race came was imagined, and as humankind came to value its existence and thus it sources, a Mother Goddess came to be revered, and feared, by her mortal children. For just as the earth received the dead, as trees held corpses in their trunks, and as receptacles preserved ointments for the dead, so female and woman were associated not only with the celebration, birth, and support of life, but also with grief, death, and the taking of life. When exuberant and generous, nature could be relied on to give, satisfy, feed, and protect, but in other moods, it might threaten, deprive, and reclaim. Whereas its bounty and beauty were to be enjoyed and appreciated, its dangerous and death-dealing epiphanies were to be confronted or escaped, overcome or transcended.

As civilizations grew in scope and complexity, the value conferred on women and men, female and male, and by extension feminine and masculine, shifted. Available for more than preservation and survival, human energy could be used for conquest, expansion, and acquisition, not just of *enough* to preserve the tribe, but of *more*, to augment its status and reputation. In most societies, women seemed more intimately connected with and thus more determined in the furtherance of continuous life. Men appeared more aggressive in combat for territory and dominance. As the race's relation to nature evolved from one of extraction and enhancement of life's necessities to the reshaping of matter through strength and domination, those energies viewed as more male than female, more masculine than feminine, were increasingly emphasized. As human groups consolidated into tribes; tribes into cities; and cities into states, kingdoms, and empires, hierarchical structures, perceived as masculine, evolved apart from nature, which was increasingly perceived as feminine. Larger tasks were undertaken with heavier tools and organized work forces in the building of cities; longer wars were fought with increasingly complex weapons and stratified armies. Physical size and strength and phallic, single-minded aggression were admired and idealized. It may well be that male bonding and men's separateness and detachment from women and children were positively reinforced for the sake of distant hunts and battles.

Such shifts in gender perspective and values were manifested in the structures of societies, in their crafts and arts, and in their mythologies and religions. As male rulers and conquerors of ascendant civilizations sought to have their agendas and appetites reinforced by male gods, goddesses in many cultures lost primary status to increasingly patriarchal and domineering father gods. As the Western world evolved, the female deities of its cultural cradles and nurseries were diminished or suppressed. The Sumerian goddess Innana, the Assyrian Ishtar and Astarte, the Canaanite-Hebrew Asherah-Anath, the Cypriot Aphrodite, the Phrygian Cybele, the Egyptian Nut and Sekhmet and Hathor, the Mediterranean Magna Mater, and the Celtic Brigid, over time, were dismembered; their inclusive, encompassing embodiments of female powers and energies were broken into fragmented images of specific female functions. When seen in an objectifying male perspective, the Great Goddesses were bound to and dominated by patriarchal deities. They became their sisters, wives, mistresses, or daughters; their religious handmaidens and saints; or their enemies, derided and denigrated as harlots and whores. Autonomous feminine libido was disallowed and therefore suspect. Particularly in those cultures where female came to be associated exclusively with the laws of matter that must be overcome—be it in the threats of nature, the beckonings of the captivating mother, the seductive mistress, or physical death—goddesses and women came to be seen as biological necessities, to be controlled and constrained but otherwise dismissed. The son cultures separated from the ancient Great Mothers. The assertions of masculine will, power, and strength; its focused and detached purposefulness; its egocentric identification with progress defined as over and against nature, became increasingly strident. The ascendant masculine values rigidified into patriarchal orthodoxies, self-consciously superior toward all that seemed to belong to women's contextual and emotional sensibilities. For a time, women's mystery cults gave expression to feminine comprehension and intensity. Then these, too, were extinguished by the established regimes, although the goddesses prevailed in covert forms among many peoples.

The goddess was neither an exotic mirage nor a passing fancy. From our modern, Western point of view, it is difficult to grasp just how long she reigned in her various epiphanies in those cultures that predated and influenced our own. In the Mediterranean, the reign of the goddesses lasted longest in Egypt, where Isis was overtly worshiped from approximately 3200 B.C. to A.D. 472, a period nearly as long as the time since Abraham until today, and nearly twice as long as the Christian dispensation. Because of their dedication to balance, with its essential pairing of opposites, the Egyptians had evolved a complex symbolism that honored both male potency and female generativity and acknowledged their interdependence. The Egyptians revered autonomous female divinities in equilibrium with the male gods, even when a father god was affirmed as the theological reinforcement of the goddess's earthly son, the ruling Pharaoh. This meant, in daily life, that Egyptian women had status and autonomy, unlike women in other patriarchal goddess-worshiping or goddess-fearing societies.

Women and men of the Judeo-Christian tradition have, until recently, had little sense of the numinosity, primacy, and power of the ancient goddesses. In both Old and New Testaments, goddesses are depicted primarily as prostitutes or dangerous females. Or we have been acquainted with them in the attenuated forms of the classical texts of Olympian Greece and imperial Rome. Deposed and disenfranchised, female personifications of power have been presented as, at best, anomalies of nature, as exotic deviations from the norm, or at worst, as perverse witches or possessions of devils. As has been frequently noted in recent times, misogynist distortions and diminutions of the full and multivalenced feminine models of our mythopoeic heritage have shaped our collective and personal histories, religions, art, and literature, as well as our relation to nature, our bodies, ourselves, and each other. Our culture's antifeminine biases have been manifest in our lives and in our psychologies.

Goddess worship in ancient cultures did not guarantee status for individual women any more than it does in contemporary goddess-conscious tribes or in cultures such as modern India. But visible goddesses provide female models with whom to identify and from whom sustenance, comfort, and a sense of belonging and worth can be drawn. As an introspective psychology bids us to find the numinous and authoritative within ourselves, to connect with the immanent as well as the transcendent, reflective women will feel the absence of female images to turn to and draw from for reinforcement as they grow toward personal empowerment. Psychologically attuned women will be keenly aware of the absence of inspiring gender role models, for they note their idealizations and projections and will attempt to humanize, resolve, and integrate them for a more mature, wider, and deeper personality. In the absence of female wisdom figures, feminine contextual and comprehensive intelligence and judgment have been labeled weak-minded and diffuse, unprincipled and amoral. Without goddesses, without great "grand" mothers to claim as ancestresses, many Western women have had little sense of a numinous and autonomous feminine tradition.

In our millennium, the females of the human species have been perceived, reinforced, and valued for their supportive connections to others—to men, children, families, institutions, and societies—rather than for the essential in themselves and for their individual destinies, work, and creativity. Women have typically sought worth by attempting to live up to externally endorsed images and roles, even when these are not innate. In such instances, what may appear to be womanly relatedness may be merely submission to an outer mandate or an internal compulsion—at the cost of authentic relation to the actual and potential in oneself and in another. Sadly, the fundamental, universal principle of the receptive, with its powerful and active generative energy, is then domesticized, as if transmuted and tamed within the constricting notion of availability.

Depth psychology implicitly challenges patriarchal authority, insofar as it suggests that individuals and groups are shaped by unconscious influences as well as by proclamations from podiums and pulpits. The fathers of our psychoanalytic schools were sons and heirs of Judeo-Christian and classical traditions. While Freud's description of psychological dynamics was couched in the masculine language of penetration and dominance, in revealing unconscious conflicts and explicating determining forces invisibly at work, psychoanalysis questioned and undermined the patriarchal notion of a rational ego's autonomy.

The pioneers of depth psychology were insightful and courageous in risking their place and time-bound egos in their descents into the psyche; but Freud and Jung were men, understandably and undeniably influenced by their cultural and social environments. Freud, for instance, described an id of unbridled instinctuality similar to the Judeo-Christian texts' view of the archaic goddesses, and he viewed the ego's regressive tendencies as a desire to commit incest with the mother. We might say, in another language, that it is as if he feared that the patriarchally formed ego might lose itself to the goddesses lying in wait in the lower depths of the psyche. His view of the id's threat to the ego has intimations of the seduction by the serpent and of Eve's seduction of Adam. Freud's reverberating question "What do women want?" might be heard as his expression of disbelief that unmothered daughters are not content with their dependence on male overseers in goddessless gardens. In the psychoanalytic tradition, some post-Freudians have challenged their founder's gender-based assumptions of male superiority and female inferiority, expressed in such assertions as penis envy and a penis-related hierarchy of women's sexual experience. They have questioned his emphasis on female hysteria, especially regarding his revision of the early seduction theory: he later attributed his female patients' memories of sexual abuse to neurotic fantasies and not to authentic recall of actual traumatic abuse.

Jung met the unconscious with more ambivalence than did Freud. In his early practice as a psychiatrist with the inpatients of a Swiss hospital, Jung's clientele were more obviously disturbed than the functioning neurotics the neurologist Freud saw in Vienna. Witnessing its destructive impact on fragile egos, Jung saw the unconscious as more fearsome than Freud did. But he also saw the unconscious as a potentially creative parent and partner in the questing ego's birth and growth. Freud's goal was to make the unconscious conscious for the sake of ego adaptation, whereas Jung focused on individuation, the wholeness of a personality achieved through the awareness and integration of seeming opposites. His approach to the psyche resembled the Egyptian and the Chinese Taoist models in their insistence on balance between opposites: conscious and unconscious, feminine and masculine, the principles of eros and logos, introvert and extravert, the four functions—two more developed or "superior" and two less developed or "inferior"—through which different personalities orient themselves to the world: thinking or feeling, intuition or sensation.

For Jung, the unconscious was not only a repository of regressed and repressed personal memories, but also the source and ground of archetypal imagery and knowledge from the collective unconscious, unbound by place and time. Jung noted that the conscious values that had informed "civilized" Western women and men in the last two millennia were masculine: authority and dominance within hierarchical structures, penetrating and focused assertion and aggression, superiority of linear cognition and detached rationality. Insofar as he believed the unconscious to have a compensatory function in relation to the cultural dominants and the established ego, it followed that the intuitive, elliptical, contextual, and emotionally charged mythopoeic language and imagery of the unconscious shared qualities and associations with those outside the prevailing order: the poets, mystics, dreamers, lunatics, lovers, and women. As the ground, source, and matrix of the psyche and its emerging ego, he saw the unconscious to be like a human mother, both experienced as having the capacity to be supportive and destructive. Insofar as the unconscious had a feminine, maternal, and transpersonal cast for Jung, he saw coiled within it not just the serpentine temptress but also the pythonic sybil.

Jung was also fascinated with the female images of his personal unconscious. In his autobiographical *Memories, Dreams, Reflections*, he described his response on hearing an imaginal woman's voice:

> I was greatly intrigued by the fact that a woman should interfere with me from within. My conclusion was that she must be the "soul," in the primitive sense, and I began to speculate on the reasons why the name "anima" was given to the soul. Why was it thought of as feminine? Later I came to see that this inner feminine figure plays a typical, or archetypal, role in the unconscious of a

man, and I called her the "anima." The corresponding figure in
the unconscious of a woman I called the "animus."

At first it was the negative aspect of the anima that most impressed me. I felt a little awed by her. . . .

But the anima has a positive aspect as well. It is she who com-
municates the images of the unconscious to the conscious mind,
and that is what I chiefly valued her for.[1]

For Jung, the whole individual contained not only ego-near—that
is, perceived as same-sexed—qualities, but also the personal and archetypal ego-distant features associated with the other sex. This required
of a man that he examine, differentiate, and integrate his own images
and projections of the feminine apart from actual women. The same
task vis-à-vis the masculine and men was incumbent on psychologically attuned women. Virginia Woolf expressed a similar idea in her
description of the creative process:

It is fatal to be a man or woman pure and simple; one must be
woman-manly or man-womanly. . . . And fatal is no figure of
speech; for anything written with that conscious bias is doomed
to death. It ceases to be fertilized. . . . Some collaboration has to
take place in the mind between the woman and the man before the
act of creation can be accomplished. Some marriage of opposites
has to be consummated. . . . The writer, I thought, once his experience is over must lie back and let his mind celebrate its nuptial
in the darkness. He must not look or question what is being done.
Rather, he must pluck the petals from a rose or watch the swans
float calmly down the river.[2]

The notion of a contrasexual component within oneself appealed to
those women in Woolf's and Jung's time who longed to transcend the
era's narrow notions of an appropriately female and feminine existence. In the name of integrating an opposite, in the form of masculine
"animus," these women could extend beyond gender-bound arenas.
Not surprisingly, many intelligent and able women were drawn to
Jung's analytical psychology—a phenomenon humorously noted by
the Swiss pun on a famous Alp in referring to the female analysts as
the *Jungfrauenverein*.

Jung's poetic and dynamic formulations of psyche are of immense
clinical value in Jungian analytic work on the personal unconscious.
Shadow figures, in their likeness of gender to the ego, are closer to
consciousness and are thus more available for integration. Qualities
experienced as more "other" are projected onto—and are mythopoei-
cally expressed through—persons, animals, and objects associated

with the opposite gender. These "other" qualities are often over or under-valued, too idealized or too negative to be part of one's conscious identity. Traits that seem forbiddingly masculine, or in conflict with a woman's conscious female self-image, might typically appear in dreams as raping, murderous, kidnapping men, overwhelming to her ego and destructive to her psyche and life. Overvalued masculine traits might be imaged as desirable, distant heroes, who while they stimulate a woman's desire for connection to another, embody certain idealized qualities assumed to be beyond her womanly capacity to grasp and to use. As a woman develops and grows beyond the given assumptions, potentially integratable psychic contents are frequently carried first by male animus figures, then by female shadow figures, and finally by the ego. A woman thus comes to know herself as a more complete personality, culpable of the darkest deeds and capable of exalted tasks.

Whereas a woman may widen and deepen her ego to enfold and thus, so to speak, "feminize" the energies of the masculine figures of her *personal* unconscious, the male or animus images of the *collective* unconscious suggest a transpersonal or archetypal otherness that may be contacted but never fully integrated by the ego. Appearing in such guises as more-than-personal males, gods and demons, wise old men and ogres, princes and clowns, the archetypal masculine embodies transcendent potencies that mobilize the individuating woman to extend toward otherness, beyond her place, time, and social strata. While fulfilling a necessary, enlarging function, these masculine figures do not express an ultimate value for a woman striving toward her realization, because, as Jung remarked in his *Visions Seminars*, "the divine form in a woman is a woman."[3] In his language, an image of the feminine self is the end point, an embodiment of essential energy for a woman. Thus, many years before it was current to suggest that God might well be a woman, Jung alluded to numinous and awe-inspiring divine representations in female form.

In his attempt to understand the unconscious through the myths and symbols of many cultures, Jung had been led to images formed by societies and psyches consciously closer to the Great Goddess. Though a Protestant, he was affected by the Catholic devotion and iconography of a mediating Virgin Mary. And through his study of alchemy and its Egyptian antecedents, he met Mary's Nile ancestress, Isis, called by the alchemists the feminine transformative aspect of their *prima materia*. Through his explorations, Jung's knowledge of the archaic, numinous females went beyond the patriarchal testaments and the conventions of twentieth-century Swiss-German Protestantism. It was, however, limited by the available findings and scholarship of his day and by his personal cultural bias. The figures and texts of ancient peoples and the customs and worship of non-European cultures were most often interpreted and introduced to Jung's world by gentlemen with Victorian sensibilities and with classical and Judeo-Christian education. It is not accidental that the recent surge toward a liberating consciousness in women in regard to the feminine principle and its values has occurred when there is greater access and deeper exposure to ancient and contemporary mythopoeic female figures and thus greater sensitivity to their appearance and meaning in dreams and imagination. Through the work of Near Eastern scholars such as Samuel Noah Kramer, and of countless Egyptologists, archaeologists, and anthropologists, we have been reintroduced to a pantheon of female divinities who had been dismissed, ignored, or forgotten. As we learn of ancient mythologies, of African and Native American religions, and of East Asian and South Asian cultures, we also meet their goddesses and broaden our understanding of the scope and spectrum of encompassing feminine energy.

The mythopoeic and inner figures, the symbolic and interior worlds that Jung described, as well as the psychological dynamics that he sketched, have been enormously important in assisting the reentry and reintroduction into modern consciousness of the feminine principle. His positing of intrapsychic poles of otherness—characterized as feminine and masculine—in each individual is of both cultural and psychological significance. From our vantage point today, however, we see the limitations and distortions in some of Jung's remarks regarding the feminine. Jung and his followers have not been consistent in their attempts to transcend the gender biases of their masculinized histories and cultures. Inconsistency is apparent particularly regarding the archetypal principles viewed as feminine, most especially receptivity and eros, and regarding the posited characteristics of anima and animus. The universal principle of receptivity is often misrepresented as a personalized, romanticized, version of love and is described as if synonymous with constant availability, rather than honored as an inspiring and generating openness to that which is struggling to emerge within as well as without, to the transpersonal and impersonal as well as the personal. This misapprehension led Jung to write: "It is a woman's outstanding characteristic that she can do anything for the love of a man. But those women who can achieve something important for the love of a thing are most exceptional, because this does not really agree with their nature" (*CW* 10: par. 243, p. 118). This view also denigrates eros, which is more fully understood as the intense engagement with, and passionate relatedness to, the actuality and potential, both within and without, in all aspects of being: soul, spirit, mind, heart, and body.

It posits an intactness and individuality implied in the ancient idea of virgin and widow expressing autonomy rather than sexual abstinence.

In another passage, Jung wrote: "Woman's psychology is founded on the principle of Eros, the great binder and loosener, whereas from ancient times the ruling principle ascribed to man is Logos" (*CW* 10: par. 255, p. 123). Today this exclusive division is seen in large part as culturally conditioned, for logos may be feminine or masculine, and eros masculine or feminine, depending on the sex of the ego and the degree of psychological integration. An underlying problem here is Jung's patriarchally informed view of pairs in "either-or" opposition rather than in the relativized contextual "both-and" juxtaposition ascribed to a more "feminine" sensibility.

When Jung's personal associations to feminine qualities and masculine qualities were projected into his analytical psychology, they became static. It is as if the archetypes fell into matter and reemerged as stereotypes. While Jung acknowledged that "what men say about feminine eroticism, and particularly about the emotional life of women, is derived from their own anima projections, and distorted accordingly" (*CW* 17: par. 338, p. 198), the distortions persisted nevertheless as Jung struggled to distinguish his anima images from specific women. He generalized from the particular feeling quality of *his* anima, in relation to his more predominantly thinking personality type, to a universal feminine "otherness." This abstraction from the specific to the general skewed his notion of the feminine per se and its manifestations in women. Certainly Jung was influenced by his personal experiences of women in his milieu, but many of these women were themselves formed and shaped by a masculine value system. Often women in patriarchal situations negotiate their worlds by becoming "anima-women." As analyst Robert Grinnell observed in *Alchemy in a Modern Woman*, "by entering into a masculine world her eros takes on something of the emotional sentimentality of a man's anima."[4]

A contradiction remained in Jung's approach to women and the feminine. He noted, correctly: "A man counts it a virtue to repress his feminine traits as much as possible, just as a woman, at least until recently, considered it unbecoming to be 'mannish.' The repression of feminine traits and inclinations causes these contrasexual tendencies to accumulate in the unconscious. No less naturally, the image of woman (the soul-image) becomes a receptacle for these demands" (*CW* 7: par. 297, p. 189). But in other passages Jung confused the unconscious feminine in himself and in other men with women as such, thereby intimating that women themselves *are* more unconscious.

Some of Jung's declarations convey an anti-feminine-individuation sensibility. For example, he once wrote: "Unconscious assumptions or opinions are the worst enemies of woman; they can even grow into a positively demonic passion that exasperates and disgusts men, and does the woman herself the greatest injury by gradually smothering the charm and meaning of her femininity" (*CW* 10: par. 245, p. 119). Although the emphasis here is on "unconscious," nonetheless such an attitude may squash a woman just as she reaches outside cultural femininity and adaptive "charm" toward assertiveness. At first, assertiveness may emerge primitively, because not yet mediated or humanized by her ego; but eventually it can be one facet within a balanced, comfortably claimed autonomy. Jung also undermined his own stunning intuition of the contrasexual dynamic and the transitional necessity of the personal animus for those women who even today are contorted by their own semi-conscious linkage of many crucial qualities with the masculine. If, for instance, a woman is culturally conditioned to see power, force, strength, and aggression as masculine, she may at first make inner contact with these energies only as she reaches toward the inner "other" in the process of integrating the animus. In thrashing about to arrive at her own individual, separate beliefs, she must be ready for the exasperation of those who would prefer that she be malleable and deferential.

Women and men alike may be grateful to Jung for opening us to the personal and collective unconscious where "other-sexed" as well as same-sexed traits exist in each human being. We may be grateful, too, for the dynamic understanding that allows persons of both sexes to move through and beyond gender projections toward wholeness. But confusion between stereotypes and fundamental archetypes becomes evident when Jung contaminates dynamics with fixed contents. Fortunately, many women have not stopped with Jung; they have gone through him back to the numinous female figures of our archetypal ancestresses, and then carried forth the evolution of the feminine within their own beings and lives.

Just as archetypal images of universal energies may aid release from a constricted ego or restrictive persona, but can no more contain than be contained by a singular human being, so no psychological theory can encapsulate a person or a life. In becoming conscious of overdetermined patterns of myth and legend, in being aware of analytic interpretations of human experience, one may connect with the realities they describe and at the same time free oneself enough from precedent to follow an individual path.

Many of Jung's contributions to the psychology of the feminine and of women have been innovative and stimulating; others have been limiting and in some instances damaging. Women may take what is of value to them from Jung's scholarship and insight and discard what does not fit their experience. As they make their own authentic connections to transcendent feminine energy and take hold of their own being, women define themselves and give expression to their own experience. If women expect and accept definition from the "fathers," or remain fixed in resentment at being ill-defined, they remain either passive or reactive fathers' daughters rather than autonomously introspective and actively self-describing individuals. Womanhood, like manhood, is not to be, indeed cannot be, conferred but is to be accomplished and lived. This is the task and the challenge that the post-Jungian woman meets, embraces, and celebrates.

# Notes

1. C. G. Jung, *Memories, Dreams, Reflections*, ed. Aniela Jaffé, trans. Richard and Clara Winston (New York: Random House, 1961), pp. 186-187.

2. Virginia Woolf, *A Room of One's Own* (Middlesex, England: Penguin Books, 1928), p. 103.

3. C. G. Jung, *Visions Seminars*, from the complete notes of Mary Foote (Zurich: Spring Publications, 1976), p. 456.

4. Robert Grinnell, *Alchemy in a Modern Woman* (Zurich: Spring Publications, 1973), p. 6.

# Enlightening Shadows

## Between Feminism and Archetypalism, Literature and Analysis

**Carol Schreier Rupprecht**

Feminist archetypal literary criticism is an emerging mode of inquiry, rich in subtlety and suggestiveness; but its brief history is already marked by controversy between "feminists" and "archetypalists" who persist in vehemently denying their kinship. The energy mutually invested in this enterprise of denial suggests the operation of unconscious forces, and investigation reveals that the roots of the controversy as well as the nature of the discourse lie in the world of shadow, in the Jungian sense of "an unconscious part of the personality characterized by traits and attitudes, whether negative or positive, which the conscious ego tends to reject or ignore."[1] As one regularly subjected to the ascription of each label in its full range of positive and negative connotation, I take up here the challenge to unleash the potential for literary criticism and psychological analysis that is at present wastefully bound up in this shadow relation.

Feminist archetypal theory began as a multidisciplinary re-visioning of the theories of C. G. Jung with the purpose of "reformulating key Jungian concepts to reflect women's experiences more accurately" and fully.[2] Such theorizing had been carried on, primarily among women, in conversations, correspondence, articles, conference presentations, and books throughout the United States for many years. In the 1970s and 1980s, scholars like Naomi Goldenberg led the challenge to Jung from women in the humanities, and the approach was finally explicitly named in the title of a book published in 1985, *Feminist Archetypal Theory: Interdisciplinary Re-Visions of Jungian Thought*. Two premises underlay the work of the volume's editors and contributors and of many scholars working in the field as well as analysts practicing in their consulting rooms. One: Jungian psychology offers "a rich, suggestive, timely, and especially comprehensive approach to the psyche" that can connect women to "the sources of energy and meaning uniquely available through the unconscious."[3] Two: a critical reappraisal of Jungian psychology from a feminist point of view is necessary because of the

problematic nature of Jung's views on sex and gender and other tendencies within his thought that limit its potential for women. Feminist
archetypal theory is now entering a new phase with the creative task
of carrying out truly interdisciplinary modes of inquiry. One of these
modes, literary criticism in relation to analysis, is the focus here.

But let me begin with a few words about the general relation between feminism and archetypalism, especially in the latter's manifestation in Jung's analytical psychology. The evolution of that relation
parallels in interesting ways the relation between feminism and Freudian psychoanalysis, which itself has been deeply intertwined with literary texts and the work of literary critics. One of these critics, Shoshana Felman, has written provocatively about the link between
literature and psychoanalysis in a way that provides a heuristic model
for feminist archetypal theory. She addresses the challenges brought to
bear on traditional forms of psychoanalytic literary criticism by contemporary critical theories, including feminist theory, through their
questioning of the very process by which meaning is constructed
through language. Such questioning discovers a subordination of literary texts to psychoanalytic theory, and uncovers the need for a fully
revised critical approach, making its dual domains more symbiotic
than hierarchical:

> the traditional method of application of psychoanalysis to litera-
> ture would here in principle be ruled out. The notion of appli-
> cation would be replaced by the radically different notion of
> implication . . . not to apply to the text an acquired science, a pre-
> conceived knowledge, but to act as a go-between, to generate
> implications between literature and psychoanalysis, to explore, to
> bring to light and articulate the various (indirect) ways in which
> the two domains do indeed implicate each other, each one finding
> itself enlightened, informed, but also affected, displaced by the
> other.[4]

Expressed or implied, the feminist challenge to archetypalism calls
for a similar response. Felman goes on to say that "in the same way
that psychoanalysis points to the unconscious of literature, literature,
in its turn, is the unconscious of psychoanalysis; the unthought-out
shadow in psychoanalytical theory is its own involvement with literature."[5] I have written elsewhere about how Jung's involvement with
literary texts, most notably Goethe's *Faust*, shaped both his own psychology and the theories he conceptualized;[6] but what is most important here is the notion of shadow, which we, unlike Felman, understand in the Jungian sense.

Feminism is indeed a shadow of archetypalism and archetypalism a shadow of feminism. To a frequently large extent, feminism directs its resources toward the political, social, and economic conditions of women and ignores or denies the existence of any forces from the collective unconscious underlying these conditions. Many feminists fear, not without cause, that acceptance of universal psychic patterns diverts attention from socio-economic determinants. Further, belief in such patterns has been and can be used to legitimate a society's gender status quo and can thus distort literary interpretation into conformity with it. The result of such a distortion, however, is that women are thus cut off from the very sources of psychic energy that could stimulate effective and lasting individual and social change. What is needed is some "unconsciousness raising" (to use Annis Pratt's term[7]), energizing contact with this unknown and often rejected other dimension of women's lives—the archetypal.

Archetypalism, on the other hand, is rooted in a male view of the human psyche; its focus on "the feminine" in man, laudable and necessary in its time, has resulted in the exclusion of female reality, both bodily and imaginal, and has led to neglect of the formative effect on the human psyche of political, economic, and social conditions that have differed dramatically according to gender across time and culture. Ironically, archetypalism is now being countered on another feminist front—the new historicism—that locates texts in embedded, often gender-biased, cultural norms. The new historicism seeks to redress the errors and omissions—notably in regard to the lives of women—of earlier critical modes and to reassert the significant shaping powers of cultural givens. But there is no acknowledgment of a possible archetypal explanation for the persistence of certain attitudes throughout times and across cultures, so any reconstitution of a historically based criticism may itself fall prey to archetypal influence. Archetypalism has also tended to denigrate and dehumanize the real female by entangling her in male experience of the anima archetype, which is so often presented in analytical psychology as inversely opposite to that unknown other called "animus"; this turns women into shadow, although the process of transvaluation is hidden under the notion of the allegedly value-neutral concept of the "contrasexual."

Archetypalists often allege that feminists are really condemning only misuse and inappropriate application of Jung's concepts and not the concepts themselves, which are above such reproach. But critical analysis of Jung's work reveals pervasive methodological, conceptual, and linguistic gender bias of a kind that fosters and reinforces just such misogynistic use and application. And the female depicted in Jung's *Collected Works* and *Letters* emerges less as contrasexual to the male than as the male's shadow, with the additional effect of casting some of the female's experience of her own unconscious into the territory of shadow.

People experienced in Jungian thought have learned ways to approach the shadow: denial is not one of those ways. In Jung's words, "Mere suppression of the shadow is as little of a remedy as beheading would be for headache" (*CW* 11: par. 133, p. 77). We do not call it names and keep it at a distance; we open ourselves to it, recognize it as our own, withdraw our projections from it, and integrate it as much as possible into the self. So to assume willingly the label of feminist archetypal theorist, as I do, is to stake out for exploration the doubly darkened ground of overlapping shadows. The exploration is not so difficult a task if one seeks out post-Jungian archetypal theorists—like James Hillman, Patricia Berry, and Paul Kugler—who have gone beyond Jung, extended his insights into broader disciplines, and re-envisioned them, thus producing an environment that is hospitable to feminist and postmodernist critiques. If one tries to stay with, or even start from, Jung's original work, however, the task is daunting; but it is necessary to start there because the force of his concepts about female experience and the language in which he articulated these thoughts can fatally constrict the woman who encounters them without a post-Jungian postmodern interpretative context.

Feminist archetypal theorists have already identified four critical limitations in Jung's thought that bear particularly on his views of the nature of woman: the tendency toward dualism; the sanctifying ontology accompanying archetypal images ascribed to the female; confusion of enculturated social roles with actual gender identity; and the tendency to define the female predominantly through her relation to the male. Jung's many discussions of logos/eros and animus/anima provide examples that are all too familiar to need citation here.[8]

Many readers will immediately call to mind Jungians who are currently engaged, and have been engaged for decades, in open-minded modification of Jungian psychology to the changing realities of the contemporary world, acknowledging and going beyond the sexism in Jung's thought. And I will agree that Edward Whitmont, writing in 1980 in the journal *Quadrant*, would appear to represent this kind of enlightened adaptation:

> Instinct, soul and spirit, anima and animus, are archetypal principles that pertain to both sexes equally. . . . Women can be and always could be deeply involved with and psychologically determined in their conscious outlook by Logos and out of touch with their affects; men can be immensely sensitive to instinct, feeling, and affect and quite at a loss in respect to Logos or for that matter

to any other of the masculine archetypes. . . . Either sex may partake in any of the masculine or feminine determinants in various
constellations or degrees, comparable to a zodiac wheel in which
any of its sections can be accentuated to different degrees in different people.[9]

This point of view, however, as admirable as it is, presents us with
another dilemma. If what Whitmont says is true, and I believe that
much of it is, then the very labels "masculine" and "feminine" have no
meaning and should be appropriately excised from our vocabulary and
replaced by new rubrics for the categories they allegedly define. While
Whitmont is softening the opposites over a spectrum, he is still holding
on to gendered dualistic language. One can do this only by staying on
the level of abstraction, of imaging women and men. To place the actual physical human body in such a paradigm as Whitmont proposed
would bring us face to face with the stark reality of radically differing
female and male bodies and the distinct possibility of radically differing psychophysical units. Jungians have begun to restore the body to
their theorizing so that we can no longer so easily expatiate about "the
feminine" or "the masculine" and ignore the physical forms we distinguish as female and male.[10]

In other contexts, Erich Neumann has described felicitously the
process by which unknowable archetypal energy enters into concrete,
cognitively perceptible manifestations:

> The archetypes of the collective unconscious are intrinsically
> formless psychic structures which become visible in art. The ar-
> chetypes are varied by the media through which they pass—that
> is, their form changes according to the time, the place, and the
> psychological constellation of the individual in whom they are
> manifested. . . . The paradoxical multiplicity of its eternal pres-
> ence, which makes possible an infinite variety of forms of expres-
> sion, is crystallized in its realization by man in time; its archetypal
> eternity enters into a unique synthesis with a specific historical
> situation.[11]

Must not then Neumann's description be extended to the sex-specific
body of the person through whom the archetypal energy is manifest?
The human person constitutes a psychophysical unit; the principal
source of our knowledge about archetypal processes and their coming
to consciousness is a psychophysical process called dreaming. Interestingly for our purposes, gender difference is an unvarying theme in the
history of oneirology in the Western world. From Greek philosophical
texts to Roman manuals on dream symbolism, from medieval and

Renaissance dream treatises to the reports of contemporary sleep lab investigators, women and men are presumed to differ in dream content, form, and context, or, when they dream in similar ways, the dream meaning differs according to gender.

Artemidorus, one of the most famous and influential of ancient oneirologists, known to and cited by both Freud and Jung, exemplifies such gender discrimination. The views in his *Oneirocritica*, or *The Interpretation of Dreams*, a treatise written in Greek in the second century A.D., are not idiosyncratic but are compiled from a multitude of contemporary and earlier texts with wide currency in his time: "If anyone dreams he is wrapped in swaddling clothes, like a little child and takes milk from a woman, whether or not he is familiar with her, it means that he will have a long illness unless his wife is pregnant. For then it means that a son will be born. . . . But if a woman has such a dream it foretells that she will have a little daughter."[12]

Initially I was skeptical about ascriptions of difference in Artemidorus because distinctions were also made in such culturally variable categories as class and social role; for example, if a slave dreams this, it means one thing; if a king, another. I was also skeptical because the range of symbolism and function ascribed to women was based on enculturated presuppositions of the time about their inferiority, proper subordination to men, and status as legal property of men:

> Another man dreamt that his mistress died. And shortly afterwards, robbed of the acquaintance dearest to him, he himself died. The same holds true if a man dreams that his mother or wife is ill; it indicates that one's business activities will be weak and disorganized. Indeed, this is by no means inconsistent, for all agree that it is consonant with reason that a craft corresponds to one's mother, since it nourishes, and to one's wife, since it is in the highest degree one's own.[13]

I was also working from an initial hypothesis of the relative similarity, a basic congruence, between women's and men's experience of archetype. This is because I had come to see that throughout Western history the premise of gender difference had led with seeming inevitability to the ascent, dominance, and alleged superiority of one sex over the other.

As I went on with my research, however, I encountered scientific dream researchers like Rosalind Cartwright observing, over 1,700 years after Artemidorus: "Male/female differences are apparent in dreams and REM sleep from childhood to old age."[14] And my hypothesis gradually shifted to one of difference, not only of obvious sex difference in the body, but also of gender difference in the imaginal, non-corporeal (or not primarily corporeal) dimensions of human life: dreams and all aesthetic creations, including literature.

But I am less concerned at this point with proof or disproof of the hypothesis of gendered noncorporeality than I am with forming archetypal methods for investigating such a phenomenon: a female imaginary. The method must be international, to accumulate evidence cross-culturally, and it must be interdisciplinary. We cannot reconstruct diachronically a history of women, because so much of women's experience has gone unrecorded or the records have been lost. Therefore, we can accumulate a meaningful pattern of evidence only synchronically, by a convergence of disciplinary perspectives, and synchronistically, with evidence gathered through continuous mediation between inner and outer worlds of the self. That is, one cannot be just a feminist archetypal *literary critic*; the dynamic moves most effectively through one's own discipline in a centrifugal and centripetal motion involving feminist archetypalists in all other disciplines and especially joining the insights from academic research with those garnered from the practice of analysis.

In over sixteen years of sustained, experimental interdisciplinary maneuvering between literature and psychology, I have worked with neurophysiologists, social scientists, sleep lab researchers, and clinical practitioners. I have also met with women from all over the world through occasions like the International Interdisciplinary Congresses on Women in Israel, the Netherlands, and Ireland, and travels through Egypt studying women's dreams in the Coptic, Pharaonic, and Muslim traditions. Such experiences—along with immersion in contemporary feminist theory, principally French and North American—have led me increasingly to view woman's psyche and all its creations, from the primarily unconscious dreams to primarily conscious literary texts, as constituting a female imaginary.

Thus for me the most heuristic approach to literary criticism is to consider the dream as a text and the text as a dream. One cannot simply apply theory, whether feminist or archetypal or a combination of both, to literature; one can only fold them in together, alert—as Shoshana Felman shows us—to the romance language roots of "implication" that denote just such an enfolding activity. In the archetypal perspective, the process resembles the intricate interfolding of the Japanese art of origami, where multiple multicolored bits of paper emerge into a design that always leaves the impression of having been inherent in the bits of material from the beginning. But this activity, in all its aesthetically satisfying and critically engaging nuance, can proceed only after the removal of certain obstacles. The first obstacle is the pervasive presence in Jungian psychology of certain concepts that are demonstrably unworkable, because they contradict, distort, or stereotype the actual experiences of women. Such concepts must be boldly discarded as they are not only useless; they are actually destructive. One of these concepts is the animus—the "penis envy" of Jungian psychology. Nothing in any of the research I have done or have seen done on women's creations convinces me of the activity of an animus archetype, *as defined by Jung*, in the psyche of women. I have been arguing this absence for years.

At present I can only warn of the dangers of the animus concept to the practicing or aspiring feminist archetypal theorist by demonstrating that despite Whitmont's wise words of 1980, the gender-specific stranglehold on Jungians of the animus concept is as powerful as ever. For example, note the following review of the book mentioned earlier, *Feminist Archetypal Theory*. The review was published in a Jungian journal in 1986:

> The book angered me. . . . [P]art of my dismay is at what I can only describe as a collective and distorting animus invasion of these scholars. It is an animus that, alas, I recognize in myself. . . . Another source is, perhaps, anger at my own conflict about writing; I want to speak with my own voice, but a negative animus inside me disparages my ambition. It tells me I have no right, no skill, and besides no one will listen, and it really isn't my own voice anyway, so I have to watch for a certain harshness and stridency and a tendency toward commando raids that want to hit and run in secret. Even worse is the bitchy voice that comes when I would have loved to write the book I'm discussing but find the writer wrote it differently. It wants to hurt, belabor, and belittle. . . . There is a snide trickster animus at work.[15]

We can see here a person imprisoned in a concept, with not only her thought processes but also her self-image and her language, her way of expressing thought, so thoroughly shaped and controlled by a single term, a single conceptual frame—the animus—that she cannot, as she herself says, find her own voice. I cannot hear a person speaking here. The consistently intense, overwhelmingly negative imagery and language, and the splitting off of this feeling into something other than her self, keep her from claiming her anger as her own, feeling free to say what she thinks and feels, free especially to analyze and criticize. One effect of feminist archetypal theory would be to break open the prison house of language that Jungian psychology has constructed for women through terms like "animus." Then one could begin to extend awareness of the human naturalness of the feelings expressed above and their distribution across gender lines. Any reader of such publications as *The New York Review of Books* or *The New York Times Book Review* would readily recognize the tone, imagery, and sentiment of this reviewer as not uncharacteristic of the genre of writing in which she is engaged. A perusal of academic journals and "Letters to the Editor" of book-reviewing periodicals would demonstrate conclusively that "commando raids" and "bitchiness" are scarcely the provenance solely of members of the female sex or of some alleged dimension of the female psyche.

The fact is that this woman does have a voice of her own, a competent, lucid, honest, intelligent voice, as she exhibits later in the same review:

> But the damage they do the Jungian field is partly the field's own fault; Jungians have not gathered a clear exposition of the development of our theory over time for scholars in other fields to consult. Our treasures are all too often hidden in our journals or in pamphlets hiding in our libraries and even most of us may be unaware of them. We seem to prefer to let our Jungian concepts arise phenomenologically from within our own psyches and we write without first reviewing our own literature. This prevents serious scholars such as these writers from gaining accurate information about the wide scope and development of Jungian theory. Part also is that there are some among us who do stick to what we think is the letter of Jung's law rather than to its heart.[16]

If we are to become feminist archetypal readers of texts and interpreters of dreams, we must leave the animus behind once and for all.

This is one way in which the feminist critique of archetypal theory removes obstacles: by demonstrating that some of what is claimed by the theory does not in fact exist in female experience, though it may be a powerful "reality" in male fantasy and in "scientific" descriptions of that experience. There are many other obstacles that, once removed, have also given way to significant findings, but I will limit my attention today to only one more: accepting the presence in literature of a recurrent, powerful pattern of images—in short, manifestations of archetypal forces—to see whether what is present in the theory and in the literature by men also occurs in the theory and in the literature by women, and whether, if present, the female version corresponds to or differs from the male version in significant ways.

Annis Pratt has shown that many twentieth-century novels by women have a quest motif as a basic narrative pattern. This kind of narrative has been traditionally identified in literary criticism as a *bildungsroman*, representing the psychological development, the education, of the protagonist. Pratt also found, however, that the quest pattern in those elements that constitute meaningfulness of the experience differs greatly according to the gender of the protagonist and the author: "When I began my research on women's novels, my initial hypothesis was that women's literature would reveal patterns parallel to the male rebirth quest with only incidental variations."[17] And indeed this was the conclusion of Jungians such as Maud Bodkin, one of the earliest writers to apply Jung's ideas to literature. In *Archetypal Patterns in Poetry* written in 1939, Bodkin suggests, for example, that Heathcliff is to Catherine in *Wuthering Heights* as Beatrice is to Dante in *The Divine Comedy*: both serve as guides, as psychopomps to the inner development of the others. As Pratt points out, however, Bodkin overlooks significant differences in outcome: the man's quest leads him through the woman's intercession to heaven, where both of them live happily in the ever-after; the woman's "guide," on the other hand, drives her first into a socially correct marriage and ultimately to her death and his own nightmarish life-as-death existence following her loss. Pratt sums up the pattern:

> Whenever women encounter erotic godlike figures in [their quests in] literature, the encounters are often natural, antisocial, and above all antimarital; the women end up mad, dead, or socially outcast. An integrated feminine self . . . is frightening to society. Thus women's rebirth literature casts its heroes *out* of the social community rather than, as in men's rebirth literature, elevating them to the status of hero.[18]

For women in much twentieth-century fiction, the quest for and of self is lonely and perilous; even if it goes well, a woman's return to society with a whole new self is doomed to failure. Bodkin's paradigm is instructive, for we see Dante's quest as a culturally sanctioned process of salvation of the male with Biblical precedents for the intercession of the idealized female. Catherine's quest, however, is aborted at every turn by pervasive social sanctions against her alliance with Heathcliff, in support of her domestication, and in opposition to the growth of her self.

If we turn for a moment to the myth of Inanna—a Sumerian tale of a female descent to the world of spirits and a return, one of the few ancient texts about such female experience that has been preserved—we find Inanna's process differs, for example, from that of Gilgamesh, a male epic protagonist of the same era, as well as from those of such Graeco-Roman figures as Odysseus, Aeneas, Orpheus, and Theseus, or of medieval figures like Dante Pilgrim in the *Divine Comedy*. But Inanna's experience is very similar to that of protagonists in the twentieth-century novels by women that Pratt has examined.

288

Jungian analyst Sylvia Brinton Perera has shown how Inanna's tale offers insights and analogues to twentieth-century women's descending and ascending processes in analysis, in her own life as a woman, and in the lives of other women she knows. Furthermore, she articulates in psychological terms the same gender difference identified by Pratt:

> The major difference in masculine development is that until recently, and then often only in the second half of life, most men have not needed to go down into the repressed depths once they have initially freed themselves from their childhood and identified with the ideals of the culture, for they have been supported by the outside world.[19]

At one point in Inanna's story, she has been stripped of everything, reduced to a hunk of meat impaled on a peg. How many of us, as analysts or as readers of literature, would exclaim upon encountering such an image for the first time in a client's dream or a new novel: Ah! A quest motif! How impressive! How inspiring! How heroic! If we were capable of exorcising from our minds an immediate Freudian phallocentric response, we might slide over into a quasi-feminist view of the internalized self-loathing of female flesh derived from an enculturated insistence on the female body as "nothing-but-matter." Archetypally interpreted, the ancient example of Inanna and the modern example of female protagonists in novels by women can teach us a re-vision of this image as one of active moving with and toward the self (in Jung's sense of wholeness, not as perfection or as development of the ego only). In Perera's words:

> Adult daughters of the father find it humiliating to see the bonds of weakness and self-hate which they share with their mothers. The insight nails them to reality, destroys their heroic, grandiose ego-ideal, and initiates a period of descent into depression as they suffer through their identity with the wounded, derogated feminine—in much the same way as Inanna rotted on the pole of the raped and derogated Ereshkigal.[20]

Then Perera eloquently links the archetypalist and the feminist perspectives, showing their mutually corroborative and informative capacities:

> Until the negative shadow qualities are seen in their wider cultural context, the daughter feels particularly cursed and hopeless. Here a feminist perspective is therapeutic. To see that all women have suffered cultural derogation means it is not one woman's

fault that she felt weak and inadequate in her own life and in supporting her own daughter. The archetypal cultural perspective removes the onus from the particular mother, and with it from a
cycle of unmet demands, of hurts, frustrations, and vengeances
which can persist into old age and prevent self-acceptance. The
feminist perspective seems to permit an attitude of sympathetic
witnessing to Self and mother that restructures the problem and
is analogous . . . to the action of Enki's mourners.[21]

Folded in together, the work of Pratt and Perera shows us an intriguing design: parallels between female imaginal processes in literature,
myth, and analysis cohering over several thousands of years and across
drastic differences in culture. It is still too early to see where all this is
taking us,[22] but for the moment this much can be said: through such
intermediation of the literary scholar's experience of the female writer/
character and the practicing analyst's experience of the female analysand around a single type of experience—the quest—we are led to hy-
pothesize striking differences between female and male. Woman's psy-
cho-spiritual development (or, in Jungian terms, her individuation)
does not proceed by way of a beloved man, as man's so often in literature and dream seems to proceed through the beloved or at least idealized woman. Rather, man in the life of woman seems a hindrance,
even a danger, to her questing self—not a helper, and certainly not a
psychopomp. A woman's return to society after fulfillment of her
quest does not mimic that of the male hero's proud reentry; instead,
she returns to find the price of reentry the sacrifice of that very self she
has so bravely sought and found.

In closing, I propose as absolutely essential a collaboration among
those of us engaged with the female imaginary: female analysts and
female academics; female analysands and female readers; the text of a
female life evoked, created, and interpreted in the interaction ritual of
analysis and the text of female life presented, represented, and recre-
ated in literature by women.[23] For even if all obstacles to female self-
understanding inherent in Jungian psychology were to be removed,
and access offered to all the treasures available there, another crucial
obstacle would still remain: the lack of communication, often the mutual suspicion—between women doing analysis, as analysts or analysands, and women doing literature, as teachers or students, as critics
or readers.

The analysts' wariness of literary analysis (i.e., their bias that theory
takes place only in the head, that literature is a product of consciousness, and that archetypes are universal and not gendered) and the academics' wariness of the practice of psychological analysis (i.e., their

bias that "therapy" is nothing-but-feeling and reinforces patriarchally constricting notions of female self and role, that dreams are invalid as data, and that archetypes are essentialist and ahistorical) need to be led out of the territory of shadow. Female analysts and academics have a common commitment to unconsciousness-raising, to valuing the imaginal life, to welcoming and honoring—and perhaps first *recognizing*—women's images, whether in dream or fantasy, myth or literature, criticism or theory. If corroborating correspondences emerge between the images of female life in analysis and in literature, such a synchronic, synchronistic source of knowledge would help us to know better the whole lives of women, including the seemingly gendered experience of noncorporeality and the possibility of a female imaginary.

If feminist archetypal theory does nothing more than dissolve the artificial boundaries between psychological analysis in the Jungian approach and literary analysis in the feminist one, and open access to the shadowland now standing between them, it will have demonstrated its value. And the evolution of feminist archetypal literary criticism will be rapid and revelatory.

# Notes

1. This is the standard definition found, for example, in the glossary appended to monographs published by Inner City Books, Toronto. Here it is cited from James A. Hall, *Jungian Dream Interpretation* (Toronto: Inner City Books, 1983), p. 121.

2. Estella Lauter and Carol Schreier Rupprecht, *Feminist Archetypal Theory: Interdisciplinary Re-Visions of Jungian Thought* (Knoxville: University of Tennessee Press, 1985), p. 3.

3. Ibid., pp. 3 and 22.

4. Shoshana Felman, "To Open the Question," in *Literature and Psychoanalysis—The Question of Reading: Otherwise*, a special issue of *Yale French Studies*, nos. 55/56 (1977): 8-9.

5. Ibid., p. 10.

6. See Carol Schreier Rupprecht, "Dreams and Literature: A Reader's

Guide," in *Sleep and Dreams: A Sourcebook*, ed. Jayne Gackenbach (New York: Garland, 1986).

7. Annis Pratt, "Spinning among the Fields: Jung, Frye, Lévi-Strauss and Feminist Archetypal Theory," in *Feminist Archetypal Theory*, p. 95.

8. Anyone unfamiliar with either Jung's writings on these subjects or the feminist critique of those writings may begin by consulting *Feminist Archetypal Theory*, especially the notes and bibliography, where reference will be found to such essential sources as the following: Naomi Goldenberg's "A Feminist Critique of Jung," *Signs: Journal of Women in Culture and Society* 2 (Winter 1976): 443-449; "Archetypal Theory After Jung," *Spring* (1975): 199-220; and "Feminism and Jungian Theory," *Anima* 3, no. 2 (Spring Equinox 1977): 14-17. See also Carol Christ, "Some Comments on Jung, Jungians, and the Study of Women," *Anima* 3, no. 2 (Spring Equinox 1977): 66-69; and reactions to Goldenberg and Christ in *Anima* 4, no. 1 (Fall Equinox 1977): 55-64. The especially pertinent passages from Jung's *Collected Works* are cited extensively in these articles as well as in Goldenberg's *The Changing of the Gods: Feminism and the End of Traditional Religions* (Boston: Beacon Press, 1979). Typical passages are cited frequently by Demaris Wehr in a chapter in *Feminist Archetypal Theory* titled "Religious and Social Dimensions of Jung's Concept of the Archetype: A Feminist Perspective," pp. 23-45.

9. Edward C. Whitmont, "Reassessing Femininity and Masculinity: A Critique of Some Traditional Assumptions," *Quadrant* 13, no. 2 (Fall 1980): 121.

10. See especially recent issues of *Chiron: A Review of Jungian Analysis,* ed. Nathan Schwartz-Salant and Murray Stein (Wilmette, Ill.: Chiron Publications).

11. Erich Neumann, *Art and the Creative Unconscious*, trans. Ralph Manheim, Bollingen Series (Princeton: Princeton University Press, 1974), p. 82.

12. Artemidorus Daldianus, *The Interpretation of Dreams*, trans. Robert J. White (Park Ridge, N.J.: Noyes, 1975), p. 24.

13. Ibid., p. 16.

14. Rosalind Cartwright, *A Primer on Sleep and Dreaming* (Reading, Mass.: Addison-Wesley, 1978), p. 22.

15. Claire Douglas, "The Animus: Old Women, Menopause and Feminist Theory," *The San Francisco Jung Institute Library Journal* 6, no. 3 (1986): 1-20.

16. Ibid., p. 2.

17. Pratt, "Spinning Among the Fields," p. 102.

18. Ibid., p. 103.

19. Sylvia Brinton Perera, "The Descent of Inanna: Myth and Therapy," in *Feminist Archetypal Theory*, p. 259, n. 69.

20. Sylvia Brinton Perera, *Descent to the Goddess: A Way of Initiation for Women* (Toronto: Inner City Books, 1981), p. 48.

21. Ibid., p. 49.

22. I am aware of many works of feminist archetypal literary criticism in progress that follow the lead of Estella Lauter's *Women as Mythmakers: Poetry and Visual Art by Twentieth-Century Women* (Bloomington: Indiana University Press, 1984). My own current project is an analysis of an Egyptian short story,

"My World of the Unknown," by contemporary author Alifa Rifaat, that demonstrates the fertility of comparative study of women's dreams in relation to literature by women.

23. Evidence that feminist archetypal activity has been gaining attention since the Hofstra conference in November 1986 includes the publication of Demaris Wehr's *Jung and Feminism: Liberating the Archetypes* (Boston: Beacon Press, 1987) and of Polly Young-Eisendrath and Florence Wiedemann's *Female Authority: Empowering Women Through Psychotherapy* (New York: Guilford Press, 1987). Although each book is distinct in its concerns and neither collaborative nor interdisciplinary, both offer new dimensions in feminist archetypal theory and practice as advocated here. See Estella Lauter's enthusiastic and insightful review in *The Women's Review of Books* 5, no. 8 (May 1988): 20-21.

# Beyond the Feminine Principle     Andrew Samuels

It is ironic, but not entirely unexpected, that my title here regarding gender and psyche owes a lot to Sigmund Freud. My main concerns are the following: first, the implications for analytical psychology of contemporary interest in femininity; second, an inquiry into the nature of femininity; and third, some reflections on the daughter–father relationship. But I also want to discuss the "post-Jungian" label because its ideas lie behind what I have to say here.[1] It must be admitted right away that post-Jungian analytical psychology exists in symbiotic relation with Jungian analytical psychology, just as postmodernism has no existence outside its contact with modernity. Nevertheless, the debt to Jung, to the "first generation" of Jungians, and to the Classical School should not blind us to the shift in overall point of view, or vertex,[2] that has been taking place in analytical psychology during the past twenty-five years. The post-Jungian vertex refers to an emotional involvement in the debates that it evokes. I mean that if one or more of the debates within analytical psychology seems of significance to you, then you are post-Jungian. Differing opinions define the field.

What has impressed me is the way in which the two apparently opposed Developmental and Archetypal Schools have reacted similarly in an iconoclastic, revisionary way to the expressed tenets of Classical analytical psychology. The two wings are attacking the center. I am not claiming that developmentally and archetypally oriented analytical psychologists agree upon their differences; they most certainly do not. But they share a common process. For example, both schools find the Classical concept of the self to be overweighted by emphasis on potential and a view of conflict conditioned by possibilities of resolution. Both schools have "earthed" the idea of individuation. In the Developmental School, this is seen as a lifelong process, discoverable even in infancy. In the Archetypal School, the psychologically infirm, psychopathic even, are regarded as capable of individuation. Crucially, both schools do not *strive* for "wholeness" as a psychological goal. Instead, a differentiation of psychic contents is stressed, equally well illustrated whether we speak of "polytheism"[3] or of the "deintegrates of the self."[4] If a person gives honest and full attention to his or her deintegrates, or energetically explores the specific images of a particular myth, unity takes care of itself. The post-Jungian vertex considers that investment in things that are less than perfect, whole, or complex constitutes a viable form of psychological functioning. Post-Jungians join with Guggenbühl-Craig's rejection of a "cult of perfection."[5]

Archetypal theory has also been rethought. A radical change has taken place in what we require of an image before we call it "archetypal." "Archetypal images" no longer have to be large, impressive, or decorous; what is archetypal is to be found in the eye of the beholder and not in a particular image itself. We can set aside preconceived schemes or hierarchies of archetypes; the archetypal experience is a state of mind. In Joseph Campbell's words, "your divinity is the only divinity there is."[6] We do not have to get hung up on the question of transpersonal, invisible, unknowable, noumenal, skeletal, crystalline, hypothetical so-called structures, held to be somehow "deeper" than ordinary human experience and imagery. When Hillman writes that "archetypal psychology cannot separate the personal and the collective unconscious,"[7] he is in the same place as unremittingly developmental writers such as Mary Williams, who also proclaimed the indivisibility of the personal and the collective unconscious.[8] There *is* a distinction: whereas Hillman searches for an archetypal perspective on the personal, writers such as Williams are committed to a personal perspective on the archetypal.

You will gather from these remarks that post-Jungian analytical psychology is part of a poststructural intellectual matrix—or, rather, that when I employ the term "post-Jungian," I am deconstructing analytical psychology. The key terms now are interaction—of psychic themes, patterns, images, behavior, emotions, instincts—and relativity—archetypes in the eye of the beholder, a dethroned self, and democratic individuation. *En passant* everything I have been saying applies clinically: microscopic examination of transference-countertransference interactions and befriending the image in all its particularity and specificity are both reactions to the same deficiencies in classical Jungian clinical technique.

The post-Jungian therapy of analytical psychology means that it is no longer necessary for analytical psychology to march in fours (four functions, four stages of life, four phases of analysis, four forms of the feminine psyche) or in reliably computable patterns of opposites. In this sense, post-Jungian analytical psychology has a good deal in common with post-Freudian psychoanalysis, whose elegant, pioneering metapsychological structures strike the contemporary theorist as reifications or as neurotic on Freud's part.

How, if at all, does contemporary preoccupation with what could be broadly called the "feminine principle" resonate with the post-Jungian phenomenon? I am not referring to the writings on women and "feminine psychology" by Jung and his early circle of followers. The problems with that body of work are well known and often repeated. But in the 1970s and 1980s, mainly in the United States, women in analytical psychology have set out to revise, or revolutionize, the early work. Such writers are struggling to be "post-Jungian" in their attempt to evaluate those of Jung's ideas that seem unsatisfactory or just plain wrong without dismissing Jung altogether. But in my view, when it comes to the subject of gender, the post-Jungian project has failed. First, I will look at the impact on analytical psychology of work on the "feminine principle," and then I will discuss the nature of femininity itself.

The necessary reason why there has been a concentration on the "feminine principle" in recent Jungian writing is that it has provided a means to celebrate the specificity of women's identity, life, and experience. In addition, the "feminine principle" helps to make a critique of culture out of personal confrontations with it.[9] The basic desire of modern Jungian writers on femininity has been to refuse and refute the denigration of women that is perceived in analytical psychology. They desire to bring the feminine gender in from the condescending margins and to promote an alternative philosophy of life to that expressed in the power institutions of a male-dominated society.

Taken as a whole, and I realize this is a generalization, Jungian feminism stands out from other varieties, with which I feel more in sympathy, in two main ways. Both of these stem from Jung's approach, resist eradication, and cause great difficulties. It is assumed that there is something eternal about femininity and, hence, about women; that women therefore display certain essential transcultural and ahistorical characteristics; and that these can be described in psychological terms. What is omitted is the ongoing role of the prevailing culture in the construction of the "feminine," and a confusion develops between what is claimed to be eternal and what is currently observed to be the case. It is here that the deadweight of the heritage of archetypal theory is felt—but as the mirror image of Jung's problem. He assumed that there is something eternal about women and, hence, about femininity.

The second point of disagreement between Jungian feminism and feminism generally has to do with the impression that much Jungian discourse on the "feminine" seems directed away from political and social action. Dwelling upon interiority and feeling becomes an end in itself. So, just as middle-class Victorian women were believed to be the repository of sensibility and confined to hearth and home, in the

Jungian manner of it, women in the nuclear age are meant to be mainly private creatures.

My concern is that much thinking and writing around the "feminine principle" has opened a secret door into analytical psychology for the return of what is, paradoxically and ironically, an overstructured approach to psyche, heavily dependent upon abstraction and decidedly moralistic. Because of this, the Jungian version of feminism that we encounter today is at odds with the post-Jungian vertex that I have outlined. What I suggest is that much contemporary Jungian effort in this area may be seen as far more of an imitation of Jung than was consciously intended. The conscious intention of rectifying Jung's mistakes and prejudices has been perverted.

Trawling the recent literature, I have been struck by the massiveness of the feminine problematic, signified in numerous phrases such as feminine elements of being, feminine modality of being, femininity of self, feminine ways of knowing, feminine authority, feminine assertion, feminine reflection, feminine dimensions of the soul, primal feminine energy pattern, feminine power, feminine response, feminine creativity, feminine mysteries, feminine body, feminine subjectivity, feminine transformation. I could have quadrupled the list; for ease of reference, I have subsumed all these terms under the general heading of the "feminine principle."

Something oppressive has come into being, not because what is claimed as the content of the "feminine principle" is oppressive but because celebrating the feminine has raised it to the status of an ego ideal, leading to a simple and pointless reversal of power positions. Further, it is the shadow of feminism generally to make women feel inadequate if they do not come up to the mark.

The "feminine principle" has acquired a hierarchical cast or aura. The problem is not with hierarchy itself, for we cannot but develop *ad hoc* ideational hierarchies. The problem is with prejudged hierarchy: graded, calibrated, a *cursus honorum* of the psyche. All the schools of depth psychology demonstrate this tendency, whether the "good" is labeled "the self," "genitality," "the image," "the imaginal," the "depressive position," "full object relations," "separation–individuation," "individuation," or the "feminine principle." If we fail to become conscious of our tendencies toward hierarchy, then we are tempted to forget that human life is not homogeneous and that each sphere of experience should rule in its own time.

We can get another angle on the problem of hierarchy by recalling that the numinosity of psychological theories lies to a great extent in their heuristic function of throwing light on present problems and guiding future action and practice. This is in contrast to their potential to provide answers to fundamental and fascinating questions of human nature. The idea of the "feminine principle" may therefore be evaluated pragmatically. Its truth would then be measured, in William James's words, by the degree to which it "helps us to get into satisfactory relations with other parts of our experience."[10] But the playing of femininity in a pragmatic and not an absolute key is a task waiting to be carried out.

One particular problem raised by the impact of the "feminine principle" on our hierarchies of ideas concerns its connection to holism. I am referring, for example, to attempts to use a "feminine" approach to proclaim an overcoming of the patriarchal scientism that had led to the old Cartesian dualisms. This is not to say that apparently "objective" science is not based on a gendered ideology; but the problem is truly about what holism does to our sense of culture.

Culture requires the marking off of certain places as special or sacred. That is why education consists to a great extent of learning to distinguish the different spaces and values of a complex civilization. A holistic viewpoint that can see everything only as connected with everything else seeks to do away with the spaces and strikes at the heart of such a civilization. Barbarism never comes into contact with these complexities; when it performs a "butterknife function"—that is, smooths things over—holism is the new barbarism.

The problem with holistic megaimages (such as a "world-soul")[11] is not that they are wrong. How could they be wrong? Nor are they unrooted in experience. The problem is that the more all-encompassing, the more utopian, the "bigger" the image, the more it devours other images, other people's images. The "feminine principle" can be such a megaimage.

A holistic vision perceives the world as inextricably united. Though I *do* doubt that such a phenomenon exists to the extent wished for, personal experiences of oneness mean that I partly share the holistic ideal. But holistic thinking tends to be utopian—what Jung referred to as "preaching" about unity and wholeness (*CW* 18: par. 1817, p. 819). There is a certain compulsiveness that gets attached to holism that then becomes an attempt to deny even the pain of *rupture*, to use Lacanian language.

So far, I have been explaining my claim that the overall effect upon analytical psychology of work on the "feminine principle" has been unfortunate. Now I want to raise and discuss constructively the question: "what is femininity?" It is difficult to discuss the subject at all without acknowledging a distinction between sex and gender, allowing for some overlap as well. *Sex* (male and female) refers to anatomy and the biological substrate to behavior, to the extent that there is one.

*Gender* (masculine and feminine) is a cultural or psychological term, arising in part from observations and identifications within the family, hence relative and flexible, and capable of sustaining change. Now in some Jungian approaches, what can happen is that a form of determinism creeps in and the invariant nature of gender is assumed, just as if gender characteristics and qualities were as fixed as sexual ones. The history of women shows that change is possible just because the social meaning of womanhood is malleable. But when this is ignored, the possibilities of change—other than as part of ordinary maturation and individuation—are lost.

Is there such a thing as a "feminine psychology"? Men and women do have experiences that vary markedly. But it is a huge step from that to a claim that the way in which they actually function is sufficiently different psychologically for us to speak of two distinct psychologies. The evidence concerning this is muddled and hard to assess. For instance, the discovery that boys build towers and girls build enclosures when they are given bricks can be taken to show a similarity of functioning rather than difference (which is what is usually claimed). Both sexes are interested in their bodies and, possibly, in the differences between male and female bodies. Both sexes express that interest in the same way—symbolically, in play with bricks. Or, put in another form, *both sexes approach the difference between the sexes in the same way*. The differences that we can see in gender role and gender identity can then be looked at as having arisen in the same manner. The psychological processes by which a man becomes an aggressive business executive and a woman a nurturing homemaker are the same, and one should not be deceived by the dissimilarity in the end product.

From a woman's point of view, what I have been describing is not a relation to an innate femininity or to an innate masculinity. Rather, I am talking of her relation to the phenomenon of difference. Then we can consider the social or cultural structures erected on the basis of that difference. Each woman lives her life in interplay with such difference. This may lead to questions of gender role (for example, how a woman can best assert herself in our culture), but these questions need not be couched in terms of innate femininity or innate masculinity, or in terms of some feminine–masculine spectrum. Rather, they may be expressed in terms of difference. In the example, the difference between assertion and compliance needs to be seen as different from the difference between men and women. Or, put another way, whatever differences there might be between women and men are not illuminated or signified by the difference between compliance and assertion.

I am aware that men are said to have access to the "feminine," or to the "feminine principle," and I used to think that such an unremittingly interior view was the jewel in the Jungian crown. Now I am not so sure for, again, I sense the muddle between the fixed and eternal on the one hand and the cultural and mutable on the other. If we are attempting to describe psychological performance, we have to be sure why terms with gendered associations and appellation are being used at all. Otherwise we end up with statements such as that "masculine" assertion is available to women via their relation to the animus, or "feminine" reflection in the man via his anima. But assertion is part of woman, and reflection is part of man. What is more, there are so many kinds of assertion open to women that even current attempts to speak of a woman's assertion as "feminine" rather than "masculine" is still to bind her as tightly as ever. Let us begin to speak merely of assertion. Gender engenders confusion, and this is made worse when gender terms are used exclusively in an inner way. When we speak of "inner" femininity in a man, we bring in all the unnecessary problems of reification and substantive abstraction that I have described. We still cannot assume that psychological functioning is different in men and women, though we know that the creatures "man" and "woman" are different.

The question of "difference" brings us to a point where we can play back these ideas into analytical psychology. From Jung's overall theory of opposites, which hamstrings us by its insistence on contrasexuality ("masculine" assertion via the animus, etc.), we can extract the theme of difference. The notion of difference, I suggest, can help us in the discussion about gender—not innate opposites that lead us to create an unjustified psychological division expressed in lists of antithetical qualities, each list yearning for the other so as to become whole. Not what differences between women and men there are, or have always been. (If we pursue that, we end up captured by our captivation and obsession with myth and with the eternal, the burdensome part of the legacy from Jung that I mentioned earlier.) But rather the fact, image, and social reality of difference itself—what difference itself is like, what the experience of difference is like. Not what a woman *is* but what being a woman is *like*. Not the archetypal structuring of woman's world but woman's personal experience in today's world. Not the meaning of a woman's life but her experience of her life. Each person remains a man or a woman, but what that means to each becomes immediate and relative, and hence capable of generational expansion and cultural challenge. All the time, the question of "masculine" and "feminine" remains in suspension—the bliss of not knowing, in David Miller's words.[12]

We also need to question whether heterosexuality itself should be taken as innate and therefore as something fundamental and beyond debate, or whether it, too, has a nonbiological dimension. I am thinking of Freud's perception of an innate bisexuality followed later by heterosexuality. Jung's view was that man and woman are each incomplete without the other; heterosexuality is therefore a given. In this sense, he differs from Freud's emphasis on bisexuality as the natural state of human beings. In Freud's approach, sexual identity arises from the enforced twin demands of reproduction and society. What I have been arguing shifts the concept of bisexuality from something undifferentiated (polymorphous or polyvalent) into a vision of there being available to all a variety of positions in relation to gender role, without recourse to the illusion of androgyny.

I would like to say a few words now about the literal and the metaphoric relations between anatomy and psychology because I will be talking again about this toward the end. A literal determinism has seduced those who seek to make a simple equation between body and psyche. We do not really know what the relation between them is, but it is probably indirect. The fact that a penis penetrates and a womb contains tells us absolutely nothing about the psychological qualities of those who actually possess such organs. One does not have to be a clinician to recognize penetrative women and receptive men or to conclude that psychology has projected its fantasies onto the body.

Animus and anima images are not of men and women because animus and anima qualities are masculine and feminine. Rather, for the individual woman or man, anatomy is a metaphor for the richness and potential of the "other." A man will imagine what is other to him in the symbolic form of a woman—a being with another anatomy. A woman will symbolize what is foreign to her in terms of the kind of body she does not herself have. The so-called contrasexuality is more something "contrapsychological"; anatomy is a metaphor for that. But anatomy is absolutely *not* a metaphor for any particular emotional characteristic or set of characteristics. That depends on the individual and on whatever is presently outside her or his conscious grasp and hence in need of being represented by a personification of the opposite sex. The difference between you and your animus or anima has to be more than the difference between you and a man or woman. (I realize that I am discussing animus and anima in their personified forms, but I bring them in as illustrative of the indirect nature of the relation between body and psyche.) What I am saying is that "metaphor" can be as seductively misleading and one-sided as "literalism." Sometimes, it is claimed that "masculine" and "feminine" are metaphors ("just" metaphors) for two distinct *weltanschauungen*, or the typical styles of operating of the two cerebral hemispheres. Why can we not just talk of *weltanschauungen*, or just of hemispheres? When we bring in either masculinity and femininity or maleness and femaleness, we are projecting a dichotomy that certainly exists in human ideation and functioning onto convenient receptors for the projections. Arguing that masculinity and femininity should be understood nonliterally, as having nothing to do with bodily men and bodily women in a social context, may be taken as an effort to come to terms with what is lost by the projection; but this has not led to a recollection of it. All the other divisions that we know about—rational/irrational, Apollonian/Dionysian, classical/romantic, digital/analogic, and so forth—all these exist in every human being. They cannot conveniently be assigned by gender (or sex), save by the kind of bifurcated projection I have depicted.

Why do we make such a projection? Surely it is more than a question of language. It could be because we find difficulty in living with both sides of our murky human natures. We import a degree of certainty and clarity, and hence reduce anxiety, by making the projection. In summary, it is in this projection that we find the origin of dualist ambitions to construct distinct psychologies for the two sexes: a failure to withdraw the projection leading to an attempt to use "masculinity" and "femininity" solely as metaphors. As I said earlier, the back door is opened for the pernicious misuse of Jung's theory of opposites as a patriarchal ploy.

I would like now to explain the experiential background that has given rise to what I have said here, especially why I have concentrated so much on the question of difference. I will be talking about the personal realm, but the personal is not a problem when it is used imaginatively. In my practice, I have been seeing several women who occupy a cultural and psychological position somewhere between the traditional and the contemporary. Two emotions stand out. First, their sense of failure at fulfilling neither the ancient nor the modern womanly ideal, the feminine principle functioning as a persecuting ideal. Second, and this is what I want to explore, their unconscious or conscious preoccupation with motherhood, whether in its presence or its absence in their lives, such preoccupation heavily coloring these women's images of femininity. Over time, I became aware of a common thread of experience for these women in relation to their fathers and, as a consequence of that, a common and troubled attitude to their mothers. I have developed an interest in how the fathers, overtly different from their daughters, have something to do with the daughters' covert differences from their mothers, which they have to discover at some time.

The following remarks on the father–daughter relationship are apt for several reasons: remembrance of the father, which is the occasion that has brought us all here; the subject of my talk; and the need to root ourselves imaginatively in what happens in lived and bodily personal experience. It is that rootedness that helps to keep the so-called meta-

phoric and the so-called literal in balance so that the notion of transformation does not prevent us, in Sylvia Perera's words, from "dealing
with things on their own matrix level."[13] It is that rootedness that prevents an intellectual enterprise from becoming abstract. This is not really to neglect all the other familial relationships in this account of
womanly experience but merely to focus this particular set of remarks
specifically on the father–daughter relationship.

We know from Jung that kinship libido has something to do with
personality enhancement and enrichment. If incest fantasy is acted out,
it becomes destructive. But if it is not present as an actual, concrete,
tangible, bodily feeling in the real family, the literal family, then I do
not think the kind of growth a girl can get out of her metaphoric relation with her father (or a boy from his mother) will take place. As
Robert Bly says, "the divine is connected with matter";[14] the ultraviolet needs the infrared.[15] Plain speaking about the body and about sexuality is neither prurient nor titillating, neither offensive nor embar-
rassing; it is necessary.

Now, boys probably do have an easier time of it than girls, because
their mothers are so used to being sexual in relation to children of either sex that they are not as frightened of their incestuous sexuality
toward their sons as fathers generally are toward their daughters. You
can see this cultural phenomenon in your own lives and, if you are
clinicians, in the lives of your patients. Look at the typical ways in
which fathers muck up the development of their daughters by not being able to cope with the erotic involvement. The first and most obvious way is actual incest. The father may not realize what he is doing,
or he has a personality and background that make it impossible for him
to hold the balance between the sexual and the symbolic, the literal and
the metaphoric. Here, we might reflect that the father who bathes his
daughter and the father who touches her up in the bath are the two
sides, substance and shadow, of that new phenomenon: the involved
father. But there are many, many more ways for fathers to damage
their daughters, and actual incest is the tip of the iceberg.

Numerous clinical problems stem from an *insufficiency* of kinship
libido or incest fantasy, not an excess of it. The father who cannot
attain an optimally erotic relation with his daughter, with the actual
bodily sensations involved in that, is damaging her almost as badly as
the father who cannot restrain himself. And you see it happening in so
many ways: excessive prohibition about her activities with boys, rules
about coming in at 8 o'clock, mocking her sexuality, making fun of
her infatuations with pop stars. These are all part of the incest theme.
She is trying to grow by close contact with Michael Jackson. If her
father says, "Take that dreadful poster down," then he is damaging her
just as surely as if he puts his hand up her skirt. Mockery, strictness,

and plain uptightness are reflected in a lack of physical involvement from the time that the girl is a baby. Lack of physical contact between father and daughter is an enormously important contemporary issue; I hope that we can begin to speak of an optimal erotic relation between them and, hence, of the pathology of a failure to achieve that. Eventually, the daughter and her father have to renounce their admitted longings for each other, and such mutual renunciation is itself affirmation of erotic viability.

I must stress that this "erotic playback," as I call it, is not at all dependent on whether the father is nice and understanding toward his daughter. I have encountered numerous women who have had erotic playback from fathers who do not fit a bourgeois description of a "good" father. My idea is that the father's literal erotic playback to his daughter permits her to break out of the bondage of the metaphorical equation: woman = mother. This equation is quite the most powerful element underlying the belief in both women and men that there is a distinct "feminine psychology." The erotic acts as a kind of liberation for the daughter so that she can begin to explore other, nonuterine female paths for herself, and maybe paths that cannot be sexed or gendered in advance: the spiritual path, the vocational path, the path of solidarity with the travails of other women, the path of sexual expression. Erotic playback promotes an attempt to challenge and overthrow the constricting aspects of the notion of a separate "feminine psychology" or "feminine principle."

Women have suffered enormously from the requirement that they be selfless creatures who relate, who are responsive to the needs of others, who react but do not act. It is true that, as *mothers*, something like that has to be done. But as *persons*, women can sniff out other vistas and ways of being. Strange as it may seem, it is the young woman's apperception of herself as a sexual creature, facilitated by her erotic connection to her father, that enables her to spin more or less at will through a variety of psychological pathways, "keeping it unresolved"[16] and enjoying the widest possible spectrum of meanings inherent in the ideogram "woman." The father's first fertilization helped to make the female baby. His second helps to bring forth the female adult who is free to drop her father when and if she needs to do so. And that female adult can, now more than ever before, be a multifaceted woman-person, not only free *from* symbiotic two-person relating with her mother, but free *to* grow in all manner of unpredictable and exciting ways beyond the feminine principle.

In a sense, I have been doing something post-Jungian in this celebration of the body in its literal, untransformed state. My claim is that untransformation, literalness, tangible physical motion are all required before transformation becomes a possibility. Metaphor can go too far, become stuck and defensive—even literal! Maybe it is time to consider whether the Jungian stress on metaphoric *transformation* might have become, first, a consummation devoutly to be wished, perhaps a badge of honor, then an addiction, and finally a restrictive moral preoccupation sometimes encapsulated by uterine associations as a "feminine" capacity. Every realm and level of existence is equally valid. All or any levels can be spiritual or transpersonal. What I am suggesting is that we try to know and value something—the body—on its own matrix level. To value the body does not require its transformation into spirit, meaning, communication, dream body, imaginal anatomy, psychosomatic symptom, or metaphor. We cannot realize spirit by the denigration and destruction of matter; that is the way of the anorexic. Things will deepen if *they* want to. Then there may occur a transformation from the sensual, earthy, and concrete to the purposeful and symbolic. We may be able to interpret that, if *we* want to.

*Acknowledgments*

I would like to thank Fred Plaut and Coline Covington for their helpful comments on the first draft, made at short notice. Rosie Parker provided a detailed critique of the whole presentation; it was really an extension of her creative influence on my evolving ideas in this area. Responsibility for the views expressed is, of course, mine.

# Notes

1. In my book *Jung and the Post-Jungians* (Boston and London: Routledge and Kegan Paul, 1985), pp. 1-22, I proposed a classification of post-Jungian analytical psychology into three schools: the Developmental, Classical, and Archetypal Schools. The Developmental School sought points of contact with Freudian psychoanalysis; clinical emphasis was placed on the analysis of in-

fancy via transference–countertransference interactions. The Classical School, by no means ossified, continued to work in the traditional way of Jung and his close followers. The Archetypal School, not identical with archetypal psychology per se, does nevertheless make use of its insights. Such a classification is a creative falsehood in that no one analyst fits neatly into any one category. But it does serve as a useful orientation. What is more, it is possible to use the classification imaginatively and metaphorically, as referring to inner strands of thought and practice within a single analyst. One special feature of the book was to point up the ways in which the Developmental School and the Archetypal School, apparently so different, share a common process when they come to evaluate Jung's original work.

2. See W. Bion, *Transformations* (London: Tavistock, 1965).

3. See James Hillman, "Psychology: Monotheistic or Polytheistic," *Spring* (1971): 193-208.

4. See Michael Fordham, *New Developments in Analytical Psychology* (London: Routledge and Kegan Paul, 1957).

5. Adolf Guggenbühl-Craig, *Eros on Crutches: Reflections on Psychopathy and Amorality* (Dallas: Spring Publications, 1980), p. 25.

6. Joseph Campbell, statement made at the "C. G. Jung and the Humanities" conference, Hofstra University, November 1986.

7. James Hillman, *Loose Ends: Primary Papers in Archetypal Psychology* (Dallas: Spring Publications, 1975), pp. 179-180.

8. See Mary Williams, "The Indivisibility of the Personal and Collective Unconscious," in *Analytical Psychology: A Modern Science*, ed. Michael Fordham et al. (London: Heinemann, 1973).

9. By *culture* I mean an assemblage, limited in time and space, of the heritage of a community of whatever size—social, material, mental, spiritual, artistic, religious, and ritualistic. "Culture" carries the connotation of a group that has, at some level, developed its own identity. By *society* (or similar words such as social or societal) I mean the political and economic structure of a particular culture, specifically its intergroup and interpersonal arrangements and how power is distributed therein.

10. William James, *Pragmatism* (London: Longmans, 1911), p. 157.

11. See Edward C. Whitmont, "Nature, Symbol and Imaginal Reality," *Spring* (1971): 64-83.

12. David Miller, statement made at the "C. G. Jung and the Humanities" conference.

13. Sylvia Brinton Perera, personal communication at the Ghost Ranch conference on "The Body in Analysis," New Mexico, June 1985.

14. Robert Bly, statement made at the "C. G. Jung and the Humanities" conference.

15. James Hillman, statement made at the "C. G. Jung and the Humanities" conference.

16. Edward S. Casey, statement made at the "C. G. Jung and the Humanities" conference.

# The Unconscious in a Postmodern Depth Psychology        Paul Kugler

## The Problematic

Perhaps nothing is more fundamental to a "depth" psychology than the concept of the *unconscious*. But what is meant by the unconscious? Is it a psychic realm topographically located "below" consciousness? Is it a psychopathology characterized by a disturbance of consciousness? Is it the representation of biological drives? Is it the locus of the imagination? The Transcendent? The Other? The Real? The Unknown? Or, is it "just" a fiction used to account for the unaccountable in personality theory? why has so much been written about the "X," the unknown element in the equation of individuality?

The problem of defining the unconscious in more than abstract terms is difficult, if not impossible, because by definition the unconscious is the *not-known*. In defining the unconscious, Jung writes: "The concept of the unconscious *posits nothing*, it designates only my *unknowing*."[1] And again in another passage, he notes: "The unconscious is a piece of Nature our mind cannot comprehend."[2] Any definition of the unconscious is simply an imago, a representation in consciousness of the not-known. Freud, in his classic paper on "The Unconscious" (1915), presents the following reflection of the problematics of coming to know this "psychic realm": "How are we to arrive at a knowledge of the unconscious? It is of course only as something conscious that we know it, after it has undergone transformation or translation into something conscious."[3]

To arrive at a knowledge of something unconscious, that content must first be psychically *represented* to consciousness as a word, an image, an emotion, or inscribed in the flesh as a psychosomatic symptom. These (re)presentations in consciousness constitute the textuality of our psychic life and are the primary focus of depth psychology. When reading and analyzing these psychic manuscripts we are, paradoxically, both author and critic of our own text. But what is implied in reading our "own" psychic images as "other"? How is an interpretation of the unconscious possible? Who *is* the author of our psychic

307

text? Who *is* the intended reader? And furthermore, on what "principle" will we "ground" the act of analytic interpretation?

To address these questions let us turn to the field of literary theory, where we find the most extensive analysis of the relation of textuality, authorship, and interpretation. We will begin with a review of some of the major shifts in theories of representation (texts) and interpretation (reading and writing) that have occurred during this century, with a particular focus on the questions that postmodern theory raises for a depth psychology.

## Modernism: A Focus on Authorial Intention

Over the past fifty years, a revolution has occurred in the field of textual interpretation. In the early part of this century, the modernist school of literary theory was guided by the assumption that a close scholarly reading of original manuscripts, biographies, and histories would lead to an understanding of the so-called true interpretation of a text. This form of "empirical" criticism imagined the subjectivity of the interpreter to be a transparent, focusable lens, through which a detached consciousness could view a stable text. The reader, as detached observer, focused primarily on an analysis of the author's *intention* as the means for deciding which of many possible meanings was the "true" interpretation of the text. The modernist hermeneutic was guided by the implicit assumption that the true meaning was to be found in authorial intention. What the creator intended in the process of composing the text is its "real" meaning.

In depth psychology, during this same period, a similar interpretative attitude was cultivated in the interpretation of dreams. The analyst, as detached observer, "objectively" viewed and interpreted the patient's dream text through a knowledge of the person's psychiatric history, psychodynamics, and free associations. Through an "objective" analysis of the clinical material, it was thought to be possible to discover the patient's unconscious intentions and, therefore, the "true" meaning of the dream text. This depth psychological approach is particularly characteristic of classical Freudian psychoanalysis.

## New Criticism: Textual Imagery as Constituent of Form

In the 1940s and 1950s, the modernist movement gave way to a new approach known as "New Criticism." Drawing heavily upon the earlier work of the modernist writers, the New Critics shifted the focus of textual analysis from history and content to form, emphasizing "imagery" as the constituent of form itself. A text was now viewed as a complex system of "forms" analyzable at different levels of generality. For example, a poem was analyzable on multiple levels—from the specific components of a poetic image or line, through the poem's genre, to that genre's place in the system of literature. The strategy adopted by the New Critics emphasized the autonomy of the text and the presence of meaning within it, shifting the reader's focus from authorial intention to a close examination of the text itself. The previous use of historical and biographical information about the author was now considered to be problematic and guilty of committing the "intentional fallacy." How could anyone really know the intention of Milton or Blake? A text reveals its own significance without needing historical or biographical information to enlighten it.

The New Critics, especially Brooks, Wimsatt, and Beardsley, produced a powerful methodology.[4] They focused the reader's attention on the conflicts and resolutions *in the text*, especially emphasizing the "unity" and "coherence" that inevitably seemed to emerge out of these internal tensions. This new style of reading attempted to disclose the existence of collective human patterns, not confined to particular times, places, and biographical facts. Where modernism reflected many of Freud's original interpretative attitudes, New Criticism echoes many of Jung's: the autonomy of the psyche, the focus on the emerging image patterns, the move to the deeper collective themes, the discovery of paradox and reconciliation, and the belief in the ultimate unity and coherence of the psyche. Although these two styles of analysis may be familiar today to many depth psychologists, for the literary and philosophical avant-garde, they are considered outdated and problematic.

In the move from modernism to postmodernism, these older styles of interpretation have been called into question, and in the process, many important issues have emerged. Not only has the author's intention become a disputable point, but the text's autonomy, unity, and ability to reveal some referential truth have also been seriously questioned.

## Structuralism: The Primacy of Structural Relations

The most significant school of interpretation to emerge after modernism and the New Critics was structuralism. The structuralists drew heavily on the work of Ferdinand de Saussure, especially his *Course in General Linguistics*. Perhaps Saussure's most significant contribution lies in his shift of attention away from the historical, etymological, and referential aspects of linguistics to a focus on how language functions as a collective system of signs. For Saussure, the basic units of language—sound and meaning, signifier and signified—are defined systematically through internal differences rather than by some correspondence to the material world or to etymological history. To demonstrate the importance of structural relations, as opposed to the previous focus on the substantive and historical aspects, Saussure suggests we compare the system of language to a game of chess. Historical and material changes in a chess piece do not affect the "meaning" of the piece. Rather, the meaning of each piece is generated by the role the piece plays and how it is used in *relation* to the other pieces. If, for example, we use fifty-year-old ivory chessmen instead of new plastic ones, the change in material substance and the historical factor have no effect on the system of structural relations, the rules of the game. If, however, we change the number of chessmen, we alter the structure or "grammar" of the game. Saussure concluded that "language is a form not a substance." Meaning is a product of structural relations, not material history.[5]

Saussure envisioned a new science called semiology that, using structural linguistics as its model, could describe all cultural phenomena through a study of the life of signs within society. From Saussure's structural linguistics, a new interpretative vision emerged in which representational qualities (i.e., the sign's ability to mirror nature or the human psyche) became much less important than how words and images work as a system of structural relations.

In 1949, Lévi-Strauss applied the structuralist insights to psychoanalysis, reformulating the Freudian topographical model of the mind. The phenomenon that Freud had earlier referred to as the "unconscious" Lévi-Strauss now subdivided into two distinct aspects. The first he referred to as the "subconscious," and the second retained the name "unconscious." In his revised formulation, the subconscious consisted of psychic "substances," memories, and imagos collected in the course of an individual life, whereas the unconscious was conceived of as "empty" and limited to the imposition of structural laws. Lévi-Strauss's reformulation is almost identical to Jung's earlier subdivision of the unconscious into a personal aspect composed of imagos and a collective aspect consisting of archetypal structures (*CW* 9i). The unconscious, for Jung and the structuralists, functions like an empty stomach that structurally digests the individual psychic substances taken in during the course of the person's life. Lévi-Strauss describes his reformulation of the Freudian unconscious this way:

One could therefore say that the subconscious is the individual lexicon where each of us accumulates the vocabulary of his personal history, but that this vocabulary only acquires signification, for ourselves and for others, in so far as the unconscious organizes it according to the laws of the unconscious, and thus makes of it a discourse. . . . The vocabulary is less important than the structure.[6]

The similarity between Lévi-Strauss's structural model and Jung's archetypal model can be seen in the following description of the function of the archetype, written by Jung some twenty years earlier.

It is necessary to point out once more that archetypes are not determined as regards their content, but only as regards their form and then only to a very limited degree. A primordial image is determined as to its content only when it has become conscious and is therefore filled out with the material of conscious experience. Its form, however, as I have explained elsewhere, might perhaps be compared to the axial system of a crystal, which as it were, performs the crystalline structure in the mother liquid, although it has no material existence of its own. . . . The archetype in itself is empty and purely formal, nothing but a *facultas praeformandi*. (*CW* 9i: par. 155, p. 79)

In 1953, Jacques Lacan, one of the most influential French psychoanalysts, adopted Lévi-Strauss's revised structural model, introducing into psychoanalytic terminology a tripartite system for "ordering" the personality. Struggling with the problematics of knowledge and self-knowledge, Lacan divided psychic experience into three orders of being: the "real," the "imaginary," and the "symbolic."[7] The object-as-such attempting to be known, Lacan refers to as the "real," and the representation of that object, the psychic imago or word, constitutes the "imaginary." On the other hand, the "symbolic" order performs a purely structural function, organizing psychic representations into meaningful units. The imagos (words and images) are structured by the symbolic order, analogous to syntax organizing lexical elements into semantically meaningful units.

## Depth Psychology's Turn Toward Language

The importance of Lacan's contribution to theories of textual interpretation lies in his emphasis on the process through which personality development is dependent on and invented in a matrix of culturally determined "symbols" (signifiers) making up our textual environment. For without the capacity for the self to represent itself, either as an image or as a word, and thereby look back at itself from another vantage point, the construction of personality and its characteristic capacity for consciousness and self-reflexivity would be impossible. The acquisition of "language" (i.e., the psychic capacity for representation) results in three significant effects. In the first place, by acquiring the ability to name an experience, the individual is able to symbolize himself or herself by replacing lived experience with a text, and thus gain consciousness of and distance from the immediacy of an event. This process establishes a realm of representations that *mediates* experience. Not only does this textual realm mediate the object world, but it also mediates self-experiences by establishing a self-representation in language through use of the first-person pronoun "I." Without this capacity for self-representation and self-consciousness, a person could not recognize his or her own self-imago in a lived dream and symbolize it in a dream text.

A second consequence of acquiring language is that through the capacity to *re-present* itself in a separate order of being, the personality is divided into an *experiential self* and a *textual self*. The textual self is a by-product of the capacity for representation. By assimilating and being assimilated by language, the speaker increasingly identifies with the textual self, the first-person pronoun "I," which is only a representative—a stand-in, in the realm of language—for the more primary self of experience, excluded from the realm of representation.[8]

This exclusion of the experiential self from the realm of representation leads to a third effect of language acquisition: the appearance of an unconscious order of experience. Although mediation is necessary for consciousness and self-consciousness, the price paid for textual mediation is the creation of a certain unbridgeable distance between text and original lived experience. The realm of unmediated experience is the realm of the unconscious.

The structuralist project focused primarily on the representational realm and worked toward developing an objective science of interpretation capable of revealing the symbolic structures underlying all psychic narratives. By the late 1950s and early 1960s, Roland Barthes, Claude Lévi-Strauss, and Jacques Lacan had extended Saussure's semiological approach to anthropology, literature, culture, and psychoanalysis. The structuralist approach maintained enormous popularity throughout the late 1960s and 1970s, until it gradually began to self-destruct from within. In one of his late works, Barthes himself began to question the structuralist tendency to catalogue all the world's narratives within a single set of archetypal structures. He concluded that the structuralist project was a task as exhaustive as it was ultimately undesirable, because through the process, the text loses its difference.[9]

In abandoning the search for structural similarities, for archetypal patterns between texts, Barthes was partially responding to a new continental philosophy rooted in the writings of Hegel and Nietzsche and epitomized in the work of the French poststructuralist philosopher Jacques Derrida. The new mode of interpretation called "deconstruction" has seriously called into question our Western metaphysical tendency to ground the act of interpretation in "absolutes" such as Truth, Reality, Self, Center, Unity, Origin, and even Author. Our Western style of thought has been committed to a belief in some "ultimate" presence, truth, or reality with a fixed, unimpeachable meaning. This fixed meaning acts as the unquestionable "ground" from which to interpret or explain all the other elements in our systems of thought.

The tendency to ground the act of interpretation in a transcendental signified is characteristic not only of Western metaphysics but of depth psychology as well. Psychoanalysis has traditionally grounded clinical diagnosis and therapeutic understanding on just such absolutes. To understand a symptom, we look to one of these ultimates to give authority to our diagnosis and interpretation. We look for the "origin" of the symptom, or we attempt to discover what "really" happened in the patient's "history," or we view the symptom from the point of view of the "self" and its innate tendency to "center" or bring "unity" to the personality. For these "absolutes" to perform their interpretative function, they must themselves transcend the very clinical phenomenon they seek to explain.

But how is this transcendence accomplished? How do we "bootstrap" the clinical material to a therapeutic interpretation? We do so by *temporally* positing the "absolute" as being either anterior or posterior (or both) to the clinical material being interpreted. The meaning of the clinical phenomenon is then either causally derived from or teleologically moved toward this first principle. Consider for a moment how depth psychology approaches a dream. To understand its significance, we interpret the dream according to a posited *a priori* or *a posteriori* absolute. If the therapist is committed to *a priori* ultimates, the significance of the case material comes about through a reduction to such absolutes as drives, the Oedipus complex, archetypes, biochemistry, the environment, family systems, childhood traumas, the analytic frame, and so on. Notice how all these absolutes are temporally located in the past.

The authority for the clinical interpretation might also be grounded in a posited absolute located in the future. For example, the clinical material might be interpreted as moving toward and referring to *a posteriori* ultimates such as the self, archetypes, wholeness, unity, spirit, soul, death, and so forth. For these first principles to perform their explanatory function, they cannot be implicated in the very system of thought and language they are being used to explain; nor can their meaning have the same semantic status as the other meanings within the system. Their semantic status must be something like the "meaning of meaning" or the "metaphor of metaphors." These *a priori* and *a posteriori* "god" terms function as the linchpins for our Western theories of clinical interpretation.

In the process of constructing a therapeutic hermeneutic, even one "purely" phenomenological and descriptive in nature, one term in this category of privileged elements is seen as the "origin" of all the other terms. For example, in traditional Jungian psychology the "self" performs this function, whereas in classical Freudian theory it is performed by the concept of "drives." Notice, however, that once the question of "origins" is evoked, it is difficult to think of an origin without wanting to ask further about the origin of the posited origin. Here we experience how language has subtly trapped us inside the logic of the "origins" metaphor, unconsciously elevating the term to a transcendental status that now attempts to account for all the other terms. The originary, explanatory principle explains everything except itself and therefore is not the *ultimate* explanatory principle. This same problem exists for absolutes given teleological status.

## The Twilight of Our God Terms

The dissolution of absolutes in our theories of knowledge had already begun at the end of the last century with Nietzsche's declaration that "God is dead." Nietzsche wrote:

> *We have killed him*—you and I. All of us are his murderers. But how have we done this? How were we able to drink up the sea? Who gave us the sponge to wipe away the entire horizon? What did we do when we unchained the earth from the sun? Whither is it moving now? Whither are we moving now? Away from all suns? Are we not plunging continually? Backward, sideward, forward, in all directions? Is there any up or down left? Are we not straying as through an infinite nothing? . . . God is dead. God remains dead. And we have killed him.[10]

The process of factoring time into a phenomenological understanding has disclosed that the ultimate grounds of Western knowledge all lapse into a temporal regress or progress. For example, Freud and the modernists attempted to explain the meaning of a text through authorial intention; Jung and the structuralists later tried to account for meaning and interpretation through unconscious psychic structures. These solutions are not solutions at all, because they do not account for the "authority of the author" or the "structurality of structure."

These accounts simply posit the author or structure as existing in time *prior* to the emergence of the text, psyche, or system of thought.

## Postmodernism: An Epistemological Crisis

The postmodern critique of the rhetorical foundations of Western epistemology has led to the realization that all conscious knowledge, as well as our theories of knowledge, work through figurative structures that render them ambiguous and indeterminate. The reader of any text is suspended between the literal and the metaphoric significance of its words, unable to choose between the two meanings and thus thrown into the dizzying semantic indeterminacy of the text.

The movement from structuralism to poststructuralism is a shift from seeing the text as a closed entity with definite, decipherable meanings to seeing the text as irreducibly plural, oscillating between literal and figural significance that can never be fixed to a single center, essence, or meaning. Contrary to the structuralist's desire to construct an objective, interpretative science, the postmodern theorist makes no such effort to create a terminology transparent to its truths. For we have come to realize that language of any sort—be it literary, philosophy, clinical, or scientific—does not allow for a transparent view to the so-called empirical world. Our theories of interpretation have no location outside language, neither objective nor empirical, and can never be a ground but only a mediation.

The modernist fantasy of an objective hermeneutic imagined the reader's subjectivity to be a transparent focusable lens through which a detached consciousness viewed the *content* of a stable text. This empiricist idea continued through the structuralist tradition, except that the focus of the "detached" observer shifted from the content of the text to its structure. This view changed dramatically with the advent of postmodernism. As the Cartesian subject–object dichotomy began to dissolve, so too did the traditional image of the separation between readers and texts, consciousness and language, meaning and the world. No longer are texts viewed as objects with a stable meaning, for in the end it is language that speaks in texts, in all its swarming "polysemic" plurality, and not the author.[11] When thinking, speaking, or writing, it is impossible for consciousness to escape the power and influence of the metaphors and "dreams" haunting the interior of our language. The lens of consciousness will always be clouded with the tropes of the text that the reader is reading or writing. The modernist-structuralist idea of a detached observer is being replaced by the idea of an intersubjectivity in which the images in the text interfuse with and alter the lens of the viewer reading the text. We not only read texts, but we read the world through texts. And it is precisely this realization that has undermined our epistemological confidence in the authority of our transcendental signifiers. The more we attempt to account linguistically for the authority of these ultimates, the more the absoluteness in our god terms begins to deliteralize, dissolve, and disappear.

## Grounds for Clinical Authority

Postmodernism with its intense focus on the problematics of self-reflection, textuality, and the process of psychic representation has revealed that these unquestionable "absolutes" are not the eternal, archetypal structures we once thought them to be, but are rather *temporal and linguistic by-products* resulting from a representational theory of language. Any such transcendental *term* is a fiction, heuristically and clinically valuable, perhaps, but nonetheless fictional. There is *no* linguistic concept that is exempt from the metaphorical status of language. No mode of discourse, not even the language of science, can be *literally* literal. All writing is by its very nature ironic, simultaneously literal and figural.[12]

The realization that our clinical ground is not as absolute as we once thought does not necessarily lead to a radical relativism or to nihilism. It leads, instead, to a psychological realism based upon the awareness that all systems of clinical interpretation gain their authority through a grounding in a transcendental "ultimate." But this "ultimate" is no longer so absolute, so ultimate, so psychologically inflated through an unconscious identification with the *deus absconditas*. In therapeutic analysis we still must, on one level, *believe in* our god term and use it *as if* it were the ultimate explanatory principle. But on a deeper level, we also know that it is not. And it is precisely this deeper level of awareness that prevents our psychological ideologies from becoming secular religions and differentiates professional debates from religious idolatry. For the ultimate ground of depth psychology is not a known god term but the ultimately unknowable, the unconscious itself. And this *is* the "absolute" ground that gives authority to all schools of depth psychology.

## A Few Questions in Closing

Postmodern theory has raised many questions concerning the processes of representation and interpretation. When these same concerns are applied to depth psychology, the following questions are raised:

1. Where is a dream being literal and where is it being figurative and metaphoric? How is this determination possible?

2. To what does the dream refer? To the outer world? To the inner world? Both? Or, is it self-referential?

3. Is the self, the wish, the soul, biochemistry, or some other transcendental ultimate the author of the dream; or, does the dream text have no author?

4. What is the relation between the discourse of dream theory and the discourse of the dream text? Is dream theory a form of metalanguage, a language about another language, that can rise above its object of study, the dream text, so as to look down and objectively examine the dream? Is this kind of metaposition ever possible in the analysis of dreams?

5. How much, if any, of the patient's dream text does the reader-analyst write in the process of clinical interpretation?

6. How does depth psychology develop a psychological theory that is itself self-conscious? In other words, how does it develop a theory capable of consciously carrying an awareness of its own figural aspects and implicit assumptions, that is, its own unconsciousness?

7. When interpreting a dream, which meaning is given primacy in our theory and practice: the literal meaning? the metaphoric meaning(s)? or both? What are the therapeutic, psychological, political, and social implications of privileging only one aspect of significance?

And, finally,

8. Is there a beginning and is there an end?

# Notes

---

1. Jung to Pastor Max Frischknecht, February 8, 1946, C. G. Jung, *Letters, Vol. 1: 1906-1950*, ed. Gerhard Adler and Aniela Jaffé, trans. R.F.C. Hull, Bollingen Series (Princeton: Princeton University Press, 1973), p. 411.

2. Jung to the Rev. Morton T. Kelsey, May 3, 1958, C. G. Jung, *Letters, Vol. 2: 1951-1961*, ed. Gerhard Adler and Aniela Jaffé, trans. R.F.C. Hull, Bollingen Series (Princeton: Princeton University Press, 1975), p. 435.

3. Sigmund Freud, *Complete Works*, vol. 14, ed. and trans. James Strachey (London: Hogarth Press, 1978), p. 166.

4. See W. K. Wimsatt and M. C. Beardsley, *Verbal Icon* (Lexington: Uni-

versity of Kentucky Press, 1954), and W. K. Wimsatt and C. Brooks, *Literary Criticism: A Short History* (New York: Alfred A. Knopf, 1957).

5. Ferdinand de Saussure, *Course in General Linguistics* (New York: McGraw-Hill, 1959), p. 122.

6. Claude Lévi-Strauss, *Anthropologie structurale* (Paris: Plon, 1958), pp. 224-225.

7. Jacques Lacan, "Le symbolique, l'imaginaire et le réel" (Paper delivered at the Conference of the French Society of Psychoanalysis, July 1953).

8. See Jacques Lacan, *The Language of the Self*, trans. and notes by Anthony Wilden (New York: Dell Publishing Co., 1968); *Ecrit*, trans. Alan Sheridan (New York: W. W. Norton, 1977); *The Four Fundamental Concepts of Psychoanalysis* (New York: W. W. Norton, 1978).

9. Roland Barthes, *Le Plaisir du texte* (Paris: Seuil, 1973).

10. Friedrich Nietzsche, "The Gay Science," in *The Portable Nietzsche*, trans. and ed. W. Kaufmann (New York: Viking Press, 1968), p. 97.

11. See Paul Kugler, *The Alchemy of Discourse: An Archetypal Approach to Language* (Lewisburg, Penn.: Bucknell University Press, 1982).

12. See Paul De Man, *Allegories of Reading* (New Haven: Yale University Press, 1979); Jacques Derrida, *De La Grammatologie* (Paris: Minuit, 1967); Paul Kugler, "Jacques Lacan and the Birth of the Post-Modern Self-Reflexive Subject," in *The Book of the Self: Person, Pretext, and Process*, ed. P. Young-Eisendrath and J. Hall (New York: New York University Press, 1986).

# Jung and the Postmodern Condition
### Edward S. Casey

Jung and the *postmodern* condition? This seems at first glance a most unlikely and unpromising topic—especially if one focuses, as I propose to do, on his conception of images. For when it comes to his treatment of images, Jung appears to be altogether *premodern*. This is above all evident in his frequent recourse to medieval and Greek terminology. In several places, he speaks of image or fantasy as *esse in anima* or being-in-the-soul. In a letter of January 1929, he writes: "I am indeed convinced that creative imagination is the only primordial phenomenon accessible to us, the real Ground of the psyche, the only immediate reality. Therefore I speak of *esse in anima*, the only form of being we can experience directly."[1]

When Jung says in *Psychological Types* that "between *intellectus* and *res* there is still *anima*, and this *esse in anima* makes the whole ontological argument superfluous" (*CW* 6: par. 66, p. 45), he invokes not only medieval nomenclature but a privileged form of medieval reasoning as well: as in the case of God, the existence of the soul (and thus of the images that proceed from soul) is contained in its very essence, its being. As if to clinch this point by a still further reversion, this time to the pre-premodern Greek world, Jung asserts in a letter of December 1949, that "I firmly believe . . . that psyche is an *ousia* [substance, essence]."[2] Since it is a root premise of Jung's that "psyche *is* image" (*CW* 13: par. 75, p. 50)—soul is not only expressed in images but *exists* in them—it follows ineluctably that images are also substances: psychic substances, possessing a "psychic reality" whose recognition, adds Jung, is "the most important achievement of modern psychology" (*CW* 8: par. 683, p. 354). From this last statement it would seem that "modern psychology" is limited to rediscovering what the Greek and medieval thinkers already knew and had better described.

There are other ways as well in which Jung presents himself as premodern—quite apart from his constant recourse to the "archaic" factor in human beings, their phylogenetic heritage. His railing against language, for example, would seem to dissociate him from the extreme sensitivity to the "linguisticality" that Gadamer, along with the French structuralists, has argued is indispensable to grasping what is distinctively human. "Our civilization," proclaims Jung, "is largely founded on a superstititious belief in words. . . . Words can take the place of men and things" (*CW* 18: par. 1428, p. 625). And of images: vis-à-vis images "the mere use of words is futile" (*CW* 18: par. 590, p. 257). To this we are inclined to respond: Yes, but. . . . And before we have answered, Jung will have intervened to add a crucial qualification: it is not a matter of separating off *all* words from images but precisely those that he calls "nebulous power-words." What kind of words are these? They are *metaphysical* words, as Jung goes on to specify: "I quite deliberately bring everything that purports to be metaphysical into the daylight of psychological understanding, and do my best to prevent people from believing in nebulous power-words" (*CW* 13: par. 73, p. 49).

With this last pronouncement, we are suddenly in a quite different language game. If Jung's suspicion of language vis-à-vis images is a suspicion of specifically metaphysical language, he is in league with Heidegger and Derrida in their assiduous efforts to deconstruct metaphysics—and this means the language of metaphysics—from the ground up. This is a very characteristic postmodern enterprise, and it goes hand in hand with a turn to phenomenology as the most meaningful alternative to metaphysics. Just as Heidegger and Derrida take inspiration from phenomenology in their common critique of metaphysics, so Jung is able to write that "Psychology cannot establish any metaphysical 'truths,' nor does it try to. It is concerned solely with the phenomenology of the psyche" (*CW* 18: par. 742, p. 309).[3]

Jung also concurs with the postmodernist philosophers' rejection of the totalizing tendency of metaphysics, especially insofar as this tendency is applied to the psyche: "the phenomenology of the psyche is so colorful, so variegated in form and meaning, that we cannot possibly reflect all its riches in *one* mirror. Nor in our description of it can we embrace the whole, but [we] must be content to shed light only on single parts of the total phenomenon" (*CW* 15: "Psychology and Literature," Introduction, p. 85).

Still more important for our purposes, this recourse to the polyformity of phenomenology in flight from the monism of metaphysics—a move that Jung shares with such other twentieth-century thinkers as Husserl, Cassirer, and Wittgenstein (all of whom also describe their philosophical work as "phenomenological")—has direct implications for understanding images. Jung remarks in a letter of September 1935 that "body is as metaphysical as spirit" and that "psychic experience is the only immediate experience."[4] If so, then the only adequate approach to images—which provide the primary content of "psychic experience"—will be phenomenology, which is designed precisely to describe "immediate experience" in detail. Indeed, Jung goes so far as to say that, strictly speaking, there can be "only phenomenology" in psychology today (*CW* 18: par. 1738, p. 774). This is to say that there can be only a phenomenology of images in a genuinely psychological investigation. And this is just what we should expect to be the case if psyche is in fact image.

Why then, you will ask, does Jung persist in employing the heavily metaphysical language of "*ousia*" and "*esse in anima*" in designating images if he is so much in step with phenomenological thinkers of this century? Is he being deliberately perverse? I do not think so. Like Heidegger (who continued to use such terms as "Being" and "essence"), Jung is making an adroit maneuver that, in focusing our attention on conspicuously premodern language, forces us to draw a crucial distinction between modern and postmodern conceptions of the image. In the explicitly *modern*, post-Cartesian view, the image is a mere "copy of an impression," as Hume put it, or in Jung's own phrase, "the psychic reflection of an external object" (*CW* 6: par. 743, p. 442). It is just this reductive approach that prevailed in Western philosophy and psychology from the seventeenth until the late nineteenth centuries—and that cannot possibly do justice to Jung's axiom that "the psyche consists essentially of images" (*CW* 8: par. 618, p. 325). Not only does the modernist conception make the image utterly subordinate to that of which it is an image—whether a sensory impression or an external object that gives rise to this impression—but it also converts the truly psychic image into a sign instead of acknowledging its symbolic status. To return to a premodern conception of images as essences, beings, or substances is thus to be reminded of the autonomy of the psyche that such images display in their symbolic power—just as this same autonomy is underlined in Jung's apparently equally regressive attempt to link image and instinct. Both moves, one expressly philosophical and the other inherently biological, serve the same basic purpose of contesting the modernist interpretation of images as bare copies or signs of that which they represent in and to the mind—a mind that is without soul, since it has become the mere container of icons deriving from external sense experience.

But if we are to grasp Jung's final dismissal of modernism in this manner, what of *post*modernism? It is one thing to suggest that earlier, premodern (as well as archaic) thought is more appreciative of the density and richness of imagistic life—its "polyformity" as I have called it—but it is another matter to bring this appreciation into line with contemporary, postmodern thinking. We have already discovered one way in which Jung manages nonetheless to accomplish such an alignment with postmodernism. This is through his spontaneous recourse to the phenomenology of the image. Another aspect of this phenomenological turn lies in his insistence that we must proceed in psychology from the outside in—and not from the inside out, as the Romantic poets and philosophers, rebelling against the Cartesians and empiricists, tried to do. He writes in 1921 that in psychology it is best "to proceed from outside inwards, from the known to the unknown, from the body to the psyche. . . . [T]here are any number of paths leading from outside inwards, from the physical to the psychic, and it is necessary that research should follow this direction until the elementary psychic facts are established with sufficient certainty" (*CW* 6: par. 917, p. 525). We are reminded here of Husserl's shibboleth for the phenomenological method: "To the Things Themselves!"—not to mention Heidegger's claim that human beings possess an essential being "outside" themselves.[5] And we are put in mind as well of Lévi-Strauss's idea that the elementary structures of kinship exist outside—independently of voluntary actions of—the members of a given social grouping: their objectivity is as "impersonal" (in Jung's term) as primordial images themselves. The structures of structuralism and the images of analytical psychology alike precede and prestructure the human persons who exist in their ambience and by their means. The "outside" of such structures and such images is a very different outside from that which figures into the early modern notion of sensory experience and its imitation in iconic signs. It belongs to a world or cosmos that is the source of symbols, just as it is the origin of the psyche itself—indeed, of the "objective psyche" as Jung came to call it.

To think in this postmodernist direction is not to eliminate the significance of the humanistic subject and its nucleus, the ego. Jung even declares that "the [objective] psyche is the greatest of all cosmic wonders and *sine qua non* of the world as an object" (*CW* 8: par. 357, p. 169), and that "the psyche is the world's pivot: not only is it the one great condition for the existence of a world at all, it is also an intervention in the existing natural order, and no one can say with certainty where this intervention will finally end" (*CW* 8: par. 423, p. 217). To say this is not to return to a Romantic inflation of self; it is to remain resolutely postmodernist—but now with a final twist. The twist, familiar to Jungians, is that the objective psyche is at the same time a collective psyche, at once prepersonal and pluripersonal (or more exactly, omnipersonal). What is perhaps less familiar is that the operative premise of structural linguistics—a premise to which not only Lévi-Strauss but Jakobson, Barthes, Merleau-Ponty, and Derrida also subscribe—is equally collective in character. In Saussure's inaugural thinking on this matter, formulated in the very years in which Jung was first thinking his own way to analytical psychology, the "speaking mass" (*la masse parlante*) is determinative for language (*la langue*) in its essential form. Language is no more a matter of an individual speech act (*la parole*) than primordial images are affairs of the isolated ego. Each proceeds from a level of the psyche that is profoundly impersonal: "collective" in Jung's preferred term, "institutionalized" in Saussure's answering notion. In this way, image and word come together in the end after all—despite Jung's sometimes heroic efforts to hold them apart. But they come together at a level of human being that has been given full recognition only in postmodernist thought. Jung and Saussure are not alone in their insistence on the collective basis of image and word that earlier modernists failed to acknowledge. They are joined by thinkers as diverse as Lévy-Bruhl and Chomsky, both of whom also assert the transpersonal foundation of imagination and language, whether in the guise of collective representations or universally shared rules of generative grammar. What matters, however, is not the history of the trend, or who in particular belongs to it. What matters is the vision it embodies. This is a vision that gives back to images, as it gives back to words, a grounding in the spontaneous action of the psyche, which *is* image as it *is* word, and, in being both at once, transcends the egological confines—in sign and copy—of the modernist conception of the human self, a conception that renders the self incapable of the symbolic activity of the psyche in its cosmic and collective dimensions.

# Notes

---

1. Jung to Kurt Plachte, January 10, 1929, C. G. Jung, *Letters, Vol. 1: 1906-1950*, ed. Gerhard Adler and Aniela Jaffé, trans. R.F.C. Hull, Bollingen Series (Princeton: Princeton University Press, 1973), p. 60.

2. Jung to Father Victor White, December 31, 1949, ibid., p. 540.

3. Cf. also *CW* 18: par. 1738, p. 774; and *CW* 15: "Psychology and Literature," Introduction, p. 85.

4. Jung to Henry A. Murray, September 10, 1935, *Letters, Vol. 1: 1906-1950*, p. 200.

5. Martin Heidegger, *Being and Time*, trans. John Macquarrie and Edward Robinson (New York: Harper and Row, 1962), p. 89. Heidegger claims that the "primary kind of being" belonging to human beings is such as to be "always 'outside' alongside entities."

# An Other Jung
## and An Other . . .   David L. Miller

## A Mystery

*Mysterium tremendum et fascinosum!* It is a mystery to me. Why is it that so many persons are astonished, empowered, amazed, inspired, provoked, and overwhelmed by Jung's so-called Personality #2? But the same persons quote, believe in, explain, and expatiate upon the jargon from Personality #1![1] Was it not Jung's view that the deep self provides the *tremendum*, the awe and insight and power? But it is ego's explanations and ideas that have been the *fascinosum*, fascinating, fastening, and fixating Jungians? Why can there not be a truly "Jungian" (#2) psychology?—that is, one that is not Jungian (#1)? Not a saying of what Jung said, but a doing of what Jung did? Will no one who pretends to believe him really believe him?

## An Other Jung

There is this other Jung. It is the Jung who said: "The concept of the unconscious *posits nothing*; it designates only my *unknowing*."[2] Again, he said: "[Y]ou cannot possibly learn analytical psychology by studying its object, since it consists exclusively of what you don't know about yourself."[3] Or, there are these words of Jung from the Kundalini seminar: "Individuation is not that you become an ego; you would then be an individualist. An individualist is a person who did not succeed in individuation: that person is a distilled egotist. Individuation is becoming that which is not the ego, . . . what you are not. . . . You feel as if you were a stranger."[4] This same other Jung also said: "the united personality will never quite lose the painful sense of innate discord. Complete redemption from the sufferings of this world is and must remain an illusion" (*CW* 6: par. 400, p. 200).

It was this other Jung for whom religion was a psychological problem: "My problem [he said] is to wrestle with the big monster of the historical past, the great snake of the centuries, the burden of the human mind, the problem of Christianity" (*CW* 18: par. 279, p. ·127). And concerning the word "God," the other Jung said: "The attribute 'coarse' is mild in comparison to what you feel when God dislocates your hip or when he slays the firstborn. I bet Jacob's punches he

handed to the angel were not just caresses or polite gestures. . . .
'Coarse' is too weak a word for it [i.e., for "God"]. 'Crude,' 'violent,'
'cruel,' 'bloody,' 'hellish,' 'demonic' would be better."⁵ Three days before he died, this Jung (#2) also said: "To this day God is the name by
which I designate all things which cross my willful path violently and
recklessly, all things which upset my subjective views, plans and intentions."⁶

These words are in keeping with the Jung who said: "The Self . . .
confronts it [the ego] with problems which it would like to avoid. . . .
[T]he experience of the self is always a defeat for the ego" (*CW* 14: par.
778, p. 546). And, to be sure, this is the same Jung who said that ego
is not a real thing,⁷ and "I don't believe such a center [as the self]
exists."⁸ At the end of his autobiography, this Jung said, quoting Lao
Tzu: " 'All are clear, I alone am clouded.' "⁹ This Jung was postmodern
before the times. He knew unknowing before Derrida's version of
Heidegger's insight that the most crucial moment is the deconstructive
one. Indeed, the other Jung invites us into the "cloud of unknowing,"
to forget our Jungian concepts and categories (#1) in order that we
may be truly Jungian (#2), listening not to Jung but to the soul, in
order that—in the manner of the saying of Coomaraswamy—we too
may have written on our tombstone: *Hic jacet nemo*, "Here lies no one."

## Mis En Abyme

But why call this other "postmodern"? Roland Barthes and William
Spanos have been useful on this question.

Barthes speaks of two experiences, or of two perspectives on any
experience, that he designates by the French words *plaisir* and *jouissance*. The experience of pleasure "contents, fills, grants euphoria." It
is an experience that "does not break with culture," and "it is linked to
what is comfortable."¹⁰ This experience is like the function of *metaphor*,
which connects. But *jouissance* is not the same as *plaisir*. (*Jouissance* really refers to the female experience of orgasm, waving and weaving
and polymorphous, rather than pointed and focused in a historical moment.) Barthes's view of "bliss" is confirmed by Julia Kristeva. It is an
experience that "imposes a state of loss . . . discomforts . . . unsettles
assumptions."¹¹ Nothing is the same. This is like the function of *me-
tonymy* in which discontinuous images are juxtaposed richly without
forcing a point, without insisting upon symbolic connections. *Jouissance* is semiotically understandable. It is *jouissance* that is the play of
the postmodern. It is the bliss of not-knowing.

Another postmodernist, William Spanos, gives an American version
of this difference (and its deferral of connection: *différance*). He speaks

of two paradigms. The paradigm of modernism is the detective story whose form has

> its source in the comforting certainty that an acute "eye," private or otherwise, can solve the crime with resounding finality by inferring causal relationships between clues which point to it (they are "leads," suggesting the primacy of the rigid linear narrative sequence). So the "form" of the . . . [modernist] universe is grounded in the equally comforting certainty that the scientist and/or psychoanalyst can solve the immediate problem by the inductive method, a process involving the inference of relationships between discontinuous "facts" that point to or lead straight to an explanation of the "mystery," the "crime" of contingent existence.[12]

On the other hand, the paradigm of postmodernism is the "anti–detective story (and its anti-psychological analogue), the formal purpose of which is to evoke the impulse to 'detect' and/or psychoanalyze in order violently to frustrate it by refusing to solve the crime (or find the cause of the neurosis)," since there is no "final solution."[13]

This postmodern talk sounds not only like the radical Freud, who defined the goal of therapy as the transformation of "hysterical misery into common unhappiness."[14] It also sounds like the Jung who defiled Basel's Christian edifice; that is, it is like his radical therapeutic saying: "Complete redemption from suffering is and must remain an illusion" (*CW* 16: par. 400, p. 200). Jung #2 is an anti-detective. He is on the side of *jouissance* and against *plaisir*, especially when one recalls Kristeva's articulation of the practical therapeutic goal of *jouissance* as "keeping it unresolved."[15] Indeed, the other Jung is postmodern before its/it's time.

## A Semiotics of Image[16]

There is an irony in this linking of Jung's *depth* psychology, his "unknowing," with postmodernism, with a radically iconoclastic movement in semiotics that comes, like surrealism, after the failure of realism, naturalism, romanticism, and symbolisms of all sorts. Jung #1 once wrote:

> Every view which interprets the symbolic expression as an analogue of an abbreviated designation for a known thing is *semiotic*. A view which interprets the symbolic expression as the best possible formulation of a relatively unknown thing, which for that

reason cannot be more clearly or characteristically expressed, is *symbolic.* (*CW* 6: par. 815, p. 474)

This is the well-known distinction between signs and symbols in Jungian, Tillichian, and other post-Kantian orthodoxies of the early twentieth century. Signs point to something known; symbols participate in that to which they point and involve depth, mystery, and the unknown. But James Hillman, among others, has pointed out that as time has gone along, symbolism has veered away from the unknown in the direction of the known. In Jungian psychological orthopraxy, we know that cats in men's dreams mean *anima*, that eggs in women's dreams mean fecundity, and so on.[17] So what has happened to Jung #2 and to the clouds, the unknowing, the depth, and the mystery?

Things have flip-flopped, something like Alice's White Knight falling off his horse and being stuck upside down because of the rigidity of his armor. First, Lacan fell off Freud's horse into Saussure's ditch, and signifiers took primacy over significations. Then, Kristeva fell off Lacan's horse and restressed the imaginary over the symbolic, noting that semiotic sign language emanates from instinctual drives and primary processes, whereas symbolic perspectives assimilate psyche's images to secondary processes, predicative synthesis, and judgment.[18] After these twists, symbolism is the domain of the known (or what the collective leads us to think we know), which leaves the sign world to be the locus of the unknown. Signs situate us in dislocations without semantic security, not in the subject or in the object, but in the abject: *mis en abyme*, say the postmodernists; *descensus ad inferos*, agrees Jung #2, speaking about the experience of the self. So, if Jung were alive today, would he not have to be a semiotician rather than a symbolist? Would he not be nearer to the French Freudians than to the American Jungians with all their hermeneutic knowledge?

Granted, it is an odd twist. But if a semiotician were asked today whether the fundamentalist discourse of Jerry Falwell were symbolic or semiotic, there would be no hesitation. It is symbolic: that is, it refers with semantic confidence to idolatrously believed-in contents taken literally. Today Christian literalism and Jungian fundamentalism are symbolic. They have become a knowing. But what Jung called symbolic, and recommended for the soul, is not this knowing. It is the paratactic, "gappy," unknowing that is today called semiotic.

## An Other . . .

What does any of this matter? It is to the end of the continual alchemical process of dynamic unsettling that allows one to see from the perspective of the Other. (Therapists in Jung's day were called "alienists," from *alius* = "other.") It is in order to deconstruct unconsciousness, ideology, and idolatry. Indeed, the other Jung opens to Otherness as a possibility in the time of the death of the ego (the subject), in the time of the death of symbolisms (object-relations), and in the time of the death of other gods as well. *Hic jacet nemo*: "Here lies no one."

# Notes

1. For Jung's own comments on these two personalities, see his *Memories, Dreams, Reflections*, ed. Aniela Jaffé, trans. Richard and Clara Winston (New York: Random House, 1963), esp. pp. 26, 33-34, 43, 44, 45, 63, 66, 88, and 225. "Personality #1" might be considered the conscious personality, whereas "Personality #2" might be considered the unconscious one, or "the Other."

2. Jung to Pastor Max Frischknecht, February 8, 1946, C. G. Jung, *Letters, Vol. 1: 1906-1950*, ed. Gerhard Adler and Aniela Jaffé, trans. R.F.C. Hull, Bollingen Series (Princeton: Princeton University Press, 1973), p. 411.

3. Jung to H. Dänzer-Vanotti, April 6, 1932, ibid., p. 90.

4. C. G. Jung, "Psychological Commentary on Kundalini Yoga," *Spring* (1975): 31.

5. Jung to the Rev. Erastus Evans, February, 17, 1954, C. G. Jung, *Letters, Vol. 2: 1951-1961*, ed. Gerhard Adler and Aniela Jaffé, trans. R.F.C. Bollingen Series (Princeton: Princeton University Press, 1975), p. 156.

6. *Good Housekeeping Magazine* (December 1961), cited in Edward Edinger, *Ego and Archetype* (Baltimore: Penguin Books, 1972), p. 101.

7. Jung to J. Allen Gilbert, January 2, 1929, *Letters, Vol. 1: 1906-1950*, p. 57.

8. Quoted in Miguel Serrano, *C. G. Jung and Hermann Hesse: A Record of Two Friendships* (Garden City, N.Y.: Doubleday, 1959), p. 50.

9. Jung, *Memories*, p. 359.

10. Roland Barthes, *The Pleasure of the Text*, trans. R. Miller (New York: Hill and Wang, 1975), p. 14.

11. Julia Kristeva, "Within the Microcosm of the 'Talking Cure,' " in *Psychiatry and the Humanities*, vol. 6: *Interpreting Lacan*, ed. J. Smith and W. Kerrigan (New Haven: Yale University Press, 1978), p. 36.

12. William Spanos, "The Detective and the Boundary: Some Notes on the Postmodern Literary Imagination," *boundary 2* 1, no. 1 (Fall 1972): 150.

13. Ibid., p. 154.

14. Sigmund Freud, *Studies in Hysteria* (London: Hogarth Press, 1893), p. 305.

15. Kristeva, "Within the Microcosm of the 'Talking Cure,' " p. 36.

16. "A semiotics of image." Paul Ricoeur has written a trenchant observation about a certain confusion. On the one hand, he argues (out of Freud) that "the universe of discourse appropriate to the analytic experience is not that of language but that of the image." Yet, on the other hand, though we possess a semiotics of language that tries to account for psychoanalytic experience (Lacan, Kristeva et alia), he thinks "we lack a theory that would account for the semiotic aspects of the image." He goes on: "I think it is mistaken to believe that everything semiotic is linguistic. At the same time, however, it is also an error to believe that the image does not arise from the semiotic order." So we have the image people and the language people in disjunction, and stupidly so, Ricoeur thinks. Our field "either recognizes the function of the image in psychoanalysis but misunderstands the semiotic dimension of its field, or it recognizes this semiotic dimension but too quickly assimilates it to the realm of language." Thus, Ricoeur calls for a semiotics of image. See Paul Ricoeur, "Image and Language in Psychoanalysis," in *Psychiatry and the Humanities*, vol. 3: *Psychoanalysis and Language*, ed. J. Smith (New Haven: Yale University Press, 1978), p. 293ff., 311. Richard Palmer has ventured that the work of James Hillman contains such a postmodern semiotics of image. See Richard Palmer, "Postmodernity and Hermeneutics," *boundary 2 5*, no. 2 (Winter 1977): 381.

17. James Hillman, "An Inquiry into Image," *Spring* (1977): 67.

18. Kristeva, "Within the Microcosm of the 'Talking Cure,' " p. 34.

Jung and
Postmodernism
Symposium

Edward S. Casey

James Hillman

Paul Kugler

David L. Miller

*Casey*: Could you, David, say more about the notion of the discontinuous, the "gappy," and how that relates to *jouissance*, and how the two together constitute the realm that you are now calling the semiotic? It seems to me to be undergoing a very interesting, indeed a radical, reinterpretation here. Could you say something by way of explication?

*Miller*: The thing that comes to mind is something that has been mentioned several times in the last two days here: namely, the image of weaving. My understanding of *jouissance* is the experience of the weave and the wave and the undulation, which fundamentally is not the centering model of ceramics or potting, but is a notion of weaving, the weave in which the texture of the textile, and what Paul called the textuality, is in the effect of the whole. There is no call for a filling in in a way that the rational mind or the conscious ego can make sense of it. One can feel the texture, or one can sense the body of the weave, whether it is in a text or a dream. It is paratactic. It may look to us like it makes a Gestalt as a whole, but it is like a fine tapestry. When you look at it closely, it begins to dissolve. It is "gappy." It is paratactic, rather than syntactic, but the body of it, the texture of it, is felt nonetheless.

*Casey*: Is that not the same thing as the "floating signifier," which seems to me to be closely related, yet not perhaps quite exactly the same idea. The floating signifier, a phrase from Lévi-Strauss, refers to the fact that signs are not related to their meanings in any one-to-one fashion. This is an effort to call into question even Saussure's model of every sign as a two-sided unity of signifier and signified. Now in the hands of Lévi-Strauss, and certainly also of Lacan and Derrida, there is an effort to show that there is no such internal unity that would lead to a predictable and determinate set of meanings, the symbolic in the limited sense. Whereas if the deconstruction of this leading linguist of the century is to be trusted, there is no such internally known-in-advance systematizable and unifiable linkage. That is, the signifier floats free from its linkage to the signified (i.e., the meaning, the concept, the notion).

*Miller*: This seems to me to accord with Jung's concern not to become seduced into a single one-sided meaning of anything, but to see always that in any meaning there is a shadow of meaninglessness, the underside. That other side is not a dualism; it is integral. Now this seems to me to be very close to what we are talking about in these humanistic debates about postmodernism.

*Hillman*: The one thing that most people identify Jung with is what Aniela Jaffé calls the "myth of meaning." That was Jung's myth, she says. The self in Jung's system is the archetype of meaning. Now when you work "meaning" over, the way all three of you have, how do you reconcile—or do you not try—the myth of meaning, which was what Jung again and again said he was concerned about, with the dissolution of meaning, of fixed meaning, of single meaning, even of any meaning (i.e., tying it to something)? How do you reconcile that?

*Kugler*: I am not going to "reconcile" it, but I will try to address the problem. For me, the question is whether we are going to "ground" the meaning of a psychic narrative through appeal to a transcendental signified, a meaning transcendent to the psyche/text, or whether we are going to ground the meaning in the unknown (the unconscious). To illustrate what I mean by grounding meaning in a transcendental signified versus grounding it in the experience of not knowing, I will tell two stories. The first is well known to Jungians. It was a story Jung often told to illustrate the importance of transcendental meaning (the self) in the establishment of psychic significance. The story is found in the eighteenth book of the Koran and begins with Moses meeting Khidr (the "Green one") in the desert. The two wander together for awhile, and Khidr expresses his fear that Moses will not be able to witness the deeds without judgment and indignation. Khidr tells Moses that if he cannot trust and bear with him, then Khidr will have to leave him. Moses agrees. After a short time they come upon a poor fishing village where Khidr sinks the fishing boats of the villagers. Moses sees this and is upset, but remembers his promise and says nothing. A short time later, they arrive at a decaying house of two pious young men, just outside the wall of the city of nonbelievers. Khidr goes up to the city wall, which is falling down, and repairs the wall rather than the house of the two believers. Again Moses is disturbed by Khidr's actions but says nothing. The story continues in this way until finally Moses sees something so intolerable that he can no longer hold back making a comment, an interpretation. This causes Khidr to leave. But before his departure, Khidr explains why he acted as he did. In the first instance, pirates were on their way to steal the boats and by sinking them, Khidr actually saved the boats from being stolen. In the second instance, by rebuilding the wall of the city of nonbelievers, Khidr actually saved the two young men from ruin because their life-fortune was hidden under the city wall and was about to be revealed and stolen. As Khidr left, Moses realized that his moral judgment and indignation had been too hasty and that Khidr's actions, which at first he interpreted as bad, were in fact not.

The second story I would characterize as a narrative representing the postmodern problematic of knowledge and meaning. It is an old Taoist story about a farmer who has a son and a horse. One day, the farmer goes outside to find that his only horse has run away. It is a small town, and the neighbors hear about it and come to visit that evening, telling him what a terrible thing it is that happened. The farmer listens to them, thinks for awhile, and responds, "I don't know." The next week the horse runs up into the mountains and takes up with a herd of thirty wild horses. After running with them for a few weeks, the farmer's horse leads the wild horses back to the corral. The farmer goes out and finds he now has thirty-one horses and closes the gate. Word gets out, and the neighbors come to see him that evening, telling him how wonderful this is. The farmer thinks for a long time and says, "I don't know." The following day his only son goes out to tame the horses. He climbs on the first horse and is thrown, breaking his leg so he cannot work. The neighbors hear about this. They all come over to the house that night and tell him it is terrible that his only son broke his leg and cannot work. The farmer thinks about this for awhile and he responds, "I don't know." The next day the country breaks out in war and the man in charge of conscription arrives to draft the son to go to the front line where he will probably be killed. He finds the son has a broken leg and tells the boy he does not have to go to war. The neighbors hear about this and come over that night and tell the farmer how wonderful it is that his son does not have to go to war. And the farmer responds, "I don't know."

The two stories illustrate the problem. The first story assumes a transcendental knowledge (meaning), and in the second, the meaning is bracketed by doubt and an attitude of not knowing. Both relativize the original story through recontextualization. But where they differ is that in the first story there is a personification (Khidr or, in Jung's psychology, the self) who "knows" (signifies) the meaning of the future, whereas in the second story there is no such personified teleological knowledge. There is only a farmer who questions the neighbors' tendency to fix a specific interpretation to an event.

*Hillman*: The meaning is generated from not knowing, and we are all quite content. Yet we are not supposed to rest content, either. The discontent is part of the experience of the *jouissance*, as you described it.

*Miller*: To follow up the lineaments of Paul's two stories, it would be just as much a one-sidedness—which is one of the definitions Jung gives of neurosis—to talk about meaninglessness as it is to talk about meaningfulness. I would take it that part of the trick in the myth of the meaning is not to dismiss it—one achieves nothing by this, and one only becomes unconscious thereby—but rather to locate all one's myths of meaning: to make them conscious and to realize that Jaffé's phrase is "the *myth* of meaning."

*Casey*: On that point, I think it is important to stress that it is not a form of semantic nihilism that is implied in this notion of not knowing. Not knowing is not knowing the definitely knowable or the metaphysically systematizable. Of course, that leaves lots of room for insight, lots of room for knowing, to recall a kind of sidereal or lateral knowing, and I use that image straight from Saussure. Merleau-Ponty said that meaning arises at the edges of signs in their internal relations with each other, and more exactly it arises in the way that strings of signifiers interrelate. This is also true of strings of "symbols," and we can certainly still go on using that word, just as we are using the word "meaning," now under a kind of double quote or "erasure," as Derrida calls it. We can go on using these words, but now the interest is in how the particular group of signs configurates, such as those we just heard in the two parables given to us by Paul Kugler, rather than in something like an overarching sense or significance.

*Miller*: We might keep in mind the common enemies that Jung and many of the postmodern thinkers have, namely, the enemy of totalitarianism of all forms, the totalitarianism of one's unconscious psychology, political totalitarianism, or literalist totalitarianism in theology. In totalitarianism, the other is split off; it is a dualistic thinking where the oppositions—instead of relating to each other, instead of being seen as a part of a dialectic or of what postmodernists call "interplay," that weaving, undulating *jouissance*, of what is split off, that is, the other nation or the other gender or sex or other person or spouse—are viewed as evil. Then that "splitness" gets us in trouble. I think those enemies are common to Jung and to many of these poststructuralist thinkers: the common enemies of totalitarianism of various sorts (ideologism) and split-off dualistic thinking as opposed to dialectical back-and-forth thinking or *coincidentia oppositorum*.

*Hillman*: Let us go back to Ed's statement for a moment. The use of the word *ousia* and *esse in anima* is a very substantive or substantiating kind of thinking. There is a whole other side of Jung that seems to me to be very important for him; it is the biological rooting, the use of biological language, giving the archetypes an infrared end in animal existence. "Instinct" he calls it. That is solidifying, is it not? What do you do with that part of Jung? The part that is not linguistic at all, the part that is outside the whole realm of the French poststructuralists and the Yale school, but is concerned with the worms and the dogs, the part of Jung that is prelinguistic, nonlinguistic?

*Casey*: Well, one thing to do with it is to say that some of those same poststructuralists that you mention have actually attached themselves to the idea of instinct, and they attempt—for better or worse—to deconstruct that, too. Let us see how they do this and whether the result of the deconstruction would still end up being anything like instinct (where instinct is linked ultimately to the Aristotelian idea of *energia*, dynamic force). I think it is that factor that Hillman wants to keep working within image, within the idea of autonomous psyche.

*Miller*: We note that *it is* working within the image. *We* do not keep it working. We note that *it is* going on.

*Casey*: It is certainly not us representing ourselves, or positing ourselves, through such things, but I wonder whether the very idea of instinct is not subject to a certain deconstruction. We could start with one of the two instincts to which Freud was finally driven—the death instinct. This has to do with dissolution in every form and fabric of our lives, not just biological destruction but every form of taking apart, separation, catabolism, in the larger sense. Instinct is not just unifying and synthesizing. At least one of the two great drives seems to be on its way to deconstruction by its very nature.

*Hillman*: Those are *Freud's* drives! I do not take them as animal drives. I never saw an animal with that kind of catabolic trait. This is a Freudian theory of instinct rather than my fantasy of chewing.

*Casey*: Yes, but your fantasy of chewing is a theory, too.

*Miller*: None of us is going to get away from being premodern, naively realistic, instinctual, or biological. We are going to be that way from time to time. We are going to be idolatrous. We are going to be ideological. We are going to make mistakes. We are going to substantialize. We are going to place our meanings in ego. We are going to use words. It seems to me one of the beauties of Jung's vision is expressed in his use of the language of alchemy. One of the alchemists' dicta for their work was *solve et coagula*, dissolve and coagulate, dissolve again and coagulate again. This implies that any idea we have coagulated will ultimately dissolve, but that another idea will emerge from the dissolution. All our ideas will fail us. But that is a part of the alchemy in which all of us are participants.

*Hillman*: We are all chewers!

*Miller*: Yes, we are all chewers, too. To think that we can get completely into feeling and to think that we can completely avoid substantialization is ridiculous. We walk down the street thinking, in spite of ourselves. So we had better do it consciously, lest we become ideologues?

*Kugler*: Yes, as Jungians we become ideologues around Jung's first principle, the archetypes, just as classical Freudians become ideologues around Freud's theory of drives. These first principles are transcendental signifieds' unimpeachable grounds. Both Freud and Jung use these "miracles" to explain the meaning and morphogenesis of psychic structure. The use of a literalized metaphor to ground interpretation is not limited, however, to psychoanalysis. Every science, and every interpretative theory, contains at least one miracle, one figural aspect that has been literalized and ontologized and thus turned into the ultimate explanatory principle. The "Big Bang" is the most popular miracle in science today. And you cannot even ask the origins question about the "Big Bang" because by definition it destroyed its origin. It is a miraculous explanatory principle, a "god" term, just as generative grammar is an explanatory miracle in linguistics, and the archetype a first principle for archetypal psychology. These ultimate explanatory terms are fictions, very useful on a practical and clinical level, but nonetheless fictional. The problem is that just here we are running up against the limits of language. No mode of discourse, not even science, can be *literally* literal. The tendency for the reader to get caught up in and suspended between the literal and the metaphoric significance of a text is given with language itself.

336

*Hillman*: So, what I am hearing now is that each and all of you would regard this basic idea of Jung as a miracle and therefore a given, not subject to what happens when Jung uses the word "instinct," what goes on in the emotion in us as readers. You would take it as a God term and as a given, one of the basics of Jung, and you would attempt to deconstruct the term in some way?

*Kugler*: One of the insights that has come out of postmodernism is the realization that whenever one reads a text, at least one element of the text must be taken literally. Everything else in the text is metaphorically pinned to (derived from, moved toward, explained by) the figural element being literalized. Now, it is possible to shift the root metaphor being used to ground the system of thought: deliteralizing the "god" term while literalizing another. James, you and Charles Boer have brilliantly demonstrated this in *Freud's Own Cookbook*. By shifting the literal element in the psychoanalytic explanatory system from sexuality to orality, you have invaginated, turned inside out, Freud's model, explaining everything, including sexuality, now in terms of orality. One of the important contributions of archetypal psychology has been its emphasis on the fictional "grounding" of all theory, including its own.

*Hillman*: No, Paul, the *Cookbook* is not literally substituting the oral for the genital. It is using the oral in imitation of Freud's use of the genital so as to deconstruct, showing the whole Freudian construct as a fantasy.

*Kugler*: Well, you seem to be quite certain about how to read *Freud's Own Cookbook*. But your "criticism" evokes authorial intention to establish the "true" reading of the book. Is this not precisely the style of reading now being called into question? The text, like an image, has a certain degree of autonomy from its creator, resulting from the inability to predetermine completely which aspects will be figural and which literal.

*Miller*: And that literal thing, you must remember, is a miracle; that is to say, it is theology. It is a matter of faith. It is not a matter of knowing. One of the things that happens as time goes on and the second generation of students finds that the miracle works is that they forget that the miracle was a matter of faith; they take it as a matter of knowledge. That is when it becomes substantialized. It becomes unconscious then, and our psychology that has worked to make us conscious becomes itself a piece of unconsciousness in us. Then we need more alchemy. We need to heat up the brew. I take it that is what we are talking about here, both to affirm the miracle and to keep its nature in view, namely, that it is a miracle.

*Casey*: But I think we need to be careful here. These really are not the same kinds of things. Miracles really are cases to become known, for which I think there is a valid place. I think that place is outside either the literal or the metaphorical. I would even contest the appropriateness of holding onto the distinction between literal and metaphorical. That is to repeat what Derrida would call a metaphysical binary opposition. It is one of the very things we need to call into question, at least in an era of postmodernism. You cannot any longer believe in the literal as literal. If you are taking this new perspective, you have to take the literal as what is positive within the system, as the opaque side of the sign, or the opaque end of the spectrum, or the fact from which we start. But now you are no longer really adhering to it, believing in it, giving credence to it as mere matter of fact. Hence it is a different literalism than it would have been had we not passed through the mesh of postmodernism or poststructuralism. You can certainly use the word "literal." How can one object to the use of words? But there is a change in the function of the concept. It is no longer a matter of obdurate fact. Fact does not seem to have a place anymore, though there is a place for the unknown and there is a place for the literal as it is inscribed within the system of signs, a sliding system of signs, having what the French call slipperiness, *glissement*. The literal slides all over the place. There is nothing to get stuck to or to get stuck on anymore.

*Miller*: It brings to mind Heraclitus's saying about the god whose oracle is at Delphi: "He neither reveals [the word is logos] nor hides [neither literal nor metaphoric], but gives a sign." And you remember in religious traditions that one of the things demanded of people is "Give us a sign." One of the things teachers and holy persons are reticent about is to give a sign, for fear the miracle will be taken as truth; that is, it will be taken as revealing something or as hiding something, rather than remaining that unnameable third "something." It is just a sign, like a texture or like a textile.

*Hillman*: When Joseph Campbell spoke about myths here, he gave the myths, these stories, a kind of heartfelt, quasi-physical quality—you used the word *dynamis* or *energia*, that quality you feel Jung is bringing to the word "instinct," that aspect of the image, its dynamic, moving, animal power. In postmodernism, where do you find that quality of impetus, or immediacy? Is that *jouissance*?

*Miller*: That is the interplay of persons, self with other, self with self, which may not refer to some thing, or a something, but is erotic; it is not anti-intellectual, not alogical, but it is nevertheless playing itself out. As Beckett said, "Something is taking its course."

*Kugler*: There is a wonderful Sufi story that carries that sense of dynamic movement you are asking about while also locating it within the context of the postmodern search for meaning. In Sufism there is a tradition of children's stories about a holy man named Mullah Naserdine. He is similar to our Uncle Remus, except he has a Zen-like sensibility. Well, one day Mullah Naserdine's friends were walking around and suddenly Mullah Naserdine comes galloping past them on his horse, intensely searching for something. A short time later, he again comes galloping past on his horse, again apparently looking for something. This happens several more times until his friends decide they are going to stop him the next time he comes by and ask if they can help him in his search. A short time later he again comes galloping past and they ask, "Mullah Naserdine, what is it that you are looking for? Can we help you?" To which he replies, "I am looking for my horse."

*Casey*: Just a note on the problem of immediacy. I think there are two different things going on in the thrust of Jim Hillman's question. One is what Bergson would call *élan vital*, creative force. That is not the same thing as what Jung is calling immediate experience. It is the latter that gets called into question by poststructuralism, especially in the form of consciousness as a spotlight, as something that can get things together coherently and lucidly in some type of determinate daylight vision. All that has been made subject to question. Saussure himself uses the image of the "life" of signs in society; there *is* life there, but it is semiological life, an intensely interrelated life. There is not life in substances separately taken but life and internal relations *between* signs, each of which is a kind of semiotic substance. The *real* life is in the interaction of the signs, and not in the signs taken separately; just as the real life is not in my consciousness, taken as the ego, but in my internal relations with my own psyche, my own unconscious and that of others.

*Hillman*: But this "real life" is also within the image. My miracle is the image. Here I am a Jungian and a Platonist and an idolatrous ideologue. I want to affirm innate substance in the images of fantasies, dreams, arts, and everyday living. They move me, "e-motion," move me out, move something from where it was, "ex." Though I do use positive language about images, and though I seem to be stuck still in prepostmodern consciousness, my method of working with images would be postmodern: I try not to make statements about what they mean. *Neti, neti*, not this, not that. You do not need to explain too much—though I love doing it—because the power of an image is right there, if you pay close attention and let it play awhile. In fact, your response is already coming from the image.

*Miller*: Also, as Wittgenstein says, the depth is in the surface. Jung objected to Freud's looking behind the manifest content of the dream for a latent content, just as the poststructuralists are calling into question the idea that for something to have energy it has to have some motor running someplace, for it to have meaning it has to have meaning behind the idea, or a structure or an archetype in back of it. No. It is right here, in the dream, as Jung said. Jung and these thinkers are very close together.

# Contributors

*Karin Barnaby* has taught German and comparative literature at Hofstra University and is pursuing doctoral studies in comparative literature at New York University. She has published an article on Schiller and Jung in *Friedrich Von Schiller and the Drama of Human Existence* and is associate editor of *Quadrant*.

Thomas Belmonte is associate professor of anthropology at Hofstra University. He has taught courses in anthropology, literature, and the theory of communications at Columbia University, The New School for Social Research, Hofstra, and Sarah Lawrence College. He is the author of *The Broken Fountain*.

*Robert Bly* is a poet, storyteller, and minstrel who has integrated Jungian and mystical insights into his work. He is the author of *The Light Around the Body* and *The Man in the Black Coat Turns*, and editor of *News of the Universe: Poems of Twofold Consciousness*.

*Joseph Campbell*, comparative mythologist, was professor of literature at Sarah Lawrence College from 1934 to 1972. He is the author of *Historical Atlas of World Mythology, The Hero with a Thousand Faces, The Masks of God, The Mythic Image*, and *The Inner Reaches of Outer Space*, among other books.

*John Carlin* practices entertainment law at the law firm of Paul, Weiss, Rifkind, Wharton, and Garrison. He has taught art history and American studies at Yale University, Connecticut College, Williams College, and Columbia University. He has also curated exhibitions on contemporary art at the Whitney Museum and elsewhere.

*Edward S. Casey* is professor of philosophy at the State University of New York, Stony Brook. He is the author of *Imagining: A Phenomenological Study*, and *Remembering: A Phenomenological Study*. A series of his articles on archetypal psychology and philosophy have appeared in *Spring: A Journal of Archetype and Culture*, and he has lectured at the C.G. Jung Institute of New York and in Zurich.

*Pellegrino D'Acierno* is associate professor of comparative literature and director of Italian studies at Hofstra University. He is the author of two forthcoming books: *The Itinerary of the Sign: Secularization and Textual Crisis in Late Medieval Culture*, and *The Labor of the Negative: Cultural Criticism and Textual Sanctuary From Vico to Foucault*. He is co-translator (with Robert Connolly) of Manfredo Tafuri's *The Sphere and the Labyrinth: Avant-Gardes and Architecture from Piranesi to the 1970's*.

341

## Contributors

*Stanley Diamond* is Distinguished Professor of anthropology and humanities on the graduate faculty of the New School for Social Research and founder of their department of anthropology. He is also the editor and founder of the international journal *Dialectical Anthropology*. Among his works are *In Search of the Primitive: A Critique of Civilization* and two volumes of poetry, *Going West* and *Totems*.

*John Patrick Dourley* is professor of religion at Carleton University in Ottawa; Diplomate Analyst, C. G. Jung Institute, Zurich, 1980; and Roman Catholic priest, member of the religious order, the Oblates of Mary Immaculate. He is author of *The Psyche as Sacrament: A Comparative Study of C. G. Jung and Paul Tillich, The Illness That We Are: A Jungian Critique of Christianity*, and *Love, Celibacy and the Inner Marriage*.

*Jean Erdman* is a dancer, choreographer, director, and producing artistic director of the Theater of The Open Eye. Her 1962 piece, *The Coach With the Six Insides* (based on James Joyce's *Finnegans Wake*), won the Vernon Rice and Obie awards.

*Leslie Fiedler* is Samuel Clemens Professor of English at the State University of New York, Buffalo. He is the author of more than two dozen books, including most recently *What Was Literature? Class Culture and Mass Society*.

*Terree Grabenhorst-Randall* is a doctoral candidate in art history at the Graduate Center of City University of New York. She has taught, lectured, and curated on a number of American art subjects, particularly those relating to abstract expressionism and women's issues. She was curator of the 1986 exhibit at Hofstra University, "Jung and Abstract Expressionism: The Collective Image Among Individual Voices."

*Mark Hasselriis* was art advisor to the Bollingen Foundation during the 1960s. An expert symbologist and Egyptologist, he has illustrated several archaeological books on Egyptian material as well as Joseph Campbell's *The Mythic Image*.

*James Hillman* practices Jungian analysis in Connecticut. He is editor and publisher of Spring Publications and is a founding Fellow of the Dallas Institute of Humanities and Culture. His many books include *Re-Visioning Psychology, Suicide and the Soul, Healing Fiction, Freud's Own Cookbook* (with Charles Boer), and *Anima: An Anatomy of a Personified Notion*.

*Linda Huntington* teaches Latin American fiction and contemporary literature at the School of Visual Arts in New York City. She has published articles in *Psychological Perspectives: A Semi-Annual Journal of Jungian Thought*.

342

*Paul Kugler* is a psychoanalyst in private practice in Buffalo and a senior training analyst with the Inter-regional Society of Jungian Analysts. He has taught at the State University of New York, Buffalo, and is the author of *The Alchemy of Discourse: An Archetypal Approach to Language*.

*Ibram Lassaw* is a sculptor working in open-space abstract sculpture and a member of the American Academy and Institute of Arts and Letters. His work is represented in the collections of more than thirty museums as well as numerous private collections.

*Neil Levine* is chairman of the department of fine arts at Harvard University and an art historian specializing in the history of modern architecture. He has been engaged in research on Frank Lloyd Wright and is at present completing a book on him.

*John M. Lundquist* is The Susan and Douglas Dillon Chief Librarian of the Oriental Divison, New York Public Library, and was formerly professor of anthropology and religious studies at Brigham Young University. He has had eleven years excavation experience in Syria and Jordan and has written articles on the temple, on excavations in Syria and Jordan, on Biblical studies, and on ancient law.

*Stephen A. Martin* is a certified Jungian Analyst and clinical psychologist. He is also a clinical assistant professor of mental health science at Hahnemann University in Philadelphia, and is the editor of *Quadrant*.

*David L. Miller* is Watson-Ledden Professor of Religion at Syracuse University. He is the author of *The New Polytheism: Rebirth of the Gods & Goddesses, Christs: Meditations on Archetypal Images in Christian Theology*, and *Three Faces of God: Traces of the Trinity in Literature and Life*.

*Dinnah Pladott* teaches American literature, innovative fiction, women and literature, and the semiotics of theater and drama at Tel Aviv University. She is working on a book on the development of American drama and theater circa 1905-1939.

*Lucio Pozzi* is an artist. He has taught at Marlboro College, Cooper Union, and Princeton University, and is currently on the faculty of the School of Visual Arts in New York City. He is the publisher of *New Observations*.

*Eileen Preston* is associate professor and chair of the department of classics at Concordia University in Montreal. She recently published an article on Eros and Psyche in *Anima: The Journal of Human Experience*.

## Contributors

*Gilles Quispel*, Knight of the Order of the Dutch Lion, is professor emeritus of religion at the University of Utrecht, Harvard University, and the Catholic University of Louvain. He acquired the *Jung Codex* with five unknown gnostic writings in 1952. He is the author of *The Gospel According to Thomas, Gnostic Studies*, and *The Sacred Book of Revelation*, among other work.

*Robert Richenburg* is a painter and sculptor. He has taught at Pratt Institute, Cornell University, Hunter College, and Ithaca College. His work is found in many public collections including The Museum of Modern Art, The Whitney Museum, The Hirshhorn Museum, The Pasadena Art Museum, The Philadelphia Museum of Art, and the University Art Museum at the University of California, Berkeley.

*Carol Schreier Rupprecht* is associate professor and chair of the department of comparative literature at Hamilton College. She is co-editor (with Estella Lauter) of *Feminist Archetypal Theory: Interdisciplinary Re-visions of Jungian Thought*, and has published articles in *Spring: An Annual of Archetypal Psychology and Jungian Thought, Signs: A Journal of Women in Culture and Society*, and *Women's Studies Quarterly*. She is a founding member of the Connecticut Association for Jungian Psychology and vice president of the National Association for the Study of Dreams.

*Andrew Samuels* is a training analyst, Society of Analytical Psychology, London, and is in private analytical practice. He is the author of *Jung and the Post-Jungians* and *The Plural Psyche: Personality, Morality, and the Father*, co-author (with Bani Shorter and Fred Plaut) of *A Critical Dictionary of Jungian Analysis*, and editor of *The Father: Contemporary Jungian Perspectives* and *Psychopathology: Contemporary Jungian Perspectives*.

*Harold Schechter* is professor of English at Queens College, the City University of New York, where he teaches courses in American literature, myth, and the popular arts. His articles have appeared in numerous journals, including *The Journal of American Culture, Studies in Short Fiction*, and *The Georgia Review*. His books include *The New Gods: Psyche and Symbol in Popular Art* and (with Jonna Semeiks) *Patterns in Popular Culture*.

*June Singer* is a Jungian analyst and a member of the C. G. Jung Institute of San Francisco. She is the author of *Boundaries of the Soul: The Practice of Jung's Psychology; Androgyny: The Opposites Within; The Unholy Bible: Blake, Jung, and the Collective Unconscious*; and *Seeing Through the Visible World*.

*Evans Lansing Smith* is professor of literature at Franklin College, Switzerland. He is revising his dissertation, "Descent to the Underworld: Towards an Archetypal Poetics of Modernism," for publication.

344

*Anne Griswold Tyng* is an archietct, a fellow of the American Institute of Architects, an associate of the National Academy of Design, and adjunct associate professor of architecture at the University of Pennsylvania. Her articles relating archetypes and creativity include "The Energy of Abstraction in Architecture: A Theory of Creativity" in *Architecture and Abstraction: The Pratt Journal of Architecture*, and "From Muse to Heroine: Toward a Visible Creative Identity" in *Architecture: A Place for Women*.

*Jos van Meurs* is senior lecturer in English and American literature at the University of Groningen, the Netherlands. He is the author of *Jungian Literary Criticism, 1920-1980: An Annotated, Critical Bibliography of Works in English*.

*Deborah Welsh* is a creative arts/dance therapist in Syracuse, New York. She practices in a psychiatric/rehabilitation center, and privately. She teaches at Syracuse University and has published articles on movement and dance in the *Journal of Physical Education, Recreation and Dance*, and in a book of essays, *Persons, Minds, and Bodies*.

*Beverley D. Zabriskie* practices as a Jungian analyst in New York City and is on the faculty of the C. G. Jung Institute of New York. She has served on the Boards of the Institute, the C. G. Jung Foundation, and the National Association for the Advancement of Psychoanalysis, of which she is a past president. She was formerly on the editorial board of the journal *Quadrant*.

*Philip T. Zabriskie* is a Jungian psychoanalyst in private practice. He is a member of the faculty and, until recently, was Chairman of the Board of the C. G. Jung Institute of New York; a past President of the C. G. Jung Foundation for Analytical Psychology; and a member of the New York and the International Associations for Analytical Psychology, and of the National Association for the Advancement of Psychoanalysis. His articles have appeared in the journal *Quadrant*.

345

# Index

Abraxas, 31

absolutes, 313, 316; archetypes as, 316; collective, 42; deconstruction of, 313; dissolution of, 314; teleological status of, 314

abstract expressionism, 208; as consciousness of the moment, 214; Jung's influence on, 185ff.; and outmoded forms, 204; recurring motifs in, 186; and the tragic sense of life, 216

Achilles, 5

Adam, 24; Qadmon, 34

Adler, Alfred, xviii

adultery: in literature, 28

Aeneas, 288

aesthetics, 87; of popular culture, 78, 85, 91

Agamemnon, 5

aggression, 4, 85

Ahab, 245

air, 16, 18, 20; Air God, 20. *See also* elements

alchemy, xxiii, 12, 27, 46; as active process, 194; and art, 212; and Christian gnosticism, 34; etymology of term, 213; and individuation, 192; Isis in, 274; Jung and, 274; language of, 336; the ouroboros in, 12; Poe's interest in, 245; and transformation, 194, 232

Alexandria, 26

Alexandrinus, Clement, 24

allegory: intrapsychic, 86; of reading, xix

Allison, Nancy, 228

American Romantics, 244, 245

amplification, xvii-xix; of symbol, 178

androgyny, 301

angel, 25, 32

anima, 56, 76, 86, 200, 241, 272-275, 319, 328; and dehumanization of the female, 281; and eros, 276; *esse in anima*, 335; as inner personality, 96; and mother image, 96; as muse, 206; positive, 24; and women, 301

*anima mundi*: universal consciousness, 257

animal, 54, 57; depictions in dance, 224; as first gods, 156; as human aspect, 196; and trickster, 50

animus, 86, 273, 275; and anima, 282; as carrier of psychic contents, 274; challenge to the notion of, 286; men and, 301

Anski, Schloime, 94; *The Dybbuk*, 92-100

anthropos, 41; rotundum, 105

anti-detective story: as paradigm for postmodernism, 327

Aphrodite, 269

*Apocryphon of John*, 24

Apophis, 18

archetypal: criticism, 242; feminist-literary criticism, 279-293; forms, 22; image(s), 11, 15, 16, 33, 50, 76, 235; literature, 82, 99; motifs, 42, 186; myths, 11; otherness, 271; patterns, 178; psychology, 295; School, 294, 305-306 n.1; tale, 49; themes in Joyce, 257; theory, 11, 295, 296

archetypalism, 274, 280; as male viewpoint, 281; as shadow of feminism, 280-281

archetype(s), xix, xxiv, 3, 5, 22, 47-50, 52, 55, 84; as absolute(s), 316; activation of, 253; and art, 177; of the collective unconscious, 15; and context, 80, 82; as crystalline structure, 106; and culture, xvi, 73; definition of, 283; and emotion, 186; father, 170; fecundity of, 40; as first principle(s), 336; impact of, 202; as innate structures, 186; and instinct, 11, 12, 335; as link between past and present, 49; literary vs. psychological, 243; mandala, 117; and matter, 49; of meaning, 119, 332; metamorphoses of, 53; mother, 170; as pantheon of gods and goddesses, 211; and popular culture, 76, 77, 89; recurrence of, 57; as reductive categories, 175; and stereotype(s), 276, 277; subjective meaning

# The Collected
## Works of
## C. G. Jung

The publication of the first complete edition, in English, of the works of C. G. Jung was undertaken by Routledge and Kegan Paul, Ltd., in England and by Bollingen Foundation in the United States. The American edition is number XX in Bollingen Series, which since 1967 has been published by Princeton University Press. The edition contains revised versions of works previously published, such as *Psychology of the Unconscious*, which is now entitled *Symbols of Transformation*; works originally written in English, such as *Psychology and Religion*; works not previously translated, such as *Aion*; and, in general, new translations of virtually all of Professor Jung's writings. Prior to his death, in 1961, the author supervised the textual revision, which in some cases is extensive. Sir Herbert Read (d. 1968), Dr. Michael Fordham, and Dr. Gerhard Adler (d. 1988) compose the Editorial Committee; the translator is R. F. C. Hull (except for Volume 2) and William McGuire is executive editor.

The price of the volumes varies according to size; they are sold separately, and may also be obtained on standing order. Several of the volumes are extensively illustrated. Each volume contains an index and most a bibliography; the final volumes contain a complete bibliography of Jung's writings and a general index to the entire edition.

In the following list, dates of original publication are given in parentheses (of original composition, in brackets). Multiple dates indicate revisions.

## 1. Psychiatric Studies*

On the Psychology and Pathology of So-Called Occult Phenomena (1902)
On Hysterical Misreading (1904)
Cryptomnesia (1905)
On Manic Mood Disorder (1903)
A Case of Hysterical Stupor in a Prisoner in Detention (1902)
On Simulated Insanity (1903)
A Medical Opinion on a Case of Simulated Insanity (1904)
A Third and Final Opinion on Two Contradictory Psychiatric Diagnoses (1906)
On the Psychological Diagnosis of Facts (1905)

* Published 1957; 2nd edn., 1970.

## 2. Experimental Researches★

*Translated by Leopold Stein in collaboration with Diana Riviere*

### STUDIES IN WORD ASSOCIATION (1904-7, 1910)

The Associations of Normal Subjects (by Jung and F. Riklin)
An Analysis of the Associations of an Epileptic
The Reaction-Time Ratio in the Association Experiment
Experimental Observations on the Faculty of Memory
Psychoanalysis and Association Experiments
The Psychological Diagnosis of Evidence
Association, Dream, and Hysterical Symptom
The Psychopathological Significance of the Association Experiment
Disturbances in Reproduction in the Association Experiment
The Association Method
The Family Constellation

### PSYCHOPHYSICAL RESEARCHES (1907-8)

On the Psychophysical Relations of the Association Experiment
Psychophysical Investigations with the Galvanometer and Pneumograph
   in Normal and Insane Individuals (by F. Peterson and Jung)
Further Investigations on the Galvanic Phenomenon and Respiration in
   Normal and Insane Individuals (by C. Ricksher and Jung)
Appendix: Statistical Details of Enlistment (1906); New Aspects of
   Criminal Psychology (1908); The Psychological Methods of Investiga-
   tion Used in the Psychiatric Clinic of the University of Zurich (1910);
   On the Doctrine of Complexes ([1911] 1913); On the Psychological Di-
   agnosis of Evidence (1937)

## 3. The Psychogensis of Mental Disease†

The Psychology of Dementia Praecox (1907)
The Content of the Psychoses (1908/1914)
On Psychological Understanding (1914)
A Criticism of Bleuler's Theory of Schizophrenic Negativism (1911)
On the Importance of the Unconscious in Psychopathology (1914)
On the Problem of Psychogenesis in Mental Disease (1919)
Mental Disease and the Psyche (1928)
On the Psychogenesis of Schizophrenia (1939)
Recent Thoughts on Schizophrenia (1957)
Schizophrenia (1958)

★ Published 1973.
† Published 1960.

## 4. Freud and Psychoanalysis★

Freud's Theory of Hysteria: A Reply to Aschaffenburg (1906)
The Freudian Theory of Hysteria (1908)
The Analysis of Dreams (1909)
A Contribution to the Psychology of Rumour (1910-11)
On the Significance of Number Dreams (1910-11)
Morton Prince, "The Mechanism and Interpretation of Dreams": A Critical Review (1911)
On the Criticism of Psychoanalysis (1910)
Concerning Psychoanalysis (1912)
The Theory of Psychoanalysis (1913)
General Aspects of Psychoanalysis (1913)
Psychoanalysis and Neurosis (1916)
Some Crucial Points in Psychoanalysis: A Correspondence between Dr. Jung and Dr. Loÿ (1914)
Prefaces to "Collected Papers on Analytical Psychology" (1916, 1917)
The Significance of the Father in the Destiny of the Individual (1909/1949)
Introduction to Kranefeldt's "Secret Ways of the Mind" (1930)
Freud and Jung: Contrasts (1929)

## 5. Symbols of Transformation (1911-12/1952)

### PART I†

Introduction
Two Kinds of Thinking
The Miller Fantasies: Anamnesis
The Hymn of Creation
The Song of the Moth

### PART II

Introduction
The Concept of Libido
The Transformation of Libido
The Origin of the Hero
Symbols of the Mother and of Rebirth
The Battle for Deliverance from the Mother
The Dual Mother
The Sacrifice
Epilogue
Appendix: The Miller Fantasies

★ Published 1961.
† Published 1956; 2nd edn., 1967. (65 plates, 43 text figures.)

## 6. Psychological Types (1921)*

Introduction
The Problem of Types in the History of Classical and Medieval Thought
Schiller's Ideas on the Type Problem
The Apollonian and the Dionysian
The Type Problem in Human Character
The Type Problem in Poetry
The Type Problem in Psychopathology
The Type Problem in Aesthetics
The Type Problem in Modern Philosophy
The Type Problem in Biography
General Description of the Types
Definitions
Epilogue
Four Papers on Psychological Typology (1913, 1925, 1931, 1936)

## 7. Two Essays on Analytical Psychology†

On the Psychology of the Unconscious (1917/1926/1943)
The Relations between the Ego and the Unconscious (1928)
Appendix: New Paths in Psychology (1912); The Structure of the Unconscious (1916) (new versions, with variants, 1966)

## 8. The Structure and Dynamics of the Psyche‡

On Psychic Energy (1928)
The Transcendent Function ([1916]/1957)
A Review of the Complex Theory (1934)
The Significance of Constitution and Heredity in Psychology (1929)
Psychological Factors Determining Human Behavior (1937)
Instinct and the Unconscious (1919)
The Structure of the Psyche (1927/1931)
On the Nature of the Psyche (1947/1954)
General Aspects of Dream Psychology (1916/1948)
On the Nature of Dreams (1945/1948)
The Psychological Foundations of Belief in Spirits (1920/1948)
Spirit and Life (1926)
Basic Postulates of Analytical Psychology (1931)
Analytical Psychology and *Weltanschauung* (1928/1931)
The Real and the Surreal (1933)
The Stages of Life (1930-1931)
The Soul and Death (1934)
Synchronicity: An Acausal Connecting Principle (1952)
Appendix: on Synchronicity (1951)

* Published 1971.
† Published 1953; 2nd edn., 1966.
‡ Published 1960; 2nd edn., 1969.

9. Part I. The Archetypes and the Collective Unconscious★

Archetypes of the Collective Unconscious (1934/1954)
The Concept of the Collective Unconscious (1936)
Concerning the Archetypes, with Special Reference to the Anima Con-
cept (1936/1954)
Psychological Aspects of the Mother Archetype (1938/1954)
Concerning Rebirth (1940/1950)
The Psychology of the Child Archetype (1940)
The Psychological Aspects of the Kore (1941)
The Phenomenology of the Spirit in Fairytales (1945/1948)
On the Psychology of the Trickster-Figure (1954)
Conscious, Unconscious, and Individuation (1939)
A Study in the Process of Individuation (1934/1950)
Concerning Mandala Symbolism (1950)
Appendix: Mandalas (1955)

9. Part II. Aion (1951)★

RESEARCHES INTO THE PHENOMENOLOGY OF THE SELF

The Ego
The Shadow
The Syzygy: Anima and Animus
The Self
Christ, a Symbol of the Self
The Sign of the Fishes
The Prophecies of Nostradamus
The Historical Significance of the Fish
The Ambivalence of the Fish Symbol
The Fish in Alchemy
The Alchemical Interpretation of the Fish
Background to the Psychology of Christian Alchemical Symbolism
Gnostic Symbols of the Self
The Structure and Dynamics of the Self
Conclusion

10. Civilization in Transition†

The Role of the Unconscious (1918)
Mind and Earth (1927/1931)
Archaic Man (1931)
The Spiritual Problem of Modern Man (1928/1931)
The Love Problem of a Student (1928)
Woman in Europe (1927)
The Meaning of Psychology for Modern Man (1933/1934)

★ Published 1959; 2nd edn., 1968. (Part I: 79 plates, with 29 in colour.)
† Published 1964; 2nd edn., 1970. (8 plates.)

369

Works of C. G. Jung

The State of Psychotherapy Today (1934)
Preface and Epilogue to "Essays on Contemporary Events" (1946)
Wotan (1936)
After the Catastrophe (1945)
The Fight with the Shadow (1946)
The Undiscovered Self (Present and Future) (1957)
Flying Saucers: A Modern Myth (1958)
A Psychological View of Conscience (1958)
Good and Evil in Analytical Psychology (1959)
Introduction to Wolff's "Studies in Jungian Psychology" (1959)
The Swiss Line in the European Spectrum (1928)
Reviews of Keyserling's "America Set Free" (1930) and "La Révolution Mondiale" (1934)
The Complications of American Psychology (1930)
The Dreamlike World of India (1939)
What India Can Teach Us (1939)
Appendix: Documents (1933-1938)

11. Psychology and Religion: West and East*

WESTERN RELIGION

Psychology and Religion (The Terry Lectures) (1938/1940)
A Psychological Approach to the Dogma of the Trinity (1942/1948)
Transformation Symbolism in the Mass (1942/1954)
Forewords to White's "God and the Unconscious" and Werblowsky's "Lucifer and Prometheus" (1952)
Brother Klaus (1933)
Psychotherapists or the Clergy (1932)
Psychoanalysis and the Cure of Souls (1928)
Answer to Job (1952)

EASTERN RELIGION

Psychological Commentaries on "The Tibetan Book of the Great Liberation" (1939/1954) and "The Tibetan Book of the Dead" (1935/1953)
Yoga and the West (1936)
Foreword to Suzuki's "Introduction to Zen Buddhism" (1939)
The Psychology of Eastern Meditation (1943)
The Holy Men of India: Introduction to Zimmer's "Der Weg zum Selbst" (1944)
Foreword to the "I Ching" (1950)

12. Psychology and Alchemy (1944)†

Prefatory note to the English Edition ([1951?] added 1967)
Introduction to the Religious and Psychological Problems of Alchemy
Individual Dream Symbolism in Relation to Alchemy (1936)

* Published 1958; 2nd edn., 1969.
† Published 1953; 2nd edn., completely revised, 1968. (270 illustrations.)

Religious Ideas in Alchemy (1937)
Epilogue

## 13. Alchemical Studies★

Commentary on "The Secret of the Golden Flower" (1929)
The Visions of Zosimos (1938/1954)
Paracelsus as a Spiritual Phenomenon (1942)
The Spirit Mercurius (1943/1948)
The Philosophical Tree (1945/1954)

## 14. Mysterium Coniunctionis (1955-56)†

AN INQUIRY INTO THE SEPARATION AND SYNTHESIS OF
PSYCHIC OPPOSITES IN ALCHEMY

The Components of the Coniunctio
The Paradoxa
The Personification of the Opposites
Rex and Regina
Adam and Eve
The Conjunction

## 15. The Spirit in Man, Art, and Literature‡

Paracelsus (1929)
Paracelsus the Physician (1941)
Sigmund Freud in His Historical Setting (1932)
In Memory of Sigmund Freud (1939)
Richard Wilhelm: In Memoriam (1930)
On the Relation of Analytical Psychology to Poetry (1922)
Psychology and Literature (1930/1950)
"Ulysses": A Monologue (1932)
Picasso (1932)

## 16. The Practice of Psychotherapy¶

GENERAL PROBLEMS OF PSYCHOTHERAPY

Principles of Practical Psychotherapy (1935)
What Is Psychotherapy? (1935)
Some Aspects of Modern Psychotherapy (1930)
The Aims of Psychotherapy (1931)
Problems of Modern Psychotherapy (1929)

★ Published 1968. (50 plates, 4 text figures.)
† Published 1963; 2nd edn., 1970. (10 plates.)
‡ Published 1966.
¶ Published 1954; 2nd edn., revised and augmented, 1966. (13 illustrations.)

*Works of C. G. Jung*

Psychotherapy and a Philosophy of Life (1943)
Medicine and Psychotherapy (1945)
Psychotherapy Today (1945)
Fundamental Questions of Psychotherapy (1951)

SPECIFIC PROBLEMS OF PSYCHOTHERAPY

The Therapeutic Value of Abreaction (1921/1928)
The Practical Use of Dream-Analysis (1934)
The Psychology of the Transference (1946)
Appendix: The Realities of Practical Psychotherapy ([1937] added, 1966)

17. The Development of Personality★

Psychic Conflicts in a Child (1910/1946)
Introduction to Wickes's "Analyses der Kinderseele" (1927/1931)
Child Development and Education (1928)
Analytical Psychology and Education: Three Lectures (1926/1946)
The Gifted Child (1943)
The Significance of the Unconscious in Individual Education (1928)
The Development of Personality (1934)
Marriage as a Psychological Relationship (1925)

18. The Symbolic Life†

Miscellaneous Writings

19. Bibliography of C. G. Jung's Writings‡
20. General Index to the Collected Works‡

★ Published 1954.
† Published 1976.
‡ Published 1979.